I enjoyed having had the opportunity to work with you closely at CCS and II recently. Also thanks for your assistance on the conference that resulted in the production of this book.

With best wishes,

Shuen-fu Lin

Although he is away, I'm sure Bob Dernberger, who is also represented in this book, would join me in expressing appreciation for all you have done for the Center for Chinese Studies during your tenure as II Director.

Yours,

Ernie Young

Constructing China

The Interaction of Culture and Economics

EDITED BY
Kenneth G. Lieberthal
Shuen-fu Lin
AND
Ernest P. Young

CENTER FOR CHINESE STUDIES
THE UNIVERSITY OF MICHIGAN
ANN ARBOR

MICHIGAN MONOGRAPHS IN CHINESE STUDIES
ISSN 1081-9053
SERIES ESTABLISHED 1968
VOLUME 78

Published by the Center for Chinese Studies
The University of Michigan, Ann Arbor

First Edition

Printed and made in the United States of America

∞ The paper used in this publication conforms to the
American National Standard for Information Sciences—
Permanence of Paper for Publications and Documents
in Libraries and Archives ANSI/NISO/Z39.48—1992.

Library of Congress Cataloging-in-Publication Data

Constructing China:
the interaction of culture and economics /
edited by Kenneth G. Lieberthal, Shuen-fu Lin, and Ernest P. Young.
— 1st ed.
p.   cm. —
(Michigan monographs in Chinese studies ; 78)
Includes bibliographical references.
ISBN 0-89264-121-5 (alk. paper)
1. China.
I. Lieberthal, Kenneth G.
II. Lin, Shuen-fu, 1943–
III. Young. Ernest P.
IV. Series.
DS706.C66   1997
951—dc21   97-27317
CIP

Contents

4 *Contents*

Preface

The Center for Chinese Studies at the University of Michigan has been a leading American center of learning on China since 1961. Established as part of the Ford Foundation's efforts to increase scholarship in foreign area studies, the Center embodies the central notion that understanding current developments in a country like China requires a knowledge of history, language, culture, and society as well as economics and politics. The Center therefore seeks to bring together scholars from various disciplines who take China as the major focus of their work and provide opportunities for them to exchange ideas and to collaborate on research and teaching. The Center also offers an interdisciplinary MA program in Chinese area studies that some students take as a prelude to PhD work and others use as a starting point for careers in education, government, business, foundations, exchange organizations, and other endeavors.

The Center has been particularly fortunate in having benefited from the contributions of four key senior faculty for more than three decades. Each one has contributed in significant ways both to the scholarship in their disciplines and to the development of the China field as a whole. These four, whose names long ago became virtually synonymous with the Center—Donald Munro in Philosophy, Albert Feuerwerker in History, Norma Diamond in Anthropology, and Robert F. Dernberger in Economics—reached retirement age in the past two years. Current Center faculty and former students wished to convey their gratitude for the contributions these four have made to their lives and their field of work over the decades.

No single effort can hope to capture entire careers. Instead of attempting such an ambitious goal, the symposium "Constructing China" reflected the kind of intellectually exciting event which always delighted the four honorees. In tribute to them, the Center, with support from the University's International Institute, convened a two-day conference from 31 March to 1 April 1995, around the broad theme of the interaction of culture and development in modern China. This conclave brought together the extended Center community—including noted graduates as well as current faculty. This volume presents the symposium papers, along with substantive introductions for each group of papers written by the respective retirees. The essays range across a wide intellectual landscape, reflecting the breadth of scholarship that the four honorees have nurtured.

On the eve of the conference William Rowe gave the annual Alexander Eckstein Memorial Lecture to the University community. His wideranging remarks struck just the right note in terms of intellectual scope and excitement. The editors are delighted that Professor Rowe agreed to include the text of his presentation in this volume.

Working on the symposium and the resulting volume has been an experience of high—and decidedly mixed—emotions: fond reflections on the years spent together in a close-knit scholarly community; keen awareness of the magnitude of the loss that these retirements represent; pride in the quality of the scholarship that is the hallmark of current and former Michigan students; and deep recognition of the value of a special community that continues to nurture both high standards and lasting friendships while encouraging serious critical exchanges. In this, the Center's history is itself like a good book—each new page adds something that is significant, but each is inextricably bound to those that precede it.

We deeply appreciate the enthusiastic efforts made by all who participated in the conclave and edited volume: those who wrote individual papers, the panel chairs and discussants, the many colleagues who attended the sessions and rose to the occasion in the toasts they presented at the celebratory dinner, and the Center staff who, as always, bore an enormous burden without complaint.

KENNETH G. LIEBERTHAL
SHUEN-FU LIN
ERNEST P. YOUNG

Economics and Culture
in Eighteenth-Century China

WILLIAM T. ROWE
The Johns Hopkins University

In this paper I want to explore the relationship of the notions of "economics" and "culture" in the thought and discourse of the mid-Qing bureaucratic elite. We might begin by considering some provocative recent comments on this subject by the Ming historian Romeyn Taylor, in an article entitled "Chinese Hierarchy in Comparative Perspective" (1989). I cite them, as you will see, in order to disagree with them, and for that reason I must stress at this point how stimulating in general I have found Taylor's recent work on what he calls the "official religion" of the Ming and Qing, and how much that work has influenced my own thinking on this subject. On this particular point, however, my research suggests that he is off the mark.

In his article Taylor declares that the conception of the economy in "nonmodern" societies—a blanket cross-cultural category in which he includes late imperial China—is not that of the "autonomous market," the way it is in the "modern" world. Rather, the economic sphere is "subordinated to other kinds of social relations." It is better understood simply as the concern for "livelihood," that is, as "an instituted process of interaction serving the satisfaction of material wants," i.e., minimal subsistence (*Ibid.*: 491). He goes on:

> In the ideology of [late imperial China], economy appeared in its substantive sense of the livelihood ... of the people. Legitimated by its subordination to the orthodox social order, it was distinguished from profit (*li*), which sprang from the vice of self-interest (*Ibid.*: 494).

Taylor concedes, of course, that in practice profit-maximizing market behavior existed, and that the cultural and political elite were not unaware of this. However, he insists that "the orthodox social order always struggled against it,

This is a slightly revised version of the Fourteenth Annual Alexander Eckstein Memorial Lecture, delivered at the University of Michigan, 30 March 1995. I am grateful to the Center for Chinese Studies, University of Michigan, for sponsoring that lecture and suggesting the topic.

by one stratagem or another," and, as a result, a modern autonomous market, while never fully subdued, was effectively contained.

Taylor's argument is obviously, and by his own account, derived from the "substantivist" theories of Karl Polanyi (1969). These hold that the notion of an economy as an entity based on market transactions, freed from cultural preconceptions of morality and of personal status, and governed by rational and binding laws, was itself a cultural invention of the early modern West. Since it has no *a priori* reality, there is no reason to presume its operation in other historical or non-Western societies. "Formalists" who reject Polanyi's argument, and who tend to see economics as a fully certified field of scientific inquiry, insist that *any* society can and should be analyzed in terms of the play of market forces. They usually assume that actors in these societies operate on the basis of some implicit understanding of the market, even when lacking the language to articulate their understanding in strictly economic terms.

I tend to agree with Philip Curtin that the substantivist-formalist controversy has not been especially enlightening, based as it is on a forced reading of each other's arguments and a largely unnecessary dichotomization of economy and culture (Curtin 1984: 14). It seems clear to me that, in *any* society (ours included), economic logic is invariably understood and articulated in the context of specific cultural assumptions, and economic policy is inescapably bent to the service of values and institutions which are themselves cultural constructions.

I would argue with even more confidence that the attempt to understand late imperial China in terms of Polanyi-type substantivist theory is misguided; it conceals far more than it reveals. As I will show, autonomous and binding economic laws *were* deeply appreciated in eighteenth-century China. Contrary to what Taylor asserts, the profit motive was respected and creatively utilized by fully orthodox Confucian elites. And an economic development that included "livelihood" (*minsheng*), but also quite a bit more, was vigorously pursued by policymakers, all in the context of good old Neo-Confucian family values.

Although one might advance such arguments on the basis a very wide range of evidence (a close reading of the Kangxi emperor's Sacred Edict might well serve as a point of departure), I ground myself here in the routine political correspondence of Chen Hongmou (1696–1771), the longest-serving provincial governor during the Qing. Although known in Western scholarship primarily as a hard-headed, pragmatic technocrat and an exemplar of the *jingshi* (Statecraft) approach to governance, it is worth noting that in Chinese scholarship Chen is even better known as one of the last great bulwarks of Cheng-Zhu Neo-Confucian orthodoxy against the rising tide of *kaozheng* philological skepticism. Chen was perhaps a bit more "economist" in his thinking than some of his colleagues, but I feel fairly safe in presenting his views as largely in step with the mainstream of mid-Qing bureaucratic thought.

Chen himself tips us off quite openly to the relation *he* sees between economics and culture. It surprised me initially to notice how frequently he uses the term *jingji*, which I had thought to be a modern neologism, to indicate economics as a field of detached scientific inquiry. But he routinely couples this with a parallel object of study—*lixue* or *lijiao*—which concerns itself with the ontological underpinnings of moral action. Locating himself in a discrete and increasingly self-conscious tradition of social-activist Neo-Confucianism, stretching from Zhen Dexiu in the Song, to Qiu Jun and Lü Kun (1536–1618) in the Ming, to Li Yong and the so-called Shaanxi school in the early Qing, Chen insists that *lixue* without *jingji* is useless (*xu er wuyong*), but, just as clearly economics without a foundation of cultural-religious values is aimless (*za er wuben*) (Chen 1839: 49: 1–2).

Chen also creates this linkage by coupling *jiao* (training the people in the ritually correct norms of human behavior) and *yang* (material nurturance, an enterprise which, as Chen makes clear, goes well beyond minimal provisioning to encompass a more activist quest for wealth and prosperity). *Jiao* and *yang* are inextricably bound; in Chen's copious writings on proper official conduct, they make up the twin missions with which any public servant is entrusted by Heaven and by his sovereign (Chen: 1936: 1: 4–5).

In many of his provincial tenures, but most notably in Shaanxi in 1745 and Fujian in 1754, Chen launched amazingly comprehensive drives for *jiaoyang*, drives which look much like Maoist political re-education campaigns, eighteenth-century mini-Cultural Revolutions (Chen 1896: 19: 21–40; 34: 20–27). The first such campaign began in response to a charge by the Qianlong emperor to all his provincial governors in the winter of 1744–45, calling upon them to itemize aspects of the local culture and economy of each county under their jurisdiction and specify what was being done to bring about improvements. The throne's stated objective was one of personnel assessment, providing governors a means to test their subordinate magistrates' level of engagement (*Da Qing*: 231: 15–16).

But Chen, who had just left for Shaanxi when he received the edict, and who had already in his previous tenures begun to proceed along similar lines, used the imperial charge less as a test of magistrates than as springboard for a genuine crusade to remold popular consciousness in his province. He drew up a list of twenty-four areas of desired reform, from upholding the *lunchang* (the norms of ritualized human interaction) and orthodox marriage and funerary customs, to more material concerns such as promotion of sericulture and land reclamation, and the search for higher-yield crops and seeds. Chen's cultural and economic desiderata were extremely precise. This was the time, he insisted, to shake the people out of generations of lethargy and habituated practice, put them back in touch with their heavenly endowed innate goodness (*tianliang*), and accomplish their transformation (*hua*) into the morally correct and materially prosperous beings their rational nature enabled them to be. Chen also prescribed the way magistrates were to accomplish this: they were to visit each village in their district regularly, call out in sequence small groups of villagers, and lead self-criticism sessions on aspects of local practice which fell short of the ideal. For years thereafter the governor browbeat his subordinates to make follow-up visits to monitor progress and offer repeated exhortation.

This seamless merger of the moral and the material distinguishes Chen's social policy throughout his career. Strikingly, he uses the same utilitarian language to legitimate both: behavior which is culturally orthodox or economically efficient is useful (*youyong*) and profitable (*youyi*), That which is morally deviant or economically unproductive is useless (*wuyong*) and unprofitable (*wuyi*). From one end of the empire to the other, over four decades, Chen campaigned to root out patterns of culture he considered dysfunctional, nearly always stressing material interests: If you people persist in the sorts of bad habits to which your region is prone—gambling, say, or wanton litigiousness—you will surely bring your families to ruin. With the elitist intolerance of the devout Neo-Confucian, Chen regularly directed broadsides against popular religious practices: pilgrimages, sacrifices to local cult deities, and so on. These are simultaneously licentious (Chen rarely uses the term heretical [*xie*] stressing instead the threat to public morality), vain and fruitless, and wasteful of heaven's bounty. More surprising, perhaps, is the quasi-populist way he directs analogous attacks against literati elites, who insist upon ostentatiously following Zhu Xi's prescriptions for family rituals to the letter, heedless of the enormous financial cost. This, complains Chen, is *too much* ritual (*guoli*), and is no less disdainful of heaven and injurious to household finances than more plebeian manifestations of religious enthusiasm.

In each case it might be argued that Chen's campaigns for moral-cultural rectification (or *hua*) turn out on closer inspection to serve an economic end: the husbanding of scarce material resources. But it works both ways. After all, he argues, it is far easier to get people to observe the dictates of ritual propriety if they are adequately clothed and fed.

Chen's persistent efforts to instill in the population "beautiful" and "civilized" customs were intended, in his words, simultaneously to uphold ritual orthodoxy (*yi dun lijiao*) and to bring about material prosperity (*yi fu caiwu*) (Chen 1826: 68: 4–6). These beautiful customs included hard work, long-term planning, and economic cooperation among local community members. They conspicuously did *not* include economic competitiveness—a cultural value opted for in the early modern West, but not in Qing China, despite the similarity of many other economic assumptions.

Perhaps most interesting among these "beautiful" customs, from our perspective, is frugality. Frugality—about which Chen Hongmou was deeply obsessed, and the mid-Qing administration only slightly less so—is interesting not merely because of its very evident parallels to the cult of "bourgeois thrift" emerging about the same time in Europe, but even more basically because in Qing discourse frugality so blatantly elides economist and moralist values.[1] The very term *jie*, meaning literally "restraint," and identified by Wing-tsit Chan and K. C. Liu with moral fervor in general (1990: 70, 79), meant most specifically in Qing usage two surprisingly linked attributes: economic frugality and widow chastity. In one policy document Chen starts off by extolling *jiesheng*—financial thrift—and then by a progressive substitution of ideographs subtly shifts his subject first to *liejian* (self-restraint, moral as well as economic), and ultimately to *lianpu* (the stoic rusticity and lack of pretense which for Chen is a paramount cultural ideal) (1896: 19: 23–24). In another text, Chen's 1746 "Proclamation Encouraging Frugality," the economic quality identified in the title soon gives way to the moral quality of *zhipu*, yeomanlike simplicity and directness (*Ibid.*: 24: 23–24). As with many early modern economic thinkers in the West, frugality is virtuous for a variety of reasons. It represents responsible stewardship of the resources granted humankind by the creator. It is a denial of personal indulgence in the broader interests of family and community. ("If you go and drink at a wineshop," Chen warns darkly, "your whole family will go hungry."[*Ibid.*: 26: 2].) And the very exercise of financial responsibility is a means of getting in more complete touch with, of realizing, one's innate moral nature. Habits of extravagance are debased and corrupting (*louxi*), whereas frugality, savings, and accumulation are genuine and substantial (*shi*—for Chen Hongmou, an all-purpose term of approval, describing both moral virtue and practical efficacy).

Below the surface level of Chen's social policy, what assumptions does he hold about the way economics, what he calls *jingji*, really works? It is most immediately and strikingly clear that Chen believes it operates according to predetermined, immutable, but rationally inferrable laws. Facing famine in Jiangxi in 1742–43, Governor Chen took the remarkable steps of prohibiting local grain export embargoes, government grain-price freezes, and confiscations of grain from private hoarders. Why? Because he believed that merchants would inevitably be drawn to make purchases in markets where prices were low, and be drawn to make sales where prices were high, hence driving the

---

1. For an analysis and critique of the notion of "bourgeois thrift" in early modern Europe, see Medick, 1982: 84–113.

price down through market mechanisms. "If rice from one district happens to be available," he writes, "merchants from adjacent districts will come and buy it *in direct proportion to its price*" [my emphasis]. This is in strict compliance with what Chen calls "the regularities of commerce" (*maoyi zhi chang*) and is in no way reprehensible. Similarly he argues that "for those who own land to harvest their grain and sell it at the optimal price is part of the natural order of things" (*yuan shu qingli*—literally, it is based on principle and heavenly endowed human nature). Nor does such conduct in any way violate the dictates of one's social role (*bingbu feifen*). When the price is at a level where sellers find it most advantageous to sell, they will inevitably (and properly) do so; buyers will buy, and sellers will sell, when the time is right (*jishi*) (1896: 12: 12–13; 1936: 2: 14). If this is not faith in the operation of an "autonomous market," it is hard to imagine what might be! That factors of supply and demand determine prices in a local market, that commodities will be drawn to the market in which they command the highest price, and that economic actors will seek to buy low and sell high are all for Chen Hongmou firmly established principles (*yiding zhi li*). These recognitions impose clear limits on the range of government activism in the economy, and Chen repeatedly counsels against policies which seem to him to contravene market realities, policies which in most cases will prove actively counterproductive. But the overall policy implication to be drawn is hardly one of laissez-faire. Rather, the very predictability of market mechanisms ensures that well-thought-out policies, which creatively *utilize* these mechanisms, will automatically (*ziran*) or inevitably (*biran*) achieve their intended result.

There is something else at work here as well. Unlike the famous eighth-century finance minister Liu Yan, who observed similar regularities in the operation of the market and referred to them straightforwardly as "laws" (*fa*),[2] Chen Hongmou and his contemporaries operated in a universe of discourse dominated by Neo-Confucian ethics and metaphysics. Consequently, the terms used to describe economic axioms are no longer Legalist ones, but those with a deep *lixue* resonance, such as *li* itself (rational principle), and *qing* (primordial human emotions, a term which had highly positive moral overtones in Chen's writings), and *chang* (the old Confucian virtue of constancy, frequently used by Chen in the compound *lunchang* to refer to the universally proper pattern of human role-relationships). Economic theory, then, is firmly embedded in a moral-ontological discourse. One important consequence of this, occasionally but not always made explicit, is that profit-maximizing market behavior, according as it does with *li, qing*, and *chang*, is for that very reason now seen as morally legitimate.

---

2. On Liu Yan see Hartwell, 1971.

But it is not only the high culture—Taylor's "official religion"—which provides the context for the operation of the economy (Taylor 1990: 126–57). Chen Hongmou is highly emphatic—indeed, it is probably a hallmark of his State-craft political style—that universal, axiomatic economic laws are observed only in local situations, which are both spatially and temporally discrete (*suidi suishi*). Government intervention in the economy, to be effective, must take into account not only the generalized economic laws themselves, but their highly particularized instantiations. And it is notable that Chen repeatedly identifies local cultures (*difang fengsu*)—localized popular tastes, skill levels, and ha-bituated practice—as one variable which officials must acknowledge in determining economic policy (Chen n.d.).

I have written elsewhere (1993) about the deep respect Chen holds for the market as the proper arbiter of prices—the sanctity of the *shilia* (market price) or *shijia* (current price). Officials should never attempt to impose price controls on items of consumer need in inflationary periods, for this is counterproductive, simply driving the goods off the market, and effectively raising prices still further. They should *never*, no matter how much it strains their official coffers, procure goods or labor for state needs at below-market fixed prices (*guanjia*), for this "harasses" (*rao* or *lei*) the people and provides an active disincentive to economic productivity. I can think of no single admonition that Chen, over his long career, more persistently imposed on his subordinates than this. Far from trying to suppress or even circumscribe the autonomous market, Chen Hongmou, at least in this regard, labored quite strenuously to protect and uphold it.

This brings us to the more general view of profit and self-interest held in eighteenth-century bureaucratic thought, and here I am put in the uncomfortable position of disagreeing with the published work of one of our honorees in this volume, Donald Munro. In a seminal 1980 article, he argued that in Chinese thought prior to Western influence, private interest (*li* or *yi*) was never seriously engaged as a philosophic issue, but instead was peremptorily denied moral value. In any discussion of economic morality it was personal responsibility, rather than interests, which was the focus of attention. The overall thrust of Chinese ethical inquiry stressed harmony—not a harmony of interests, but a harmonization of individual strivings to fulfill potentially conflicting social obligations.

There is of course no dearth of evidence for such views, from at least Mencius onwards. But as scholars such as Mizoguchi Yūzō (1980) and Yu Yingshi (1987) have argued, a long-standing countercurrent to such thought began to achieve renewed prominence in the early modern era. Parallel to their common rehabilitation of human desires and their denial of an intrinsic opposition between heavenly principle (*tianli*) and human emotion (*renqing*), scholars such as Li Zhi, Lü Kun, Gu Yanwu, Huang Zongxi, and Dai Zhen, each in his own way, contributed to a new revaluation of the role of self-interest (*si*) in pursuit of the collective good (*gong*). Without delving too deeply upon moral philosophy, there is no denying that in his ethical writings Chen Hongmou wrestles very forthrightly with this problem and emerges with a very considerable value attached to *si*, or self.

More to the point here is the fact that in their discussions of the economy, Chen and his eighteenth-century colleagues, including the Qianlong emperor, show themselves to be quite aware of the social value of self-interest. Far more often than not, the term *li* (profit or advantage in the most material sense) is used in a positive way. Often enough, it is true, the profit referred to is that for the society as a whole, the *dali* or greater benefit. Chen regularly uses *li* in this way to refer to the material benefits he anticipates arising from his various regional development schemes. But, though he is not unaware of the potential for conflict between private and public interest, he is clearly not troubled overmuch by this. Even in cases where profit for the individual household seems clearly in opposition to the collective good—as when households withhold grain in times of dearth in expectation of still higher market prices—private profit-seeking is explicitly defended as normal, rational, and hence in accord with principle.

Like most of his contemporaries Chen was not at all reluctant to use the profit motive to get local populations to fall in line with his various economic development projects—extension of irrigation works, introduction of new commercial crops, building new roads for commercial traffic, and so on. In a formulation not too distant from Adam Smith's "invisible hand," Chen tells his constituents on one occasion that his current project will bring profit to all (*liren*), precisely to the extent that it brings profit to oneself (*zili*) (1896: 19: 31–32). And in a letter of 1740 to Jiangsu Salt Commissioner Ni Xiangkai, Chen advises Ni not to be overly concerned about the admonition in the classics to "take ethical propriety as the true form of profit" (*yi yi wei li*). Since human acquisitiveness is a universal given, the wise official more appropriately exploits the profit motive (*yin li cheng bian*) to "turn the useless into the useful" (1936: 1: 10). Chen, I may add, was a master of the art.

Neither Chen Hongmou, nor many of his colleagues, exhibit the sort of knee-jerk antimercantile bias that is sometimes imagined to pervade Confucian officialdom. Although they of course condemn instances of gross merchant misconduct, commercial exchange and circulation (*huxiang liutong*) is in and of itself a socioeconomic good, and its agents are, for the most part, *maoyi liangmin,*" good folks who happen to engage in trade.[3] What may set Chen

---

3. On the generally positive role assigned to commerce in Qing economic policy, see for example Feuerwerker 1966: 13–45.

apart from some of his fellow-bureaucrats is the *degree* of his concern that any government policy calling for merchant participation show solicitous care for these merchants' profits (*shangli*) and working capital (*gongben*). He voices this concern repeatedly throughout his career, for example, in his long and ultimately unsuccessful campaign to have Yunnan mine owners paid sufficient prices for copper they sold to the state to keep them in business. And it was his strident pursuit of a government bailout for capital-starved Guangdong salt merchants in 1758 that cost Chen his one, long-coveted shot at a governor-generalship.

Without going in any depth into Chen's various regional economic development schemes, programs for which he was justly celebrated in his day, I would simply stress two points. First, such programs as mining development in the south and southwest, promotion of a silk textile industry in Shaanxi, and market integration of the northwest frontier demonstrated a conception of regional economic health that went well beyond agriculture to encompass substantial commercial and industrial sectors of investment and employment. Second, Chen's goals notably included fostering a continuing and self-generating process of the production of wealth (*shengcai*). Whether this constitutes a notion of economic growth is perhaps debatable—Chen never articulates an ideal of rising per capita productivity, though this may well have been in his mind—but it goes well beyond simple concerns for provisioning and subsistence.

Moving yet one layer deeper, we can consider what Chen Hongmou's economic policies were ultimately designed to protect. Upon reflection, one of the most striking things about Chen's economic discourse is the pervasiveness of the notion of property—expressed either as *ye* (a term whose meanings also include employment and business enterprise, meanings which are elided very creatively in Qing rhetoric) or the less ambiguous *chan*. Chen speaks frequently, for example of the *minye* (a shorthand form of the contemporary idiom *xiaomin dongye*, assets of the common people). These, according to Chen, have been greatly augmented by the solicitous policies of our glorious dynasty and must be vigorously safeguarded by officials.

Chen argues that private property derives either from the patrimony of one's ancestors (*zufu yiji*) or from one's personal labor and savings (*benren ginlian*). In either case, one's rights to such property are very nearly inviolable (1896: 15: 20–23, 20: 18–19; Xu 1830: 4: 25–26). My use of the term "rights" will certainly raise eyebrows, but I consider it defensible. It has often been observed (accurately, so far as I can determine) that no notion of personal rights of any kind was ever articulated in the Chinese lexicon until its importation from the West, in perhaps the 1870s (Xiong 1986: ii). Nevertheless, as Philip Huang (1996) has recently shown on the basis of county magistrate's citations of the Qing code in civil cases, a clearly understood (though unstated) principle of the code was that property rights existed and were to be defended by the state. Chen Hongmou may come closest to giving this notion concrete expression when he argues that the concept of private property ownership "derives ultimately from rational principle" (*yuan shu qingli*).

Political authority is obliged to defend private property both because it is heaven's will, and for instrumental reasons associated with governance. Those persons without a stake in the economic and moral order—those who are *wu-chan wuye*—are self-evidently threatening to society, but they can be reclaimed through state policies aimed at restoring their *ye* (*guiye*). For these same reasons, as we've seen, Chen constantly browbeats his constituents not to gamble, litigate, or do anything else which may bring about their own loss of property (*shiye*).

A related set of terms Chen constantly uses—*mingao* and *minfei* (literally, "the fat of the people")—suggests that his theory of proprietorship incorporates the concept of accumulation of surplus. (He even from time to time uses the modern term *ziben*, capital assets). Private wealth, he argues, represents "the blood and sweat of the people," and the property-holder's right to dispose of it at will must be protected. Even in situations of dearth, he vigorously prohibits government or community seizures of private grainholdings, and disguised seizures in the form of forced sales at below-market prices. Government fiscal and procurement policies, too, must always be formulated "on the basis of respect for private accumulation" (*yi xu mingao*). Chen insists that private wealth contributes to the public good by constituting a reserve that society can draw upon in lean years, and by providing the purchasing power that stimulates the society's overall economic health (Chen 1769: 4: 12).

All of this, it seems to me, bears significant resemblance to early modern Western theories of property, most notably that of John Locke. Quite obviously, the political and cultural circumstances in which Chen and Locke operated were very different, and I would not want to push this comparison too hard. Still, Chen Hongmou, would likely agree with Locke's positions (1) that property ownership is a fundamental right conforming with the natural order of the cosmos; (2) that proprietorship makes one socially accountable and responsible; (3) that one's labor is one's property, and is therefore freely marketable; and (4) that accumulated surplus is largely the consequence of the labor one has invested in its production, and that this fact reinforces one's right to dispose of the surplus as one sees fit. For both Chen, as a devout *lixue* adherent with a faith in heaven's agency, and Locke, as a God-fearing Christian, all these principles are a reflection of the divine plan on earth (Locke 1980).

In suggesting that economic thinkers in both mid-Qing China and the early modern West were operating with somewhat similar notions of property, I do not mean to imply that such notions are universal. Far from it. Property, conceived in this way, seems hardly a given, but rather a highly particularized cultural construction. The fact that similar constructions could appear in two relatively (but by no means completely) isolated societies does lead me to suspect that some significant material and cultural affinities existed which helped bring them forth. Yet the equally striking differences in the Chinese and the Western constructions of property suggest equally striking variances in cultural context.

The most dramatic difference is in the presumed locus of proprietorship. In the West—at least for our friend John Locke—proprietorship was vested most basically in the *individual;* it was the cornerstone of what C. B. Macpherson famously termed "the theory of possessive individualism." The individual's proprietorship of his/her body, granted by God, was the point of departure for Locke's theories both of the accumulation of capital and of popular sovereignty (Macpherson 1962: esp. chap. 5). It should go without saying that such a construction of the "individual" is itself a highly selective cultural choice, to say nothing of the myriad ways Locke and his intellectual heirs in the West (including the neoclassical economists) chose to run with it.

Although my study of Chen Hongmou has suggested to me a number of areas in which one might see a new appreciation of individualism injecting itself into his consciousness, there can be no question that Chen and his contemporaries did not operate with anything like the construction of the "individual" that found favor in the early modern West. Certainly, the "individual" was not for them the locus of proprietorship. That locus was the *family*, and not just any family, but rather the highly particularized, multigenerational, Chinese-style family prescribed by the Confucian canon.

I think it is critical to understand that, for someone like Chen, the Chinese household is at once the heavenly mandated, morally correct foundation of the sociocultural order and the most efficient unit of economic productivity—the optimal vehicle to achieve maximal employment of heaven's bounty. He explicitly defended his famous campaigns among non-Han populations in the southwest to replace indigenous kinship structures with the Chinese-style household on both moral and economic grounds. Similarly, at the other end of the empire in highly developed Jiangnan, Chen campaigned vigorously against such family practices as conspicuously elaborate funerals on the grounds that they were culturally deviant and threatened the financial integrity—the *jiaji*—of the households involved.

Put most directly, it is this *jiaji*, or capital accounting at the household level, which Chen sees as the basic foundation of both the economy and society. Whereas others in the Neo-Confucian tradition might have insisted that the proper conception of the family was a ritual/moral, rather than material one, this distinction doesn't trouble Chen Hongmou in the least. For him, *jiaji* is an

indispensable component of the "regulation of the family" (*zhijia*) identified by
the *Great Learning* as one of humankind's most basic moral imperatives. The
culturally orthodox "way of the family" (*jiadao*), Chen notes, is simultaneously
the surest path to the material well-being of society—the *dali*" (1769: 4: 12).
He constantly reminds his local-level subordinates that their most basic tasks
are to root out harmful cultural practices and to instill in their constituencies
the rudiments of "small household budgetary planning."

For Chen property is—like the family itself—culturally constructed not as a
static thing, but rather as a living entity persisting over time. Household assets
cannot be calculated in monthly or even annual terms, he argues, "since what is
recklessly used up cannot be bequeathed to one's descendants." Household
budgeting is therefore a matter of heavenly principle. It is also a matter of deep
public concern, since the material extinction of any patriline is "a calamity for
the entire world" (*Ibid.*: 3: 22).

Those same rootless creatures who threaten society because they have no
property (*wuchan wuve*) are even more threatening because they have no family
(*wuiia*). They are to be feared because they have "lost their place" (*shisuo*). *Suo*
here is one of those spatial metaphors which, following Munro (1985: 265–66),
I believe offer us powerful clues to understanding late imperial social thought.

Again we must not be either economically or culturally reductionist in our
reading of Chen's consciousness. He rails on the one hand against excessive
ritual nicety and extravagant gifting in wedding ceremonies; what constitutes a
proper dowry is, very simply, a gift of land that will serve as the continuing
basis of the nuptial household's economic productivity. And yet in arguing
elsewhere for the desirability of rural households involving themselves in the
market, he makes his case above all on their need for cash to finance the orthodox rituals of family reproduction: weddings and funerals.

With this in mind, I think we must acknowledge the limits set on the economic development schemes of Chen and the many other activist officials of his
era by the primacy they accorded to the family in both the moral and the economic realms. However vigorously Chen might pursue his economic development projects, he would never, I believe, have deliberately entertained schemes
that might render obsolete the household as the basic economic unit. That
would have run counter to his most basic assumptions and negated the very
purposes for which he worked.

I have argued that substantivist models do a great disservice to our attempts
to come to grips with either the economic or the cultural premises of the late
imperial Chinese official elite. An autonomous market, governed by rationally
inferrable laws of economic behavior, was understood to exist, valorized, and
creatively utilized as a tool of administrative policy. Private interests and the
profit motive were taken as givens and welcomed for the incentive they might

provide for popular compliance in the achievement of state goals. Commerce was seen as a positive good and an instrument in the pursuit of wealth and material comfort for all. But all of this was embedded in a cultural system which imposed certain constraints on the way this increase in wealth might be pursued.

Where, then, does this leave us? Are we back in the 1950s and 1960s, in the heyday of a logic of "modernization" which decried the particularist familism of "traditional" China while celebrating the universalist individualism of the progressive West? I certainly hope not. I believe that since that time we have gained a much more useful appreciation of culture. Culture, I hope, is no longer a black box in which we place all factors which make no logical sense, or worse, an orientalist tool by which we assign to other peoples nonrational behaviors or preferences we don't see in ourselves. I hope I have made clear my own belief that most, if not all, notions about the working of an economy, however enabling or however constraining they might prove in the cause of efficient production, represent cultural choices.

In Albert Hirshman's *The Passions and the Interests* (1967) he argues that the early modern era in the West saw the emergence of a new and powerful view of human acquisitiveness. Pursuit of private economic advantage (now termed "interest"), though perhaps every bit as selfish as carnal desire or emotional excitement (that is, "passion"), was now seen as far more socially useful, precisely because it was calm, dispassionate, and above all in accord with "reason." To the extent that this "rational" (and hence divinely inspired) calculation of economic self-interest could be made to supplant sinful, hotheaded passions, the cause of social order would be advanced. An interest-governed world would have the virtues of "predictability" and "constancy." In Hirshman's view, it was this kind of moral and cultural argument for self-interest, not the somewhat later economic argument of Adam Smith (the famous "invisible hand"), that effectively paved the way for what he calls the "triumph of capitalism."

Is it reasonable to see in Chen Hongmou's notions of the market as operating in accordance with heavenly principle and of private profit-seeking as a predictable constant rooted in innate human rationality (*qingli zhi chang*) a conceptual move potentially as powerful as that which Hirshman sees in the early modern West? Maybe so. But however tenuous the parallel may be, the European case certainly tells me one thing. Subtle shifts in cultural understandings of the economy—shifts which by no means necessarily extract the market from a context of culturally defined values and assumptions—can pave the way for profound and unanticipated changes in that economy's basic structure. I suggest that mid-Qing bureaucrats such as Chen Hongmou, in both their concrete economic policies and, no less, the cultural language they appropriated

to legitimate them, were laying the groundwork for structural change, whether
they wanted to or not.

References

Chan, Wing-tsit, trans. 1967. *Reflections on Things at Hand: The Neo-
    Confucian Anthology Compiled by Chu Hsi and Lu Tsu-ch'ien*. New York:
    Columbia University Press.
Chen Hongmou. 1769. *Xunsu yigui* (Sourcebook on reform of social practice).
    Guilin.
————. 1826. "Fengsu tiaoyue" (Regulations concerning local customs)
    1760. In *Huangchao jingshi wenbian* (Writings on statecraft from the pres-
    ent dynasty), edited by He Changling. Changsha.
————. 1839. "Preface" to *Daxue yanyi Daxue yanyibu jiyao* (Abridged
    edition of the *Daxue yanyi* and the *Daxue yanyibu*). Reprinted in *Guochao
    wenlu* (Prose works from the present dynasty), edited by Li Zutao, juan 44.
————. 1896. *Peiyuan tang oucun gao* (Draft writings from the Peiyuan
    Studio). Wuchang.
————. 1936. *Chen Wengong gong shoudu* (Letters of Chen Hongmou).
    Beijing. Letter to Guangxi prefect, 1738.
————. n.d. Memorial of Qianlong 9.3.1. Number One Historical Archives,
    Beijing.
Curtin, Philip B. 1984. *Cross-Cultural Trade in World History*. Cambridge:
    Cambridge University Press.
Da Qing Gaozong Shunhuangdi shilu (Vertiable records of the Qianlong reign).
Feuerwerker, Albert. 1984. "The State and the Economy in Late Imperial
    China." *Theory and Society* 13, no. 3. Reprinted in Albert Feuerwerker,
    Studies in the Economic History of Late Imperial China. Ann Arbor: Uni-
    versity of Michigan Center for Chinese Studies, 1966.
Hartwell, Robert M. 1971. "Historical Analogism, Public Policy, and Social
    Science in Eleventh- and Twelfth-Century China." *American Historical Re-
    view* 76, no. 3 (June).
Hirshman, Albert O. 1967. *The Passions and the Interests: Political Arguments
    for Capitalism before its Triumph*. Princeton: Princeton University Press.
Huang, Philip C.C. 1996. *Civil Justice in China: Representation and Practice
    in the Qing*. Stanford: Stanford University Press.
Liu, Kwang-Ching. 1990. "Socioethics as Orthodoxy." In *Orthodoxy in Late
    Imperial China*, edited by Kwang-Ching Liu. Berkeley: University of Cali-
    fornia Press.

Locke, John. 1980. *Second Treatise of Government*. Indianapolis: Hackett.

Macpherson, C.B. 1962. *The Political Theory of Possessive Individualism: Hobbes to Locke*. London: Oxford University Press.

Medick, Hans. 1982. "Plebeian Culture in the Transition to Capitalism." In *Culture, Ideology, and Politics*, edited by Raphael Samuel and Gareth Stedman Jones. London.

Munro, Donald J. 1980. "The Concept of Interest in Chinese Thought." *Journal of the History of Ideas* 41, no. 2: 179–97.

————, ed. 1985. *Individualism and Holism: Studies in Confucian and Taoist Values*. Ann Arbor: University of Michigan Center for Chinese Studies.

Polanyi, Karl. 1969. *Primitive, Archaic, and Modern Economies: Essays of Karl Polanyi*. Edited by George Dalton. New York: Anchor

Rowe, William T. 1993. "State and Market in Mid-Qing Economic Thought." *Études chinoises* 12, no. 1 (Spring): 7–40.

Taylor, Romeyn. 1989. "Chinese Hierarchy in Comparative Perspective." *Journal of Asian Studies* 48, no. 3 (August).

————. 1990. "Official and Popular Religion and the Political Organization of Chinese Society in the Ming." In *Orthodoxy in Late Imperial China*, edited by Kwang-Ching Liu. Berkeley: University of California Press.

Xiong Yueszhi. 1986. *Zhongguo jindai minzhu sixiang shi* (History of modern democratic thought in China). Shanghai: Renmin.

Xu Dong. ca. 1830. *Muling shu* (Handbook for local officials).

Yu Yingshi. 1987. *Zhongguo linshi zongjiao lunli yu shangren lingshen* (Modern Chinese religious theory and the mercantile spirit). Taibei: Liangjing.

Yūzō, Mizoguchi. 1980. "Chūgoku ni okeru kōshih gainen ni tendai" (The evolution of the concepts "public" and "private" in China). Shisō 669: 19–38.

Glossary

benren qinjian	本人勤儉	*min'gao*	民膏
bingbu feifen	並不非分	minsheng	民生
biran	必然	*minye*	民業
chang	常	*qing*	情
Chen Hongmou	陳宏謀	*qingli*	情理
dali	大利	*qingli zhi chang*	情理之常
difang fengsu	地方風俗	*rao*	擾
guanjia	官價	*renqing*	人情
gong	公	*shangli*	商利
gongben	工本	*shengcai*	生財
guiye	歸業	*shi*	實
guoli	過禮	*shijia* (current price)	時價
hua	化		
huxiang liutong	互相流通	*shijia* (market price)	市價
jiadao	家道		
jiaji	家計	*shisuo*	失所
jianpu	儉樸	*shiye*	失業
jiaoyang	教養	*suidi suishi*	隨地隨時
jie	節	*suo*	所
jiejian	節儉	*tianli*	天理
jiesheng	節省	*tianliang*	天良
jingji	經濟	*wuchan wuye*	無產無業
jingshi	經世	*wujia*	無家
jishi	及時	*wuyi*	無益
kaozheng	考證	*wuyong*	無用
lei	累	*xiaomin dongye*	小民東業
li (principle)	理	*xu er wuyong*	虛而無用
li (profit)	利	*yi dun lijiao*	以敦禮教
li (ritual)	禮	*yi fu caiwu*	以富財物
lijiao	禮教	*yi xu min'gao*	以恤民膏
liren	利人	*yi yi wei li*	以義爲利
lixue	理學	*yiding zhi li*	一定之理
louxi	陋習	*yin li cheng bian*	引利乘便
lunchang	倫常	*youyi*	有益
maoyi liangmin	貿易良民	*youyong*	有用
maoyi zhi chang	貿易之常	*yuan shu qingli*	元屬情理
minfei	民肥	*za er wuben*	雜而無本

zhijia	治家
zhipu	直僕
ziben	資本
zili	自利
ziran	自然
zufu iji	祖父貽積

Coexistence and Variety

DONALD J. MUNRO

The University of Michigan

What a joy it is to learn from my students. They sometimes help me avoid falling into big holes, but mostly I gain insights, perspectives, and interpretations I had not thought of before. That is how I feel about the following three works.

Whenever we talk informally about China's current economic modernization, we usually refer to the helpful or harmful impact of the past, using words such as the influence of "the tradition" or "Confucianism." Often this is unavoidable shorthand. But when precision is important, we need to make distinctions. In "Confucian Role-Ethics and China's Economic Modernization" Sin-yee Chan opposes a common position shared by Marxists and others. She finds "Confucian" role ethics is not incompatible with values that facilitate modernization, that it contains aspects of individualism, a collectivist approach to promoting group interests, authoritarianism coupled with the delegation of power, and strong personal ties that promote small economic units. She reasons persuasively that compatibility does not mean that the Confucian texts give intrinsic worth to those new values. She has an original and significant view of what those other intrinsic values of Confucianism are. But what is Confucianism?

For Chan Confucianism comprises the standards that appear in the *Analects* and *Mencius*. Let me call this "philosophical Confucianism" while reminding readers of the obvious, that over the centuries many different schools of philosophical Confucianism appeared and many individual thinkers. But it is fair enough to treat the Confucius and Mencius who appear in those two pre-Qin works as sacred founders, the standard-bearers, so to speak, and treat their teachings as philosophical Confucianism. It is how they have been regarded since the twelfth century.

Chan's contribution is to focus on the personal nature of the relationships that constitute Confucian role-ethics, especially the "five relationships" mentioned by Mencius. The enormous number of people who have accepted such teachings have justified their actions by appealing to relationship duties, not individual duties or rights. Even today, the practice of forming such relationships, inside and outside the family, persists, as, for example, in the mentor relation that has always characterized the interaction between some people in a

Chinese workplace.

To speak of the relationships as personal immediately brings readers to the core of philosophical Confucianism and shows that this ethical system is not the same as a sociologist's description of pre-modern Chinese society. People are not mere role occupants. They do not have relations with abstract groups. Rather, they relate to individual persons with unique traits. This is why Chan is able to identify the values underlying philosophical Confucianism as caring, reciprocity, emotional connection, and particularity. We would not experience these values as duties to mere role occupants. And they are quite different, though not, she argues, incompatible with the values required by modernization.

I believe, however, that other Confucianisms in China do not fall under Chan's umbrella, and their values differ sharply from those of the *Analects* and *Mencius*. One is imperial Confucianism. This ideology may claim to anchor its teachings in those two books, and in other sacred classics as well, but its teachings exist to promote the survival and strength of China as an empire and of the emperor as a person. Imperial Confucianism begins in the Han dynasty, with Dong Zhongshu (179?–104?) as its best-known architect.

Imperial Confucianism elevates one relationship above all the others, namely, that between ruler and minister. The virtue associated with this relationship is the loyalty or obedience of the minister, or the people whom the minister symbolizes, to the ruler. The supremacy of this relationship was not acceptable to many philosophical Confucians. However, it was a position for which emperors sought justification in the classics and in commentaries by certain Song and Ming Ruist (Confucian) writers.

In its twentieth-century manifestation imperial Confucianism promotes a value that may impede modernization. Obedience or loyalty to the person of the emperor was also to the collectivist group, the unity of heaven/nature and humans represented by the emperor. In the modern period obedience and loyalty are owed to the Party or the person of the Party leader. The emperors and their officials, or Party leader, would define selflessness as obedience and being of the same mind with or agreeing with the ruler. Selfishness is defined as individual interest or beliefs that diverge from the ruler's, and they are to be overcome. Such definitions can impede modernization by dampening initiative and creating terror in the innovator. Imperial Confucians do not hesitate to impose sanctions on deviants.

Although philosophical Confucians expected emperors to be moral exemplars, delegating much of their authority, many actual emperors disagreed. They had some textual justification for doing so, for the sage kings were generally activists. Activist emperors, such as the first Ming ruler, considered themselves to be Confucians, but they cut the feet off people who objected to any exercise of autocracy.

Popular Confucianism refers to the practices of the family ethic that has its textual rationale in the ancient texts. Its tenets have been conveyed over the centuries in stories and plays. In these practices and the writings about them by members of the gentry who considered themselves good Confucians, we encounter values that diverge from philosophical Confucianism. As Patricia Ebrey (1983) and others have shown, the landed gentry often did not recognize much worth in anyone outside the nuclear family, not even poor clan relatives. They tended to ignore the general love of humankind advocated by philosophical Confucians. Their charity was often self-interested, to preempt violence in the underclass. This narrow view and practice is inconsistent with the obligation of a modern ruler to look out for the people's welfare. Sun Yat-sen spoke of the principle of the People's Livelihood, and the Communist leaders acknowledge the peoples' right to subsistence.

Popular Confucianism recognizes the superiority of local official families, because they are the emperor's representatives. In the old days this meant the families of patriarchal elders; nowadays it means the families of Party Secretaries. Today, they possess a power to run small enterprises that is not equally shared by other families. Such absence of fair competition may not be a good thing for modernization. Privileged families can use their control of power and resources to form networks, within which preferential treatment becomes a salable commodity unrelated to community welfare. Short-term profit nearly always takes precedence over long-term consequences, as China's dismal environmental record in water and air pollution attests. The privileged families often have charge both of running profitable enterprises and of enforcing environmental rules.

China has inherited all three kinds of Confucianism, with norms safely anchored in prestigious texts or heroes or sayings. Many Chinese today operate simultaneously on three levels that draw from these quite different traditions.

Robert Eno's contribution, "Selling Sagehood," reminds us that philosophy is a commodity that may help nation-states survive and become wealthy in the process. Some very influential Chinese writers in the late nineteenth century and twentieth century treated it as such. While not sounding as dignified as saying that philosophy is "a search for basic principles in nature, ethics, and knowledge," philosophy as commodity may earn more money. Robert Eno's investigation of the pre-Qin period brings new, and very plausible, thinking to that somewhat sacred but troubled period.

Let me cite a modern example. Yan Fu (1853–1921), a name familiar to those who read modern Chinese history, introduced J. S. Mill's *On Liberty* and other seminal Western works in translation to the Chinese audience (Schwartz 1983). Mill had treated freedom primarily as the absence of constraints on the individual's beliefs and lifestyle. As such, liberty is intrinsically valuable and needs no additional justification. At the same time, Mill held that such freedom promotes human progress, as the best individual beliefs compete and then flourish. At the hands of Yan Fu, in contrast, liberty becomes a commodity to peddle to China's leaders and opinion-makers as something that could promote the strength of the Chinese nation-state. The individual dropped out of the center of the picture as freedom became the removal of constraints on the energies of the people as a whole, permitting them to create wealth that in turn would benefit the state. Yan Fu's motives were not as self-serving as those Eno attributes to the pre-Qin philosophers; his motives were in large part patriotic. But he did promote a philosophical doctrine as an immediately useful commodity, rather than as the fruit of a search for basic epistemological or ethical principles.

This patriotic motive permeates the work of many philosophers in the 1930s and 1940s. Many focused on the term *cheng* (integrity, sincerity) as it appears in the *Doctrine of the Mean* and in the works of certain Song dynasty thinkers. On the cosmic level, *cheng* describes heaven's ceaseless life-giving process of production and reproduction. On the individual level, it can be tapped as one of life's motive forces, manifest in self-discipline. The writers would then say that the way to nurture this energy is to carry out the life-enhancing program that Sun Yat-sen called "People's Livelihood," as interpreted by the Guomindang leaders. Here are some old metaphysical and ethical basics transformed into a commodity to strengthen China. Jiang Jieshi's sometime minister of education, Chen Lifu, was only the most politically prominent philosophical writer to take this position.

Eno has a marvelously simple way of describing the arts that the pre-Qin philosophers peddled: "to learn how to win friends and influence people [cultivate *de* or virtue]; learn how to do the right thing at the right time; learn how to turn your body into a spiritual vessel [cultivate your vital energy *qi* that is coextensive with the cosmic energy]; learn a perfect management system; learn how to harness the rhythms of the cosmos and make them work for you."

We can divide these arts into two sets, which gave officials or merchants on the operational firing line a choice. They could focus on their own character development, namely, cultivating their *de* or a state of equilibrium in their *qi*. This approach does not require exhaustive study of objective conditions. Or they could perfect a management system and study processes of change the better to know when to intervene. This does require the collection of facts, either by learning them oneself or through co-opting those who know them (for example, merchants who know the logistics involved in the movement of goods). As my friend Michel Oksenberg has shown, many Chinese officials both perfected management styles and cultivated their own character development, depending on the rewards and circumstances (Munro 1996: esp. 26–29). This was true in the pre-Qin period and is true today.

Eno provides several examples to illustrate that pre-Qin philosophers often depended on patrons. This remains the case in China today. Xiong Shili (1885–1968), one of the most respected of modern philosophers in China, worked out doctrines that were inspired primarily by the Idealistic or Consciousness Only School of Buddhism, Neo-Confucianism, *The Book of Changes*, and, to a lesser degree, the French philosopher Henri Bergson. There is not a trace of Marxism in all the pages he wrote. Yet he was untouched by the authorities because he had a patron, Dong Biwu, a friend from anti-Manchu days in Wuhan. Unlike the philosophies that offer officials tools to strengthen the state or themselves materially, Xiong Shihli wrote philosophy as basic principles. It is probably of no commercial value to anyone. So even today the different forms of philosophy coexist.

In "Do Human Rights Apply to China?" Chad Hansen thinks that he is pretty much steering clear of economics. While I respect his approach, I suggest that interesting ties with economics really do exist.

Hansen is careful to remind us that we should distinguish the Chinese tradition, which is diverse and comprehensive, from Confucianism. The two are not the same thing, although politically conservative East Asian leaders, such as Lee Kuan Yu of Singapore, often treat them as equivalent. I would add further that these leaders are in fact usually talking about imperial or state Confucianism, which favors loyalty to emperor and state over concerns with smaller units. It differs from philosophical Confucianism, in which the interests of individuals sometimes have prominence. The philosophical tradition differs from imperial Confucianism in spawning ideas that may be compatible with a doctrine of universal rights, even though no such term as rights was known in China prior to the waning days of the last dynasty.

Most readers would agree with Hansen that the Chinese and Western traditions part company in the priority that the latter assigns to liberty as a supreme value. Given the place of "rights" in his title and the prominence of "liberty" in his narrative, it would appear that he equates them. This centers rights on the individual's freedom from government control of his or her decisions and actions. In short, it seems to focus on freedom of speech and religious belief. However, such an equation hides the areas where even the most conservative East Asian leaders would agree immediately with Westerners on the existence of universal rights. This is the first point where economics rears its head.

China's supreme leaders have already joined the world's club on universal rights. They did so in a State Council document entitled, "Human Rights in China," published by the State Council in 1991. They treat subsistence (*sheng cun*) as the primary right, defined in terms of food, clothing, dwelling, and transportation. Though they do not make the point, this right can be derived from much in the Chinese tradition, Mencian and otherwise. There is also some compatibility, as those leaders are aware, with the Four Freedoms honored in the United States: freedom *from* fear and want, and freedom *of* speech and religion. Subsistence is another way of referring to freedom from want. This is an economic matter.

Economic considerations also spur the movement in China towards freedom of belief and speech. Newspapers and magazines, which publish weekend editions for profit, publish not only scandalous gossip but unorthodox opinion, because it sells. Entrepreneurs insist on freedom from official intrusion into their economic beliefs and practices because they are responsible for the budget's bottom line. These forces incidentally promote Western priorities. But other groups do it consciously.

I can only praise Hansen for arguing that Westerners should vigorously defend their own belief in the primacy of certain rights, so long as their views remain open to modification. Such discussion promotes the harmony that facilitates social cooperation. I praise this view because it recognizes that societies are dynamic; they change. We can use talk of certain specific rights as a tool, just as the Jackson-Vanick amendment was used to induce change in the old USSR. Societies change in part because they have different constituencies. There are young people in China today who accept many aspects of liberty that have Western origins and focus on rights other than subsistence. These younger people are the agents of the societal change. They oppose the conservative leaders who want to restrict rights to rights of subsistence. They question the assumption that recognizing other rights may generate chaos. For young people the time to stop government intrusion into beliefs and lifestyle and voluntary organization is now.

The differing priorities among East Asian leaders and ourselves, to which Hansen alerts us, are a product of differing views about what it means to be human. We derive our set of rights from assumptions about human needs and abilities. These change over time as well. So there is opportunity continuously to enrich and perhaps to change each other's perspective on this matter.

But political actualities must be a part of any harmonization of attitudes. No Westerner will be satisfied with harmonious *attitudes* about rights unless the rights themselves are actually protected. Since that requires a regional enforcement mechanism, Asian, East Asian, or locally Chinese, philosophy and politics must remain bedfellows as they always have been in China.

References

Ebrey, Patricia B. 1983. *Family and Property in Sung China*. Princeton: Princeton University Press.

Munro, Donald J. 1996. *The Imperial Style of Inquiry in Twentieth-Century China: The Emergence of New Approaches*. Ann Arbor: Center for Chinese Studies, University of Michigan.

Schwartz, Benjamin. 1983. *In Search of Wealth and Power: Yen Fu and the West*. Cambridge: Harvard University Press.

Confucian Role-Ethics and China's Economic Modernization

SIN YEE CHAN*

University of Vermont

Introduction

In a sense the relationship between Confucian ethics and China's economic modernization is an empirical issue outside the scope of philosophical investigation. To analyze and explain the actual practice of Confucian ethical ideas in society and their interplay with economic forces would require the concerted efforts of sociologists, anthropologists, economists, and historians, but probably not ethicists. However, from another perspective, ethicists can contribute to the investigation of the issue by facilitating a deeper understanding of the ethical ideas themselves. Ethical ideas are behavior-guiding. In uncovering the basic assumptions of ethical ideas, examining their justifications and tracing out their implications, ethicists can help to interpret, clarify, and, if necessary, redefine the normative orientation and constraints on people's behavior. And when two normative systems interact, ethicists can help to compare and contrast their meanings and evaluate their compatibility.

I believe that the values embodied in Confucian ethics do not conflict with the values necessary to facilitate the economic modernization of China. Moreover, these values have significant implications for the particular direction economic activity will take.

---

* I am grateful to Roger Ames, Chad Hansen, and Robert Eno for their useful comments on this essay. I am also very much indebted to David Christensen, Arthur Kuflik, Don Loeb, and Derk Pereboom for commenting on earlier drafts of this work, as well as for their generosity in spending so much time discussing the issues with me. I also want to thank Leslie Weiger for helping me to edit this paper. Above all, I owe my deepest gratitude to Professor Donald Munro for his unfailing support and intellectual inspiration.

Confucian Role-Ethics: Ethics of Love and Engagement

Confucian role-ethics

In role-ethics, an individual's duties are essentially generated by the part or role the individual plays, not by the individual per se. It is important to note that the roles which are relevant to the Confucian account of ethics are roles within human relationships, not social roles as such or professional roles.

> This was a subject of anxious solicitude to the sage Shun. He appointed Qi to be the Minister of Instruction to teach the relations of humanity: how, between father and son there should be affection; between sovereign and minister, righteousness; between husband and wife, attention to their separate functions; between old and young, a proper order; and between friends, fidelity. (*Mencius* 3A: 4)

In this passage Mencius points out the five relationships central to Confucianism: father-son, ruler-minister, husband-wife, old-young, friend-friend. These five relationships started to occur as a special term in the Sung Dynasty (A.D. 960–1279) (Hsu 1960). The first three relationships had also been named the Three Bonds by the Han scholar Dong Zhongshu around A.D. 79 in the book *Baihu tong*. Both the Five Relationships and the Three Bonds were officially endorsed by the state and became the sacred socio-moral code in China from the thirteenth to the early twentieth century.

By Confucian role-ethics I do not refer narrowly to the ethics related to the Five Relationships or the Three Bonds. I include the entire ethical system which takes the Five Relationships and the Three Bonds as paradigms and extends from them to include all sorts of personal relationships, such as those between relatives, clan members, neighbors, and so forth.

Central to Confucian role-ethics is the ideal of *ren*, which can be interpreted as the ideal of loving, "the man of *ren* loves people" (*Analects* 12: 22). As I interpret it, the ideal of *ren* has two components: relationship love, i.e., the love one has towards specific people with whom one has personal relationships; and general love, i.e., the love one has for people regardless of their relationship to oneself. In other words, general love is the love that applies to people in the world (*tianxia*), including strangers. The component of relationship love is intrinsically valuable:

> The actuality of benevolence (*ren*) is the serving of one's parents; the actuality of righteousness (*yi*) is obedience to one's elder brother; the actuality of wisdom (*zhi*) is to understand the two and to hold fast to them; the actuality of propriety (*li*) is the regulation and adornment of them (*Mencius* 4A;27).

But relationship love is also the path to the cultivation of general love:

> A superior man is devoted to the roots (*ben*). When the root is firmly established, the Dao will grow. Filial piety and brotherly respect are the roots of *ren*. (*Analects* 1: 2)

> When the personal life is cultivated, the family will be regulated; when the family is regulated, the state will be in order; and when the state is in order, there will be peace throughout the world. (*The Great Learning*)

Perfecting oneself in family relationships is the prerequisite for bringing benevolence to all the people in the world, regardless of their relationship to oneself.

Confucian role-ethics and engagement

So what exactly should be counted as relationship love? What should a person do in order to fulfill the ethical demands of the Five Relationships? The Confucian texts point to numerous specific duties. For example, a son should support and be obedient to his father. A younger brother should defer to the wish of the elder brother. But what values underlie the specific duties?

Analysis of the *Analects* and the *Mencius* suggests that the underlying values are *caring, reciprocity, emotional connection,* and *particularity.* In other words to fulfill the ethical demands of the Five Relationships, the individual has to *care* for the person she is related to. Among other things she should actively promote the well-being of that person, that person's weal and woe should have direct emotional impact on the individual. Second, people related to each other should *reciprocate*. They should return good for good. For the benevolence a father confers on a son, a son should reciprocate with filial piety. Third, people in a relationship should be *emotionally connected*. There should be affection between them. In appropriate circumstances the individual should empathize with the related person, delight in her company, and be affected by her emotions. Finally the individual should take the related person as well as the relationship as *irreplaceable particulars.* That is, the individual should conceive of the related person and the relationship incapable of substitution. The individual should appreciate the relationship as a unique common good shared only between herself and the related person. In other words the related person is not a mere role-occupant who is interchangeable with any person who might occupy the same role. Having a different person occupy the same role can only mean the conclusion of the original relationship and the creation of a new and different common good between the individual and the new person. Since the relationship embodies mutuality between two particular individuals, each relationship is unique and contingent on the contribution of both partners.

What is interesting about the four values is that all, with the exception of particularity, can be applied to general love. One can care, reciprocate, and have an emotional connection with people who are unrelated to oneself. But it is not obvious that particularity can be applied to people unrelated to oneself. It is difficult to imagine taking a stranger as irreplaceable unless one believes, which the Confucians do not seem to believe, that every individual is a unique person with distinctive characteristics. For this discussion we do not need to worry about this aspect of particularity. It is sufficient to note that since most of the values underlying the ethical demands of the Five Relationships can be applied to the practice of general love, it is no wonder that relationship love is seen as instrumental to the cultivation of general love.

Confucian role-ethics orients an agent towards engagement in close personal relationships. Yet it also orients an agent to aspire to transcend the relationship boundaries. And both relationship and general love stem from and are informed by the same kind of perspective: the outlook of a person who is engaged with certain individuals in deep and close personal relationships. It is the perspective of a person who cares, reciprocates, and appreciates the particularity of others and of relationships, and who is emotionally connected.

Problem One: the lack of support for individualism

The first worry is that Confucian role-ethics is incompatible with individualism, whose acceptance helps to promote economic modernization. Individualism directs people to value the individual's rights, choices, and interests, and encourages them to exert themselves to pursue and protect these values. Thus people adhering to individualism are ready to participate in free competition in pursuit of their diverse goals, hence contributing to the economic dynamism of modern society.

Admittedly, individualism is an extremely intricate, complex issue, taking many different forms: political, economic, ethical, religious, and method-ological. Each form of individualism has its own specific claims, but I will examine the two most relevant to the issue of economic modernization: the dignity of individuals and autonomy. Do they conflict with Confucian values in any important way?[1]

---

1. For an interesting discussion of individualism in Chinese philosophy, see Munro 1985.

To respect the *dignity* of an individual is to conceive of the individual as having an intrinsic value independent of her role, status, and function in society. More importantly, dignity implies that sometimes an individual's interests—and in particular her rights—have priority over the mere larger aggregate sum of other people's interests.

At first glance Confucian role-ethics does not imply any value that contradicts respect for the dignity of individuals. It is wrong to say that Confucianism does not value individual persons intrinsically. To a Confucian, the ideal way to regard each individual is as brother or family member. Confucius says that all within the four seas are brothers (*Analects* 12: 5). Mencius suggests that one should treat the elders in other families as the elders in one's own family (*Mencius* 1A: 7). Each person is to be valued as each family member is valued. Indeed it may even be argued that every adequate moral theory must show some appreciation of the intrinsic value of individuals in order to justify things like prohibitions against imposing gratuitous suffering on individuals and setting the prima facie goal of promoting the well-being of individuals.

Still we may not want to say that Confucian role-ethics embodies the same sort of respect for individual dignity as individualism does because it assigns ethical priority to the social category of relationships, not to individual interests. It requires an individual to fulfill her relationship duties before she pursues her own interests, and blames and punishes her for failing to fulfill those duties.

However, social role-duties are not lacking in individualism. Individualists ranging from an egoist like Thomas Hobbes to a liberal like John Rawls do not dispute the duty of a citizen to the state. Hobbes even advocates the subordination of individual interests to an autocrat. And individualists like John Stuart Mill and Rawls endorse other social role-duties, such as duties to one's friends, spouse, and children.[2] Moreover, individualists need not see these social role-duties as having only instrumental value in furthering individual interests. Rawls, for example, acknowledges and endorses the emotional connections among members of associations, including families, and sees social engagement as having intrinsic value (Rawls 1971: 467–472, 522–523).

Still there are important differences, if only of degree, between Confucian role-ethics and individualism. While both acknowledge the constraints imposed

---

2. In *On Liberty* Mill claims that people deserve reprobation and even punishment for breaching their duties to their families; see Mill 1947: 138. Rawls discusses the obligations one assumes when one participates in social institutions in *A Theory of Justice* (1971: 111–14).

by social role-duties, the *primary* concern of individualism is the articulation and protection of individual freedom to pursue one's own interests (within those constraints). Thus we find that Mill devotes a whole book to the subject of liberty. And Rawls makes equal liberty the first principle of his two principles of justice. To carefully define individual liberty and suggest rules and mechanisms to protect individual liberty are the main themes of many individualists.[3] The concept of rights is thus deeply rooted in individualism. Consequently we find in individualist societies systems which aim at protecting individual liberty against violation. The criminal justice system in the United States is a good example.

Since Confucian role-ethics, on the other hand, focuses on the elucidation of the meaning and importance of relationship duties, it is no accident that until recently China had no concept of rights. An individual's interests can always be weighed against the value of relationships: a son may be required to divorce his wife, a minister may have the moral obligation to commit suicide. Even if sacrificing individual interests is not required by relationship duties, it is sometimes still considered the right thing to do. We find Mencius endorsing Zhang Zhi's action to send away his wife and son as a punishment of himself for alienating his father (*Mencius* 4B: 30). Not only Zhang Zhi's own interests, but those of his wife and son as well, are sacrificed to the greater good of filial virtue.

Another contrast has to do with the justification individualists give for social role-duties. First of all, individualists assume that social role-duties require justification. They are not seen as given or natural. This is not to imply that individualists may not conceive of individuals as intrinsically social; in fact many of them do. But to say that one has concern and need for other people is different from saying that one has obligations towards them. Obligations, as constraints on an individual's pursuit of her interests, require justification on the part of individualists, but not from the standpoint of Confucianism.

The justifications reflect the individualists' view that individuals, rather than social relationships, are primary. They appeal to the individual's choices and interests to justify social role-duties. Hence, we find that many individualists are contractarians. Social role-duties are binding only if individuals have chosen or would choose them in the state of nature. Rawls, for example, explicitly holds that persons in the original position—the hypothetical

---

3. Not every individualist emphasizes individual liberty, of course. Hobbes advocates the relinquishing of individual interests for the sake of security. He prizes individual interests over other things, but regards security as the paramount individual interest, for the sake of which other interests can be given up.

counterpart to the state of nature in traditional theories—do not have obligations to third parties. Instead all obligations have to be derived from the choices people make when they reflect about their own conditions behind the veil of ignorance, that is, when they are deprived of knowledge of their own particular personal characteristics such as gender, age, economic class, religion, and natural assets like intelligence, physical strength, etc. (Rawls 1971: 128). Moreover, Rawls is a double contractarian in the sense that most social role-duties are seen as generated out of one's voluntary undertakings, such as forming associations with others or accepting the benefits of the arrangement (after one comes out of the veil of ignorance). These duties based on voluntary choices should be distinguished from natural duties (such as the duty not to harm others), which are binding on everyone regardless of individual choices (*Ibid.*: 111–15). Likewise, Mill, though not a contractarian, justifies family obligations in terms of a person's responsibility for having voluntarily undertaken the relationship (1947: 138).

Relationships and their correlated obligations in Confucian role-ethics, on the other hand, are seen as given and requiring no justification.[4] Relationship duties constitute the content of the cardinal Confucian virtues of benevolence (*ren*), righteousness (*yi*), propriety (*li*), and wisdom (*zhi*) (*Mencius* 4A: 27). To Mencius, human nature is good because humans are born with the tendency to fulfill these relationship duties: for example, humans have innate love for their parents and respect for their elder brothers (*Mencius* 7A: 15). In brief, one has to perform the paternal duty just because one is a parent in the parent-child relationship. The social category of relationships is not only conceptually prior to the individual in the sense that it provides the background against which one understands what a person is. Nor is it just causally prior in the sense that experiences in relationships shape the personality of an individual. Relationships are *ethically* prior because they provide the ultimate ethical justification for one's actions. One justifies one's actions by appealing to the relationship duties or to the meaning of these actions in relationships or their impacts on relationships.[5]

But we should not conclude that Confucian role-ethics ignores individuals' interests. Mencius makes it clear that rites (*li*), which can be seen as largely relationship-based, are more important than food and sex. But, as he points out, this does not mean that one should necessarily starve to death or forego having a wife if getting food and sex involves some violation of *li*. The choice depends

---

4. This does not mean that one cannot evaluate the specific content of relationship duties.

5. George Sher distinguishes between conceptual, causal, and ethical priority in defending ethical individualism (1989: 133–57).

on weighing the importance of food or sex against the importance of the particular kind of *li* that is violated. If the *li* is inconsequential and the lack of food means death, then comparing the two is just like comparing the weight of the gold in a clasp with that of a cartload of feathers (*Mencius* 6B: 1). Similarly, both Confucius and Mencius see the desire to seek official position as a legitimate interest, but Mencius warns that one should not seek it by dishonorable means (*Mencius* 3B: 8), and Confucius advises that one should also help others to become prominent if one wants to be prominent oneself (*Analects* 6: 30).

The value of reciprocity which underlies Confucian role-ethics is another means to guarantee the interests of individuals. While reciprocity may not imply strictly equal exchange between parties, it does imply some mutual claims. Even if Confucian role-ethics required the agent to ignore her own interests in favor of the interests of her related others, the requirement of reciprocity makes it likely that others would in turn look after her interests. After all failure to reciprocate constitutes failure to fulfill one's relationship duties and can justify the termination of the relationship.

Indeed, in the ideal situation, the other values embodied in Confucian role-ethics serve to guarantee each individual's interests. Since agents are required to care for each other and be emotionally connected to each other, everyone's interests will be taken care of if everyone follows the prescription.[6] Thus the ideal itself implies the promotion of individual interests.

It might be objected that these elements of reciprocity, mutual caring, and emotional connection need not imply a high regard for individual interests. It may be that those elements are cherished for their own sake. The promotion of individual interests is a natural by-product of practicing those values, but it is not valued by Confucian role-ethics as such.

This objection displays a lack of understanding of the concept of caring. For caring is premised on recognizing the importance of the interests of the person one cares for. Typically one cannot care for someone and consider that person's interests as unworthy of being taken into account. One may think that caring embodies a more significant moral value than the claim of individual interests, but one cannot consistently prescribe the value of caring and dismiss the claim of individual interests.

Respect for an individual's *autonomy* means respect for the individual's right to be her own master. It means freedom from unjustified external interference and obstacles, and the ability to implement one's plans and fulfill

---

6. When reality falls short of the ideal, the reciprocity element should operate to solve the problem of free-riders, i.e., people who benefit from others' care but do not reciprocate.

one's goals. Unjustified external interference includes more than just concrete obstructions, like denial of access to resources, but also subtle ones, like certain forms of social influence. To promote her freedom from social influence, an autonomous individual will comply only with norms which she has critically evaluated and accepted.

Again Confucian role-ethics and individualism diverge, but only in subtle ways. Autonomy is important in Confucianism, and the will of a person is very important. To Confucius, "the commander of three armies can be taken away, but the will of even a common man cannot be taken away from him" (*Analects* 9: 25). Moreover, the portrait of a Confucian agent is of an autonomous agent who examines and reflects on her motives, feelings, and behavior (*Analects* 1: 4) and acts according to her own judgment. A Confucian agent does not blindly follow others' demands. She judges whether their demands are legitimate or not. The sage Shun decides to go against his parents' wishes and gets married without their permission because his parents' wishes are unjustified and because compliance with them will result in his not achieving the important relationship of husband and wife. (*Mencius* 5A: 2). Furthermore, a Confucian agent is guided by the idea of *shu* (taking oneself as analogous to others). She treats others in the way she wants others to treat her, and she helps others to achieve what she herself values. She relies on her own judgment in deciding how to treat others.

Indeed, as a component of Confucian agency, autonomy can even be said to be indispensable. After all, one cannot truly embrace certain values unless one autonomously chooses to ratify or adopt those values as one's own. When an individual is brainwashed, conditioned, coerced, or deceived into accepting certain values, the individual does not stand in the right relationship with them: the individual is not moved by the values themselves and does not accept them for their own sake. But it is of paramount importance that a Confucian agent should be moved by the intrinsic goodness of relationships and accept relationship duties based on nothing other than this moral apprehension.[7] Confucius claims that if one is not moved by the values of *ren*, following ritual rules does not count as practicing the ritual (*li*) (*Analects* 3: 3). Autonomy is important in Confucian role-ethics because it is the presupposition of Confucian agency.

Still autonomy as such need not be seen as valuable. The value of autonomy depends on the value of the content of one's autonomous choices. Thus,

---

7. Autonomous choice in Confucian agency therefore does not require the availability of alternatives of equal value. It does, however, require, the availability of alternatives, and the agent's ability to differentiate and compare the moral values embodied in the alternatives.

autonomy is only valuable when the *correct* values are autonomously embraced. An autonomous agent who deviates from the Confucian path will not be praised for her autonomy. For example, although he encourages a student to make an autonomous choice about whether to shorten the mourning period of three years, Confucius nevertheless sneers at the student as not being a person of *ren* when he chooses to shorten it (*Analects* 17: 19). Thus, the Confucian endorsement of autonomy is a qualified one: the value of autonomy is derived from the role it plays in Confucian agency.

Individualism, on the other hand, values autonomy for its own sake. Taking this value to its extremity, the existentialists believe that autonomy is the basis of one's existence: one's existence is realized in the making of autonomous choices. Thus, autonomy is not just seen as having value in itself independent of the value of the content of the autonomous choice. It even confers value on the options it selects.[8]

For Kant, autonomy is also intrinsically valuable. It is the basis of human dignity: "Autonomy is thus the basis of the dignity of both human nature and every rational nature."[9] For in virtue of autonomy, an individual becomes self-legislating. She is under no law except those which she herself legislates. In other words, she is subject to no authority except her own. This capacity to be her own master accounts for her dignity.

One might argue that in encouraging an agent to choose her own values, Confucian role-ethics is also promoting self-mastery, for when a Confucian agent chooses her own values, she is also her own master. But this claim is misleading. For Kant, being one's own master is the intrinsic value which grounds one's dignity. The Confucian case is different. Although a Confucian agent can be seen as her own master in choosing her values, the self-mastery itself is not the value a Confucian agent prizes or aims at achieving. She aims only at doing the right thing for the right reasons. Autonomy, a precondition for that, is valued, but only instrumentally. Indeed, given the authoritarian nature of Confucian relationships, it is hard to imagine how Confucian role-ethics could encourage an agent to cherish self-mastery intrinsically.

Apart from self-mastery, however, Kantian ethics and Confucian role-ethics do not differ substantially on the issue of the intrinsic value of autonomy. They hold different conclusions only because they have very different conceptions of autonomy. Kant regards an autonomous choice as a rational choice, a choice based on reasoning. This concept of autonomy is thicker than the Confucian

---

8. See Jean-Paul Sartre, 1957.

9. Note that Kant's sense of dignity is different from the sense of dignity in individualism. It focuses more on respectability than on giving priority to an individual's interests (1959: 54).

one in that it requires rationality, not mere reflection and the absence of constraint. Autonomy is intrinsically valuable because morally right choices are essentially autonomous choices (Kant 1959: 22–64). But the Confucian conception contains no inherent connection between autonomy and morally right choices and therefore has no reason to regard autonomy as intrinsically valuable.

We should be careful in drawing conclusions about what Confucian role-ethics would say about autonomy. Not valuing autonomy as such does not imply the acceptability of interference or the imposition of rules on deviants. Confucius does not attempt to force the student to comply with the mourning rule. Abstaining from interference may be justified on pedagogical grounds. Seeing that autonomy lacks intrinsic value does not prevent one from seeing its instrumental value, for autonomy is the precondition for acting virtuously. Furthermore, a Confucian may weigh the costs of interference, such as resistance, rejection, and over-reliance, and other instrumental values of autonomy such as the effectiveness of learning from one's mistakes and cultivating one's initiative. The decision to respect autonomy or to interfere is a contextual and pragmatic one which depends on the empirical considerations in each case. In sum, a Confucian may not diverge much from an individualist when it comes to the practice of respecting autonomy.

Clearly Confucian role-ethics diverges significantly from the individualist values of dignity and autonomy. However, it may still have enough overlap with individualism to accommodate economic competition and the assertiveness of individuals. Though Confucian role-ethics does not respect the dignity of individuals in the sense that it does not accord first priority to individual interests, it still recognizes their importance. Similarly, while there is no intrinsic valuing of autonomy as such, autonomy is seen as good if the content of the autonomous choice is right. Hence one can autonomously pursue one's economic interests for oneself and one's family, if one does it in the right way.

The lack of support for collectivism

The second worry starts at the other end of the spectrum. Perhaps individualism is not essential for economic success. Even if it were, it might entail too high a social price, such as social disruption, alienation, short-sighted economic endeavors, and so forth. Perhaps the right model is the Japanese one, which places primacy on groups rather than individuals and subordinates the interests of individuals to those of groups. Collectivism induces cooperation and economic success as well as social cohesion and solidarity. The problem is that Confucian role-ethics does not imply collectivism. The Five Relationships are all relationships between individuals, not between groups or between an individual and a group.

It might be objected that this worry is groundless because Confucian role-ethics does embody collectivism. It emphasizes the interests of a social group—the family (*jia*). Three out of the Five Relationships are familial relationships, so in a sense Confucian role-ethics is primarily family ethics. Family was always the primary social and economic unit in traditional China. Farming was family-based, family members shared the economic resources, and the financial control was exercised by the head of a family, usually the father or grandfather. Family interests often seemed to take priority over the interests of individual family members. And the importance of family persists in modern China. According to the survey made by Chu and Ju in Shanghai and the rural county of Qingpu, 79.8 per cent of the respondents claimed that the most important goal in life was to have a warm and close family.[10] Hence, one can attribute a group orientation to Confucian role-ethics.

Appreciating the importance of family in Confucian role-ethics, scholars have attributed "familism" to the Asian countries of Japan, Hong Kong, Taiwan, Singapore, and South Korea, all of which share a Confucian heritage.[11] By familism, they mean the extraordinary preoccupation with family solidarity and interests. The familial characteristics they describe include filial piety, ancestor reverence, patriarchal authority, female subordination, respect for the elderly, intergenerational continuity, long-term planning, and fear of collective dishonor. But the term may actually imply different things in different countries.

Whether familism in Japan expresses a group orientation or not, familism in China does not. First, it is dubious whether family is really understood as a group unit, or whether it is primarily seen as a repository of familial relationships. It is undeniable that the word "family" does denote a collective unit in traditional China. As Patricia Ebrey points out about the Chinese family system in the Song Dynasty, a family (*jia*) could have economic assets (1984: 219–45). It dealt with the outside world as a unit and continued through time despite the deaths of individual members. It could have rules (*fa*), teachings (*xun*), records (*bu*), reputations (*sheng*), and power (*shi*). And it is undeniable that people often did things for the sake of family as a group unit. People acted carefully to protect family reputation. They worked hard to bring honor and

---

10. The survey's 2,000 respondents included 1,199 from metropolitan Shanghai, 304 from two towns in Qingpu, and 497 from 20 villages in the four nearby rural districts; see Chu and Ju 1993: 174.

11. See, for example, Rozman 1991: 31.

wealth to family. And they were concerned about the preservation of family teachings and rules.

What is not obvious, however, is whether this collective entity is the thing that constitutes the locus of the Chinese style of familism. For what the group unit really refers to is the "family-household," that is, the independent economic and social unit. But family, the unit which includes the three relationships of father-son, elder brother-younger brother, husband-wife need not coincide with the family-household. Daughters marry and become members of family-households of another surname. Adult younger sons set up independent family-households. Bad sons and daughters can be expelled from family-households. Nevertheless all these people are still considered to be members of family, and they are still bound by ethical obligations and emotional ties to other members of the family. What Confucian role-ethics is about and what the Chinese deeply cherish seems to be family, not family-household.

Does this sense of family apply to a group unit? I doubt it. As pointed out by Fei Hsiao-tung, Ambrose King, and others, the concept of a group (*qun*) is an elusive one in China; the boundaries of any Chinese grouping, including family, are always ambiguous and undefined.[12] A family boundary, in particular, is highly elastic. Family membership can extend beyond the nuclear family to include members of a lineage or a clan. This fact tells against the existence of a group orientation in China, for it is hard to imagine group solidarity existing given such nebulous group boundaries. It is even harder to imagine that individual members will subordinate their interests for the sake of such an indefinite group.

Even the importance of having a male heir, for the sake of which a childless wife can be divorced, should be seen more as a means to fulfill the moral obligation to the parents and ancestors than as a means to perpetuate an abstract group unit called family. Mencius describes not having a male heir as the greatest violation of filial duty (*Mencius* 4A: 26). Ebrey points out that the importance of a male heir was not so much to ensure the descent line as to ensure performance of the sacrificial rites to the ancestors (1984: 235). The well-being of the ancestral spirits depended upon regular performance of the sacrificial rites, which explains, Zhu Xi says, Mencius' claim about filial duty (Zhu 1985: 109).

The greatest punishment meted out by a family is the termination of relationship with the offending person. This is more serious than expulsion from family which merely cancels one's entitlement to family property and

---

12. King cites Fei Hsiao-t'ung in arguing this point (1985: 61).

excludes one from participating in family functions and ceremonies. When the relationship is terminated, the individual can no longer pay sacrifice to the deceased parents, and one's siblings treat one as a stranger. One reason why the Cultural Revolution is so abhorrent to the Chinese is because many people were coerced to "draw a clear line" (*huaqing jiexian*), that is, to terminate their relationships with family members who were considered class enemies. Note that the action is expressed as a termination of relationships, not as a withdrawal from family or a changing of one's family name.

When justification is required for the sacrifice of relationships (in family contexts), one never appeals to the interests of the family.[13] Sacrifice of relationships often happened, especially in traditional China. People divorced their wives and sold their children (mostly daughters). The justification was made in relationship terms. Wives were divorced because they had failed their role-duties as wives: for example, they were infertile, or they did not maintain filial piety towards the husbands' parents. Children were sold because the parents could not support them, or because the parents could not support both the children and the grandparents. When dilemmas occur in a family, they are dilemmas between the specific relationships within the family, not dilemmas between a person and a group unit called a family. One is never just a member in a family; one is a son, a husband, a brother, or a father in a family.[14]

Although Confucian role-ethics does not embody collectivism, it may still be congenial to collectivism. One might assimilate a group into the relationship nexus and create a sixth relationship—the relationship between a person and a group of which she is a member. The idea of establishing this sixth relationship has been widely discussed in Taiwan (King 1985: 65, n. 60). One can also point to the Japanese model where enterprise loyalty is equated with family solidarity. Kinship terms are extended to companies, and the individual identifies her interests with the company's interests just as she identifies her interests with her family's. The spirit of harmony, mutual understanding, and

---

13. Sacrifices of familial relationships are often made when there is conflict with another moral obligation: for example, the conflict between loyalty and filial piety. Thus one sometimes speaks of sacrificing one's kin for the sake of the greater ethical duty (*dayi mieqin*).

14. The New Confucianist Liang Shou-ming and the sociologist Ambrose King both refer to the relationship orientation of Chinese society and distinguish it from collectivism. Liang points out that the Chinese society does not have groups, nor individuals. It is a relationship-based society. According to King a role-relationship is a relationship between concrete individuals. See Liang 1963: 78–95; King 1985: 64.

solicitude extends from families to companies (Rozman 1991: 32; Clark 1988: 105).[15]

There is no obvious reason why a group cannot be assimilated into the relationship nexus. Confucian role-ethics values can apply to a group. One can care about a group, interact with it according to the principle of reciprocity, be emotionally connected to it, and even see it as an irreplaceable particular and cherish the relationship one shares with it as not capable of substitution. Students care immensely about the victory or defeat of their school football team. One recalls President Kennedy's famous dictum, "Ask not what your country can do for you. Ask what you can do for your country." Individuals and a group unit can reciprocate. And one can love one's former school, miss it, or feel ashamed of it.

But assimilation of a group into the relationship framework is not equivalent to collectivism, for collectivism requires the accordance of primacy to a group and the subservience of individual interests to those of a group. In the suggested model, the engaged individual need not be submerged in a group just as she is not submerged in a relationship. She can be an independent agent actively defining her relationship with the group and balancing her own interests with the interests of her related group, as she does with a related individual.

Perhaps modernization does not require collectivism as such, but only the recognition of the importance of group interests. If that is the case, assimilating a group into the relationship framework is sufficient, but not necessary. For example, an individual can see the instrumental value of promoting group interests and attain them through good coordination of individual efforts. It is not necessary to care for or to be related to a group. Moreover, it remains to be seen whether Confucian role-ethics can be extended to cover a group without distorting its spirit. After all, Confucian role-ethics is about relationships among concrete individuals, and not with an abstract entity like a group.

Backdooring

The third worry is that since Confucian role-ethics encourages and allows elasticity of relationships, it paves the way for backdooring, the unethical seeking of advantages by using human relationships in a way that violates relevant rules or the spirit of those rules. Suppose I work for a company whose policy requires me to hire the most qualified applicant. If because of friendship,

---

15. Masa Okano pointed out to me that personal relationships also play an important role in creating harmony among colleagues in Japanese companies.

I give the job to a person who is not the most qualified applicant, this is backdooring. It is an unethical form of preferential treatment which should be distinguished from networking and from certain types of family favoritism. For example, in many family businesses, family members rather than the most qualified fill the top positions, but since the owner has the prerogative to set up the rules of appointment and promotion, provided that the rules do not violate the law, the practice is ethically acceptable, if not economically advisable. This problem of backdooring is prevalent in China as anyone with experience living there knows.

It is true that Confucian role-ethics encourages relationship building because it sees engagement in relationships as intrinsically valuable. And it is also true that relationship building in Confucianism is flexible and elastic, allowing significant room for an individual to maneuver. Of the Five Relationships, only two are "natural" rather than chosen, namely, the father-son and elder brother-younger brother relationships. Of course, individuals often did not choose the husband-wife relationship in traditional China. But the relationships between ruler and minister and between friends are voluntary. An individual can choose to remain a hermit and abstain from official positions, and one can cut the mat one shares with another person and terminate the friendship. Although the Five Relationships are intrinsically valuable, there are circumstances where it is better, or at least permissible, not to engage in the voluntary relationships. Confucius praised Wei Zi (*Analects* 18: 1) and Mencius praised Bo Yi (Mencius 5B: 1) as virtuous individuals who abstained from office. And the Confucians are ever so earnest that people should shrink from bad company. No one is obligated to cultivate a relationship just because one interacts with a person. Moreover, by manipulating the reciprocity element in relationships, one can decide to what extent the relationship should develop. Confucius demonstrates this deft art when he goes to visit the sender of a gift to express his gratitude, knowing all along that the person is not at home (*Analects* 17: 1). Ambrose King rightly points out that a Confucian agent does not passively fulfill obligations imposed by the various roles, but rather, plays a dynamic role in defining the scope and the degree of the interactions (1985: 57–68). Thus the ability to establish connections with others (*la guanxi*), and to court friendship (*pan jiaoqing*) become an art to many Chinese.

While not disputing an inherent connection between backdooring and the relationship orientation of Confucian role-ethics, we still believe that the problem is not inevitable. While Confucian role-ethics encourages relationship building, it does not encourage the manipulation of relationships for unjust gains. The fact that relationships are intrinsically valuable and that preferential treatment among relations is acceptable in certain circumstances does not mean that all forms of preferential treatment of family and friends are equally acceptable and justified. Some forms of preferential treatment violate values such as justice and efficiency and should not be endorsed.

Confucian texts recognize the need to draw distinctions between acceptable and unacceptable forms of preferential treatment. The sage Shun appointed Yu rather than his son to be his successor (*Mencius* 5A: 6). The text points out that ideally the throne should be passed on to the (most) virtuous rather than to one's relatives. Shun also shared wealth and honor with his brother Xiang by endowing Xiang with a fief. But because Xiang was not virtuous, Shun made sure that he was not allowed to take any action in his fief. Officials were appointed to administer the fief, so that Xiang could not mistreat the people (*Mencius* 5A: 3). The idea of putting the public duty before the private affair is clearly pointed out in Mencius's discussion of the ideal of the well system. "Only when they have done their public (*gong*) duty dare they turn to their private (*si*) affairs" (*Mencius* 3A: 3). Confucius as a teacher showed no preferential treatment to his son Li as a student (*Analects* 16: 13).[16]

In sum, while the orientation towards relationships may encourage people to give preferential treatment, it does not imply indiscriminate endorsement of preferential treatment. Hence, we do not need to steer away from it in order to combat backdooring. It suffices to make the significant distinction between acceptable and unacceptable forms of preferential treatment.

Since respect for the distinction between acceptable and unacceptable preferential treatment can be promoted by people's respect for laws and regulations, we also need to see whether Confucian role-ethics discourages a respect for rules. But Confucian role-ethics cannot downplay the importance of respecting rules. Ritual rules (*li*) are central to Confucian role-ethics. Confucius admonished his students for suggesting that he should sell his carriage in order to give his son a decent funeral. To do this would force him to travel without a carriage, and that violated a ritual rule (*Analects* 11: 8).

Moreover, laws and rules deter, regulate, and coordinate within each orientation: individualism, collectivism, or the relationship orientation. For example, good rules of an organization inform people of the parameters they have when interacting with colleagues. Guided by the rules, one cannot refuse to perform a task just because the task involves interaction with a colleague whom one loathes. Nor should one give one's favorite colleague confidential company information if she does not have the right to know this information.

---

16. Indeed the tradition has always seriously condemned the practice of favoritism, nepotism, and factionalism. Formal organizations of factions were suppressed. The policy of avoidance (*bixun*) prohibited the appointment of a person to serve as a governor in his native province, and another policy forbade an official to give appointments to his relatives.

Within the rules one can choose to go an extra mile to help a colleague or can do only what is required. A Confucian agent can certainly accept rules as constraints on her practice of preferential treatment.

The Chinese saying that "Laws are nothing more than human sentiments" (*falü bu wei hu renqing*) should not be interpreted as meaning that emotional or relationship ties are to be achieved at the expense of laws. Nor does it mean that the application of laws should be supplemented by considerations about emotional or relationship ties. The words "human sentiments" refer to the reality of the whole range of human emotions, not just emotional or relationship ties. Rather than advocating favoritism, the saying should be seen as expressing the idea of discretion (*quan*) (Mencius 1A: 7; 4A: 18; 7A: 26). That is, one should not follow the rules strictly, but should carefully weigh all relevant factors in a situation.

Authoritarianism

Unlike the previous three worries, which stem from considerations about the nature of relationship ethics, the fourth worry is about the actual content of relationships prescribed by Confucian role-ethics. Confucian relationships are authoritarian, and authoritarianism induces inefficiency. Authoritarianism requires subservience of those occupying an inferior position to those in a superior position, which dampens the initiative and incentives of subordinates and inhibits their independent decision-making, self-reliance, and sense of responsibility.

It might be objected that Confucian role-ethics does not imply authoritarianism, but the Three Bonds do suggest asymmetrical relationships. The term "bond" implies authoritarianism in that strict obedience is expected of the son, minister and wife to the father, ruler, and husband respectively. The latter group has the power to make decisions about every aspect of the lives of those in the former group. But if we turn to the Five Relationships, we see they are more symmetrical. Mencius describes the Five Relationships as "love between father and son, duty between ruler and subject, distinction between husband and wife, precedence of the old over the young, and faith between friends" (*Mencius* 3A: 4). All but one description involves reciprocity. A similar reciprocal element is illustrated in the *Book of Rites* (*Li ji*). "The father be affectionate, the son be filial. The elder brother be virtuous, the younger brother be obedient. The husband be righteous, the wife be docile. The senior be kind, the junior be compliant. The ruler be benevolent, the minister be loyal." (*Li ji*, "Li Yun").

But one should not equate reciprocity with equality. Although a degree of symmetry between relationships is guaranteed by reciprocity, the authoritarian element may still remain. Reciprocity ensures only that good is returned for good, not the exchange of a good of the same nature. One reciprocates affection and respect for protection and guidance. While nobody need be shortchanged in this transaction, nonetheless one party has authority over the other. Authoritarian relationships can be compatible with reciprocity.

There is textual support for the view that Confucian relationships are authoritarian. From the quotation in *Li ji*, we can see that the younger brother, the wife, and the junior are expected to be obedient, docile, and compliant. And although filial piety and loyalty do not obviously imply subservience, some illustrations in *Analects* and *Mencius* suggest subservience. A son can remonstrate against the parent, but he still cannot act against the parent's wishes (*Analects* 4: 18). And loyalty may require that a minister commit suicide as his only legitimate means of remonstrating the ruler (*Analects* 18: 1).

However, a more careful examination will show that authoritarianism in Confucian role-ethics does not run very deep. Mencius explicitly says that authority can be overridden. Parents' wishes can be acted against if they are gravely mistaken (*Mencius* 5A: 2). A minister can legitimately overthrow a bad ruler if his justified remonstrations are regularly ignored (*Mencius* 5B: 9). This antiauthoritarian sentiment is also implicit in the *Analects*. While committing suicide exhibits paramount loyalty, leaving a bad ruler is seen as equally virtuous. The guiding rule is serving the ruler according to the virtuous way, the *Dao* (*Analects* 11: 22). One should leave the ruler-minister relationship if the ruler requires one to transgress the *Dao*.

Above all, the importance of autonomy in Confucian agency challenges authoritarianism in Confucian role-ethics. It might be objected that authoritarianism still has a significant hold here. While there is evidence that Confucian role-ethics sanctions autonomy in judgment, it is not obvious that it sanctions autonomy in action as well. If authority can be challenged in action only when grave mistakes are made, and if the only means of expressing the challenge to less serious mistakes is to leave the relationship, the subservient party is far from being an independent, effective agent.

But it is misguided to think that the Confucian agent has freedom of thought without freedom of action, even if there is not much room for challenging the authority in action. First, we should note that dialog is built into the system of Confucian authoritarianism. To remonstrate is part of the duty of loyalty and filial piety. Respecting the opinions of the minister is part of the duty of the ruler; it is part of treating the minister with ritual (*li*) (*Mencius* 4B: 3). Second, we should remember that Confucian role-ethics does not assume frequent conflicts between the related parties. Requiring remonstration and communication helps to resolve some conflicts. But in most cases, the extent of autonomy in action, as opposed to autonomy in judgment, depends on how much power the person in the superior position delegated to the person in the subordinate position.

Authoritarianism permits a high degree of delegation of power on expediency grounds such as efficiency. Or delegation may be made after considering the instrumental value of autonomy, such as the importance of learning from one's own mistakes. Confucian authoritarianism endorses a high degree of delegation. This is not surprising, given the importance of autonomy in Confucian agency. A child should respect parental wishes, but the parent can also want the child to make independent decisions. The ideal Confucian ruler is not a dictator or a busy executive; he is a moral exemplar who takes no (unnecessary) action (*Analects* 15: 4).

Authoritarianism may still be objectionable on moral grounds. But it is not obvious that Confucian authoritarianism, with its stress on communication and a high degree of delegation of power, will undermine individual initiative or efficiency.

Finally, we should note that authoritarianism is not essential to the spirit of Confucian role-ethics, which has the ideal of loving engagement with others. Reciprocity is an essential element of that ideal, but reciprocity is neutral on the issue of authoritarianism. Though authoritarianism has been part of the traditional Confucian role-ethics, it need not continue to be.

Confucian Role-Ethics and Small Economic Units with Personal Ties

The Confucian stress on close personal relationships tends to facilitate the development and healthy maintenance of small enterprises. Mutual caring encourages the pooling of manpower and capital from families and relatives to help start and later sustain small economic enterprises. Moreover, relationship networking paves the way both to resources and clientele. A person's skill in initiating and consolidating relationships translates easily into an economic asset, especially in a context which emphasizes and values relationships. The high percentage of small-scale, family-based manufacturing units in Taiwan and the flourishing over the past decade of "individual-households" (*geti hu*) in the trading markets of mainland China testify to this impact of Confucian role-ethics.

The stress on close personal relationships also has important implications for people's interactions in the workplace. Since the economic context is also a social context, relationships are not seen in purely economic terms. Instead, a Confucian agent plays a dynamic role in establishing her relationship nexus, determining with whom and to what extent she will build personal relationships in the workplace. The orientation of Confucian role-ethics towards relationships, however, definitely encourages people in the direction of actively building up personal bonds among colleagues.

In the workplace the Confucian influence on personalizing relationships among colleagues can best be seen in the mentor relationship. While the formal institution of this relationship in China (including mainland China, Taiwan, and Hong Kong) is rare, its actual practice is pervasive. The relationship can hold between a supervisor and a subordinate, between an experienced worker and a novice, or between an old-timer and a newcomer. Experience transmission, training, and supervision are only part of the purpose of this practice. Its main function is to establish the newcomer in the workplace by securing a relationship for her. The activity is relationship-oriented rather than task-oriented. The values that govern the relationship are those governing personal relationships: concern, sincerity, consideration, respect, appreciation, and gratitude. A newcomer looks to a mentor for personal support as well as for guidance. Even more important, a mentor provides a starting point from which the newcomer develops her own relationship network. The mentor is responsible for introducing the newcomer to other colleagues and facilitating the newcomer's integration into the existing relationship network. The Chinese saying "teacher/ mentor for a day, teacher/ mentor for a whole life." (*yiri weishi, zhongshen wei shi*) illustrates the personal nature of this relationship very well. For further evidence of the personal ties among colleagues in China, one need only recall the mah-jongg games, the group lunches, the widespread gossiping, and more recently the karaoke mania which bond people in the workplace together on a personal basis.

Conclusion

Confucian role-ethics is not incompatible with the values supporting modernization. It has enough overlap with elements in individualism to facilitate economic competition. It is also congenial to the collectivist approach of promoting the interests of groups. Given the orientation of Confucian role-ethics towards relationships, backdooring is a natural, but not an inevitable problem. Confucian agents need to recognize the distinction between legitimate and illegitimate forms of preferential treatment for family and friends. Although authoritarianism is inherent in traditional Confucian role-ethics, the stress in Confucian authoritarianism on dialogue, autonomy of judgment, and delegation of power can reduce its negative impact on efficiency. Finally, the orientation towards relationships facilitates the development of small economic units based on familial or other close personal ties and promotes the development of personal relationships in the workplace.

Chinese culture has often been praised as a culture of humanism. Confucian role-ethics has made an important contribution to the development of this characteristic. With a little luck, its continual influence will help the Chinese society to preserve this valuable quality while it undergoes the process of economic modernization. Let us hope that in the century to come, China progresses not only in the economic sphere, but also in the production of caring and engaged persons.

References

Chu, Godwin C., and Yanan Ju. 1993. *The Great Wall in Ruins*. Albany: State University of New York Press.
Clark, Rodney. 1988. "The Company as Family: Historical Background." In *Inside the Japanese System*, edited by Daniel Okimoto and Thomas Rohlem. Stanford: Stanford University Press.
Confucius. *Analects*.
Ebrey, Patricia. 1984. "Conceptions of the Family in Sung Dynasty." *Journal of Asian Studies* 43: 219-45.
Hsu, Dau-lin. 1960. "The Myth of the Five Human Relations of Confucius." *Minzhu ping-lun* (Democratic critique) (Hong Kong) 11 (April).
Kant, Immanuel. 1959. *Foundations of the Metaphysics of Morals*. Translated by Lewis White Beck. New York: Bobbs-Merrill.
King, Ambrose. 1985. "The Individual and the Group in Confucianism." In *Individualism and Holism: Studies in Confucian and Taoist Values*, edited by Donald J. Munro. Ann Arbor: University of Michigan Center for Chinese Studies.
Liang Shou-ming. 1963. *Zhong guo wenhua yaoyi* (The essence of Chinese culture). Taipei: Zheng Zhong Book Company.
Mencius.
Mill, John Stuart. 1947. *Utilitarianism, Liberty and Republican Government*. New York: Everyman's Library.
Munro, Donald J., ed. 1985. *Individualism and Holism: Studies in Confucian and Taoist Values*. Ann Arbor: University of Michigan Center for Chinese Studies.
Rawls, John. 1971. *A Theory of Justice*. Cambridge: The Belknap Press of Harvard University Press.
Rozman, Gilbert. 1991. *The East Asian Region: Confucian Heritage and its Modern Interpretation*. Princeton: Princeton University Press.

Sartre. Jean-Paul. 1957. "Existentialism is a Humanism." In *Existentialism from Dostoevsky to Sartre*, edited by Walter Kaufmann. New York: Meridian Books.

Sher, George. 1989. "Three Degrees of Social Involvement." *Philosophy and Public Affairs* 18: 133-57.

Zhu Xi. 1985. *Sishu jizhu: Collected Commentary on the Four Books*. Taipei: World Book Store.

Glossary

Baihu tong	白虎通
ben	本
bixun	避巡
bu	簿
dayi mieqin	大義滅親
fa	法
falü bu wai hu renqing	法律不外乎人情
geti hu	個體戶
gong	公
huaqing jiexian	劃清界線
la guanxi	拉關係
li	禮
pan jiaoqing	攀交情
quan	權
qun	群
ren	仁
sheng	聲
shi	勢
si	私
tianxia	天下
xun	訓
yi	義
yiri wei shi, zhongshen wei shi	一日爲師終身爲師
zhi	智

Selling Sagehood:
The Philosophical Marketplace
in Early China

ROBERT ENO
Indiana University

When we speak of the marketplace of ideas we generally use the phrase figuratively, referring to free intellectual competition through which the validity of ideas is tested. In analyzing the development of early Chinese thought we may appropriately use the phrase with a more explicit, economic meaning. The men whom we now identify as China's first philosophers were not initially viewed as pure thinkers, but as men who possessed ideas of tangible value, political or personal, to the economic elite of the era. Their *dao*s (teachings) were commodities and our understanding of early Chinese thought can be enriched if we better understand the ways in which market forces governed the development of ideas and doctrines.

Among the economic constraints that bore on the growth of philosophy in Warring States China, the most fundamental were related to the centralized state structures that grew from new agricultural and military technologies following from China's entry into the Iron Age. Cho-yun Hsu demonstrated in great detail thirty years ago that the demand for talented men created by these changes fatally undermined the monopoly that China's traditional hereditary elite held on positions of power and status (1965). The implications of Hsu's findings for the emergent structures of Chinese thought were formulated by Donald Munro, who correlated them with the general belief in the descriptive equality of men that shaped the most basic doctrines of both Confucian and Daoist schools (1969). These beliefs, and the consequent claim that any man with useful ideas or good character should receive patronage and employment, were axiomatic to the intellectual marketplace of ancient China.

This essay explores smaller scale economic and social factors that shaped the market of ideas during the Warring States and Qin periods. For this kind of analysis, issues of theoretical debate between schools and individuals, normally at the focus of our interest in discussions of early thought, are less central. Instead, we will seek some perspective on the ways in which the philosophical community as a whole shaped its enterprise in response to those people whose patronage provided thinkers with economic livelihood and social position. As a consequence of this sociological orientation, our analysis will tend to stress similarities rather than distinctions among philosophical schools. Our principal goal is to outline the contours of early philosophy as a socially located profession providing a range of goods, rather than to delineate the varied forms of the philosophical goods themselves.

Five Basic Commodities

If we are to consider early Chinese thought as a marketplace, we need to propose at least a provisional list of commodities that were offered for sale by its participants.[1] After formulating a starting list, we will see how its items differ from a full inventory of the major ideas of early Chinese philosophy.

While there is a great diversity among the early Chinese philosophical schools, there was also significant overlap in terms of key concepts. For example, a number of schools laid great stress upon the importance of *de* (character, virtue, power) in connection with personal, social, or metaphysical transformation. The specific way in which *de* was to be understood varied according to the doctrinal contexts of the various schools—which is why, in part, the word is so difficult to translate—but the basic notion that by cultivating a quality referred to as *de* one could attain a form of personal excellence and social leverage was common to several types of thought. The theory that personal virtue could endow a man with the ability to attract, lead, and transform others was a widespread social and political notion.

In using the marketplace analogy to discuss early Chinese thought, it will be useful to distinguish between concepts such as *de* and the ideological contexts in which they appear. *De* was a marketable commodity: a thinker appealing to a potential patron might offer a *dao* for the attainment of *de*. The thinker might be distinguished within a community of peers for the uniqueness of that *dao*, but from the standpoint of the wealthy or powerful consumer, the commodity of interest was the *de* and the social leverage that it would provide.

For example, the appeal that early Confucianism might have for a person in a position of power would not likely lie in the attractiveness of ritualism or the imperatives of filiality and benevolence, but rather in the claim that in adopting such behaviors a person might gain increased moral sway over local and neighboring populations.[2] The Mohists, opponents of Confucian ritualism and

---

1. I refer to these intellectual goods as commodities because they became subject to forms of explicit exchange, typically for patronage stipends or disciple tuition, during the Warring States period. Earlier, such intellectual goods in the possession of well-placed patricians or hereditary functionaries might have enhanced their stature, but not in the context of conceptually defined exchange.

2. Mencius repeatedly made this argument in his appeals to kings. It seems unlikely that most potential patrons of Confucians would have made a clear distinction between embodying virtues, which is the way we ordinarily think of the term *de* in a Confucian context, and being looked upon as a benign source of grace by others, which seems to have been an earlier and more common meaning.

narrow filiality, promoted the ethical ideal of the universal-minded ruler. To the degree that rulers may have responded to Mohism, that response would not have been to the moral imperative of universality, but to Mohist arguments that ritual *li* would impoverish a state and alienate its people, while rulers implementing the policies of universality would gain the type of personal; ascendance over others that would yield social leverage and secure power.[3]

Among the basic marketable commodities offered by early Chinese thinkers, we may note five that predominated and spread widely among the different schools. The notion of transformative *de* was one of these. The others include the following: the notion that one could learn to control all situations through arts of proper timing, variously referred to as "timeliness" (*shi*) and "situational propensities" (*shi*);[4] the belief that *qi* (vaporous energy) could be harnessed to gain leverage over objective constraints generally beyond the power of an individual to overcome; the idea that administrative design could produce social order and make power secure; and the belief that correlative natural categories could be manipulated to order society and gain leverage over the natural world.

To change idioms for clarity, the following five hooks were the principal ways in which philosophers attracted patronage: learn how to win friends and influence people; learn how to do the right thing at the right time; learn how to turn your body into a spiritual vessel; learn a perfect management system; learn how to harness the rhythms of the cosmos and make them work for you.

During the Warring States period, practical formulas for these aims seem to emerge as dominant commodities in roughly this order, packaged differently by various schools in each case. This is not by any means to say that early Chinese philosophy is limited to these ideas. Many of its most powerful philosophical ideas, such as its identification of the problematic aspects of language, are not among the basic notions listed here. This is because such ideas, while philosophically significant, had little practical appeal for potential patrons and so did not directly affect the market.

Abstruse philosophical arguments could, however, be commoditized as esoteric exotica which could raise the status of the patron who endorsed them by virtue of their strangeness. The status of the philosopher of language Gongsun Long at the court of the warlord Pingyuan Jun in Zhao, for example, could be seen as a case of a thinker being engaged not because he offered a *useful* commodity, but because it

---

3. The Mohists do not much use the term *de*, and as an "action ethics" Mohism is less concerned with personal attributes than with behavior. However, the social outcome Mohists claimed for adherence to their universalist maxims is identical in essentials with that claimed by Confucians for virtue cultivation: the attraction and transformation of others.

4. I borrow the term "propensities" from François Jullien, who has pointed out that the notions of "timeliness" and recognition of propensities are complementary concepts framed in metaphors of time and space. See 1992: 11n.

enhanced his lord's stature to be seen patronizing a "luxury item." In this sense, we may add as a sixth basic commodity the notion that high quality intellectual arts or *dao*s were in themselves valuable, and so marketable without regard to their specific content.

Basic Stages of Market Development

The philosophical market developed through five stages: 1. the period of Confucius's later career (about 500–480 [all dates are B.C.]), during which the roles of itinerant minister and master of a *dao* become linked; 2. a phase that begins with the decision of Marquis Wen of Wei, in the second half of the fifth century, to base the composition of his court on the recruitment of wise men from other states; 3. the establishment of the Jixia Academy in Qi about a century later, which formalized the practice of government patronage of wise men without a fixed linkage to ministerial duties; 4. the devolution of patronage during the mid-third century from state courts to the households of major warlords; and 5. the establishment of the *boshi* (erudite) system, which under the Qin made the state not only the patron of philosophy, but its regulator.

Confucius: The First Salesman

Confucius (551–479) seems to have been the first man to be recognized as basing his economic sustenance and social persona on the role of freelance instructor.[5] Clearly, knowledge was transmitted by specialists prior to Confucius's day and there is no persuasive reason to believe that such transmission had never occurred in private contexts. But because Confucius was explicitly training men in generalized patrician skills that would earlier have likely been transmitted by family members or tutors in residence with wealthy or powerful families, the freelance and mobile nature of his social persona seems to have attracted notice.

Confucius's students were clearly aiming at economic rewards and social position.[6] Confucius accepted tuition and may have had little else to live on for periods of his life.[7] At times Confucius did receive the benefits of patronage. Such treatment, however, was a consequence of his standing as a wise man, rather than

---

5. All dates for philosophers' lifetimes are according to Qian 1935, and should be viewed as provisional.

6. "A student willing to study three years without taking a position is hard to come by" (*Analects* 8.12). (*Analects* passages are cited by Harvard-Yenching Institute concordance numbers.)

7. "From those who have offered as little as dried sausages on up, I have never refused anyone instruction" (*Analects* 7.7). The *Analects* and Confucius's *Shiji* biography agree that he was at times reduced to penury.

of the attractiveness of his *dao*, which turned out to be marketable only to his student audience.[8]

In seeking for patronage and employment at the various courts of eastern China, Confucius was hoping to make use of the precedent of "guest ministers" that had been established during the Spring and Autumn period by such men as Baili Xi in Qin and Confucius's contemporary Wu Zixu in Wu. But Confucius differed from these men in that he sought position not on the basis of his worthiness alone, but on the basis of his *dao*: a set of ritual prescripts that were designed to transform both individuals and states. The distinction between patronizing a person because of his worth and because of his *dao* was a necessary foundation to the establishment of the philosophical market.

After Confucius's death his disciples dispersed, and most of those who became leading figures in the nascent Confucian community initially replicated their master's pattern of seeking economic sustenance by becoming private teachers.

The Court of Marquis Wen of Wei

While Confucius established the model that would become the basis of the professional philosopher in China, the lack of appeal of his particular program prevented him from opening a broad market. The next step towards the establishment of such a market occurred several decades after his death, and it was a consumer who took the lead.

In 446 the newly enthroned ruler of the upstart state of Wei, Marquis Wen, issued a call for men of talent to serve him at his court. The marquis's motives seem to have been two-fold. Wei was one of the three successor states of Jin, and as a usurper state not yet acknowledged by the Zhou royal house, Wei was undoubtedly anxious to enhance its legitimacy by establishing a reputation as a haven for worthy men. In addition, the balance of power between Wei and the two other Jin successor states, Han and Zhao, was unsettled, and Wei was in search of military and administrative talent that could give it an edge.

The call of Marquis Wen changed the nature of the phenomenon of the guest minister. Whereas such ministers had earlier been appointed to court positions on the basis of the unique circumstances that took them from their home states to another, Marquis Wen's ministers were recruited, and Wei's personnel policy became consciously interstate in nature.

Moreover, the case of Wei illustrates complex patterns of patronage that bore upon the structure of the philosophical marketplace. The *Shiji* recounts how the political stature of natives of the Wei court was determined, at least in part, by the number and quality of the "guests" whom they introduced into the Marquis's

---

8. For example, see the case of the stay in Qi recounted in *Analects* 18.3.

service (44.1840).[9] The philosophical figures of the Warring States period needed
to fashion their approach to powerholders in terms of a multilevel culture of
courtiers, which could involve tailoring one's message for a succession of
patrons.[10]

Among those who responded to Wei's recruitment was the prominent
Confucian disciple, Zixia (507–420), who became court tutor. However, the
outstanding member of Marquis Wen's court was not Zixia but Li Ke (455–395),
who eventually served as prime minister.[11] Li Ke is associated with a technocratic
system of agricultural administration that seems, in many respects, a precursor of
later Legalist models, and he is sometimes referred to as a father of Legalism.[12] The
Shiji attributes the rise in warfare during subsequent generations to his state designs
(30.1442). Yet Li Ke is elsewhere classed as a Confucian, the pupil of Zixia.[13] This
puzzling reference is paralleled by the example of Wu Qi (440–381), a general of
Wei initially recommended by Li Ke, whose name is attached to one of the major
militarist texts attributed to this period. Wu Qi, who was eventually assassinated
while serving as prime minister to Chu, is characterized as "greedy and lustful," but
is also listed as a student of Confucius's disciple Zeng Zi and a transmitter of the
Spring and Autumn Annals in the Confucian classical tradition.[14]

---

9. The specific events narrated may be apocryphal, but the social dynamic appears
credible.

10. The "Wen" chapter of the *Guan Zi* notes as an issue the number of courtiers in a state
who serve the ruler while simultaneously retaining a position in a grandee household
(*qun chen you wei shi guan-dafuzhe*, following the interpretation of Shi 1988: 251). The
complexities of Warring States patronage, in particular the relation between patronage as
a retainer (*shike*) and as a courtier (*binke*), has been analyzed by Aihara Junji (1960: 223–
50).

While this essay employs the metaphor of the marketplace, a more nuanced
presentation might compare the impact of the courtier role on philosophical discourse to
that described by Mario Biagioli with regard to Renaissance science (1993).

11. I am identifying Li Ke and Li Kui, following common practice.

12. Li Ke's policies are recorded in the *Han shu*, "Shihuo zhi" 24a.1124–25. Concerning
his characterization as a Legalist, see Hu 1962: I.265 (subsequent pages include a very
detailed analysis of his economic policies). The notion of a Legalist "precursor" often
focuses less on theories of law in government than on the design of new and efficient
systems to improve social order, economic output, and military strength. Li Ke's success
in Wei helped prepare the ground for the idea that technocratic theory should be a part of
philosophical discourse, which became very powerful after the fourth century reforms of
Shang Yang in Qin.

13. The *Han shu*, "Yiwen zhi" lists a *Li Ke* in seven *juan* under the Confucian category,
and identifies the author as a disciple of Zixia.

14. Characterization: *Shiji* 65.2166; as Zeng Zi pupil: 65.2165; on the tradition of Wu as
transmitter of the classics, see Qian (1935: 192–95) (Qian dismisses the claim). He is also

How do we account for such men being classed as Confucians and what could this imply concerning the scope of the early philosophical market? Perhaps two complementary conclusions may be drawn. First, during the mid- to late fifth century, Confucians were forced to diversify their audiences from those who wished to acquire the master's *dao* to all who would pay to acquire polished skills useful at court. Second, those whom Confucian teachers provided with the teaching's prized commodity, the path towards social leverage through ritual *de*, sought out other goods to sell upon finding that there was no realistic market for *de*: in the case of Li Ke, administrative design, in the case of Wu Qi, military tactics.[15]

A variety of other worthies appear in the lists of men at the court of Marquis Wen: Tian Zifang, a disciple of Confucius's pupil Zigong; the reclusive Duangan Mu, who is said to have once been a great merchant; and others associated with various strengths of government.[16]

This evidence allows us to suggest that the opening of an interstate market for guest ministers in Wei may have triggered diversity in the philosophical marketplace, as associates of the luckless Confucians abandoned the Master's ritual pieties in order to develop expertise in non-Confucian fields that allowed them to create new intellectual commodities more appealing to men of wealth and power.

Packaging the Commodity: The Invention of Philosophical Texts

One key development in the marketing of wisdom during the Classical period is the invention of the philosophical text. Texts, of course, had the practical value of storing *dao*s in conveniently retrievable form. However, they also could possess value as commodities. Wisdom texts are among the objects that we recover from the graves of the elite, and the treasured status which made them suitable grave goods would also have endowed them with market value for the living. But although the appearance of texts as a marketing vehicle is an important step in the evolution of the market, the date and early significance of this invention are difficult to determine.

The *Analects* is often believed to include passages recording the recollections of Confucius's own disciples, and its earliest phases of composition would, if this were true, date from no later than the mid-fifth century. But the *Analects* was clearly not composed to be marketed to an audience external to the Confucian group itself. Many of its cryptic passages make little sense without the support of a

---

listed as a pupil of Zixia (*Shiji* 121.3116). Qian argues that he was not a pupil of Zeng Zi but of his son (1935: 156). This is surely the correct way to read the evidence.

15. Wu Qi's *Shiji* biography (65.2165–68) portrays him as thoroughly evil from youth, yet the latter portion of the text offers a strikingly different portrait which is in some respects quite close to Confucian values, even including a speech concerning the priority of *de* over strategy in war.

16. A full list with discussion is found in Qian 1935: 129–34.

dense teaching tradition; moreover, paradoxical ambiguity and understated modesty, two of its recurrent themes, seem unlikely tools for marketing to wealthy patrons.

The example of the *Analects* highlights the possibility that well-defined schools of thought may not have required texts that presented an expository description of their ideas. In fact, such schools would not necessarily have benefited from the production of such texts, as this would have removed control of the teaching from the teachers, and, in essence, allowed for tuition-free transmission. Perhaps for this reason the earliest and most highly developed of the pre-Qin schools, Confucianism, seems not to have produced an expository philosophical text until the *Xun Zi* was edited during the mid-third century.[17]

It is not currently possible to come to definitive conclusions about the dates of composition of most early texts and any theory concerning the period at which texts were first packaged for consumers at large will necessarily be speculative. However, claims that any specific texts reached such form before the middle years of the fourth century appear to me unlikely. Even so crudely formulated a text as the *Mo Zi* appears not to have reached written form until after the Mohist cult split into three factions, in the early fourth century.[18]

I suggest, then, that somewhere close to 350, original thinkers and disciples of masters first packaged the *dao*s which became their paths to wealth and status as physical commodities, a concrete token of the value that these men promised to

---

17. As I will explain, I regard the *Daxue* and *Zhongyong* as Qin period texts.

18. I am following Graham (1989a: 35). Graham elsewhere suggests 350 as a closing date for the formulation of the central Mohist theses (1978: 5n7). Another philosophical text for which a very early date has been claimed is the *Yan Zi chunqiu* (see Stephen Durrant's discussion in Loewe (1993: 486–87). I am not very familiar with this text and can only offer a concurrence with Durrant's observation, in support of Liang Qichao's late dating of the text, that its style fits very well the literary environment of the late Warring States.

An important recent argument in this connection concerns the *Sun Zi*, for which some would now claim a fifth-century date, based on portions of the text recovered at the Yinqueshan site in Shandong; see Wu 1975: 7, and Yates 1988: 217–18. The passage in question is translated in Ames 1993: 174–76. Ames nevertheless dates the period of composition to 400–320 (*Ibid.*: 24). A passage in that manuscript predicts that the state of Zhao will reunify the former territories of Jin, an outcome which never came to pass. This has led some scholars to argue that the passage could not have been written after 403, when the Zhou royal house officially acknowledged the legitimacy of all three Jin successor states. However, since the force of the prediction is only to assert that Zhao will, at some future time, prevail over Wei and Han, it seems to me that the date of 403 bears no significance. The passage suggests only that this redaction was composed as a marketing tool in the state of Zhao at a time when its relations with Han and Wei were strained, which was quite often the case. It may have been this regional marketing feature of the passage which led to its absence from other transmitted editions.

potential patrons.[19] If the date is correct, it seems beyond coincidence that the profusion of texts should coincide with the establishment in Qi of the Jixia Academy during the reign of King Wei (357–320).[20] The creation of the academy marks a major change in the conditions governing the philosophical market. It is the first example of government patronage of an interstate corps of philosophers without an entailed relationship to government responsibilities, a change which liberates philosophers from the allure of political ambition (though not from dependence on political actors).[21]

The Intellectual Commodities of the Early Fourth Century

Before examining in more detail the significance of the Jixia Academy, I would like to consider the major philosophical ideas that had emerged by the time of its creation in terms of the five major intellectual commodities enumerated earlier (the sixth item, doctrines as exotica, does not play the same sort of role).

The earliest forms of Confucianism and Mohism do not seem to have attracted support beyond an audience of disciples because the most powerful lure they offered placed too great a demand on the ethical commitment of potential patrons. Both schools offered paths to success that required unremitting moral effort, and this approach has historically had few takers. During the fourth century, however, Confucians, and perhaps Mohists, seem to have assimilated more marketable ideas, which they shared in common with other thinkers.

In the case of Confucianism, one major development was the emergence of the doctrine of timeliness, a theme of restricted scope in the early portions of the *Analects*, but a basic notion for Mencius. The concept of timeliness—that there existed attainable skills that would allow a virtuoso actor infallibly to read proper imperatives out of the apparent randomness of particular circumstances—spread far beyond Confucianism in the fourth century. It is a major feature of the *Sun Zi*'s art of the general, particularly if timeliness is understood as embracing the counterpart

---

19. While disciples of the largest and best established schools, namely, Confucianism and Mohism, could have, and eventually did, market their texts under the names of the leading figures of their schools, thinkers not associated with schools sanctified by tradition generally enhanced their texts by ascribing them to figures of mystery or historical authority.

20. The historical texts give contradictory information concerning the date of the founding of Jixia. Qian Mu argues well but not conclusively for the beginning of King Wei's reign (Qian 1935: 232–33). For evidence of an earlier founding date, see Kanaya 1987: 304–5.

21. The interstate nature of Jixia patronage distinguishes it from the custom of "honoring worthies" which was said to be a feature of the court of Duke Mu of Lu (r. 415–383). The duke's policies in his small state seem to have been an attempt of the court to enhance its legitimacy chiefly by linking itself to the growing posthumous reputation of Confucius, a native son.

notion of responding to situational propensities (*shi*).[22] The concept of timeliness is basic to the entire notion of sagehood as it was construed during the late Warring States period, and the proliferation of competing claims by schools to possess the unique route to these skills suggests its appeal to consumers.[23]

The fourth century also seems to have seen the rise of interest in the notion of *qi* across a number of philosophical divisions. Texts dating from this period that show an interest in the concept include the militarist *Sun Zi*, which discusses its manifestation among massed troops, the quietist proto-hygiene *Nei ye* text, the *Zhuang Zi*, in tales such as the Cook Ding story, and the *Mencius*, which links the cultivation of *qi* with the figures of virtuoso martial artists. While *qi* already possesses many dimensions of meaning by this time, its most marketable feature was not likely to have been its cosmological significance, but rather the various sorts of physical prowess which were said to be consequences of harnessing its power, along with its potential for increasing longevity.[24]

The philosophical market, then, began to broaden during the first half of the fourth century in large part because philosophers began to offer two new and attractive products—control over timing and situational propensities, or power distributions, and control over *qi*—in a variety of theoretical and practical packages.

As the century came to a close, however, a very different kind of philosophical product appears to make its first important impact on the market. The notion that government systems design could reach the technical level of a *dao* seems to emerge in the wake of the famous successes of Shang Yang in the state of Qin, where he enacted his revolutionary reforms during the period 359–338. The

---

22. See Jullien 1992: esp. 23–32. While militarists may not have been the first to isolate the concepts of timeliness and situational propensities, the obvious marketability of their works in the context of Warring States period demand for innovative military strategy and coordination very likely gave militarist terminology a leading role in the philosophical competition for patronage.

23. It seems to me legitimate to see the doctrine of timeliness as a source for such action prescriptions as *wuwei* in the *Dao de jing*, *bu de yi* in the *Zhuang Zi* (particularly in the chapter "Renjian shi"), and *shun* in Huang-Lao texts.

24. While Mohist texts do not engage the concept of *qi* in any substantive way, it is possible that patrician interest in *qi* enhanced the attractiveness of Mohist paramilitary retainers because Mohists were viewed as a cult that had mastered the mobilization of *qi*. Mohists were famous for subduing ordinary dispositions in favor of the often fatal imperatives dictated by their uncompromising universalism, and I have elsewhere argued that their ability to do so was viewed as a product of *qi*-cultivation (Eno 1990: 260 n56). While Mohists seem to have opposed the viciousness of *qi*-crazed bravos like Bogong You, described by Mencius, their own fanatical behavior may have appeared to be the consequence of powers of *qi* cultivated through devotion to their own brand of righteousness. Mark Lewis presents portraits of warriors with excessive *qi* in *Sanctioned Violence in Early China* (1990: 222–26) and includes a passage indicating the Mohist attitude towards them. For the most famous instance of Mohist fanaticism, see Graham 1989a: 44–45.

growing crescendo of technocratic writings from the end of the fourth century through the following century, which command compendia such as the *Guan Zi*, invade Confucian texts such as the *Xun Zi* (and perhaps some early ritual texts), and form the distinguishing substance of Legalist texts, reflects the impact of this new philosophical product just as the Jixia period reaches its first flourishing.

Moonlighting and Nontraditional Students

An issue that deserves investigation but for which evidence does not seem to be abundant is the means by which philosophers eked out a living when patronage was scarce. As noted earlier, the disciples of Confucius seem to have, from the time of their master's death, established themselves as a professional group specializing in cultural training, literary tutoring, and performance of ritual ceremonies necessary for gracious living in the elite stratum of society. These activities, though clearly related to the cult's philosophical teachings, constituted a nonphilosophical form of professionalism that cushioned the school against difficult times when major government patronage was not forthcoming.[25]

In time, the Confucian school seems to have been deflected from both its political idealism and its original ambitious designs for self-transformation by increasing immersion in and patronage of its textual program, a phenomenon we will encounter further below. Xun Zi, who attacks what he regards as false Confucians with a bitterness surpassing that directed even at Mohists, clearly views these men as cynical and self-interested manipulators of the good reputation of their school.

Mohists, like the Confucians, turned extraphilosophical professional skills sanctioned by their doctrine to economic advantage, in their case by pioneering the science of defensive warfare. I would not want to suggest any cynical motive in this on the part of individual Mohists, who were surely the least self-regarding members of early Chinese society. But by fashioning a profession from their doctrinal obsessions they ensured themselves an acknowledged role in society and undoubtedly earned rewards of honor and esteem that were uniquely sustaining to the psychology of their group.

It is not the economic aspects per se that make the extraphilosophical activities of these men of interest, rather these activities suggest that philosophy in early China generated spin-off products that became secondary, and in some cases primary, professional engagements of the philosophers. Thus it seems logical, although direct evidence may be less than complete, to anticipate that the men who carried the messages we now label Daoist earned patronage on the basis of their personas as hermits,[26] that cosmologists specializing in models of *qi* and, later, yin

---

25. I examine these aspects of Confucianism in more detail in 1990: 60–62.

26. Aat Vervoorn, in his *Men of the Cliffs and Caves*, explores many forms of eremitism in early China and discovers during the post-Warring States era many ways in which

and yang, were among the same men who earned the patronage of the wealthy by providing them training in or treatment with various forms of physical, dietary, medical, and sexual hygiene, and that the specialists in natural categories whom we will encounter shortly, pocketed substantial fees by marketing new and improved forms of knowing the future.[27]

Along with this diversification of secondary products, we may expect that there was a parallel attempt to discover new and diverse consumer groups. Student tuition was unlikely to have been a fully rewarding source of income during times of sparse patronage (witness Mohist descriptions of impoverished Confucians). In sustaining themselves, the early schools may well have searched for formulas that would earn them access to new markets.

One possibility that may have been overlooked is the role that the increasingly wealthy merchant class may have played in sustaining philosophy. It would not be unusual in world history for a class of nouveau riche to seek the patina of social legitimacy through patronage of the intellectual arts. Apart from the merchant-turned-prime-minister, Lü Buwei, whom we will mention again later, the *Shiji* does not record such patrons. However, this may in part be due to the ambivalent attitude of Han society towards merchants; after all, Sima Qian has very little to say about the class in any respect. However, among the few pre-Qin figures discussed in the *Shiji*'s account of great merchants, at least three do seem to suggest connections with the philosophical market.

The most famous of these is Confucius's prominent disciple Zigong (Duanmu Si, 520–450), who is said to have become wealthy as an itinerant merchant after the death of the Master (*Shiji* 67.2201; 129.3258). The *Analects* includes an apparent reference to Zigong's mercantile skills even before Confucius's death ("Si has not received any official commission, nevertheless goods proliferate with him" [*Analects* 11.18]). The wording of the passage is difficult to interpret. It is possible that the phrase is an insertion into a preexisting characterization of Zigong as a clever speaker and predictor of events, which accords with the *Zuozhuan* accounts of his activities during Confucius's lifetime.[28] While it may be true that Zigong became a merchant, it is also possible that his reputation as a merchant reflects a pattern of interaction between the Confucian faction which was associated with him

---

playing the hermit could lead to social prestige and even material reward (1990). The tale of Bo Yi and Shu Qi, cited in the *Analects* and elsewhere, would already have established the possibility for hermits to "extort" patronage in return for the political benefits of having a righteous recluse nest at one's court.

27. The peculiarly nonphilosophical flavor of much Han Dynasty learning may be the result of a general displacement of the primary enterprise of the early philosophical community by the more easily marketable secondary products that developed from these closely related but extraphilosophical pursuits.

28. The *Lüshi chunqiu* also pictures Zigong as a wealthy man while a disciple (*Cha wei* 16/6) (Chen 1984: 1003).

in the state of Qi and merchant-patrons there.[29] Confucians in Qi may have found that packaging the founder of their faction with a merchant reputation improved their ability to attract patronage from this increasingly influential class.

Two other biographical passages in the *Shiji* suggest interactions between philosophy and the merchant class. The strange story of the Yue militarist minister Fan Li is the more elaborate. Fan Li is known as the minister whose advice to King Goujian led to Yue's famous victory of vengeance over Wu in 482, and the *Han shu* lists him as the author of a militarist text (30.1757). Several accounts of his life tell us that after Yue's great triumph, Fan Li chose to sail off from Yue to start a new life, traveling first to Qi, where he acted as prime minister and was known as Chiyi Zipi (the "Leather Bag"), and then wandering off again, this time to the town of Tao in eastern Shandong, where he became a very wealthy merchant known as Lord Zhu (*Shiji* 129.3257).[30]

Fan's decision is said to have been based in part on the observation that the principles that were put into practice to revive Yue economically and prepare it for victory could also be applied to ensure personal success and wealth. These principles are attributed in the *Shiji* to "Ji Ran" ("Thus calculated"), which was traditionally understood to be the name of Fan Li's teacher, but may equally well be understood as a text title (*Shiji* 129.3256; Qian 1935: 103–7).[31] The brief description of the principles of "Ji Ran" read very much as a Huang-Lao style guide to state fiscal policy. The first sentence reads, "If one understands conflict then one prepares in advance. If one is timely in expenditures then one understands goods. When both these are manifest then the true nature of the myriad commodities comes fully into view." The text goes on to discuss in detail relationships between cycles of timing and market practices.[32]

The tale of Fan Li is not very coherent as history. But it forges a folkloric link joining a class of potential patrons with a hero of the Huang-Lao cult and some of

---

29. The role Zigong played in the transmission of Confucian teaching is unclear. The possibility that he fostered the spread of Confucianism in Qi is explored in Kimura 1971: 200–1.

30. It is hard to avoid the impression that the image of the leather bag signals a folktale conflation of Fan Li with his adversary Wu Zixu, whose body was cast adrift in a leather bag by King Fuchai of Wu. Fan Li is said to have cast himself adrift in a boat as he went off to Qi (variously sailing the sea or up the Yangzi). The *Lüshi chunqiu* says, at one point, "Thus were Fan Li and Zixu floated off (exiled)" (*Liwei, Xin shu*, "Erpi" says that he committed suicide).

31. Qian also contends that the assignation of the name "Leather Bag" to Fan Li is a conflation with another man of Qi.

32. Du Zhengsheng has analyzed apparent relationships between the "Ji Ran" text and calendrical cosmology of the period (1990: esp. 486–95). His arguments suggest that common techniques for speculation in crops had been displaced into arcane formulas that would require merchants to consult intitiates.

its ideas concerning timing.[33] The message of the tale is that ideas that thinkers may initially attempt to sell to those who hold power and office may be equally applicable to those who are in a position to employ them for their own personal benefit. Were we to analyze texts more consistently for their economic implications, we might find within them many hints of messages of this nature, stretching the appeal of certain doctrines, such as timeliness, to new audiences.

Another merchant biography with similar philosophical overtones concerns Bo Gui, a political leader in Wei who appears several times in the *Mencius*. Bo Gui, like Fan Li, is said to have relied on a set of timing practices resonant with Huang-Lao ideas. He is quoted characterizing himself as the merchant equivalent of a string of figures who represent ideas congenial to that cult. "My method of control over produce resembles the strategies of Yi Yin and Lü Shang, the military tactics of Sun Wu, and the legal designs of Shang Yang" (*Shiji* 129.3259).

The Jixia Academy and the Formation of a Market Community

When, about 350, the rulers of the usurping Tian clan in the state of Qi elected to follow the example of Marquis Wen in trying to strengthen their position by patronizing philosophy, they carried their experiment further than had been the case in Wei. The academy of scholars that they founded disengaged the marketing of *dao*s to government from issues of state appointment. Scholars appointed to Jixia received a stipend from the Qi government but were under no political obligations (although some such scholars, such as Chunyu Kun, seem to have performed services for the court as individuals).[34]

The establishment of the academy also had the effect of physically settling a wide variety of thinkers within a limited neighborhood, and this, more than any other phenomenon, may have given rise to the notion of the *zhuzi* (scholars) as a distinct group of people engaged in a uniform type of activity.[35] It may well be that it was during the early decades of Jixia that focused intellectual attacks of one school against another first emerged.[36] While this sort of adversarial advertising was intended by each school to advance its interests at the expense of its

---

33. We will discuss Fan Li's status as a Huang-Lao figure below.

34. Some interpreters hold that Jixia scholars were obliged to meet in convocations and advise the rulers of Qi (see, for example, Zhang 1990). This idea seems to be inspired by a late passage in *Yantie lun* "Lun Ru" that projects the government activities of Mencius and Chunyu Kun as standard for Jixia scholars in general; see Zhang 1991: 13).

35. If we accept the suggestion of Guo Moruo that the *Guan Zi* "Dizi zhi" chapter includes rules of behavior that were meant to apply universally in the academy, its cohesive identity would appear all the stronger (see Kanaya 1987: 314–15).

36. For example, one of the most famous and sustained of these, the *Mo Zi*'s attack on Confucianism in its "Fei Ru" chapter, describes Confucius's actions in the state of Qi and makes the Qi minister Yan Ying its chief spokesperson.

competitors', it may also be viewed as a recognition of certain features of community shared among all members of the Jixia group.

The advent of the close philosophical community at Jixia heightened competition among schools, and by the opening decades of the third century it had engendered intellectual cross-fertilization on a scale far surpassing that of the previous century. This accounts for the rapid diffusion among different schools of the ideas of yin-yang and the five forces, the last of the major new product lines to emerge during the Warring States period.

The features of Jixia discourse and the resulting eclecticism that is visible both in the works of individual thinkers such as Xun Zi and in the *Guan Zi* text, often regarded as at root a Jixia compendium, are too well known to require detailed discussion here.[37] The possible linkage of the Tian clan, which claimed Huang Di as its lineage ancestor, and the development of Huang-Lao ideology also suggests that this sole example of a truly syncretist school may also have owed its development to the environment of Jixia.

The nature of Jixia patronage, which seems to have been entirely gratuitous and extremely broad, makes the trends of Jixia less subject to new insights through the application of a market model: the types of competition spurred by the academy would have related more specifically to intellectual than to economic issues. However, it may be that increased awareness of shared professional identity among the members of *zhuzi* teaching traditions created a new sense of the need to distinguish the products of philosophy from those of non-philosophical wisdom peddlers: doctors, diviners, astronomers, shamans, and so forth. As the ideas of *qi* cultivation and the cosmologies of yin-yang and five forces theory increasingly bridged these two types of groups after 300, maintaining the distinction would have required some effort. The "Jin shu" chapter of the *Lüshi chunqiu*, which appears to be the product of a hygiene cult centered on the concept of *qi* nurturance, makes the following comment, expressing a low opinion for nonphilosophical approaches to health, "Nowadays, men value divination and shrine prayer, hence diseases come with increasing frequency . . . . Shamanic doctors and poisoned herbal concoctions cure illness only by driving it out [once it is established], hence the ancients scorned them as superficial" (Chen 1984: 137).

The transition in Chinese thought that coincides with the Jixia era is one which moves from a period when individual thinkers with their disciples seek to make a place for themselves and their teachings in society to a period when the manufacture and marketing of philosophical *dao*s is viewed as a respectable Chinese industry. The members of the philosophical community now understand the nature of the market and of their competitive position within it, and have developed some awareness that they possess a shared set of interests as well.

---

37. A good survey of Jixia debates appears in Zhang 1990: 82–86. The nature of his list illustrates how far beyond the limits of our five "commodities" debates ranged within the confines of the philosophical community.

The Economics of Yue as Background to the Rise of Fangshi

The sharpest conflicts between the philosophical and nonphilosophical communities seem to have arisen during the post-Jixia period with the advent of learning traditions that go under the generic name of *fangshi*. The *Shiji* implies that the major ideas that lay behind *fangshi* arts were derived from the Jixia community through the philosopher Zou Yan (305–240). His teachings, we are told, were misunderstood by the *fangshi* of the coastal regions and perverted into superstition and immortalist doctrines (*Shiji* 28.1369).

After the Jixia period, the greatest market challenges to individual philosophical schools may not have come from competing schools, but from these *fangshi* cults, which appealed to rulers and the wealthy with exciting products such as foreknowledge, spirit control, levitation, and immortality. This key change in the market may have been the direct consequence of making the Qi capital at Linzi so prominent a center of philosophical discourse, and may also point to an important indirect connection between the history of philosophy and the economy of the early Warring States state of Yue.

Linzi, in the northern region of the Shandong Peninsula, is located near to the coastal regions where the *fangshi* cults flourished during the late third and second centuries. These cults, and in particular their notions of the flying immortals of the east, seem to be regional inheritances of the culture of the former states of Wu and Yue, which had flourished suddenly in the sixth and fifth centuries, only to die out abruptly under the spreading influence of Chu.[38]

Perhaps the greatest geographical anomaly of the Classical period in China is the fact that seven years after Yue completed its conquest of Wu in 473 and consolidated itself in the Yangzi delta as the dominant power of eastern China, it relocated its capital hundreds of miles north of its base territory to the coastal outpost of Langye, on the southern edge of the Shandong Peninsula. The capital remained in Langye for about fifty years, separated from the Qi only by the permeable barrier of the central Shandong mountains.[39]

The cultures of Wu and Yue, unlike those of the central states, were noted for their reliance on water transport and skills in sea navigation (Dong 1988: 274–81). Of the five major Warring States coastal ports, the southernmost two, Kuaiji (modern Shaoxing) and Gouzhang (modern Ningbo) were within the heartland of

---

38. In following discussion I am much indebted to current dissertation research by Chia-li Luo, who is tracing the history of cultural interactions between the peoples of the Taihu region, where the states of Wu and Yue were located, and other regions of early China.

39. As Chen Wei has recently pointed out, the history of Yue in Langye is not well documented, and the duration of the capital's location there may be questioned (1993: 57–58). Qian Mu offered extensive arguments that the site of the Yue capital was not at present-day Langye, but some 50–100 km. further south; his arguments are reasonable but neither convincing nor called for in light of the maritime significance of Langye (Qian 1935: 110–14).

the Wu-Yue consolidated state.[40] The relocation to Langye, which was the central coastal port, seems cogent only as a strategy for enhancing Yue's control of coastal trade and allowing it greater access to the markets of the two northern ports, which were located in the states of Qi and Yan.[41]

I speculate that the coastal *fangshi* cults are probably the product of heightened contact between Yue seafarers and local populations, and that the ideas that came to be associated with Zou Yan at Jixia were, in fact, probably originally inspired by these cults, rather than the other way around.[42] While much work needs to be done to identify specific features of Wu-Yue culture which may have formed the basis of the *fangshi* cults, the likelihood that such a cultural link existed is reflected in accounts of the First Emperor of Qin's romance with immortalism, which locate his various rendezvous with those in search of the immortal isles at the former Yue capital of Langye (*Shiji* 6.247, 263).

If Wu-Yue culture lies behind the *fangshi* traditions, then the fact that it was the rulers of Qi rather than the competitor patrons of the Wei royal house who succeeded in attracting so great a portion of the philosophical community would appear to have had a dramatic impact on the course of intellectual history.[43] Together with the economic policies of the fifth century court of Yue, Qi's geographical location may have determined the direction of philosophical discourse after 300 as much as any other aspect of social or political history.

The Diffusion of Patronage

Between the final collapse of the Jixia Academy in 265 and the consolidation of China under Qin rule in 221, the philosophical market seems to have fragmented. No other single court managed to replace the role that the Tian clan had played in

---

40. Dong discusses the major seaports of the period (1988: 278).

41. Note the resonance between this political move and the tale of Fan Li's seafaring departure from Yue as a militarist and reemergence in Qi as a merchant, discussed earlier.

42. A similar point might be made concerning the relationship between Huang-Lao thought and these cults. The *Huang Di si jing* texts excavated at Mawangdui show intense borrowing from the *Yue yu* II, which Qian Mu speculated is the lost "Book of Fan Li" (1935: 453), and this may suggest the impact of Yue-influenced *fangshi* cults on early Huang-Lao thought. The *Wenwu* editors of the silk texts cite seventeen instances of textual overlap, which occur in three of the four Huang Di texts (not all are significant, but some not noted are). By contrast, Graham notes that the *Heguan Zi* includes more instances of overlap than any other text, with twenty (1989b: 508); yet the *Heguan Zi* is many times longer than the *Yue-yu* II, indicating denser borrowing from the latter.

43. King Hui of Wei (r. 370–319) appears to have attempted to recruit scholars during the era of Jixia, but without the success that characterized Qi.

Qi, and many philosophical professionals seemed to have searched out patronage away from the courts of legitimate rulers.[44]

These were the decades when the great warlord-ministers dominated the politics of a number of states, from Lord Chunshen in Chu, the patron of Xun Zi, to Lord Pingyuan in Zhao, the patron of Gongsun Long. In the west, the merchant Lü Buwei, having succeeded to the office of prime minister of Qin, and seeking to compete with the great warlords of the east, also established a reputation as a great patron of thinkers. This is said to have been the origin of the *Lüshi chunqiu*.

Although this was a period of significant philosophical innovation, particularly in the articulation of Legalist and Huang-Lao types of thought, our information concerning the nature of the philosophical market is sparse. Any changes that may have begun to emerge during this period would, in any event, have been quickly terminated with the Qin conquest, which radically altered the shape of the marketplace of ideas.

One possible reflection of the new patron audiences that philosophers were addressing may be the gradual rise in the proportion of historical anecdote included in philosophical texts. Perhaps this is the consequence of a renewed need for philosophers, as aspiring guests at the courts of warlord patricians, to entertain in their persuasions and in the texts that they offered as commodities in exchange for patronage. In the *Han Fei Zi* we find a group of chapters in which tales are categorized together under headings of political or philosophical points that they may be used to illustrate (the various *chu shuo* or "stored up stories"). Perhaps in these final decades of the Classical era, when philosophers were competing most acutely with swordsmen and other martial artists for the favors of less-than-erudite warlord patrons, a new premium on the amusement value of intellectual packaging gave a decisive push to the anecdotal genre of philosophical writing, which makes many later Han works engaging despite their uneven quality as philosophy.

The Qin Conquest and the Regulated Market

The Qin is usually viewed as an antiphilosophical dynasty, which set out to destroy learning in order to implement a Daoist-Legalist policy of making the people ignorant. It is certainly so that in 213, at the urging of the prime minister Li Si, the First Emperor issued an order banning many philosophical texts and certain books that had come to have canonical status among a wide range of intellectuals. But as Derk Bodde has pointed out, the event took place late in the emperor's reign and is unlikely to have had the devastating effect that is often attributed to it (1986: 72–73).

---

44. Zhang Bingnan describes records of a Wuyang Academy established by Yan in preparation for its invasion of Qi which attracted prominent men, such as Zou Yan, and persisted for some time (1990: 91). The fact that records of this academy are preserved only in the *Shuijing zhu* (6th c. A.D.) suggests that its influence was small.

The Qin conquest eliminated all the established sources of patronage for philosophy, and the abolition of feudalism removed the courts that had been home for so many thinkers. The wealthy families that had supported wise men all over China were relocated to the capital region in the far west for easier control, and the powerholders who replaced them were civil or military appointees, without the resources or mandate to patronage philosophers. While the philosophers would still have had recourse to the extraphilosophical professions that had sustained them throughout the Warring States era in times when patronage was scarce, they would now have been competing with *fangshi*, who had developed alternative systems of divination, hygiene, and so forth, and were, perhaps, in a better position to capture customers through their willingness to incorporate a greater body of popular tradition in their rationalizations.

However, the Qin soon moved to create an entirely new market, adapted from Jixia. This was the *boshi* or erudite system, a body of official appointments reserved for men outstanding in their knowledge.[45] This state-sponsored bureau of *boshi* is the heart of the small, closely regulated, but important philosophical market of the Qin. It is likely that members of all intellectual traditions, which surely shared a sense of awe that they were living in a generation that had seen the end of over 500 years of multistate warfare, looked upon service to the new government as an opportunity to take part in the future, while reaping the benefits of Qin rank and privilege in the process.

The *boshi* represented a relatively large number of high-ranking officers. In 213, at the convention of *boshi* that led to the policy banning certain books, seventy *boshi* were in attendance, and we must recall that these men had students who assisted them (*Shiji* 6.254).[46] It is clear from the scattered references to individual *boshi* and their activities in the historical sources that the *boshi* were a diverse group of men, including Confucians, *fangshi*, and others. No apparent attempt was made to limit *boshi* to Legalists or to men agreeing with Qin policies.

While we do not have any detailed description of the normal duties of the *boshi* outside of advisory conclaves, the *boshi* "were in charge of comprehending (*tong*)

---

45. Qian Mu concludes that the office predated the Qin. He traces the origins of the office back to the court of Duke Mu of Lu, nearly two centuries before the Qin conquest, and discovers examples of *boshi* in Qi in the Jixia era as well (1978: 165–66; see also Zhang 1990: 80). However, Qian does not make a strong case for interpreting these early instances of men who may have possessed the title *boshi* as precursors of the Qin system. The Qin *boshi* were not merely men titled in consequence of their wide knowledge, they were an appointed bureau of official advisors, on call for consultation and expected to maintain a library of resources that would allow them to provide to the state the most informed opinions available in the empire. The institution as thus described does not seem to predate the Qin.

46. The fact that *boshi* had followers is confirmed by the biography of Shusun Tong, a Qin *boshi* who transferred his allegiance to the Han. At the time that he did so, his followers are said to have numbered over one hundred (*Shiji* 99.2721).

the past and the present."[47] This suggests that the task of the *boshi* was to assemble knowledge of the past so that it could, where warranted, assist the Qin program.[48] While one would expect that this would result in the generation of texts, none are listed in the "Yiwen zhi." Because the *boshi* do not appear to have produced philosophical works, not much attention has been paid to them, and we may well ask whether the institution was a philosophical market of ideas at all.

I do not have a definitive answer, but I would like to suggest a hypothesis concerning the function of the *boshi* which proposes a way in which the office formed a bridge between the contending schools of the pre-Qin period and the highly text-based period that followed in the Han. I want to argue that the function of the *boshi* was to compose encyclopedic catalogues of the knowledge of the Classical period, representing the doctrines of all schools in anthologies and authoritatively comprehensive new digests, for use by the Qin emperors and courts of the future. Such projects would have imposed closure on the intellectual history of China prior to Qin control and would have been fully congenial to the spirit of the dynasty to unify, circumscribe, and control the cultural region of China.

If such was the encyclopedic project, where then are the texts? I suggest that the principal product of this project was the *Lüshi chunqiu* in its current form. The text is said to have been completed under the supervision of Lü Buwei by his own courtiers in 239, but it includes passages that must postdate Lü's death, and we may question how Lü, during the ten prior years of his prime ministership, could ever have lured to the western outpost of Qin so diverse and outstanding a group of scholars and literary talents as would have been required to produce a text such as the one which bears his name. It seems far more likely that the text that Lü "displayed at the gate of the Xianyang market," consisted of the "monthly ordinances" of the *ji* section of the text, which form a complete almanac. These, and perhaps the essays attached to them, correspond far better than the whole text to the claim reported in the *Shiji* that not a word could be added or subtracted to improve them. The *Lüshi chunqiu*, with its encyclopedic and topically cogent arrangement, nearly standardized formats, relative unity of diction across different schools, and broadly balanced presentation of pre-Qin schools, is the sort of comprehensive product that the Qin government might have found appropriate to bring the past to closure.[49]

---

47. Qian, quoting the *Han shu, Baiguan biao* (1978: 166).

48. The relation of the past and the present was a major issue for the Qin. The Qin conquest was a greater revolution than had been seen before in China, particularly after the First Emperor chose to follow the antifeudal policies of Li Si. The book-burning edict of 213 was undertaken in response to a criticism of these policies by a Confucian *boshi*, and its specific purpose was to put a stop to those who would "use the past to reject the present" (*Shiji* 6.255).

49. On passages postdating Lü's death, see Carson 1980: 435. Carson's entry on the text in Loewe notes a divergence of linguistic patterns between the *ji* and other sections (1993: 325-26).

In addition to the *Lüshi chunqiu*, outstanding unattributed texts such as the *Daxue* and *Zhongyong* make excellent sense as products of a *boshi* literary bureau. The *Daxue*, which cites as canon the "Qin shi" chapter of the *Shang shu*, supposedly the words of Duke Mu of Qin (r. 659–621), would be unlikely to exalt such a text had it been composed during any other period. The *Zhongyong*, which appears to fit so well as a complement to the *Daxue* and clearly blends elements of the teachings of both Mencius and Xun Zi, would equally represent the type of summative synthesis—the best of the Confucians—which such a model of *boshi* activity would entail.[50]

Moreover, if the "Qin shi" seems an odd text for the Confucian *Daxue* to cite, how much odder that it appears in the *Shang shu*, many sections of which had clearly attained canonical status prior to the Qin. Duke Mu, though a hero of Qin history, was the ruler reviled in the *Shi jing* poem "Huang niao" because of his dying order that his most courageous men-at-arms be killed and buried with him. In view of the inclusion of this chapter in the *Shang shu* text, would it not be reasonable to see this collection, which closes with the "Qin shi," as reaching its broadest state as a *boshi* compendium. After all, Fu Sheng, the man who hid the *Shang shu* text at the time of its ultimate proscription and became the source of its later transmission, was a Qin *boshi* (*Shiji* 121.3124).[51]

The evidence for this argument is not strong enough to do more than suggest that it represents a reasonable hypothesis. But it should be obvious that if this were the case, the Confucians would have been anxious not to advertise during the

---

50. Dating the text to the Qin would explain the problematic phrases, "In the world today, carts are identical in axle width; texts are identical in script; conduct is identical in roles" (section 28). Some previous scholars, noting such issues, have dated the text to the early Han (see Tu 1976: 13–14), but once the notion that Qin intellectual trends excluded Confucianism is questioned, the phrasing most naturally suggests a Qin date.

51. Regarding the *Shang shu* as a compendium completed by the Qin *boshi* could explain the puzzling fact that none of the chapters in the canonical version of the text which modern scholarship considers to be genuine (all located in the "Zhou shu" section) are cited in other pre-Qin texts, with the exception of the "Kang gao." It may well be that these texts, which resemble early Western Zhou bronze inscriptions, had been preserved near the old Zhou homeland in the Wei River valley, the region of the Qin capital of Xianyang. The scholars of the *boshi* corps, whose pre-Qin predecessors had generally sought employment in eastern China, could have been the first scholars granted access to these texts, which may have been stored in the Qin palace archives (destroyed in 207).

Though the Qin state clearly withdrew its approval of the *Shang shu* and outlawed its possession, this was by no means necessarily the case with other texts which the *boshi* may have assembled. The *Lüshi chunqiu, Daxue*, and *Zhongyong* appear unscathed after the fall of the Qin. Qian Mu has argued that the literary proscription extended to a relatively narrow range of texts, and also points out that it did not include copies in the possession of the *boshi* (1978: 167–68).

subsequent era of the Han Dynasty that important portions of their textual corpus were sponsored by the Qin state and produced by Confucian collaborators.[52]

If the philosophical marketplace during the Qin was as I have suggested, it would account for certain features of post-Qin intellectual history. First, given the extraphilosophical trade of Confucians as masters of a textual tradition and teachers of the literary graces to young men of good family, it is likely that Confucians would have featured more prominently among the *boshi* than would the representatives of other schools, perhaps accounting for the fact that despite their "persecution," Confucians emerged from the Qin-Han transition much stronger than all but a few pre-Qin schools. Moreover, the transition of philosophical activity from an era of creativity and debate to one of canon closure and interpretation would have been well facilitated by a decade in which the marketplace of ideas became a forum for categorization, selection, and editorial digestion.[53]

Conclusion

The perspective of the economics of the philosophical marketplace brings to the foreground aspects of the history of early Chinese philosophy not often attended to. Among the phenomena at least partially tied to issues of the market are the branching of Confucian disciples into new areas of marketing, such as administrative systems design (Li Ke) and militaristic strategy (Wu Qi), the creation of a philosophical community (as a consequence of Jixia patronage), the influence of *fangshi* cults on philosophy (a delayed result of economic policies in fifth-century Yue), and the transformation from an era of philosophy to an era of textual classicism (as a consequence of the *boshi* bureau activities under the Qin). While this brief account does no more than survey prospects for fruitful inquiry that

---

52. Confucians continued to keep appointments as *boshi* even after 213, as is shown by the presence of the Confucian ritualist Shusun Tong at a convocation in 209 (*Shiji* 99.2720). It seems best to withhold sympathy from the Confucians as a persecuted minority under the terror of the Qin, given the ambiguity of the evidence and the contributions they made to the construction of the historical account, particularly after 135. The picture of Confucians as Qin loyalists would help explain the aversion that the Han founder Liu Bang expressed towards them, and the fact that the proscription against the Confucian canonical texts was left in place until 191, over a decade after the Han assumed control of all China.

53. John Henderson has noted the importance to the fixing of a closed canon of some experience of sharp break with the past, and observes that the Qin provides this function in China (1991: 39–40). He means by this that the literary and institutional destruction associated with the Qin alienated the past from the present. But it may be that we should look at the Qin's closure of the past as a more positive response to the political revolution of Li Si's policies. The past was not alien because it was unreachable, but rather it had been closed off by the encyclopedist's urge to commoditize and control it.

a more nuanced market analysis of early philosophical activity could provide, I
believe further research will show that the promise of this perspectival experiment
is more than empty advertising.

References

Aihara Junji. 1960. "Sen-Shin jidai no 'kyaku' ni tsuite" (On retainers of the
pre-Ch'in era). In *Chūgoku kodaishi kenkyū*, edited by Mikami Tsugio.
Tokyo: Yoshikawa kobunkan.

Ames, Roger T. 1993. *Sun Tzu: The Art of Warfare*. New York: Ballantine
Books.

Biagioli, Mario. 1993. *Galileo Courtier: The Practice of Science in the Culture
of Absolutism*. Chicago: University of Chicago Press.

Bodde, Derk. 1986. "The State and Empire of Ch'in." In *The Cambridge History
of China*, Vol. 1, edited by Denis Twitchett and Michael Loewe. Cambridge:
Cambridge University Press.

Carson, Michael. 1980. "The Language of the *Lu-shih ch'un-ch'iu*: Some
Characteristic Features of Grammar and Style in a Third Century B.C. Text."
Ph.D. diss., University of Washington.

Chen Qiyou. 1984. *Lushi chunqiu jishi* (Collected explications of the Lushi
chunqui). Shanghai: Xuelin chubanshe.

Chen Wei. 1993. "Guanyu Chu-Yue zhanzheng de jige wenti" (A few questions
concerning the war between Chu and Yue). *Jiang-Han luntan* 4.

Dong Chuping. 1988. *Wu-Yue wenhua xintan* (New explorations of the cultures
of Wu and Yue). Hangzhou: Zhejiang renmin chubanshe.

Du Zhengsheng. 1990. "Zhanguo de qingzhongshu yu qingzhong shangren"
(Commercial methods and mercantile speculators of the Warring State
period). *Bulletin of the Institute of History and Philology*, Academia Sinica
61, no. 2.

Eno, Robert. 1990. *The Confucian Creation of Heaven*. Albany: State University
of New York Press.

Graham, A.C. 1978. *Later Mohist Logic, Ethics and Science*. Hong Kong: The
Chinese University Press.

————. 1989a. *Disputers of the Tao*. La Salle, IL: Open Court.

————. 1989b. "A Neglected Pre-Han Philosophical Text: *Ho-kuan-tzu*."
Bulletin of the School of Oriental and African Studies 52, no. 3.

Han shu. 1962. Beijing: Zhonghua shuju.

Henderson, John. 1991. *Scripture, Canon, and Commentary*. Princeton:
Princeton University Press.

Hsu, Cho-yun. 1965. *Ancient China in Transition*. Chicago: University of
Chicago Press.

Hu Jichuang. 1962. *Zhongguo jingji sixiang shi* (History of Chinese economic thought). Shanghai: Renmin chubanshe.

Jullien, François. 1992. *La propension des choses*. Paris: Editions du Seuil.

Kanaya, Osamu. 1987. *Kanshi no kenkyū* (Studies on the Guan Zi). Tokyo: Iwanami Shoten.

Kimura, Eiichi. 1971. *Kōshi to Rongo* (Confucius and the Analects). Tokyo: Sobunsha.

Lewis, Mark. 1990. *Sanctioned Violence in Early China*. Albany: State University of New York Press.

Loewe, Michael. 1993. *Early Chinese Texts: A Bibliographical Guide*. Berkeley: Society for the Study of Early China and the Institute for East Asian Studies.

Munro, Donald J. 1969. *The Concept of Man in Early China*. Stanford: Stanford University Press.

Qian Mu. 1935. *Xian-Qin zhuzi xinian* (Chronology of pre-Ch'in philosophers). Shanghai: Commercial Press.

—————. 1978. *Liang-Han jingxue jin-guwen pingyi* (Critical analysis of New and Old Text classicism in the Han Dynasty). Taipei: Dongda tushugongsi.

Shi Yican. 1938. *Guan Zi jinzhu* (New annotations of the Guan Zi). Beijing: Zhongguo shudian.

Shiji. 1959. Beijing: Zhonghua Shuju.

Tu Wei-ming. 1976. *Centrality and Commonality: An Essay on Chung-yung*. Honolulu: University of Hawaii Press.

Vervoorn, Aat. 1990. *Men of the Cliffs and Caves*. Hong Kong: The Chinese University Press.

Wu Shuping. 1975. "Cong Linyi Hanmu zhujian Wu wen kan Sun Wu de fa jia sixiang" (Sun Wu's Legalist thought, as seen in the Wu Wen bamboo text excavated from the Han tomb at Linyi). *Wenwu* 4.

Yates, Robin. 1988. "New Light on Ancient Chinese Military Texts." *T'oung Pao* 74, no. 4–5.

Zhang Bingnan. 1990. "Jixia xuegong yu baijia zhengming" (The Jixia Academy and the Hundred Schools). *Lishi yanjiu* 5.

—————. 1991. *Jixia gouchen* (Exploring the Jixia Academy). Shanghai: Shanghai guji chubanshe.

Glossary

Aihara Junji	相原俊二	"Ji Ran"	計然
Baiguan biao	百官表	Jin	晉
Baili Xi	百里奚	Jixia	稷下
binke	賓客	Kanaya Osamu	金谷治
Bo Gui	白圭	"Kang gao"	康誥
Bo Yi	伯夷	Kimura Eiichi	木村英一
Bogong Yu	北宮黝	Kuaiji	會稽
boshi	博士	Langye	瑯琊
bu de yi	不得已	*li*	禮
Chen Qiyou	陳奇猷	Li Ke	李克
Chen Wei	陳偉	Li Kui	李悝
Chiyi Zipi	鴟夷子皮	Li Si	李斯
Chu	楚	Liwei	璃謂
chu shuo	儲說	Linzi	臨淄
Chunshen	春申	Liu Bang	劉邦
Chunyu Kun	淳于髡	Lu	魯
dao	道	Lü Buwei	呂不韋
Daxue	大學	"Lun Ru"	論儒
de	德	Lü Shang	呂尚
Dong Chuping	董楚平	*Lüshi chunqiu*	呂氏春秋
Du Zhengsheng	杜正勝	*Mo Zi*	墨子
Duangan Mu	段干木	*Nei ye*	內業
Duanmu Si	端木賜	Pingyuan	平原
"Erpi"	耳痹	*qi*	氣
Fan Li	范蠡	Qi	齊
fangshi	方士	Qian Mu	錢穆
Fu Sheng	伏勝	Qin	秦
Fuchai	夫差	"Qin shi"	秦誓
Gongsun Long	公孫龍	*qun chen you*	群臣有位事
Goujian	句踐	*wei shi guan-*	官大夫者
Gouzhang	句章	*dafuzhe*	
Guan Zi	管子	*Shang shu*	尚書
Guo Moruo	郭沫若	Shang Yang	商鞅
Han	韓	*shi*	勢
Han Fei Zi	韓非子	(propensities)	
Han shu	漢書	*shi* (timeliness)	時
Heguan Zi	鶡冠子	"Shihuo zhi"	食貨志
Hu Jichuang	胡奇窗	Shi Yican	石一參
Huang Di si jing	黃帝四經	*Shiji*	史記
Huang-Lao	黃老	*shike*	食客
ji	紀	Shu Qi	叔齊

Shuijing zhu	水經注
shun	順
Shusun Tong	叔孫通
Sima Qian	司馬遷
Sun Wu	孫吳
Sun Zi	孫子
Tao	陶
Tian	田
Tian Zifang	田子方
tong	通
Wei	魏
Wu	吳
Wu Qi	吳起
Wu Shuping	吳樹平
Wu Zixu	伍子胥
wuwei	無爲
Wuyang	武陽
Xin shu	新書
Xun Zi	荀子
Yan	燕
Yan Ying	晏嬰
Yan Zi chunqiu	晏子春秋
Yantie lun	鹽鐵論
Yi Yin	伊尹
"Yiwen zhi"	藝文志
Yue	越
Yue yu	越語
Zeng Zi	曾子
Zhang Bingnan	張秉楠
Zhao	趙
Zhongyong	中庸
Zhou shu	周書
Zhu	邾
Zhuang Zi	莊子
zhuzi	諸子
Zigong	子貢
Zixia	子夏
Zou Yan	鄒衍
Zuozhuan	左傳

Do Human Rights Apply to China?
A Normative Analysis of Cultural Difference

CHAD HANSEN
University of Hong Kong

I am pursuing a modest and limited philosophical goal. I want to work out how we can talk about this issue in a way that does justice to the two conflicting intuitions. The intuitions, which I also share, are widespread in Hong Kong: 1) that human rights clearly do apply to China and 2) the appeal to Chinese tradition in resisting emphasis on individual rights has serious normative force. I characterize it as modest because it merely gives us a perspective on the problem, not *the* answer to the question and limited because it will be of interest to someone who shares these two intuitions.

I start with John Rawls's two principles of justice, first enunciated during the Cultural Revolution in China. They now rank among the most familiar words of contemporary philosophy.

The first statement of the two principles reads as follows:

First: each person is to have an equal right to the most extensive basic liberty compatible with a similar liberty for others.

Second: social and economic inequalities are to be arranged so that they are both (a) reasonably expected to be to everyone's advantage, and (b) attached to positions and offices open to all.[1] (Rawls 1971: 60)

The principles were not revolutionary, but at the time he formulated them, thinking in a disciplined way about normative issues was. Before Rawls, the accepted philosophical view was that normative ethics was only a marginally respectable enterprise—more suitable for advice columnists than for serious philosophers. Rawls was revolutionary in part because he offered not only a

---

Many thanks to Donald Munro, Roger Ames, and Sin Yee Chan for their reading and helpful comments on earlier versions of this manuscript. Any errors that remain are the responsibility of the author.

1. John Rawls, *A Theory of Justice* (Cambridge: Harvard University Press, 1971), p. 60. Rawls has continuously revised the wording of the two principles. The latest is in his 1993. Nothing in my argument will turn on subtleties in formulation.

substantive theory of justice, but also a seemingly powerful new form of argument for normative theory—reflective equilibrium:

> In searching for the most favored description of this situation, we work from both ends. . . . By going back and forth, sometimes altering the conditions of the contractual circumstances, at others withdrawing our judgments and conforming to principle, I assume that eventually we shall find a description of the initial situation that both expresses reasonable conditions and yields principles which match our considered judgments duly pruned and adjusted. This state of affairs I refer to as reflective equilibrium. It is an equilibrium because at last our principles and judgments coincide and it is reflective since we know to what principles our judgments conform and the premises of their derivation (*Ibid.*: 20).

Rawls's argument form was compelling because the technique of reflective equilibrium coincided vaguely with the emerging post-positivist view of scientific reasoning. It undermined the view of science as "absolute empirical proof." The insight that reasoning in science and ethics were essentially similar ushered in a heyday of moral objectivism in metaethics. Rawls found a way to combine ethical theory with a counterpart of "data" or "facts" for the theory to explain. He argued that we could reason in ethics in a way that is similar to the way we reason in science.

> There is a definite if limited class of facts against which conjectured principles can be checked, namely, our considered judgments in reflective equilibrium (*Ibid*: 51).

Rawls argued that his two principles of justice brought our considered judgments about liberty and equality into coherent harmony. He thus defended a theoretical perspective that we have come to know as "deontological individualism"—an heir of Kantian "respect for the individual" and Christian "worth of the individual soul." Rawls argued that utilitarianism failed similarly to harmonize our judgments. It was a form of reasoning more appropriate to individual prudential calculation than to a moral theory and did not take the differences among individuals as seriously as our moral intuitions do.

First statement of the problem:
intuitions and reflective equilibrium

The idea gripped me at the time that an idealized Chinese critic of injustice might share the "considered judgments" reflected in Rawls's second principle. The philosophical roots of Chinese "intuitions" about equality seem as strong as or stronger than are those of the Western tradition—a central point of Donald Munro's analysis of the Chinese concept of person. Munro argued that all the classical schools shared an assumption that humans have an equal moral potential. The principle of maximizing liberty, however, which for Rawls was "lexically prior" to the distributive principle, hardly figured in the rhetoric of political reform whether in traditional or in modern Maoist China.

Many Western scholars of China have called attention to these differences between the historically dominant Confucian communalism and Rawlsian individualism. We assume both are expressions of a broadly shared moral orientation. Rawlsian individualism draws on Greek, Judeo-Christian, and Kantian roots as Confucian tradition draws on its sources of Daoism, Legalism, and Mohism. Theodore DeBary (1988) and Roger Ames (1988) draw special attention to the historical context of the emergence of individualism. Other social changes accompanying the rise of industrial capitalism, science, the conflict of church and state, and so forth are all crucial to telling the story of the emergence of individualist moral values in Europe and America. Such historicist reflection on the question of human rights in China raises worries about our implicit ideal of objectivity in normative judgment. It suggests that while the value of equality in the distributive justice might be a plausible cultural universal, the priority of liberty could turn out to be a Western peculiarity.

Historicity and Objectivity

These worries about the historicity of Rawls's "moral facts" dovetail with an obvious temptation to the rulers and governments of Asian states. They can appeal to a respectable intellectual line of thought to condone their resistance to international pressure for human rights. The 1993 "Bangkok Declaration" exemplifies this response. I reproduce part of it here as an approximate model of what I want to call the Bangkok attitude or Bangkok *objection* to human rights[2] (Davis 1995: 205):

> [We] . . . .
> 8. *Recognize* that while human rights are universal in nature, they must be considered in the context of a dynamic and evolving process of international norm-setting bearing in mind the significance of national and regional particularities and various historical, cultural and religious backgrounds. . . .

---

2. The model is only approximate because 1) the declaration was a compromise with other Asian states who insisted on acknowledging the universality of human rights and 2) their formal subscription to U.N. treaties dealing with human rights restricts available wording. The usual form of the complaint does not put it in clear normative terms. It emphasizes the historical contingency of the emergence of Western individualism and leaves the normative conclusion implicit. I assume the conclusions should be: "Human rights do not apply to cultures where they are not the outcome of their historical, cultural, and religious background." One issue is the relevance of history and another is what counts as an "outcome." A copy of the Bangkok declaration is reprinted in the appendix of Davis 1995.

The statement falls short of the usual norm of philosophical precision.[3] I propose to read it as a straightforward normative claim. It appeals to comparative ethics to justify a kind of value relativism. Different cultures *have* different normative rights. The internal political debates in Hong Kong and in greater China reverberate with this practical, normative tone. The internal question is whether we (speaking within the Hong Kong community) should adopt a system of basic liberties or rights. That internal deliberation is the counterpart of the external controversy: "Do human rights apply to China?" I suggest we can best analyze and evaluate the Bangkok objection to human rights if we treat the two questions as intimately related. One is formulated between cultures and one from within a culture.

The external question perplexes Westerners partly because it seems difficult to find a neutral way to formulate it. A "scholarly" sensitivity to formulations that suggest arrogant moral superiority ("Orientalism") inhibits reflective thinkers. Otherwise, the tempting answer to the question would be, "Of course human rights apply to China. Its population consists of human beings." The fact that Chinese tradition did not or does not value liberty is irrelevant to the normative issue. It simply confuses epistemology and metaphysics. Moral objectivists should treat a culture's rejection of rights as scientists do the beliefs of flat-earth societies and we all do the practices of cannibals. That a group of people believes something fervently does not make it true. Simply put, people may have rights of which they are not aware. They may have rights they do not claim or do not believe they have. They may even have rights they could not justify using the community's forms of discourse.

That answer to a Bangkok attitude is both simple and theoretically sound. However, if we have felt any normative pull from the objection, it is obviously unsatisfying. It feels as if we have brushed off some genuine moral force of the Bangkok objection. The declaration demands a kind of respect for traditional moral attitudes that our dismissive analogy to cannibalism or flat-earth societies rules out. The declaration implies that we should give a higher normative status to conventional beliefs and practices than moral realism usually allows.

The problem is the notorious incoherence of relativism. It requires us to treat normative respect, like any other normative attitude, as being relative to some moral perspective. The very formulation of the objection seems to license our rejecting it from our "realist" moral perspective. "While we *recognize* that

---

3. Notoriously, diplomats use vagueness to help paper over disputes. Historical, predictive, sociological, and epistemological readings are clearly possible. That is, one may take it as noting that some cultures do not have a rights tradition, or are unlikely to adopt one, or that one would fit differently in their social structure. Alternatively, one may take it, epistemologically, as asserting that someone from certain cultures may have trouble recognizing what human rights are normatively required. Part of the heat in discussions of this issue results from confusing these various readings of the "Asian values" claim.

moral respect is due to all traditions, we must bear in mind our historical, cultural, and religious backgrounds." From our Rawlsian perspective, we are disinclined to respect sexism, authoritarianism, paternalism, and moral arrogance. Acknowledging cultural difference seems to give us little reason to resist the first, quick response.

If comparative philosophy has any significant role to play in answering these cross-cultural questions, then an adequate comparative account should explain why an ostensibly sound answer is normatively inadequate in this specific cross-cultural context. Why do we sense that an otherwise philosophically sound answer has missed something of normative importance? Can we find a description of the situation that accounts for the appearance of a conflict of moral judgments?

One normative approach is to attack the Rawlsian theory itself—say from a communitarian perspective. Henry Rosemont (1988) exemplifies this comparative approach. He has argued that our "taste" for ethical individualism is not merely a cultural peculiarity; it is a cultural bias that is morally dubious.[4] It rests, he thinks, on a seriously flawed conception of the individual—flawed because it is unrealistically abstract. Confucianism, he argues, has a more realistic conception of human nature—one that recognizes the inherent involvement of social relations in the characterizations of persons.

> For the early Confucians there can be no me in isolation, to be considered abstractly: I am the totality of roles I live in relation to specific others. I do not play or perform these roles; I am these roles. When they have all been specified, I have been defined uniquely, fully, and altogether, with no remainder with which to piece together a free, autonomous self (Rosemont 1988: 177).

Other comparative scholars confine their discussion to formally descriptive, historicist claims about Chinese thought. They avoid formulating the repressed normative conclusion (Ames 1988). Rosemont's approach has the advantage that it is explicitly normative and clearly targets the question: "Do (or should)

---

4. Rosemont's arguments are complicated not only by his challenge to Western background beliefs, but also by his way of characterizing morality and his related arguments about relativity. These are complicated issues that deserve fuller discussion. I cannot address these issues in the detail they deserve here. I will have to make do with noting where I agree with and depart from Rosemont on these deeper issues and continue my focus simply on the availability of the judgment that governments should allow their citizens extensive and equal liberty. I should stress that I present Rosemont's views with considerable respect first, for the courage they show in the face of widespread anti-China sentiments in the U. S. media, second for their subtlety and complexity, and third for his wider analysis of the situation in China surrounding the Tiananmen protest, with much of which I agree. (Rosemont has a deep respect and affection for China and is a defender of greater liberty in China) Thanks to Roger Ames for reminding me of the need to make the respectful context of my disagreement clear.

human rights apply to China?" However, it does not help with the broader question. Is comparative philosophy relevant to this normative issue and if so, why?

The problem with the communitarian attack for my purposes is this. If it succeeds, then comparative philosophy will play no role in settling the normative issue. It tells us to abandon the Rawlsian (Western?) perspective for a communitarian (Chinese?) one. It does not tell us how to mediate the disagreement between the two. If the attack is sound, then it's sound whether Confucius took that position or not. If it succeeds, then there are no human rights . . . period. It tells us neither anything in particular about China nor why we should see a difference in the normative status of Chinese liberty. Confucius' philosophy becomes irreverent, and technically the Bangkok position is false. Conversely, if the criticism fails, we would simply revert to the Rawlsian conclusion, "Chinese moral beliefs are wrong."

I propose, therefore, that we seek our statement of the relevance of comparative philosophy and the moral pull of the Bangkok objection within the Rawlsian perspective and in Rawlsian language. I offer the following reasons for this approach:

1. I suspect Rawls is right that his principles harmonize the intuitions of most Western liberals. (Technically, communitarians might disagree.) These warring intuitions arise within a Rawlsian perspective when we reflect on Chinese ethical theory. Rawlsian method, so to speak, owes us a solution.

2. Even if the communitarian attack on Rawls fails, my intuition is that the Bangkok attitude will continue to have normative "pull."

3. Reflective equilibrium already has helped us clarify the problem. If Chinese moral thinkers start from different intuitions, a reflective equilibrium might lead them to different conclusions. We should see what other resources the analysis can bring to deeper insights into the comparativist's puzzle.

4. Rawls is the most frequent foil for traditionalist arguments. Absent a neutral "view from nowhere," the best we can do may be to show that we can account for the normative force of the Bangkok attitude from within the "opposing" moral point of view. We will have an agreed conclusion even if we reach it from different starting points.

Rawls's position, however, did come with the hint of ethical objectivism that underlies the earlier unsatisfying response.[5] The Bangkok attitude, by contrast, strongly suggests ethical relativism. We may join them in being skeptical about the claim that metaphysically independent moral facts make our moral claims true the way physical facts make our physical theory true.

---

5. I doubt Rawls was ever committed to such a strong universalism. He originally presented his theory as harmonizing the intuitions of liberal democratic society. In any case, his move to a "political not metaphysical" analysis suggests he is amenable to the thrust of the compromise that emerges here.

Abandoning this still-live philosophical posture would give us some common ground. I do this here for the sake of argument. It may be possible to pursue the line of argument I am about to give even if there are metaphysically straightforward, independent moral facts, but I will not attempt to do so here.

I propose this to open us to the focus on social traditions inherent in the Bangkok view. We represent morality as the standards that justify our society's shared evaluations—our praising, blaming, excusing, feeling guilty or angry, and so on. This is not to confuse them with idealized descriptions of *actual* social behavior or actual moral beliefs. We characterize neither Chinese nor our own morality by our respective behavior patterns. Nor do we equate morality with either the proclamations of current political figures or the existing moral beliefs of the population. We can maintain the distinction between philosophy and sociology and still formulate intelligibly the claim that different cultures may have a different morality.

Morality consists of a culture's way (*dao*) of reasoning about what is right. We are interested in each culture's higher *standards* governing *evaluation* of behavior. We accept the hypothesis that these standards are the evolutionary outcome of normative discourse within historical moral communities.[6] Such evaluations, we can allow, may be more alike within any moral community than across different ones. We reason with our neighbors about ways (*dao*s) to evaluate, guide, and harmonize our actions. Here we can follow Gibbard and speak of "dialectical equilibrium" in the place of Rawls's "reflective equilibrium." It is still reflective, but we carry on moral reflection in groups and naturally adjust our attitudes to harmonize with those of others in our community. The purpose of moral discussion and communication is the harmonization of attitudes that facilitates social cooperation.

This is, admittedly, a perspective shift in Western moral reflection that brings it closer to Chinese moral framework. We can illustrate the traditional difference in perspective at the separate "originating moments" of ethical reflection. Socrates doubted traditional attitudes (hearsay, popular beliefs) and formulates the task of ethics as "know thyself." Given my community's possibly wrong attitudes, what should I do really? Mozi, starting with the same skeptical insight about social attitudes, asks instead how we should change society's moral discourse. Socrates' view can generalize to "what should we do," but Mozi's still has the more explicit recognition that philosophical discourse about *dao*s asks how we should modify the community's guiding discourse. He

---

6. See Gibbard 1990. Gibbard does not deny that some moral standards may be genetic adaptations, but the most important one is the adaptation to engage in moral discourse, to be moved by other's judgments, and to expect them to be moved by ours. See also Kitcher (1993) for an excellent discussion of the evolutionary issues surrounding the genetic disposition to qualified altruism.

reflects on moral issues to engineer changes in social attitudes while Socrates reflects to free himself from social attitudes.

This difference is mainly in emphasis. The two intellectual projects are closely linked. Mozi surely has to decide *independently of existing attitudes* what the attitudes ought to be. Socrates assumes that moral principles would hold equally for everyone so, ideally, all should reason as he does.

Traditionally, Western moral theory has resisted the social emphasis because it invites the threat of relativism and that threat undermines the implicit goal of eventual rational agreement. On the other hand, we can locate part of our sense of morality's *objectivity* within this social conception. Morality is not simply how I *feel*, but how the standards and a language of evaluation shared by my linguistic-moral community *guide* my feeling. We expect the norms guiding moral intuitions to gather wide support and yield agreement in attitudes and reactions. We characterize as 'moral' only those normative reactions that we expect others in our community to take as seriously regulative.

This means we still distinguish morality from conventional *mores*. Morality retains its reflective character. Moral reasoners in a community do not simply agree on evaluative attitudes. They also discuss and share second-level standards for justifying those attitudes, deeper reasons for those standards, and so forth. Our social standards "supervene" on the facts. Thus, moral judgments are world-guided and constant. Still, we give up the hint of straightforward moral facts in our earlier "abrupt" reply. The role of moral discourse is guiding and coordinating our evaluative attitudes and reactions, not merely expressing attitudes or describing normative facts.

Confucius may be a borderline case, but from Mozi on, Chinese moral reasoning, like Western reasoning, accepts that morality applies objectively to all people whether or not they know or understand it. The standards of justification are themselves social, but, again, neither Western nor Chinese philosophy justifies second-level norms *simply* on the ground that society uses them.[7] We understand right and wrong as depending on whether an action is justified. The mere prevalence of a pattern of action is not the issue. Therefore, this conception of morality should neither abandon serious normative reasoning nor substitute sociology or history for reflective normative thinking. It does accept that 'reasonable', as applied to moral attitudes, is a public, shared concept, which may differ in different moral communities. Provisionally, we can allow that those differences reflect the effects of history and tradition.

---

7. Some may use this criterion to distinguish between moral and legal claims. Legal claims, they may argue, are justified by second-level standards, but those standards themselves have no justification. They are the standards of the legal system in virtue of their being institutionalized. This posture is relevant to Rosemont's more complex claims about moral relativism and the presence or absence of a concept of morality in Chinese thought. Again, I will not address these questions directly here.

One of Rosemont's formulations now links up with our social discourse conception of the development of moral attitudes (Rosemont 1988: 176). He observes that Western *arguments* for rights, which seem compelling to Western reasoners, would not have convinced Confucius. Ames suggests that the very concept of "rights" is unintelligible to someone within a *genuinely* Chinese moral-conceptual framework (1988: 203). Would any argument for human rights "work" internally? Could we make conceptual sense of and justify to someone culturally Chinese (given their first-level intuitions and second-level norms) a political morality that maximizes equal liberty and freedom from state coercion? Could we imagine that conclusion emerging from discussion *within* a Chinese community of moral reasoners, given their initial shared attitudes and high-level norms of judgment?

This question has normative content because we accept the epistemic norm of reflective equilibrium. People *should* make moral judgments in accord with the standards of reasoning that best justify their existing, considered moral judgments. A Westerner's own commitment to this version of rational autonomy requires her to respect different moral points of view as long as they are seriously and sincerely reflective. She still has room to say the other community is wrong. She must, however, grant they have reasoned rightly by their own lights and further grant that so reasoning is precisely what they *ought* to do. By our lights, they would get the wrong answer, but our moral epistemology should hold them blameless. Western reasoners should conclude that Chinese reflective moral reasoners would be wrong *internally* to simply accept Western standards.

So we can appreciate and identify the normative force of the Bangkok attitude while still judging that moral human rights apply in China. The normative force falls in the realm of excuses. We may simultaneously judge that something is objectively morally wrong yet subjectively right. What the Bangkok attitude invites us to consider is that, guided by their best lights and reasons, the Chinese moral community may have reached a different dialectical equilibrium from the West. We can simultaneously say that their evaluative process was correct, but their conclusion is wrong. They make a mistake but reason correctly and responsibly—just as they should.

As we saw, the mere fact that someone else disagrees has no relevance to the truth of the disputed claim. *Mere* disagreement warrants no special normative respect. Our appreciation that continuous, cultivated, and wise reflection generates disagreement does merit respect. A reflective community may be wrong, but their disagreements do *and should* give us pause. That pause is the mark of normative respect. Comparative philosophy grounds that respect by exhibiting it as a rich tradition that is not merely different, but reflective and self-critical.

The relativism of this result is not theoretically problematic. It is the familiar result of a single principle producing different judgments in different conditions. A common, shared norm of warrant produces, when applied according to the varying epistemic norms of different cultures, different moral attitudes. It would be unacceptable from within a Rawlsian moral perspective to regard Chinese moral reasoning as deficient simply because it reaches a different conclusion from ours. It demands of Rawlsian reasoners a plausible story explaining why the disagreement is there.

Locating the normative force in the realm of excuses (subjective epistemic rightness) captures our intuition that a Bangkok objection is relevant while still regarding it as wrong or inconclusive. The remaining problem for comparative philosophy, however, is that this kind of respect puts an argumentative burden on apologists alleging that rights do not apply to China. It is not enough to show that the actual attitudes are different. Apologetic comparativists need to show that the alleged judgment is valid—warranted by the higher norms of Chinese reasoning. They must present it as a justified outcome of a dialectical equilibrium within the moral community, not merely a conclusion of which political authorities approve. Lee Kwan Yiu cannot carry on his debate with Hillary Clinton and Chris Patten. He needs to prove his claims to the likes of Wei Jingsheng, Fang Lizhi, Wang Dan, Christine Loh, and Gladys Li.

I will not survey Chinese moral philosophy at any great depth here. We have already noted one important point. Given this conception of subjective rightness, it is not enough merely to describe what moral attitudes people actually have. Any survey should show what attitudes that moral perspective warrants. It means proving that conclusion, not merely showing some Chinese thinkers sincerely believe it. It is, therefore, strictly irrelevant whether China actually had a tradition of human rights before the Qing dynasty.

Even a consensus of *actual* moral judgments of the existing community is irrelevant. We can see this if we imagine it as a response to a Chinese rights activist. Her goal is to convince her community to exchange its historically basic institutions in the direction of a democratic rule of law. It would be simply obtuse to argue against her that the community is not already convinced. Finally, she is not engaging in sociological *predictions* about what rights will survive in Hong Kong or will eventually be adopted in China. Her question is a practical, ethical one—what should *we* (the Hong Kong community) now do?

Common academic apologists for the Bangkok attitude usually carefully limit their scope to Confucianism and, in particular, to classical Confucianism. For a normative claim of subjective rightness, however, those interpretive analyses, even if sound, would be irrelevant. The practical question arises today in Hong Kong, not two thousand years ago in Loyang or Chang'an. "Chinese tradition" is a rich concept of which Confucianism is only a part—however important a part. Hong Kong now has a tradition of abiding by the rule of law that is about as old as the abolition of slavery in America. It may suit Chinese authoritarians to accuse dissidents of being tainted by Western ideas, but it is a red herring in the internal debate.

By itself, therefore, Rosemont's observation that we could not convince Confucius of human rights has exactly the normative status as the observation that we could not persuade the Pope to accept abortion. It does not show the judgment is an ideally coherent product of the higher-level norms of Chinese reasoning. If we put Confucius on a sacred pedestal as a sage (religious authority) and ignore the objections made by Mohists, Daoists, and Legalists, we would undermine the basis for the respect we just averred.[8] Other members of the Chinese moral community made those objections and all accepted that they were legitimate (whether or not answerable) objections. Neither Sinologists nor Chinese authorities can fairly characterize them as foreign.

Donald Munro drew our attention to the shared Chinese assumption of essential equality of humans (1969). Ronald Dworkin argues that the core of Rawls's argument for liberty is an assumption that we should show people equal concern and respect (1977: 180-83). It would be hard to show that a tradition with such a view about human equality could not get a justification of equal liberty off the ground. The normative conclusion that a wide scope of decision and action should be free from governmental control is one that different Chinese thinkers reached repeatedly throughout their history.

I will not attempt a more detailed analysis of the philosophical tradition here. I tend (more than most comparative scholars) to find the justification of Confucian piety to be weak *by indigenous Chinese philosophical grounds.* The analogy with Christianity in the West seems apt. Both are the single largest religions and both have influenced the moral attitudes of almost everyone in their respective communities. Ethical thinkers in both traditions, however, find ample grounds for skepticism about their religious morality. A full account of Chinese thought would probably support the idea that reasonable moral reflection from the assumptions and norms of a Chinese community would lead to some different results. However, it could not show that, on principled grounds, Chinese ethical thinking must fail to value a scheme of equal liberty. That result, of course, should surprise no one, since reflective and thoughtful Chinese moral thinkers have advocated greater liberty—going all the way back to Zhuangzi.

One correct way to show respect for Chinese tradition of this type would be to give greater weight to the integrity of the discussion internal to the Chinese community. We should clearly distinguish this internal debate from any China-

---

8. Other bases of respect may be justified by separate arguments, say, merely of "right to their opinions" etc. and that kind of respect would presumably survive. Chan Sin Yee has pointed out (in conversation) that Confucianism has been dominant in China so the dialectical equilibrium today would not include input from these classical perspectives. I doubt that the ideas and principles of reasoning "died out" when the social movements or ongoing philosophical school did. One cannot delete validity merely by destroying a social movement. For the argument that these inputs survived in Chinese consciousness into modern times, see Needham 1954.

West dialogue. Blurring them short-circuit's the internal debate by inviting the authoritarians to treat their internal discussants as proxies for the West.

We should also avoid treating human rights as some kind of international demand to which the Chinese community must bow because of an allegedly superior status of an international consensus. Rhetorically, such a consensus may undermine confidence in a local community morality, but it is irrelevant to reflective internal ethical inquiry and begs the question in the context of cross-cultural dialog. Politically, in urging that these are either international standards to which Chinese must conform or parochial Western attitudes that do not fit China, we give intellectual cover to the authoritarian fallacy within the internal discourse.

Another way of showing this respect, however, appears to pull in the opposite direction. In cross-cultural dialog, to credit another community with competent moral authority is to justify including them within the circle of moral discourse. This means openly addressing our judgments, criticisms, attitudes, and arguments to them. We do not cite the fact they are ours (or shared with others) in support or those judgments. We give the principles themselves and, if challenged, defend them. We do not accept "our principles are different" as an excuse. We ask what the rival principle is and how it justifies the moral attitude in dispute.

We naturally seek to enlarge our community of moral agreement. To exclude or shield them from the normal assumptions of our moral discourse signals a lack of respect for their competence as moral judges and reasoners. If we think the members of the other community are competent moral judges capable of reflective adjustment of moral attitudes, we should engage them in moral discourse as we do each other.

The balance for this tension between lies in being clear about the tone of our open discourse. Clearly, a lecturing tone is wrong, but a direct, even combative, critical tone shows more respect than historicist apologetics. Treating one's interlocutors as prisoners of their history violates the principle of moral respect we justified here even if we similarly describe ourselves. Ironically, therefore, taking refuge in a communitarian's or comparativist's attitude of accepting differences as warranted *simply because the community holds* them suggests we do not credit the other community with reflective normative authority. An excessively protective or paternalistic valuing of Chinese culture suggests some insecurity that it cannot interact on an equal footing with full-blown robust normative discourse.

I worry when comparative philosophy tends toward this condescension. When critics offer rational objections to a Chinese philosophical or moral view, the field responds too often with an attack on the narrowness or prejudice of the questioner. It avoids the reasons given Western philosophers offer for their views and fails to elicit from their interpretation similarly strong reasons for the other culture's view. Comparativists are too easily tempted to become anti-

Western in their own attitudes and to celebrate the irrational "quaintness" of Chinese thought. We should be doing more to uncover the depth and coherence of Chinese thought, not merely to use it as a relativist stick with which to beat Western liberal individualism.[9]

Western apologists sometimes mimic the biologist arguing for preserving species or the anthropologist arguing for conserving old cultures. Ethically such an attitude is paternalistic in a way inconsistent with the justification given here for moral respect. We may have reasons for preserving Neolithic cultures, but freezing them in time as museum pieces is incompatible with moral respect. As authentic, reflective moral communities, they will change and evolve.

Another consequence of normative respect further explains why we should avoid this paternalistic preservationist attitude. Widening our moral community means engaging in open, frank moral discourse. We must do this in a way that leaves us open to the possibility that our own moral attitudes will change. The knowledge that a fully reflective moral community has a different moral structure should upset our own reflective equilibrium of normative attitudes. Similarly, given the Chinese conception of morality as "natural intuitions," acknowledging a rich, reflective, but divergent Western morality should equally upset their moral equilibrium.

The consequence of respect should be that each reflective tradition initially has a lower confidence in their inherited attitudes. We add this to our set of moral beliefs: a fully competent, reflective moral community has reached a different dialectical equilibrium. We now have to bring that belief into harmony with our other moral beliefs and our faith in the method of reflective equilibrium.

This result emerges from a distinguishing feature of moral reasoning. We reach our moral views in discourse governed by appeal to higher norms and reasons. So we are likely to (and in both cultures do) operate under a "one right answer" assumption. That is, communities with well-developed second-level discursive support for their moral attitudes are likely to regard them as adequate to settling moral issues. Neither is likely to treat the answers to moral questions as relativistic historical prejudices.

Both are likely, therefore, to be objectivists about moral inquiry. Both accept the value and importance of moral debate. Both assume such open discussion has a point, i.e., that it tends to the improvement of the community's

---

9. I do not mean to rule out the appropriateness of questioning Western assumptions about deontological individualism and the priority of liberty, nor, in particular, the use of Chinese thought to illustrate or motivate such questioning. Thanks to Roger Ames for reminding me to introduce this caveat here. I do explore that use of comparative philosophy in the next section. Even in this use, however, the intellectual value of introducing Chinese ethical thought still requires getting its position right and spelling out its relevance for our own ethical reflection.

moral discourse (*dao*). Prima facie, both would be inclined to suppose that if a moral position could capture the sound normative insights of both, it would have a strong claim to be a more correct morality than either taken alone. This explains the perennial mutual interest in a still unrealized synthesis of East and West.

This synthesis will not be the intellectual product of comparative philosophers, but of the two communities interacting. Beyond mere coherence, any synthesis must work in practice and attract wide community agreement. Comparative philosophy can and should supply the appreciation of the coherence and workability of the other viewpoint to its home culture. Ordinary normative discourse and debate will test the coherence of any emerging synthesis.

References

Ames, Roger. 1988. "Rites as Rights: The Confucian Alternative." In *Human Rights and the World's Religions,* edited by Leroy S. Rouner, 199–214. South Bend: University of Notre Dame Press.

Davis, Michael C., ed. 1995. *Human Rights and Chinese Values: Legal, Philosophical, and Political Perspectives.* Oxford: Oxford University Press.

De Bary, William Theodore. 1988. "Neo-Confucianism and Human Rights." In *Human Rights and the World's Religions,* edited by Leroy S. Rouner, 183–98. South Bend: University of Notre Dame Press.

Dworkin, Ronald. 1977. *Taking Rights Seriously.* Cambridge: Harvard University Press.

Gibbard, Allan. 1990. *Wise Choices, Apt Feelings: A Theory of Normative Judgment.* New York: Oxford University Press.

Kitcher, Philip. 1993. "The Evolution of Human Altruism." *Journal of Philosophy* 90(10): 497–516.

Munro, Donald J. 1969. *The Concept of Man in Early China.* Stanford: Stanford University Press.

Needham, Joseph. 1954. *Science and Civilization in China.* Cambridge: Cambridge University Press.

Rawls, John. 1971. *A Theory of Justice.* Cambridge: Harvard University Press.

Rosemont, Henry, Jr. 1988. "Why Take Rights Seriously? A Confucian Critique." In *Human Rights and the World's Religions*, edited by Leroy S. Rouner, 167–82. South Bend: University of Notre Dame Press.

————. 1991. *A Chinese Mirror: Moral Reflections on Political Economy and Society.* La Salle, IL: Open Court.

Rouner, Leroy S. 1988. In *Human Rights and the World's Religions*, edited by Leroy S. Rouner. South Bend: University of Notre Dame Press.

A History Composed of Many Histories

ALBERT FEUERWERKER

The University of Michigan

It is a truism that China's history is composed of many Chinese histories. This macro-history/micro-history syllogism has numerous possible dimensions. In its simplest guise it reminds us that geographically China is a very large and diverse country. To write its national history as, say, a narrative of the intricate politics of the capital, not only omits or underplays other dimensions of what properly constitutes history—economic, intellectual, and cultural developments, among others. It also neglects the potentially enormous variability between what may be transpiring in Beijing and what occurs or is apprehended at the multiple levels of the regions, provinces, counties, cities, and villages that constitute China.

China's cultural diversity beyond the geographical dimension includes a substantial range of local religious expressions, among which the numerically small but strategically significant Chinese Christian communities are to be counted. And similarly, with respect to economic-occupational heterogeneity, the role of businessman or merchant is an omnipresent occurrence.

What is especially interesting about the following three contributors is not that they are aware—as they obviously are—of the near impossibility of writing convincingly about China without taking account of such distinctions as I have suggested. Daniel Bays, Keith Schoppa, and Andrea McElderry also partly turn the syllogism on its head. Of course China is composed of many Chinas, but it is precisely the integration of these parts—through the process of creating communities at each of the loci that constitute the fabric of Chinese history and society—that makes it possible to speak of China at all. The three essays share an underlying concern to explain what it was that contributed to constructing a community in that patch of local history—recall, all history is local and a province is not only a geographical conceit—which they are explicating.

At the height of the late imperial era, it might be argued that China was unified by an impressive degree of commitment to the basic values of Qing society as expressed in the dominant Confucian religious ideology. At least among the literate elite, at the capital and in multiple localities, there were few dissenters, no "Sunday" Confucians. Here was a genuine conservatism dedicated to continuity not as a reaction to modernist challenges, but from commitment to a religious-philosophical orthodoxy that claimed to comprehend the

97

total meaning of life and humanity. In the course of the nineteenth century, as the political and economic institutions of the Qing dynasty showed themselves unable to cope with the weight of combined internal and external challenges, this universality of Confucian belief also began to crumble. Although some of the old values and behavior persisted even after 1911, in the twentieth century we face the remarkable circumstance that of all the great historical religions of the world—Buddhism, Islam, Hinduism, Judaism, Christianity—Confucianism alone has expired as the principal expression of the values and beliefs of the society that it had once both explicated and justified. In what can one believe in China today, with Marxism-Leninism Mao Zedong Thought now also totally in shambles? Can the cramped contemporary message to *zhuan yidian qian* ("make a little money") long suffice to nourish and integrate hearts and minds in a nation with so long a history and so rich a culture?

While the dominant Confucianism glued Chinese society together before the present century, the actual fabric of religious experience and commitment was not so simplistic. Buddhism and Daoism, with substantial variations in doctrine and ceremony, were widely present, often in combination with local religious traditions of multiple origins, sometimes as components of sectarian movements with millenarian beliefs. These too, in the many local Chinas, were the basis for community and cohesion at levels below that of the greater China. Buddhism especially, and sometimes Daoism as well, at times provided intellectual or aesthetic alternatives for the Confucian elites out of office. Only very small results ensued from Jesuit and other Catholic missionary activity in China, itself subject to sporadic persecutions, in the seventeenth and eighteenth centuries. After the treaties imposed upon China following the mid-nineteenth-century Opium Wars, however, which in effect made the foreign victors protectors of missionaries and their converts, both Catholic and Protestant proselytizing achieved some greater results. But the numbers were still limited: never as many as one percent of the Chinese population accepted Christianity before 1949.

Daniel Bays suggests that notwithstanding the small number of its adherents, Christianity in the twentieth century—he is writing only about Protestants; the circumstances of the Catholic community were not entirely comparable—could form the basis of local community, especially after the larger Confucian religious ecumene had been dissolved. In other places Bays has studied local sectarian movements based on Protestant Christianity that were in every way comparable to the "indigenous" religious sects that have attracted the attention of most scholars. In his essay here, he examines the creation of a Protestant Christian urban community in Shandong in North China in the early twentieth century, which grew originally out of education at a notable missionary-operated school, but which acquired an autonomous Chinese character when it was no longer controlled by the Protestant missionaries who had launched it. By implication, this Shandong example might be one of a number of such instances, the most remarkable one recently being the salience of an indigenized Protestant Christian community in the rapid economic growth of the city of Wenzhou in Zhejiang province in the post-1979 era of Deng Xiaoping's reforms. I am certain that Bays does not expect that Christianity, or any imported set of beliefs however sinicized, will simply replace Confucianism or Mao Zedong Thought in the twenty-first century as the source of genuine identity and value for the men and women of a truly modern China. But that caution surely does not rule out the local participation of Christian believers as components in constructing that larger Chinese community yet to come.

It was nationalism, specifically anti-Japanese nationalism in the context of Japan's brutal war on China which broke out in full force in 1937, that provided one of the bases for the construction of new political community in the unoccupied areas of Zhejiang province, still under Guomindang leadership but distinct from the prewar provincial configuration. Keith Schoppa's portrayal of Yongkang county, formerly a peripheral district but now the seat of the refugee provincial government, is not just local history. What he constructs is an alternative framework, another quality of mesh, through which it becomes possible to view wartime events in unoccupied China. He questions any putative direct connection *for all of China invariably* between the agony and destruction of the 1937–1945 Sino-Japanese war and the victory of the Chinese Communists over their Guomindang adversaries in the civil war of 1946–1949.

In Zhejiang, in any case, the wartime provincial government appeared able to gain and hold general support, to provide assistance to refugees from occupied areas while simultaneously furthering economic development through a successful refugee textile mill project, to encourage transport and communications and the circulation of newspapers too, and to undertake some aspects of "nation-building" by carving out a new county adjacent to Yongkang. This was still a Guomindang-dominated government, still closely linked to provincial and local elites—indeed it was because of and through this linkage that its economic projects were effective at all—but without many of the disabilities that are frequently ascribed to the wartime Guomindang and said to prefigure its collapse in the civil war. Some strands in the Guomindang agglomeration seemingly were able to adopt to the periphery, to the interior of China, when they were driven from the southeast coastal cities by the Japanese army. And the Guomindang defeat may perhaps be sought as much in the character and local events of the civil war itself as in the trying wartime years that preceded it.

The contributions by both Bays and Schoppa are, among their several qualities, also pieces of local history in a normal geographical meaning: treating Shandong province in one case and Zhejiang in the other. Locality as a quality is more diffuse in Andrea McElderry's essay. What she is investigating are the institutional arrangements that linked "local"—in the sense of unrelated by kinship or by other primary ties—economic actors into networks for the flow of personnel, information, goods, and funds that constituted the Chinese economy in operation in the late-Qing and early Republican eras. In "the transition from rural-based to urban-based enterprise and from small family-centered businesses to larger modem-style enterprises," she states, the use of guarantors facilitated these transitions by reducing risk in a manner that drew upon the resources of the prevailing Chinese culture and also evolved as the culture and economy were transformed in the twentieth century.

McElderry's discussion focuses on the role of guarantors in employer-employee relations, but also considers broader guarantor functions. It becomes evident from her examples and analysis that guarantorship was not just a throwback to "traditional" means of doing business and hence to be judged "backward" in foreign eyes. While in principle it was inconsistent with the operation of a free labor market, in practice the use of guarantors supported the development in China of just such an impersonal labor market in circumstances when "modern" legal institutions were still in their infancy. Guarantorship could facilitate the beneficial application of other particularistic relations in new and complex circumstances where family ties alone, for example, had become inadequate bases for enterprise expansion and economic growth. Thus we may conclude that an unqualified application of the Weberian universalistic-particularistic distinction to China or East Asia is not always helpful. The remarkable recent economic growth of the Asian "Four Tigers"—and possibly some aspects of the People's Republic economy too—are testimony to the efficacy of the right mix of Weberian economic rationality with attenuated and controlled utilization of lubricating particularistic relations.

The three authors, once students and now colleagues and friends of whom I am exceedingly proud, have nicely fulfilled their assignments to spark our attention to the manifold processes by which "China" is constructed and her culture and economy linked.

A Chinese Christian 'Public Sphere'?: Socioeconomic Mobility and the Formation of Urban Middle Class Protestant Communities in the Early Twentieth Century

DANIEL H. BAYS
University of Kansas

At the turn of the century there emerged in some cities self-conscious Chinese Protestant urban communities that had grown out of the Protestant foreign missionary-managed institutions and activities. This clearly visible and steadily growing element of Chinese urban society between 1900 and 1920, especially after 1911, had its own voice and increasing economic and administrative independence from foreign missions. In the Shandong example which I examine here, this group formation was closely linked to modern education and the economic mobility derived from it. In addition, there seem to be some lines of continuity between these early twentieth-century communities and the recent re-emergence of urban Christian communities in China since the early 1980s.

In June 1995 a *Wall Street Journal* reporter devoted an entire column to the 10 percent of the population of Wenzhou, Zhejiang Province, many of them quite wealthy, who constitute a set of dynamic local Christian communities:

> Just as they drink Coke and carry Motorola pagers, entrepreneurs show off their cosmopolitan savvy by erecting the finest houses of worship. Taxi drivers sermonize passengers. Factory foremen lure their workers to Sunday services. So the Chinese people are discovering what Max Weber theorized long ago: Capitalism and Christianity can be self-reinforcing (Kahn 1995).

Earlier in the 1990s, another American observer in Wenzhou, one very familiar with Chinese churches, also cited Weber and noted, "Both capitalism and Protestantism are flourishing in Wenzhou, and one cannot help thinking that there is some relationship between the two. . . . Economic and Christian vitality seem to go hand in hand" (Wickeri 1990: 582).

Today in Wenzhou and other cities, especially in coastal and riverine China, many Christian communities have resources to fund the social and ritual activities that provide group solidarity. They are able to take some initiative in apolitical (that is, not threatening to the state) social activities, as well as in entrepreneurial economic endeavors. They have, in effect, carved out a niche for their communities, although like other such groups in China today they are still vulnerable to arbitrary acts of suppression or harassment by state authorities.[1]

I believe that the historical process of forming urban Christian communities with growing economic power not dependent on foreign missionaries, although at first it took place in an overall framework of foreign-mission-dominated Christianity, began in the late nineteenth century and accelerated between 1900 and 1920.

Research on Chinese Christianity: From a Religious to a Socioeconomic Focus

Some years ago when I began research on modern Chinese Christianity, my aim was to discover how Christianity, especially Protestantism, which was so dynamic in the 1980s, had come from being viewed as a foreign religion, under foreign missionary control, to attracting several million new adherents even after three decades (approximately 1950–1980) of stringent control or outright suppression by a strong secular state. Was there a process at work in the first half of the twentieth century which would explain this phenomenon? My initial research and that of other scholars revealed strong impulses towards autonomy or even full-fledged independence for Chinese Protestant congregations soon after 1900. These trends resulted in several independent Protestant movements between about 1910 and the 1930s, some of which were nationwide in scope.

These movements and their leaders seemed to me of particular interest as potential historical repositories of the dynamism and resiliency of Christian faith that has resurfaced in recent years. They include groups such as the True Jesus Church, the Jesus Family, the China Independent Church, the Assembly Hall (also called the Little Flock), and others. Leaders, many of whom used English given names in addition to their Chinese names, included John Sung (Song Shangjie), Watchman Nee (Ni Tuosheng), Marcus Cheng (Chen Chonggui), Leland Wang (Wang Zai), Andrew Gih (Ji Zhiwen), Wang Mingdao, and Jing Dianying (Bays 1993, 1995, 1996). These groups and leaders are not names we encounter in most accounts of modern Chinese history, but we must focus on them if we want to explain how Christianity survived and adapted in modern China. I have examined their religious origins, the development of their theological and doctrinal ideas, their relationships with missionaries, and those cultural features which perhaps made them more "Chinese" than the missionary-

---

1. For a profile of Protestant communities in China today, see Hunter and Chan 1993. Brief profiles of local Christian communities, most of them Protestant, appear regularly in *Bridge: Church Life in China Today*, published bi-monthly by The Christian Study Centre on Chinese Religion and Culture, Hong Kong. It should be noted, however, that the majority of Christian communities in China as a whole, especially in the countryside, are rather poor.

led mainstream, which I call the "Sino-foreign Protestant Establishment." This research endeavor has been exciting for me, partly because it has revealed "new" historical actors and partly because it is directly linked to the life histories of many older Christian men and women whom I have been privileged to meet in China in recent years.[2]

In none of this previous work on Chinese Christians did I particularly stress a historical socioeconomic analysis. However, such an analysis could and should be done. In fact, in reviewing the scholarly literature of the last few decades I find one overall weakness has been its failure to consider at least some Christian groups as parts of Chinese society, with important characteristics going beyond their connections with foreign missions. It is not easy to do this sort of analysis. Foreign missionary records are remarkably poor in detail on Chinese Christians, and Qing government records often portray Chinese Christians in stereotyped pejorative terms.

In the period from the 1860s to the early 1900s, we have either some overly broad generalizations or a mélange of anecdotal detail on personalities and incidents. Paul Cohen's characterization twenty years ago, that in the late nineteenth century Chinese Christians "were confined almost entirely to poor peasants and townspeople, criminal elements and other unsavory types, and deracinated individuals in the treaty ports," is a vast overstatement that is probably not valid past the 1860s (Cohen 1978: 560). Cohen's other work, on "Christian reformers" of the late Qing, as well as other scholars' research into compradors, social groups in Hankou, and an analysis of the writings of Chinese contributors to the *Jiaohui xinbao* (Church news), provide specific insights into interesting individuals among the urban Christians, but almost no real data about the communities of which they were a part (Cohen 1974).[3] Even the recent work by Kwok Pui-lan on the ideas, roles, and activities of Chinese women converts, while pathbreaking and immensely important, does not directly consider Christian congregations as communities in a wider social and political setting. The one work which provides at least a cursory profile of nineteenth-century urban Christians, including many biographical sketches, is on Hong Kong, so its conclusions must be carefully used with regard to China (Smith 1985).

---

2. I have had informal interviews and conversations with Christians I have met at urban churches or to whom I have been introduced by mutual friends almost annually since 1985. These have been in over a dozen cities and county-level towns in North China and the Yangzi Valley.

3. Hao 1970: 183 mentions a few "Christian compradors." There are tantalizing references to some Hankou shopkeepers, including a "prosperous baker," becoming Christians in the early 1880s in Rowe 1989: 201. Bennett (1983) has a section analyzing Chinese contributions to the *Jiaohui xinbao*. A carefully done set of biographical studies of Chinese Christian leaders, including some from the late nineteenth and early twentieth century (Zha 1983), has little or no data on the Christian communities of whom these men and women were leaders.

Past scholarship concentrating on foreign missionaries and the missionary enterprise in China during these decades also fails to inform us about the nature of the Chinese Christian congregations growing in China's cities. Whether in looking at institutional developments such as schools and colleges, or in analyzing, sometimes brilliantly, missionary personalities, scholars have tended to assume that the Chinese Christian community was an extension of, or encompassed by, the missionary community.[4] Of course, the missionaries themselves usually assumed that to be the case. Even an otherwise excellent study of the YMCA, the single missionary-related institution that made a strong effort to indigenize its leadership and management, gives us no sense at all of the urban Chinese Christian communities which by their participation and financial support undergirded the YMCA presence in scores of cities (Garrett 1970).

Chinese scholarship in the PRC on the role of Christianity in modern Chinese history has until very recently been constrained by the imperative to characterize all pre-1949 Christian activities as imperialist (though a category of benign imperialism was acceptable after 1980) and to portray Chinese Christians as part of the foreign missionary-imperialist presence.[5] But much more nuanced and thoughtful publications began appearing in the 1990s. These include essays on the Christian colleges and on Christianity and culture, and especially a fine study by two young historians at Shandong University, on the role of Christianity in modern Shandong society, which analyzes the changing social composition (*shehui goucheng*) of Shandong Protestant Christians against the backdrop of broader changes in society at large (Zhang and Waldron 1991; Zhu 1994; Tao and Liu 1995).[6]

In addition to the inclination and ability of Chinese scholars to treat Christian themes in more depth than previously, a whole range of materials has become available since the 1980s which makes it possible for both Chinese and foreign scholars to analyze much more effectively the social and economic composition of late Qing and early Republican Chinese Christian communities. The most important single category is that of *wenshi ziliao*, or local history collections. These publications often have individual articles on the history of local churches or on prominent local Christians. Some localities, for example Ji'nan, have

---

4. See, for example, discussion of the origins of education and the Christian colleges in Lutz 1971. Two studies full of insights on missionaries and very thin on Chinese Christians are Hyatt 1976 and Hunter 1984.

5. See, for example, Gu 1991. For a very useful chronological listing of books and articles on Christianity in China published in the People's Republic from 1949 to 1993, see Zhu 1994: 429–89.

6. Tao and Liu have a chapter on "historical analysis" (*lishi fenxi*) of Shandong Christians over a period of several decades which is especially insightful on matters of social composition, careers, and mobility.

published volumes of these materials specifically for religion, or even more specifically for Christianity.[7] The great difference between our picture of the Chinese church derived from these materials and the picture we derive from foreign missionary records is that the former often record the names, occupations, and life histories of prominent local Christians, including elders and deacons as well as pastors. Missionary records notoriously omit details about, or even the names of, Chinese Christians, especially lay people.

Published documentation can often be enhanced by interviews with older Chinese Christians. Some from long-standing Christian families are delighted to trace their family lineage back several generations for the benefit of the interested listener. Finally, the growing ability of Chinese and foreign scholars to obtain access to provincial and local archives in China makes it possible to trace the career patterns and social mobility of Christians in the late nineteenth and early twentieth century and to make some estimates about their accumulation of wealth, status, and resources of social networking.[8]

General Patterns

Before presenting a Shandong example of the socioeconomic approach to the study of Christian communities that I am suggesting, let us look at what we know of the general features of Chinese Protestant Christians in the decades of the late Qing and the early Republic. There were only a few hundred Chinese Protestants in 1860; in 1905 they numbered over 250,000. It has been remarked that this is a tiny number in terms of China's total size, which of course is true. But I suggest that it is not such a small figure when we take into account the cultural demands of conversion during these decades.

These Chinese Christians, moreover, were not just passive recipients of what the missionaries offered, but were important participants in all that the foreign missionaries did. Christianity was from this early period already a Sino-foreign joint enterprise. Mission records usually seriously understate the Chinese role, often not even naming Chinese participants. But as we know from various Chinese-language sources, some available only in the past two decades, the Chinese played key roles in all religious activities, as assistants, preachers, and

---

7. See, for example, individual articles in various issues of *Shandong wenshi ziliao xuanji* (Shandong local history collection) from the 1980s; an earlier Ji'nan publication, *Jidujiao* 1962; an important recent study is Ruan and Gao 1992, which contains more than 160 pages on Catholicism and in excess of 240 pages on Protestantism.

8. Much of the documentation in Tao and Liu 1995, for example, comes from archival sources within the province. Ryan Dunch, a doctoral student of Jonathan Spence at Yale, is writing a dissertation on changes in the Fuzhou Protestant community from the 1880s to the 1920s, using provincial archival materials such as the Fuzhou Imperial Maritime Customs and post office personnel records. See a preliminary report on these materials and their usefulness in Dunch 1994.

translators. They also staffed the thousands of mission stations which had no resident missionary, and by 1900 the mission schools were producing a steady stream of ordained Chinese pastors, who in most missions gradually took over much of the direct evangelism and preaching duties.

Similarly, Chinese participation was crucial in the growth of nonreligious mission activities like general education, medicine, and publishing, where they did the lion's share of the real work. In most schools missionary educators were far outnumbered by Chinese teachers, themselves graduates of the Christian school system. As hospitals developed and raised standards, mission doctors and nurses became dependent on Chinese medical personnel to handle the volume of patients. And Chinese writers, translators, and assistant editors were essential to the production of both Christian and secular literature at the mission publishing houses. Thus all areas of endeavor became Sino-foreign in composition.

Even though many Christian converts were attracted by the religious and spiritual aspects of Christianity, careers in the Christian sphere, and opportunities for training of various kinds, point to a key effect. Many Chinese found occupational and socioeconomic mobility through association with Christianity. This mobility most often resulted from the Christian school system. Tao and Liu's discussion of social composition, career paths, and mobility among Shandong Christians, for example, concludes that the generation of Chinese Christians who were educated in mission schools between about 1880 and the early 1900s became the core of an increasingly prosperous and assertive Shandong Protestant community, visible especially in Ji'nan and Qingdao (Tao and Liu 1995; chap. 4). In the cities Christian schools facilitated the entry of many into secular areas such as private businesses and trade, government agencies (the customs and the post office, for example), interpreting, and (after 1900) teaching in the new Chinese government school system.

These Christian school graduates (or attendees—many did not graduate), whether believers or not, made a large contribution to changes in the urban economy and society at the turn of the century and after. Of course, not all mission school graduates who found mobility in the occupations enumerated above were members of Christian communities. Some never became Christians and others dropped their Christianity as they advanced in their careers. But—and this is the key point—apparently a significant number did remain Christians, and they constituted the social and economic foundation of an increasingly assertive, nonmissionary, Chinese Protestantism later in the twentieth century.[9]

---

9. Some scholars maintain that missionaries turned to educational efforts in the 1870s and 1880s out of frustration at their lack of success in evangelization; see, for example, Lutz, 1971: 12. And they see the graduates of Christian schools as being trained for service in the institutions run by the missionaries. But much of the pressure for creating a school system came from the Chinese Christian communities themselves; this demand is visible as early as the late 1860s and 1870s. See Bennett 1983: 140, 212; and Robert 1996.

One striking impact on the creation of Chinese Christian communities early in the twentieth century came from schools for girls and women. The socioeconomic result was not most dramatic in what the missionary educators intended—creation of appropriately educated spouses for Chinese pastors and church workers, and the leavening of Chinese society with Christian values instilled in the "women's sphere." Instead significant numbers of women who attended Christian upper middle schools and colleges delayed marriage and motherhood, or never married, so that they could be self-sufficient and have satisfying careers, usually in education or social service endeavors (Hunter 1984; Kwok 1992; Ross 1996; Liu and Kelly 1996). Married or single, they often brought an independent income or at least partial personal economic autonomy to those Christian communities of which they remained a part.

Broadly speaking, the period from just after 1900 to the early 1920s was the golden age of foreign Protestant missions. During these years, as China apparently moved decisively towards reform and modernization, missions and Christianity seemed to be in the vanguard of progress. Moreover, after 1900 the Chinese church, especially several prominent individual Chinese Christian leaders, became visible, albeit against the backdrop of a Protestant scene still largely dominated by foreign missions. Thus there emerged what I call the "Sino-Foreign Protestant Establishment"—a more public collaboration between missions and Chinese Christians as compared with the nineteenth century, and a more balanced, though by no means equal, one.

An example makes this transition clear. In 1907 the China Centenary Missionary Conference was held in Shanghai, commemorating the centennial of the arrival in Canton of the first Protestant missionary, Robert Morrison; over 1,100 delegates attended. In keeping with the focus on the missionary, not the Chinese Christian, there were only six or seven Chinese present—although the program was replete with topics *about* "the Chinese church." But this meeting, which followed the example of its predecessor meetings of 1877 and 1890, was the last such nationwide conference where foreigners did all the speaking for Chinese Christians. The next, in 1922, was called the National Christian (not missionary) Conference, and it had a majority of Chinese delegates, although in many important ways the foreign missionary bodies still directed its business.

This was indicative of the times: a whole generation of well-educated Chinese Christian leaders had come into its own in this period. Some worked in mission or church institutions, as pastors, theologians, teachers, or YMCA and YWCA leaders. But others were teachers at government schools, or professionals such as doctors or lawyers, or businessmen. It was this latter group who constituted the core of maturing Chinese Protestant congregations, and as

---

Moreover, some of the graduates or trainees clearly did not take mission employment, but entered other careers.

local leaders were in many ways the essential element of a Christian movement based increasingly on Chinese society, not on foreign missionary structures.

Shandong as an Example

At this point I wish to turn to a more extended discussion of Shandong, particularly eastern Shandong and the area of the U.S. Northern Presbyterian Mission (though English Baptists and American Southern Baptists were also active in this general area). First, I wish to acknowledge some very interesting material given me several years ago by Irwin T. Hyatt, professor of history at Emory University and author of a 1976 study on some of the American missionaries in Shandong (1976a). One of these missionaries was the Presbyterian Calvin W. Mateer, founder of the Wenhuiguan ("Tengchow College") at Dengzhou (Penglai). The Wenhuiguan was one of the most successful of all missionary schools in China; after 1900 it became a core element of Shandong Union College, which in turn became Shandong Christian University and finally, in 1931, Cheeloo University, the latter two institutions both being located at Ji'nan.

Hyatt's material was extremely useful in answering questions about the social and career mobility and growing economic resources of Christian communities.[10] The graduates of the Wenhuiguan had all been recruited from Christian families, and almost all of them were from rural areas. Of the 170 graduates recorded from the classes between 1876 and 1904, 156 were from rural backgrounds, representing 107 villages in 29 different *xian*. Many were from poor families or families of modest means. In this regard they differ significantly from the graduates of the twentieth-century Christian colleges, many of whom were from non-Christian urban families. For the rural Shandong Christian youths of the late nineteenth century, their education at Mateer's school made a dramatic difference in their lives. In 1912, not one of the 170 was listed as a farmer, and only 21 were noted as having rural addresses (including last addresses of some of the 25 deceased) (Hyatt 1976b: 173).

The move of so many Wenhuiguan graduates up and out of the village is measurable in their subsequent careers. In 1912, of the surviving 145 graduates, by far the largest group, 87, had teaching jobs; 26 were in religious positions,

---

10. Hyatt sent me a long section of manuscript which was originally intended to be part of *Our Ordered Lives Confess* and does appear there as a one-paragraph summary, 229. In the more extensive version he did a close analysis of the career patterns of graduates of Mateer's school over more than thirty years, covering all the graduating classes from 1876 to 1904. He carried the discussion forward to 1912, when his main source, an alumni history of the school (*Wenhuiguan zhi*), was written.

In addition to his own manuscript draft, Hyatt sent me a copy of those sections of the *Wenhuiguan zhi* (1913), which had been his source of data on the careers of the graduates.

and 32 were scattered in other professions such as medicine, business, the civil service, and "literary work" (including interpreting and translating, printing, or editing). Some had more than one career; of those not teaching in 1912, over half had done so at some time. Moreover, geographical mobility was common; the 146 who were teachers at some time after 1876 held a total of 380 appointments in eleven provinces and Manchuria. Of the 87 who were still teaching in 1912, 31 were in government schools, at 25 different institutions all over the country but with the largest concentrations in Ji'nan and Tianjin.[11]

More so than the later graduates of other Christian colleges, this group seems to have remained committed to a Christian identity. They willingly took up leadership roles in the Protestant Christian community, especially in Shandong, where most of them remained. At the same time, their success in various professions brought higher economic status and a broadening of the resource base of the growing Protestant communities in the cities in which the graduates settled—these were often the termini of the German railway, Qingdao and Ji'nan, and cities on the line such as Weixian (today's Weifang). A few underwrote various Christian projects, including several financially independent Shandong Protestant churches in the twentieth century. An example was Liu Shoushan (1863–1935), who came out of abject poverty as son of an opium addict and eventually became a real estate tycoon in Qingdao. At Chefoo (Yantai) in the 1890s, as his jewelry business prospered, he repaid the American Presbyterians, with interest, every cent spent on his upbringing and education. Between 1911 and his death in 1935 he gave large sums of money to several churches in addition to funding other Christian institutions such as schools and hospitals and helping individual Chinese preachers, YMCA workers, and the like.[12]

As men like Liu Shoushan began to assume natural leadership roles in the Protestant communities, and as the economic resources of the community became sufficient, some congregations began to chafe at continued foreign missionary leadership. They wanted to choose and pay their own Chinese pastors, and to manage and support their own programs. This tendency began before the Revolution of 1911, but it was especially visible after 1912, when the national constitutions of the early Republic adopted the Western-derived concepts of freedom of religion and separation of church and state. Prior to this time, although there were some nineteenth-century edicts reestablishing the legality of Christianity, most of the legal protections for Chinese Christians derived from the treaties with the foreign powers. Until the end of the Qing, Christians were legally called *jiaomin* (people of religion), not the usual *pingmin*

---

11. Hyatt 1976b: 156–57, where he comments, "Across the board one gets an impression of mobility and diversity, and of Christian-graduate status as a sort of profession in itself."

12. Liu's career is summarized in Hyatt 1976b: 181–84, 186.

(common people or subjects), and did not have the legal right to build and own churches under their own names. Under the Republic, Christians were simply *guomin* (citizens) like everyone else and were free to register churches and other religious properties under their own names (Zha 1993: 9–10; Chao 1986: 63–65). This is undoubtedly one important reason why, after early 1912, a very pronounced movement towards autonomy or full independence took place in several Chinese Protestant churches formerly administered by foreign missionaries.

Shanghai, Beijing, and Tianjin were the sort of developed metropolises where one would expect to see early manifestations of this phenomenon, and indeed it occurred in all of these places. In Shanghai, the process was already well along by 1906 or so, and in Tianjin the initiative was taken in 1910 by a group of influential Chinese led by Zhang Boling, founder of the Nankai Middle School and later Nankai University, who had just become a Christian in 1909. Advised by the Tianjin group, the first independent congregation appeared in Beijing in 1912.[13]

A similar movement took place in several cities in Shandong Province after the 1911 Revolution. And when the first loose federation of independent Protestant churches in the province emerged in 1912–1913, it was the graduates of the Wenhuiguan who played a leading role in organizing and financially supporting it. Of the nine founders of the Shandong Independent Christian Church (Shandong Jidujiao zilihui) in these years, seven were former students of the Wenhuiguan, graduating in the years between 1884 and 1904. Foremost among them was the wealthy Liu Shoushan, whom I have described above. Three of the other eight founders were also businessmen, two of them Wenhuiguan graduates (Wang 1986). Here, in my opinion, is a case of the graduates of the Christian schools helping to create a new urban social and economic entity, the middle-class Protestant congregation.

During the past decade I have visited three times the large church building constructed in the 1920s by the Ji'nan congregation belonging to this Shandong church federation. This was the first Protestant church building in Ji'nan to be reopened after 1980, and it is still the largest in the city today. Its present staff of old pastors, born between about 1910 and the early 1920s, point with pride to this sturdy building being constructed by an independent congregation so early.

---

13. There is a fair amount of documentation on these events, including some on the Chinese leaders (or "instigators," as some suspicious foreign missionaries saw them), in publications of the Sino-Foreign Protestant Establishment. These include its monthly, *The Chinese Recorder*, and the annual *Christian Mission Year Book*, also the Chinese-language equivalent of the latter, *Zhonghua Jidujiaohui nianjian* (China Christian yearbook), which began publication in 1914 and often was substantially different from the English-language version. This documentation is brought together in a discussion of the Shanghai, Tianjin, and Beijing independent movements in Chao 1986: 74–85.

Wenhuiguan graduates were themselves at least second-generation Christians, for they had to be Christian to be admitted to the school. I cannot prove that their families remained middle-class Christians all the way down to the present, but I have met living proof that one did. In 1986, in retrospect an open year for interviewing in China, I spoke with a retired Christian army medical doctor, originally from Shandong, who was living in retirement in Kaifeng, Honan. Born in 1903, a 1928 medical graduate of Shandong Christian University, he had been a zealous Christian since the 1930s. He had had much intercourse with one of the indigenous sectarian churches I was researching at the time, the Jesus Family, actually living with them and having a leadership position for a few years in the 1940s.

Dr. Feng was a remarkable character. The People's Liberation Army "drafted" him out of the Jesus Family during the fighting in Shandong after 1945. He rose to a high position in the PLA medical establishment, all the while remaining a devoted Christian. This affiliation cost him a demotion in the anti-Rightist movement of 1958, but he survived well enough. By the 1980s, in retirement, he was respected and comfortable; he showed me a laudatory 1980 *Henan ribao* (Henan daily) article on his career (which of course did not mention his religious faith). Now, in the mid-1980s, he had become a leader in the Kaifeng Protestant community, often preaching in the churches of the city and even evangelizing in public parks; his prestige was sufficient to protect him from harassment.

Dr. Feng was perhaps most proud of the fact that his family was an unbroken line of Christian believers for six generations, from his grandfather to his great-grandchildren. He mentioned that his father had graduated from the Wenhuiguan in Dengzhou around 1900. Later, upon examining closely the detailed list of names and origins in the 1912 Wenhuiguan alumni gazetteer, I discovered just how involved in the school Dr. Feng's family had been. Not only had his father, Feng Wenxiu, graduated in 1901; apparently two uncles graduated in 1904, and two more uncles in 1912, by which time the school had moved to Weixian and changed its name. All five of these individuals have the same first character of the given name, and all are listed as being from the same village, Tianyukou, of the same district, Linqu, of Qingzhou prefecture.[14] From my interview with Dr. Feng in 1986 I had learned that his grandfather had been an elder in his local Presbyterian church and that his father had likewise been an elder in his Presbyterian church until his death in the 1960s.[15]

---

14. *Wenhuiguan zhi* 1913: 89, 104, 106. I suppose it is possible that this pattern of names could also indicate that the five were cousins, not brothers.

15. The phenomenon of generational continuity of religious affiliation among China's Catholic Christians down to the present constitutes a similar pattern of Christian family resiliency and loyalty. This is dealt with insightfully in Madsen 1989: 103–20. The ethic of respect for ancestral practices confirms the religious faith of descendents of Christians.

I am fond of this family story, but I have included it for more than personal reasons. I think that it makes concrete the concept of a maturing Protestant Christian community, which in the last years of the Qing and the early years of the Republic moved geographically to the towns and cities and upwards in socioeconomic terms, mainly propelled by education.

Another interesting piece of information on early twentieth-century Chinese Christians comes out of the 1912 data on the Wenhuiguan graduates. It sheds light on the related question of whether Christianity or a Christian education denationalized young Chinese. An 1898 graduate, Feng Zhiqian, probably a relative of the Feng family I have been discussing, had been a leader of the college singing club, and later became a peripatetic mathematics teacher and a poet; he died young, in 1908 (*Wenhuiguan* 1913: 86; Hyatt 1976b: 184–88). Two of his songs are recorded in the 1913 alumni history volume, not in the part available to me; but Irwin Hyatt arranged to have one translated, entitled "Recovery" (*Huifu zhi*), and used it to conclude the section of his original manuscript on the careers of the Wenhuiguan graduates (Hyatt 1976b: 188–89). In thirteen stanzas, two of which are reproduced below, it clearly reverses the impression that Chinese Christians were somehow less nationalistic than non-Christians. After bemoaning China's near-extinction under foreign pressure, Feng sounds a call to action in stanza seven, and in stanza nine begins to foretell China's future glory and power, this last theme being continued for the rest of the poem.

> (7) To build a mighty army,
>   To manage victorious affairs,
>   We will give our lives.
>   To save our leaders and benefit our people,
>   We will not love money.

> (9) From summits of Arab mountains our great guns will
>   roar, shaking all Western heavens,
>   and turning their world into an endless bloody sea.
>   We will expand our domain and push our frontiers,
>   Until we match our founding dynasties.[16]

The context of the changing Protestant communities from about 1890 to about 1920 was a China in which new sources of status and wealth were also linked to changing patterns of political power and political participation.[17] If

16. Capitalization as in translation in Hyatt 1976b; I cannot explain what the "Arab mountains" are in stanza 9.

17. Tao and Liu have an excellent section on the changes in society during these decades and the position of Chinese Christians in those changes, although they do not go on to trace direct Christian involvement in the political system through, for example,

Protestant communities were creating urban middle-class identities in Shandong and other places, was this reflected in the political arena? Were there Christian representatives in the Shandong provincial assembly of 1909? How many Christians were there in government office at the provincial level and in cities like Ji'nan and Qingdao in the early Republic? There were a number across the country as a whole, and the new access to provincial and local archives may make it possible to answer these questions.[18]

More broadly, was there a distinctly Protestant Christian element of participation in the development of a public sphere in late Qing and early Republican China (to the extent that this is a meaningful concept when applied to China)?[19] We do know, for example, that Chinese Christian leaders, both religious and lay, were prominent in the nationwide campaigns of the early Republic in favor of retaining constitutional religious freedom and against establishing Confucianism as a state religion, as well as against the monarchical schemes of Yuan Shikai (Zha 1993: 37–38; Keller 1992). And Jessie Lutz has recently argued that the YMCAs in some cities became meeting grounds for many diverse Chinese social and economic interest groups or constituencies, perhaps thereby constituting or facilitating expression of a form of public sphere or civil society (1994).

More broadly still, it is important to remember that the dynamics of twentieth-century Chinese history changed immediately after the period we have been considering here, and as a result the historical trends I have described were slowed or arrested. All parts of the Christian community in China, especially the foreign missionary sector but also Chinese believers and even independent Chinese churches, were devastated by the nationalistic political tides of the 1920s. This is of course another story, for the most part, and not an unfamiliar one. Let me just suggest that the Christian communities which built up a resource base and upwardly mobile leaders early in the century, and then suffered such a blow from the anti-imperialism of the 1920s, took a long time to re-emerge and recover their confidence. Yet recover they did after 1980. It may be possible to see today's Christian scene as a continuation, or a resumption, of trends of seventy to one hundred years ago, at least in those cities with middle-class Christian communities.

---

officeholding. See the section entitled "Shehui bianqianzhong de Jidujiaotu" (Christians amidst social change) 1995: 144–56.

18. For a listing of some Christians in office in various places soon after 1912, see Chen 1914.

19. This concept (and its accompanying concept of civil society) first began to be applied to China in the late 1980s, in works by William Rowe, Mary Rankin, and David Strand. Its applicability to China has been hotly debated in the 1990s. See in particular Rowe 1990, and a series of essays in a dedicated issue of *Modern China*, the first of which is Wakeman 1993, followed by articles in response by Rowe, Rankin, and others.

References

Bays, Daniel H. 1993. "Christian Revivalism in China, 1900–1937." In *Modern Christian Revivals*, edited by Randall Balmer and Edith Blumhofer, 159–77. Urbana: University of Illinois Press.

————. 1995. "Indigenous Protestant Churches in China, 1900–1937: A Pentecostal Case Study." In *Indigenous Responses to Western Christianity*, edited by Steven Kaplan, 124–43. New York: New York University Press.

————. 1996. "The Growth of Independent Christianity in China, 1900–1937." In *Christianity in China, the Eighteenth Century to the Present*, edited by Daniel H. Bays. Stanford University Press.

————, ed. 1996. *Christianity in China, The Eighteenth Century to the Present*. Stanford: Stanford University Press.

Bennett, Adrian A. 1983. *Missionary Journalist in China: Young J. Allen and His Magazines, 1860–1883*. Athens: University of Georgia Press.

Bridge: Church Life in China Today. Bi-monthly publication. Hong Kong: Christian Study Center on Chinese Religion and Culture.

Chao, Jonathan T'ien-en. 1986. "The Chinese Indigenous Church Movement, 1919–1927: A Protestant Response to the Anti-Christian Movements in Modern China." PhD diss., University of Pennsylvania.

Chen Chunsheng. 1914. "Jidujiao duiyu shiju zuijin zhi gailun" (A general discussion of Christianity and recent events). *Zhonghua Jidujiaohui nianjian* 1: 10–14.

Cohen, Paul A. 1974. "Littoral and Hinterland in Nineteenth Century China: The 'Christian' Reformers." In *The Missionary Enterprise in China and America*, edited by John K. Fairbank, 197–225. Cambridge: Harvard University Press.

Cohen, Paul A. 1978. "Christian Missions and their Impact to 1900." In *The Cambridge History of China*, Vol. 10, *Late Ch'ing 1800–1911*, Part I, edited by John K. Fairbank. Cambridge: Cambridge University Press.

Dunch, Ryan. 1994. "Archival Sources for Fujian History: Notes on a Year in Fuzhou." *China Exchange News* 22, no. 3 (Fall): 18–21.

Garrett, Shirley S. 1970. *Social Reformers in Urban China: The Chinese Y.M.C.A., 1895–1926*. Cambridge: Harvard University Press.

Gu Changsheng. 1991. *Chuanjiaoshi yu jindai Zhongguo* (Missionaries and modern China). Revised edition. Shanghai: Renmin chubanshe.

Hao Yen-p'ing. 1970. *The Comprador in Nineteenth Century China: Bridge between East and West*. Cambridge: Harvard University Press.

Hunter, Alan and Kim-Kwong Chan. 1993. *Protestantism in Contemporary China*. Cambridge: Cambridge University Press.

Hunter, Jane. 1984. *The Gospel of Gentility: American Women Missionaries in Turn-of-the-Century China*. New Haven: Yale University Press.

Hyatt, Jr., Irwin T. 1976a. *Our Ordered Lives Confess: Three Nineteenth-Century American Missionaries in East Shantung.* Cambridge: Harvard University Press.

————. 1976b. manuscript collection.

Jidujiao shiliao xuanji (A compilation on Christian history). 1962. Volume 2. Ji'nan: Shandong Jidujiao sanzi weiyuanhui..

Kahn. Joseph. 1995. "China's Christians Mix Business and God: Wenzhou Church Thrives on New Capitalists' Wealth." *Wall Street Journal* (June 16).

Keller, Charles A. 1992. "Nationalism and Chinese Christians: The Religious Freedom Campaign and Movement for Independent Chinese Churches, 1911–1917." *Republican China* 17, no. 2 (April): 30–51.

Kwok Pui-lan. 1992. *Chinese Women and Christianity 1860–1927.* Atlanta: Scholars Press.

Liu, Judith, and Donald P. Kelly. 1996. "'An Oasi in a Heathen Land': St. Hilda's School for Girls, Wuchang, 1928–1936." In *Christianity in China, The Eighteenth Century to the Present*, edited by Daniel H. Bays. Stanford: Stanford University Press.

Lutz, Jessie G. 1971. *China and the Christian Colleges 1850–1950.* Ithaca: Cornell University Press.

————. 1994. "The YMCA-YWCA and China's Search for a Civil Society," In *Jidujiao yu Zhongguo xiandaihua guoji xueshu taolunhui lunwenji* (Proceedings of the international symposium on Christianity and China's modernization), edited by Lin Zhiping, 621–53. Taibei: Yuzhouguang.

Madsen, Richard. 1989. "The Catholic Church in China: Cultural Contradictions, Institutional Survival, and Religious Renewal." In *Unofficial China: Popular Culture and Thought in the People's Republic*, edited by Perry Link, Richard Madsen, and Paul G. Pickowicz, 103–20. Boulder: Westview Press.

Modern China. 1993. 19, no. 2 (April). Issue dedicated to the public sphere debate.

Robert, Dana. 1996. "The Methodist Struggle Over Higher Education in Fuzhou, China, 1877–1883." *Methodist History* 34, no. 3 (April): 173–89.

Ross, Heidi A.. 1996. "'Cradle of Female Talent': The McTyeire Home and School for Girls, 1892–1937." In *Christianity in China, The Eighteenth Century to the Present*, edited by Daniel H. Bays. Stanford: Stanford University Press.

Rowe, William T. 1989. *Hankow: Conflict and Community in a Chinese City, 1796–1895.* Stanford: Stanford University Press.

————. 1990. "The Public Sphere in Modern China." *Modern China* 16, no. 3 (July): 309–29.

Ruan Renze and Gao Zhennong, eds. 1992. *Shanghai zongjiaoshi* (Religious history of Shanghai). Shanghai: Renmin chubanshe.

Shandong wenshi ziliao xuanji (Shandong local history collection) 1978–. Ji'nan: Shandong renmin chubanshe.

Smith, Carl T. 1985. *Chinese Christians: Elites, Middlemen, and the Church in Hong Kong.* Hong Kong: Oxford University Press.

Tao Feiya and Liu Tianlu. 1995. *Jidujiohui yu jindai Shandong shehui* (Christian churches and modern Shandong society). Ji'nan: Shandong daxue chubanshe.

Wakeman, Jr., Frederic. 1993. "The Civil Society and Public Sphere Debate: Western Reflections on Chinese Political Culture." *Modern China* 19, no. 2 (April): 108–38.

Wang Shenyin. 1986. "Shandong Jidujiao zilihui jianjie" (A brief introduction to the Shandong Independent Christian Church). *Shandong wenshiziliao xuanji* (Shandong local history collection) 21: 190–95. Ji'nan, Shandong.

Wenhuiguan zhi (History of Wenhuiguan). 1913. Edited by Wang Yuande and Liu Yufeng. Weixian.

Wickeri, Philip L. 1990. "Christianity in Zhejiang: A Report from a Recent Visit to Protestant Churches in China." *China Notes* 28, no. 2–3 (Spring-Summer).

Zha Shijie [James Cha Shih-chieh]. 1983. *Zhongguo Jidujiao renwu xiaozhuan* (Concise biographies of Chinese Christians). Taipei: Zhonghua fuyin shenxueyuan chubanshe (China evangelical seminary press).

————. 1993. *Minguo Jidujiaoshi lunwenji* (Essays on the history of Protestantism during th Republic). Taibei: Yuzhouguang.

Zhang Kaiyuan and Arthur Waldron, eds. 1991. *Zhongxi wenhua yu jiaohui daxue* (Christian universities and Chinese-western cultures). Wuhan: Hubei jiaoyu chubanshe.

Zhu Weizheng, ed. 1994. *Jidujiao yu jindai wenhua* (Christianity and modern culture). Shanghai: Renmin chubanshe.

Glossary
(not including provinces, major cities)

Chen Chonggui	陳崇桂
Feng Wenxiu	馮文修
Feng Zhiqian	馮志謙
guomin	國民
Huifu zhi	恢復誌
Ji Zhiwen	計志文
Jiaohui xinbao	教會新報
jiaomin	教民
Jing Dianying	敬奠瀛
lishi fenxi	歷史分析
Liu Shoushan	劉壽山
Ni Tuosheng	倪柝聲
pingmin	平民
Shandong Jidujiao zilihui	山東基督教自立會
shehui goucheng	社會構成
Song Shangjie	宋尚節
Tianyukou	田峪口
Wang Mingdao	王明道
Wang Zai	王載
Wenhuiguan	文會館
wenshi ziliao	文史資料
xian	縣
Zhang Boling	張伯苓

The Capital Comes to the Periphery: Views of the Sino-Japanese War Era in Central Zhejiang

R. KEITH SCHOPPA
Valparaiso University

For more than three decades scholars of Chinese history have viewed the Sino-Japanese War (1937–1945), primarily through the lenses of the Communist victory which it preceded. Studies like Lloyd Eastman's *Seeds of Destruction* (1984)and Ch'i Hsi-sheng's *Nationalist China at War* (subtitled "Military Defeats and Political Collapse") (1982) have seen the war as chiefly significant in setting the stage for the Guomindang collapse. Other works—from Chalmers Johnson's *Peasant Nationalism and Communist Power* (1962) through Chen Yung-fa's *Making Revolution* (1986) to Odoric Wou's recent *Mobilizing the Masses* (1994)—have studied localities during the war years as a way of explaining the Communist success. All this scholarly activity has justified itself by demonstrating that the war contributed to the social and political dynamics that produced the Communist victory and the Guomindang defeat.

Interpreting the war years as primarily the prelude to revolution is not, however, the only fruitful or instructive way to characterize or analyze the period. How does the era look if one examines its events and developments in their own contexts rather than in the context of events to come or if one sees it in relation to events, trends, and developments that it followed—as culmination, continuation, or reversal? How does it appear in the localities, where, as I have argued elsewhere (1992), established paradigms of a period often do not approximate the actual dynamics of specific local social and political situations? This last point is significant because the war in Zhejiang was marked by considerable spatial and temporal variability. Some counties or parts of counties were controlled by the Japanese for almost eight years, some for three, and a few not at all, a reality that meant that some areas were governed by the Japanese military, some by Chinese puppets, some by the Guomindang government, and some by Communist partisans. The experiences of different localities thus varied enormously, making generalizations about the war era and its general impact difficult.

Map 1

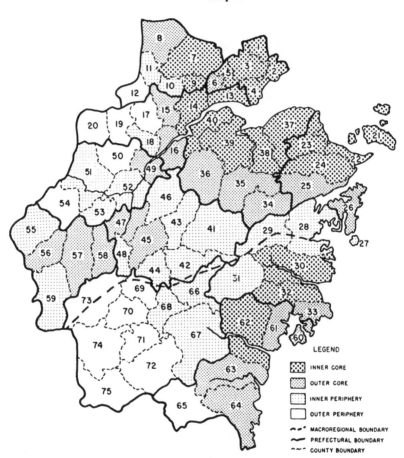

Zonal distribution of Zhejiang prefectures and counties

Counties			Prefectures	
Dongyang	41		Ningbo	21-27
Jinhua	45		Shaoxing	34-40
Jinyun	66		Jinhua	41-48
Lanqi	47		Chuzhou	66-75
Lishui	68			
Longquan	74			
Shaoxing	39			
Wuyi	44			
Xianju	31			
Yiwu	43			
Yongkang	42			
Yunhe	71			

Here I want to examine various wartime experiences in Yongkang county, which served as site for the provincial Guomindang government's capital-in-exile from 1938 to 1942 (see Map 1). When the capital moved to this less prosperous and less developed area of the province, the "periphery" in G. William Skinner's regional systems model, many people became forced sojourners, having to adapt at least temporarily to a new context. How did these sojourners react to their wartime situations; what were the relationships between the sojourners and the local population; and, most importantly, what impact did the sojourners and the experience of serving as provincial capital have on the county and its development?

Wartime Sojourning and Issues of Social and Political Identity

The war reversed at least temporarily the twentieth-century trend of population movement from rural Zhejiang to urban centers, whether of elites seeking greater opportunities in the urban sector or of laborers hoping to find a better livelihood in industrializing cities. Now as the Japanese seized important cities and towns from Shanghai and Nanjing to Hangzhou, many fled to the countryside and to the mountainous periphery of central and southern Zhejiang. The initial wave in the late summer and early fall of 1937 was of elites returning to their native places (Ruan 1980). Men like Hu Yimin, for example, came back to Yongkang to start a business (*YKX*: 761). Xu Luan returned to teach at an elementary school; Hu Zikang returned to become principal of a middle school (*YKZ*: 63, 285). They were not refugees; Hu Zikang, for example, had not been in a war zone before coming home but had been serving as magistrate in the neighboring county of Wuyi.[1] These men returned to ride out the storm by continuing careers or establishing themselves in the locality for an indefinite period. The war served, in short, as catalyst to return and to revive their identity with their native place at this time of national crisis.

For others, however, displaced by the war, their panicked migration forced on them a loss of their established identity. Two such dislocated "others" were the Zhejiang provincial government itself, which became an institution sojourning in the periphery and the flood of civilian refugees striving to survive the personal catastrophes of flight. Though the first bombing attack on Hangzhou came on August 14, 1937, the capital did not fall to Japanese troops until Christmas Eve. Hangzhou's capture was the culmination of the autumn military campaign that took the province's former three northern prefectures

---

1. In the two recent Yongkang county gazetteers, there are many others whose biographies note their return at the beginning of the war. In *YXZ*, see biographies of Xia Jiliang (109), Hu Baitang (64–65), and Li Dekang (100–101); in *YKX*, see the biography of Cheng Jian (754). Other materials suggest that this was a more general pattern. See, for example, the biography of Luo Xiatian, provincial official, who returned to the peripheral county of Yuqian, in *Zhejiang yuekan*, 12, no. 6 (June 1980): 23.

(Xinbian 1989: 286–92). The decision had been made to remove the organs of government to Jinhua, a former prefectural capital located on the Zhejiang-Jiangxi Railroad line and on the Wu River, a major tributary of the Qiantang (see Map 2). With its convenient transportation and communications and its prior status as a political, military, and economic center, it was a logical site for the temporary government headquarters (Huang 1991: 367–68). But the source of Jinhua's appeal—ease of access—created problems for its defense. With Hangzhou now a Japanese base, Jinhua was within close bombing range; and its location on the railroad line made it a potential target of attack should the Japanese seize the railroad. In addition, an increasing tide of refugees from Shanghai and northern Zhejiang flooded the city, creating much disorder and fear; as merchants closed their shops, food became scarce.

After some deliberation, Governor Huang Shaohong decided that a better location for the capital was the famous pilgrimage destination of Fangyan at the village of Yanxiajie, located sixteen kilometers northeast of the Yongkang county seat (see Map 3). The site seemed to have several advantages: it was relatively close to Jinhua and the railroad line (seventy kilometers), but far enough away to allow time to move again in a military emergency, and it was located near several highways connecting Yongkang to neighboring counties. It also seemed to offer sufficient numbers of hotels for government functionaries and even mountain caves to serve as natural air raid shelters. Moving the most important party and government organs to Fangyan came in early January 1938.

But the site turned out to be infelicitous.[2] With the temple of Song dynasty official Hu Zizheng attracting tens of thousands of pilgrims annually, the several dozen hotels in this village of less than one hundred households could not accommodate both pilgrims and government functionaries.[3] The main government offices were located at a renowned local academy, but its tiny rooms made cramped and inadequate offices. In addition, since the village did not have electricity, working at night required use of rapeseed oil lamps—a constant reminder of how far away in developmental time the new capital was from

---

2. The following descriptions are based on Huang Shaohong, 1991: 369 and Ruan Yicheng, 1976, cited hereafter as *Nianpu*.

3. A Yongkang native, Hu became a jinshi degreeholder in 989 and served for many years as an upright official in civil and military capacities before his death in 1039. The temple drew pilgrims from Zhejiang, Shanghai, Jiangsu, and Fujian. See Wang 1981: 35. See also *YKX*: 4 of introduction. Innkeepers were loath to rent out rooms for office space because many had built up loyal clients over the years, having adopted the practice of meeting pilgrims at Jinhua and Lanqi and accompanying them to Fangyan (*YXZ*: 325). See also the account of the builder and manager of the largest hotel in Yanxiajie for a fuller description of this practice (*YXZ*): 296–97. Susan Naquin and Chun-fang Yu note that already in the early modern period "associations developed that promoted [pilgrimages] and cared for ... pilgrims." See Naquin and Yu 1992: 19. For the cramped office conditions, see Ru 1982: 124.

Hangzhou (*Nianpu*: 13). The mountain caves, initially touted as splendid natural air raid shelters, seemed small and inadequate, and they did not provide air raid shelter for many (Huang 1990: 369).

Map 2

Zhejiang river systems

Map 3

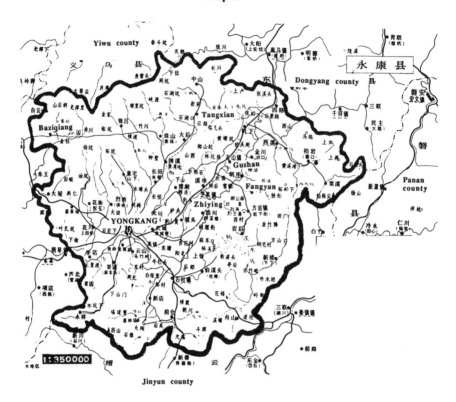

Yongkang County

The inhospitable conditions at Yanxiajie made it necessary to locate many government bureaus and offices elsewhere. The military organs remained in Jinhua. The four provincial bank offices and several subsidiary offices like the silk regulation bureau were moved to the county seat or neighboring market towns; and the education and reconstruction ministries relocated to the county of Lishui many miles to the south (Ruan 1982: 3–5).[4] Such dispersion of government bodies especially at a time of slow communications could certainly not have created a sense of coherence and joint action. Why, then, was Fangyan chosen as capital? The writings of Huang Shaohong and Minister of Civil Affairs Ruan Yicheng (1905–1988) suggest that the ultimate reason for the selection was to assert the government's identity in exile and, in that identity, legitimacy at a time of flight and sojourning. The provincial government had ignominiously been forced to flee Hangzhou. In order to prevent the Japanese from enjoying a rapid pursuit, it had destroyed the Qiantang River bridge, an engineering feat completed only months earlier after years of construction. Government prestige and self-confidence were in tatters.

Ruan wrote, "Fangyan is in eastern Zhejiang's scenic district; if we are to talk about culture, Zhu Xi studied at the Five Peaks Academy; if we are to talk about people's customary beliefs, there is the temple commemorating Hu to which pilgrims come every spring and fall" (Ruan 1978: 84). Locating at Fangyan meant continuing the tradition of a scenic provincial capital: Hangzhou to Fangyan, an acceptable transition.[5] More significant, the site linked the provincial government to traditional Chinese culture embodied in figures like Zhu Xi and Hu Zizheng. The roots of this government thus stood in contrast to Japanese puppet rule in Hangzhou. The construction of a stele commemorating the "resistance war and the reconstruction of the country" and the war dead was erected in July 1939 in front of the academy, where annual commemoration services were held on July 7 (*YXZ*: 5; *YKX*: 11 introduction). The goals of the Guomindang government—to resist Japan and reconstruct the country—were thus linked physically to this symbol of traditional culture. The site of the new capital also underscored that the roots of this government stood in contrast to the Communists in non-occupied Zhejiang. It is likely no coincidence that a Communist partisan effort had waxed and waned nearby over the previous ten years. Moving the provincial Guomindang capital into the county area where Communist activity had been the strongest would have been a potent political signal to any would-be revolutionaries or inciters of unrest.[6]

---

4. The relocation of the education and reconstruction ministries came because of the crowded conditions in Fangyan. See Huang 1991: 368.

5. Ruan, for one, openly compared nature and scenery in Fangyan with that of Hangzhou, *ibid.*: 84-85 and *YXZ*: 6.

6. In October 1928 under the direction of the county Communist party bureau a Yongkang Farmers Revolutionary Army (*Yongkang nongmin geming jun*) of more that

If the government itself had to establish an identity with links to the past and with a particular political persuasion as an expression of legitimacy, the refugees also faced loss of identity precipitated by their flight from homes, jobs, and, above all, by the severance of their connections to neighbors, kin, and community. Unlike the situation in urban central places for prewar migrants, there were no native place organizations in the counties of the mountainous periphery to tide refugees over temporarily or to facilitate adaptation to a new kind of life. Thrown into areas where the dialect was unintelligible and local customs and social structures unknown, they became rootless, faced with the task not only of survival but also of creating a new identity for an indeterminable future.

Though we have no specific data on the numbers who fled from Shanghai, Jiangsu, and northern Zhejiang into the provincial interior on the Qiantang River, estimates put the number in early 1938 as thousands per day.[7] The largest number of refugees tended to flock toward the new provincial capital, first to Jinhua, then to Yongkang. From the government's perspective, relief for the increasing numbers of refugees was necessary for its continued political legitimacy, but it posed ever greater costs. While some of the initial refugees were moved into Fujian to reclaim and develop new land, this opportunity was obviously restricted. Because the relief expense had no offsetting income, the government hit upon the idea of establishing a refugee textile mill that could make cloth and clothes for provincial public workers, provincial and county police, and military units. The government relief agency (zhenjihui) began the project but was stymied by various complications involving regulations and procedures, so Governor Huang asked Lu Gongwang (1879–1954), who had served as Zhejiang's military and civil governor in 1916–1917, to direct the project (Tao 1987: 4). With a loan of 100,000 yuan arranged by the government from the Farmers Bank of China and with the help of local elites in the town of Zhiying where he decided to locate the mill, on April 11, 1938, Lu commandeered Zhiying temples to house both the refugees and the Refugee Dyeing and Weaving Mill.

Although some refugees resisted having to work for their food and shelter, the benefits of mill work and the feeling of security in a settled place produced a growing sense of identity with the mill and its system. Lu says that when

---

400 men used the area around the nearby town of Zhiying as a base. They killed a "local bully" at the village of Rutang, four miles southwest of Fangyan, seizing his wealth and distributing it to poor farmers. Then in May 1930 a short-lived Yongkang Soviet was established at Xiazhai, slightly more than a mile to the northeast of Fangyan, and in October 1932 an agent from the Communist Party Central established a county committee at Paiqi, less than a mile north-northeast of Fangyan, YKX: 8–9, introduction.

7. Lu 1991: 780. Unless otherwise noted, the material on the refugee experience comes from Lu's account, 780–83.

refugees first came, lice covered their bodies and the stench of dirt and filth made them unapproachable, so their bodies, hair, and clothes all had to be washed thoroughly before they were allowed to begin work in the mill. A public nursery, kindergarten, and elementary school were established for refugee infants and children under thirteen *sui* in order to free the parents for work. Night classes were held for illiterate youths. The elderly who could not work in the mill performed alternative tasks. Lu, acting for the provincial government, took a strongly paternalistic stance vis-a-vis the refugees, distributing printed directions and restrictions and offering instructions in military preparedness. In addition to the main mill, there were twenty-one other work sites in the county seat and at seven towns and villages around the county. The mill and these work sites provided work, relief, and education for between 3000 and 4000 persons a year from 1938 through 1942.

Lu contends that through work at the mill refugees could forget the bitterness of their plight and that they came to identify the mill as their wartime household (Lu 1991: 781). The importance of this new identity was underscored by their actions in the exodus from Yongkang preceding the Japanese seizure of the county in May 1942. In that month the Japanese launched a major East China campaign to destroy the Zhejiang-Jiangxi railroad and any airfields that might serve as bases for bombing raids against Japan (Ch'i 1992: 160–61). The offensive moved with lightning speed; Yongkang and much of central Zhejiang fell within a week *Xinbian* 1989: 321–22). For this emergency, the workers had been mobilized to dismantle, pack up, and move the mill's machines along three pre-established routes and to carry with them the not-yet-distributed finished clothes and the cloth and yarn reserves.[8] Pursued through the mountainous terrain by Japanese soldiers and ambushed by straggling soldiers and thugs, Lu and the workers endured the threat of death and personal injury and the seizure of large quantities of their cloth cargo (Lu 1991: 781; *YXZ*: 29). In difficult days, aware only of the necessity of heading south, they continued their trek without radios or newspapers to apprise them of the enemy's whereabouts. In October they reached the town of Chishi in Yunhe county, where the provincial government moved after the collapse of Yongkang (Ruan 1972: 14–15). Lu reported that many refugees who had followed the mill with such doggedness that it indeed seemed to have been their new household never arrived in Chishi because they were killed by Japanese bombs and buried along the road.

Guomindang Officials and the Governed

When the capital came to the periphery, the sojourning government and refugees were forced to leave the "plentiful and prosperous" core zones of the

---

8. Some machines had been moved in the summer of 1941 when the Japanese took neighboring Dongyang county and bombed Yongkang from the air, Lu 1991: 781.

Lower Yangzi region for the mountainous interior where "food was insufficient, communications and transportation were blocked [by natural obstacles], and culture was backward."[9] Yongkang was on the watershed between the Qiantang River system draining into Hangzhou Bay and the Ou River system draining into the East China Sea; it faced the Qiantang, having only one of its rivers flowing into the Ou system (*Zhejiang fenxian* 1984: 629, 632). The county also lay on the macroregional border between the Lower Yangzi and the Southeast Coast regions (see Maps 1 and 2).[10] Mountains cover 81 percent of the county's land area, with plains making up only 17 percent.[11] In 1936 over 78 percent of the county's households made their living on the land. The mountainous land/farm population ratio suggests that Yongkang was not a prosperous agricultural county.

It was also not a flourishing commercial county. Boat transport had never been very important: only the Yongkang River was navigable as it flowed toward Jinhua to the west (*Zhejiang fenxian* 1984: 638). Although several roads connecting Yongkang to neighboring counties had been constructed in the 1930s, these counties were reportedly even less commercial than Yongkang.[12] The county commercial system was based upon periodic markets, though by the 1930s there were specialty markets in cattle, rice, wood, and bamboo shoots (*YKX*: 260–61). Seven elementary schools (of undisclosed size and duration) had been constructed in the county during the Republican period and lineages had established some district (*qu*) and private schools, but there was only one county middle school (*YXZ*: 20–22). Underscoring the relative poverty of the county, the gazetteer notes that financial resources for education were lacking (*Ibid.*: 24).

The attitude of government officials to the people of Yongkang reflected their elite bias and suggests what seems a rather arrogant Guomindang approach to the periphery and its peoples. As visitors to the culture of the periphery, these officials interpreted what they saw and experienced in light of their lives in urban settings. It is not therefore surprising to read their reactions couched primarily in discourse about decreased standards of living: in Fangyan, small homes constructed of earth and wood, a paucity of glass for windows, no electricity, no civilian hospital, no health workers, and the "ancient practice" (*gufeng*) of periodic markets (*Nianpu*: 204, 207). About the difficult living

---

9. The phrase and sentence are from *Nianpu*: 11, 37.

10. Macroregions are physiographic regions into which G. William Skinner divided agrarian China; he calls them "the 'natural' vessels for territorially based socioeconomic systems." This model has had a great impact on the study of traditional Chinese society and economy: see Skinner 1977: 11.

11. These and the following figures come from *Zhejiang xinzhi* 1936: 167b–168b.

12. For the road construction, see *YKX*: 359, and for the commercial state of these counties, see *YXZ*: 15.

conditions and dealing with the masses, the government leaders publicly displayed a kind of stoicism. Governor Huang said that "even though I was disappointed [about the surroundings in Fangyan], in the wartime situation it was best to embrace the idea, 'Since we're already here, let's make ourselves at home.' We could settle down, lessen our desires, and reduce expenses. This kind of life could train our general office workers in a simple life and a spirit of enduring hardship" (*Ibid.*). Despite government leaders' claims about adapting to an austere life, a government secretary later remembered another side to that life. Enervated by boredom stemming from insufficient work and nowhere to travel, many functionaries drowned their ennui in drink or spent their time in gambling (Zheng 1984: 91).[13]

The officials who have written most extensively about their roles in the government-in-exile ascribed to the masses, whether refugees or the inhabitants of Yongkang, strikingly negative traits. The masses were lazy, dirty, and untrustworthy; it was the role of a paternalistic government and its bureaucrats to reshape them. Lu Gongwang noted about the refugees at the Zhiying mill:

> Because refugees were given a place to stay and because they could eat in idleness for a rather long period, they had gotten used to being lazy. They had not intended to work at spinning and weaving, and we had to induce them to work. . . . We asked the provincial government to issue regulations banning vagrancy and laziness (Lu 1991: 780).

The masses were also ignorant and superstitious. Huang derided those who believed that Fangyan escaped serious bombing because the *fengshui* was good: "[therefore it was said that] the spirit of Hu [Zizheng] came to protect it. When enemy planes flew above, Hu appeared powerful: he mounted the clouds and rode the mists; he clouded the enemies' eyes, preventing them from bombing" (Huang 1991: 369).

Because no extant sources reveal how the refugees and the local residents of Yongkang regarded the government, we cannot deal very satisfactorily with their side of the matter. They were groups that have historically spoken through their actions rather than words. Yet there are no records of outright disturbances or protests. Those who wrote about these years—Huang, Ruan, Lu, and other officials—would not have been expected to emphasize the problems they caused the locals. Certainly at the very least, the presence of large numbers of government figures, military men, and civilian and military refugees in counties with few resources to begin with was a great burden on the localities and their people. Ruan admitted that the government's demand for rooms in the hotels at Fangyan strained the local supply that had always been reserved for pilgrim

---

13. Zheng's memories came from his experience in Yunhe where the government moved after the Japanese seizure of Yongkang, but they reflect the kind of conditions also found in Yongkang.

guests. Not only were lodging rooms and meeting rooms required for the daily business of government, but during the years at Fangyan there were two all-province administrative conferences, one all-province police administrative conference, and one all-province land administration conference, all "well attended," according to Ruan (*Nianpu*: 12; *YXZ*: 5).

For the local inhabitants a more serious problem created by the sojourners' presence was inflation. Ru Guanting, a Civil Affairs Ministry functionary, noted that when the government arrived, prices were low: one yuan could purchase seven catties of pork. Within a few days that amount of cash could buy only five catties. Even though within several weeks the Yanxiajie shops increased in number, providing food and daily commodities brought from elsewhere, the paucity of available foodstuffs forced prices higher, creating a heavy burden for locals. Years later Governor Huang admitted that becoming provincial capital "added many responsibilities and much suffering to the local populace" (Huang 1991: 370).[14] Perhaps the complaints of Ruan, Lu, and Huang about the laziness and untrustworthiness of the local populace and the refugees at the textile mill reflect not only elite bias but evidence of rather successful tactics by the weak: refusal to work as much as or as energetically as their overlord sojourners wanted.

From biographical accounts and from descriptions of political and economic developments in the counties, it seems clear that the relationship of the provincial government officials to local elites was positive and symbiotic. When the provincial government wanted to staff sensitive positions even if the work went beyond purely county concerns, they tended to look to natives of Yongkang. One Xu Dafu, trained at military schools, was selected to deal with the potentially difficult problem of the treatment of wounded soldiers; his local elite status is underscored by his subsequent elections to the chairmanship of the county assembly (*canyihui*) in 1944 and 1946 (*YKZ*: 462; *YXZ*: 55–56). (Ruan Yicheng has noted that most who served in local nonmilitary posts during the war, even in rear areas, were military men [*Nianpu*: 56].) Other examples were the appointments of educator Xu Luan to a key position in the provincial mobilization office and of policeman Li Dekang to an important propaganda post with the task of stemming collaborationist tendencies within the county (*YXZ*: 100–1, 285).

One of the clearest examples of local elites working together with Guomindang government elites was the refugee mill established and managed by Lu Gongwang. The success of this venture lay in Lu's ability to mobilize local resources to help in the organization, additional funding, and management; there were reportedly over 140 men involved in the management of the mill over its seven-year existence (Tao 1987: 4; YKX: 503). It is most likely that Lu chose

---

14. Huang was referring specifically to Yunhe, but the remarks apply as well to the people of Yongkang.

the town of Zhiying as the site of the mill because of his knowledge of the local power situation. A market town existing from the early Ming dynasty, it was the home of the Ying lineage, one of the most powerful and economically and politically successful in the county.[15] When the Qing dynasty fell in autumn 1911, Ying Yigao of Zhiying served as magistrate until April 1912 (YKX: 446). When the county Chamber of Commerce was established in the early Republic, it was initiated by merchant Ying Rufa; and on its seven-man Board of Directors sat three from the Ying lineage (*Ibid.*: 416). The head of the county assembly (*xianyihui*) elected in 1922 was Ying Huaisen, and of nine men elected to the provincial assembly in late 1923, two were Yings (*Ibid.*: 462). On receiving the mill assignment, Lu contacted Ying Wenlong (1881–1950) who had served previously as mayor of Zhiying and head of the tax office for Youxian district (*qu*) where Zhiying was located. The administrator of the Ying lineage temple, he had become known in the county for mediating disputes (*YXZ*: 102–3).[16] Wenlong led the way in responding to Lu's request and made large and small temples in Zhiying available for the mill and living quarters; he divided them into three units: spinning and weaving, child care, and dispersal (for finished goods). He appealed to his fellow elites for subscriptions to be used for managing the enterprise and for the purchase of machines and materials.[17] Local elites also became more integrally involved in mill management roles and several years later in branch workshops of the Zhiying mill that were established in four other market towns.[18] On the whole, then, local elites seemed willing allies of the government in dealing with the refugee situation and other war-related problems in the area held by the Guomindang government.

The War Era and State-Building in Yongkang

A scholarly (and popular) focus in recent years—especially in the context of the war's 50th anniversary—has been on the nature and extent of the brutal destructiveness of the Japanese military.[19] In his preface to *China's Bitter Victory*, James Hsiung notes that the "story of how [the Chinese people]

---

15. So synonymous was the Ying lineage with the town of Zhiying that Ruan Yicheng wrote the wrong character for "ying," substituting the lineage name for the "ying" meaning "outstanding." See Ruan 1980: 9.

16. Ying was executed by the Communist victors in January 1950.

17. These were elites like Huang Xunjie (b. 1906) from the nearby village of Zoushanxia. A graduate of Fudan University, he was from the wealthiest family in the village. His elder sister was married into the Ying lineage in Zhiying. See *Ibid.*: 274–75.

18. See the biographies of Chi Changgeng and Xia Jiliang in *Ibid.*: 281–82 and 109, respectively. Note also the account on 292–93.

19. See, as examples, the *Journal of Studies of Japanese Aggression Against China* from the early 1990s; Chi 1987; Wang 1973.

survived [the war] has not yet been fully told" (Hsiung and Levine 1992: ix). Certainly the most obvious change wrought by any war is death and destruction; for Chinese who lived through these traumatic times, these were certainly the dominant ones. But as Quincy Wright noted in his magisterial *A Study of War*: "the function of an activity may. . . be broader than its intention" (1942: 249). War is also an agent of other social and political changes that are shaped and defined by the particular impacts of wartime experiences.

The politically chaotic war years (Ruan Yicheng notes the difficulty of effective government rule in areas that kept falling out of and then back under Japanese control) could hardly contribute in a positive fashion to the making of a modern state. But the years 1938 to 1942 saw no fighting in Yongkang and only one episode of bombing, an attack on the county seat and the market town of Gushan in March 1939 that resulted in almost a hundred casualties (*YKX*: 534). During this time there were some elements of political change in Yongkang that were long-lasting and that even could be denoted as state-making. Charles Tilly has noted the "connections among state-making, the building of armed forces, and the maintenance of internal control" (1975: 74). He argues that the act of building an effective military machine (or, we could argue here, an effective military defense) "tended to promote territorial consolidation, centralization, differentiation of the instruments of government, and monopolization of the means of coercion, all fundamental state-making processes" (*Ibid.*: 42). Wright notes as well that war often stimulates political integration (Wright 1942: 255).

Before probing the political effects in Yongkang of its becoming the wartime capital, one can ask how much the county had been pulled into the discourse of nationalism and progressive change. In July 1919, following the May Fourth incident, Yongkang middle school and girls' normal school students participated in patriotic meetings supporting the student movement in Beijing and calling for the boycott of Japanese goods. Students marched in the county seat and then sent representatives to Zhiying, Tangxian, Qingweijie, and other market towns to popularize the boycott (*YKX*: 5–77, introduction). In the 1920s Yongkang students received telegraphed reports of student turmoil in Hangzhou and experienced their own substantial troubles in local educational institutions.[20] The older established elites in the county assembly were also involved in national political issues, sending in 1923 a telegram to the provincial assembly, condemning Beijing government traitors, and one to the National Assembly, arguing that power in a Republic belongs to the people (*Shibao*, 17 December 1923). In the May Thirtieth Movement all "circles" in Yongkang established a May Thirtieth Association which promoted strikes by students, workers, and merchants and boycotts of Japanese goods. From 1927 through 1930, county

20. See, for example, accounts in *Shen Bao*, 12 April 1920 and 21 June 1924, and in *Shibao*, 25 December 1923.

elites and masses had also been touched by efforts at mass mobilization of women, workers, and farmers and by a sporadic Communist movement in the area around Fangyan and the eastern third of the county. These efforts had resulted in many arrests, the deaths of at least 137, and the destruction of more than 380 homes in 1930 in Wuping district south of Fangyan (*YKX*: 6, 8–9). The elites of Yongkang (including its students) and some nonelites, for all the general isolation of the county, had been pulled into the larger social and political discourses of the day.

Despite this involvement in the political issues of the 1920s and 1930s, Yongkang had no newspapers until the war years. From February 1938 until January 1940 Communist partisans published a mimeographed bulletin, using other newspapers to relate the course of Communist activity in areas around the country; another paper, dates unknown, described current military campaigns. The county government published the *Yongkang Daily* from 1940 to 1942; and in the closing days of the war, the county party bureau and government published the *New Yongkang Weekly* (*Ibid.*: 10, 614). We can assume that such papers informed readers of national developments and that, at least in their coverage of the war, they enhanced the sense of the national plight.

It was in the coming to Yongkang of provincial newspapers, however, and in the consequent insertion of national and provincial factional struggle into the local scene that newspapers had most political effect on the county. When the exodus from Hangzhou occurred, the city's main newspaper, the *Southeast Daily*, and the paper of the Guomindang provincial committee, the *Zheng Bao*, moved to Jinhua, where they remained even after the capital moved to Yongkang. Both newspapers were under the firm control of the party's CC clique. Governor Huang, who did not have good relations with that clique, subsidized the establishment in early 1941 of a Zhejiang government organ, the *Zhejiang Daily*, to be published in the Yongkang county seat; that paper became embroiled in bitter verbal struggles with the Jinhua papers.[21] Huang had worked approvingly in support of the Communists during the united front; the *Zhejiang Daily* was a progressive newspaper, reporting news from "liberated" areas, a policy that enraged the Jinhua papers and the news bureau in occupied Hangzhou as well (*YKX*: 784). For newspaper readers in Yongkang, who had had no newspapers until the war, the contentiousness that developed cannot but have helped to politicize them. The Yongkang paper became a focal point and front for local Communist party members and other "progressive" county natives. A survey of the twenty people who worked on the editorial staff is suggestive about the political changes the county was beginning to undergo. The county's large established lineages—the Ying, Cheng, Hu, Wang, and Zhou— filled the rosters of Republican period organizations and contributed members in

---

21. For the relationship of Huang to the CC clique, see Xu 1988. For an account of the *Zhejiang ribao*, see *YKX*: 783–85 and *Nianpu*: 32.

key political and economic activities, but only six of those associated with the newspaper were from those lineages. The rest seem to represent a new breed of leadership.[22] In the end, there is considerable irony in the fact that the coming of the provincial capital made it possible for county Communists to center their activities in the county seat itself.

Certainly the capital's presence constrained and shaped the actions of the Yongkang county government as they had not been previously. Yongkang was one of the first counties to undergo the reforms of the new *xian* policy in 1939 and the first county in the province to establish a county assembly (*canyihui*) in April 1944.[23] The dates of the establishment of assemblies in contiguous and surrounding counties reveal the importance of the capital's site for the pace of political change in Yongkang: Yiwu county, March 1945; Xianju county, September 1945; and Wuyi county, October 1945.[24] The war and its effects thus stimulated political development in those affected rear areas.

The concern for provincial government security also led to fuller political integration of part of eastern Yongkang into the province as the new county of Pan'an in the rugged Dapan Mountains where five counties converged.[25] During the Guangxu period of the late Qing, it had become a sufficiently threatening bandit base to induce the government to establish a special Defense Office. In 1935 the Guomindang government established the Dapan Mountains Pacification District, but the close proximity of the provincial capital prompted the establishment of the new county in July 1939.[26] Civil Affairs Minister Ruan worked to establish the infrastructure of government and necessary services as quickly as possible to forestall or deal with any unrest. One after another, offices

---

22. Information in the county gazetteer seems to point to the likelihood that these Communist partisans tended to come from lineages that were not wealthy or politically powerful. This data is only suggestive since it is based in part on lineage population figures from the 1980s (*YKX*: 74–79); I would argue that it is likely that lineage population generally reflects prosperity and that the numbers of lineage population likely reflect the approximate lineage rank from the 1940s. The population of all of the five elite lineages numbered above ten thousand in the 1980s. Two of the fourteen newspaper editors who did not come from lineages active in many areas of public life also came from lineages numbering above ten thousand; five came from lineages numbering between one and ten thousand; two, from those numbering between one hundred and one thousand; and five, from those numbering less than a hundred.

23. The new *xian* program emphasized strengthening the administrative role of counties and using various procedures to ensure high-quality official personnel, encouraging local self-government, and organizing and mobilizing the populace to resist Japan and carry on the war; see Ch'i 1982: 132–40.

24. For Yongkang county, see *YKX*: 462, and Chen 1975: 17; for Yiwu, see *Yiwu xianzhi*: 373–73; for Xianju, see *Xianju xianzhi* 1987: 311; for Wuyi, see *Wuyi xianzhi*: 479.

25. The counties were Yongkang, Dongyang, Xianju, Jinyun, and Tiantai.

26. This account is based on Ruan 1982b: 7–8.

for new services never enjoyed by the mountainous area were established: police, township schools, telephone, sanitation, and credit cooperatives. Ruan claimed that he sought out able officials to oversee the government efforts and increased their pay as an incentive to go to the undeveloped county. With its rugged terrain, Pan'an was never held by Japanese forces and thus became the destination of many refugees. Throughout the war it remained peaceful. Still a county in Zhejiang today, Pan'an stands as an example of political integration and development stimulated by war and the effects of war.

War and Yongkang's Economic Development

On first glance, economic development in a country where war is being waged seems a farfetched possibility. Yet the longest-lasting changes in Yongkang county were in the economic realm; in a sense, when the capital comes to the periphery, the periphery becomes at least temporarily a core.

There were different kinds of economic change brought by becoming the capital county. The most noticeable was the temporary economic boom created in the service industries by the huge influx of population. But this boom continued only so long as the capital remained located there. In the first years of the Republic the Yongkang county seat had twelve hotels; the tourist site of Fangyan had twenty, including the imposing Chengchenxing, with total accommodations for up to two thousand guests.[27] During the war the several dozen hotels and inns at Fangyan and the county seat were packed and business flourished. After the Japanese offensive of May 1942, many of them closed. By 1949 there were about forty in the county, but this was still more than before the war. Similarly, restaurateurs experienced a great wartime boom. In the early Republic the county had twenty-three restaurants, but the number of eating and drinking establishments grew significantly. Reportedly along every street and at street intersections in the county seat and Yanxiajie (but almost certainly in towns in the vicinity like Zhiying and Gushan) were congee stalls and *dianxin* shops, especially patronized by refugees. With the Japanese offensive many of the restaurants and taverns closed; the street stalls and shops lost most of their clientele. While some restaurants and stalls reopened in 1945, eating establishments in the county in 1947 numbered only twenty-four restaurants, five teahouses, and little more than one hundred household-run street stalls (*YKX*: 251).

---

27. See *YKX*: 251 and *YXZ*: 296–98. These two sources give different details on the size and numbers of staff of the hotel. The statistics in *YXZ* come from an account by the grandson of the owner and for many years the manager of the hotel, Cheng Zhaosu; I have assumed his figures are more accurate. He says that the hotel had a staff of 80 regular employees and more than 200 during the spring and autumn pilgrimages.

The most important economic change brought by relocation of the capital was the establishment of an infrastructure to undergird the development of business and industry in the county.[28] By 1934 highways connecting Yongkang to neighboring counties had been built, construction that paved the way for passenger bus service between Yongkang and several counties (*Ibid.*: 344, 359). By 1936 the introduction of the rickshaw had already necessitated some widening and repair of intracounty roads. But moving the capital to Yongkang produced the need for even more roads both to provide security and to ease the traffic congestion caused by the incoming waves of population. After the capital's move, seven rickshaw roads (ranging in length from 3.5 to 25 kilometers) were built, linking the county seat to various market towns and the market towns to each other. Even more significant was road construction in mountainous areas that linked Yongkang market towns to towns in Jinyun, Yiwu, and Dongyang counties; together with the major roads built in the 1930s, these intercounty roads linked the county more closely with other central Zhejiang counties in the upper reaches of the Qiantang drainage system, a road system with Jinhua and Lanqi at the hub. The gazetteer comments that every town and township found that this wartime construction made transporting crops and daily necessities much more convenient; by 1947 the county had 315 kilometers of highways (*Ibid.*: 346). Also facilitating transportation and commerce were the razing of the Yongkang city wall in 1940 and the concomitant widening of city streets (*Ibid.*: 11, introduction).

When Yongkang county became the provincial capital, it became as well the provincial center for government procurement, shipping, and trade. The number of land and water transport businesses expanded rapidly. Before the war there had been only three such companies, but after 1938 no fewer than thirty transport companies of varying size sprang up. While military goods constituted the major cargo, civilian goods were also transported. It is important to note that unlike the hotel and restaurant business, which collapsed during the Japanese occupation almost back to its prewar level, the transport business, although diminished, maintained a much higher level of activity than before the war. In 1947 the county still had ten shipping firms. Like the physical highways and roads that linked counties in the region together, these shipping companies had made important business connections to large and well-known firms in key cities like Jinhua, which helped to create a transportation network that facilitated

---

28. Economic development in the early Republic had been haphazard. A telegraph office had been established in 1912 and a telephone line to Jinhua set up in 1932. An electric company, built in 1922 in the county seat, provided coal-generated electricity (36,000 kilowatt hours per year) for merchant shops and about 160 households each day from 5 until 11 p.m.; but after the Japanese seizure of the county, the company closed. See *YKX*: 167. The county government rarely became involved in direct action to support the economy, an exception being a county export office established in 1914 to oversee the selection of special products for the Panamanian Exposition. See *YKX*: 7, introduction.

the relatively rapid and free passage of goods (*Ibid.*: 357). Another indicator of the increased transport links came when the central government's Finance and Trade Ministry (*Caimao bu*) prompted the establishment of the Yongkang Transport Office in March 1940 (*Ibid.*: 11, introduction).

Also noteworthy is the expansion of the postal system. Before the 1930s Yongkang had only two post office units, a second-class office at the county seat (established in 1902) and a postal agency at the market town of Gushan. In the 1930s before the war, postal agencies had been set up in thirteen additional towns. During the war nine more postal agencies were formed, including a second office in the county seat. Moreover from January 1933 to October 1947, letter boxes were established at fourteen other sites. Such increases would have necessitated more mail sorters, office workers, and mail deliverers on the routes that were serviced by bicycle or on foot (*Ibid.*: 361–62, 364). As in other businesses and in road and highway construction, the people of the county stood to benefit from the expansion.

With the provincial capital in the county, Yongkang's commerce flourished. Scattered data exist for the number of county retail businesses, the total cash value of trade, and the total capitalization of businesses, but comparable data over time are not available. Extant data do suggest a thriving county economy from 1938 to 1942. Early in the Republic the county seat reportedly had only seven dry goods stores, five Southern goods stores, five herb shops, and two tobacco shops. In 1941 there were 680 individually owned retail businesses, 300 jointly capitalized businesses (including cooperatives), and five companies in the county. One hallmark of the wartime economic expansion was the flourishing of cooperatives. Based on the successful coops established before the war under the leadership of Hu Qinmei (1889–1952), merchant-entrepreneur from Baziqiang in northwestern Yongkang, credit, production, marketing, and shipping coops thrived in county seat and market towns.[29]

After 1942 many larger businesses moved, stores and coops closed, and merchant activity slumped sharply. In 1945–1946, however, merchant activity revived and the coop fervor was renewed: individually owned county retail businesses grew to 500, jointly capitalized ones to 200, and there was one company—the totals being altogether down about 30 percent from the period 1938 to 1942. But by 1949 the rampant inflation and chaotic market conditions reduced the county total to only 535 retail businesses—down some 24 percent from 1945–1946 (*Ibid.*: 220). The years 1948–1949 also saw the dissolution of most of the co-operatives. These data suggest that it was easier for Yongkang

---

29. For Hu's biography, see *YKX*: 748; see also 223 for the general picture of Yongkang coops. Hu's enterprises spread beyond the county: he established an indigo dye factory in Xuanping county, a firewood shop in Lanqi, a repair shop for irrigation equipment in Lishui, a ham factory in Jinhua, and a brewery and rice mill in Zhiying.

merchants to recover from war and occupation than from the economic problems that devastated Guomindang control during the trauma of civil war.

An analysis of county industrialization reveals a striking shift that seems connected to the history of the refugee textile mill.[30] Indeed, the two recent Yongkang gazetteers speak of the refugee textile mill as the real beginning of industrialization in the county; the gazetteer printed in the Republic of China calls it the "beginnings of modernization" (YXZ: 14; YKX: 187). In 1933 there were twenty-three small textile mills in the county.[31] With the aid of local elites Lu Gongwang had been able to launch the refugee mill quickly and smoothly in early 1938. In the beginning both raw cotton and some yarn were purchased and shipped from the former prefectures of Ningbo and Shaoxing without any political or fiscal obstacles to hamper their receipt. The main mill at Zhiying and the twenty-one additional work sites were quickly producing yarn and clothes ordered by government workers, police, and soldiers. Originally the mill installed 1000 looms, but with the work expanding and more refugees available, an additional 200 were purchased.[32] In 1938 the mill produced 27,903 bolts of cloth; in 1939, 72,688; in 1940, 100,206. The mill and its satellite units successfully performed their prescribed functions of providing relief for refugees and cloth for government agencies.

The next phase of mill history, the decentralization of the manufacturing process, involved the local populace more integrally. In the early months of 1941 the Japanese extended their control over most of the cotton- and textile-producing counties in Ningbo and Shaoxing. With both Shanghai and Hong Kong closed by the Japanese as well, the mill's very survival came into question: how could it purchase the cotton needed to continue the spinning and weaving? Laboring as usual under bureaucratic difficulties, Ruan reported that the traditional procedures prescribed by the government's Audit Office for purchasing materials could not be followed under the new circumstances. In light of the difficulties the provincial relief agency decided to establish seven branch factories under the direction of local elites, with each factory responsible for obtaining its own materials. After the Military Provisioning Office placed its order, managers of the Zhiying mill and the seven factories agreed on a division of labor and decided on the money to be allotted for purchase of cotton.[33] It is

---

30. The history of the textile mill in Yongkang and Yunhe counties follows the account of Lu 1991: 780–83, and Ruan 1972.

31. The largest of these had twenty looms and twelve sewing machines. Other industries included the electric company, five rice-husking mills, fifteen paper-manufacturing firms, a soy sauce brewery, and a soap factory; see YKX: 206.

32. Huang reports that the spinning was done by hand (1991: 460).

33. Profits and losses were to be the responsibility of each branch factory. The mill at Zhiying was in charge of sales, taking 1 percent from each branch's profits for administrative expenses.

apparent from later developments that the boundaries between occupied Zhejiang and Guomindang Zhejiang were very porous and that the seven branch factories were probably able to obtain the smaller amounts of cotton they needed from occupied areas more easily than if the mill maintained centralized control.[34] Raw cotton was distributed for spinning in the three counties of Yongkang, Dongyang, and Jinyun; since the spinning was not mechanized, villagers could be freely hired for the work. It obviously benefitted the seven satellite factories to purchase cotton and to arrange for spinning as cheaply as possible. The seven factories were located at market towns in the northern half of the county. There is no detailed account of how the system worked, how the factories actually purchased the cotton, and whether any or all turned a profit in 1941. In addition to an unspecified amount of yarn, the factories produced 56,361 bolts of cloth, 56 percent less than in 1940—a reduction most certainly stemming from the decentralization and the difficulty of obtaining cotton. The Japanese offensive forced evacuation of the Zhiying mill in May 1942.

The evidence is circumstantial, but it seems likely that decentralization of the mill set the stage for a substantial shift in the county's economic profile. The mobilization of economic resources and managerial expertise in Zhiying, in the towns of the dispersed work sites after 1938, in the towns and villages where the factories were established in 1941, and where spinning was let out to the local communities provided local lineage leaders with experience that they could utilize in the expansion of cottage textile operations. The prerequisites for establishing such local factories had been achieved—establishing connections to sources of raw cotton, establishing networks of spinning households, and deriving hands-on experience. It is not surprising to learn that in 1947 the Zhiying Dyeing and Weaving Producers Cooperative was established and quickly began producing 400 bolts of cloth per month (*YKX*: 205). Nor it is surprising that of the seven most important textile mills in Yongkang in 1987, three were in towns that had been factory sites in the 1940s. Whether we can draw lines directly from today's factories to specific factories in 1941–1942 is not so important as the experience and expertise gained at that time and put to use in the late 1940s. As noted by the county gazetteer, the expansion of textile manufacturing from 1947 to 1949 was the prelude to further expansion during the People's Republic (*YKX*: 205–6).

It seems likely that the refugee textile mill and its satellite work sites and factories considerably changed the face of the county economy. In 1937 the

---

34. When the mill was moved to Yunhe in 1942, the mill managers had to develop a scheme of bartering tong oil for cases of yarn from Japanese-controlled Shanghai. In "Facets of an Ambivalent Relationship: Smuggling, Puppets, and Atrocities during the War, 1937-1945," Lloyd Eastman notes the extensive trade between Shanghai and the provinces of Zhejiang and Fujian even though trade contributing to the Chinese war effort was prohibited (1980: 278, 281). For reference to the trade from Shanghai to interior Zhejiang, see also Wakeman n.d.: 8–9, n21.

reconstruction department of the Yongkang county government registered county commercial and industrial enterprises; the results showed 20 industrial firms and 985 commercial firms, for a total of 1005. There is much we do not know about this registration, especially the definitions of industrial and commercial and any qualifying criteria relating to the size or structure of the enterprise. Be that as it may, in 1947 the county government undertook another registration of county firms which produced a total of 960—but 434 of those were listed as industrial and 526 as commercial.[35] In this 1947 registration list the numbers of many specific industrial enterprises seem consistent with those specified in a 1933 study.[36] It is the textile industry that skyrockets, from 23 to 165—over 600 percent more than in 1933; in 1947 almost 40 percent of the county's industrial enterprises were textile mills, almost all certainly of the cottage variety. It seems clear that the county's economic development and profile was shaped in large part during the war years when the refugee textile mill played a pivotal role.

Conclusion

If the Sino-Japanese war is interpreted primarily as the event that spawned the Communist revolution, then questions about the secret of Communist success and the nature of Guomindang failure will continue to dominate our understanding of the war era. However, if we assume that many significant dynamics are at work in any historical period and that the revolution is only one lens through which to interpret the war, then we need to analyze the developments and trends of the war years in various regions and localities under widely divergent political and economic situations.[37] I have focused on how communities and institutions in one rear area transformed by the war and the requirements of war. The case of Yongkang county was not typical any more than Communist base areas were typical. To understand the war era and its meaning, we must look at the entire range of historical experiences.

In *Chinese Elites and Political Change*, I argued that in early twentieth century Zhejiang there was an implicit (though imperfect) correlation between economic and political change and that economic development came "not only through the natural growth of a regional economy but also through the intervention of outside political forces" (1982: 24). The coming of the provincial

---

35. The conclusions argued here depend on whether the same criteria were applied to the firms and their registration as in 1937; I have made that assumption.

36. *YKX*: 220. There were five rice-husking mills, a soy sauce brewery, and a soap factory in both lists; twenty paper-making firms in 1947 compared to fifteen in 1933; and one printing company in 1947 compared to two in 1933.

37. It seems obvious in light of Chen's and Wou's analyses of the period that these trends and developments were marked by wide local and regional variations.

capital to the periphery was such a dramatic intervention; its sojourning years played a crucial role both in the state-building process relating to the county and in its economic development. The rapid rate of directed political institutionalization and Yongkang's greater political integration are evidences of state-building, with the establishment and integration of Pan'an county the most important example. What we are unable to measure is the extent to which the political experience of Yongkang's elites and masses during the war contributed to the county's postwar incorporation into the new Communist state.

The contribution of the presence of the provincial capital to economic development and the shape of economic change in Yongkang is notable. Road and highway construction, with the subsequent development of transport companies, were basic elements for the county's defense and military support but also for the increased commercialization that tied Yongkang more tightly into regional networks. The experiences and expertise gained in the establishment and functioning of the refugee textile mill and its satellite factories substantially shifted the county economic profile (at least in numbers of concerns) from almost completely "commercial" to 45 percent "industrial." This "beginning of [industrial] modernization" was a transformation directly linked to refugee relief. The changes begun within the capital county spread into neighboring counties, linking them physically and experientially. This linkage can be seen not only in the wartime spinning networks and satellite factories but also in the flourishing of cooperatives in neighboring Yiwu and Wuyi counties, some of which were begun by men from Yongkang.[38]

The years 1938 to 1942 in Yongkang present a case study of the interaction during crisis between the center and its Guomindang bureaucratic elites and the locales and their elites and masses. Thrust into poor mountainous reaches, the center tried to assert its legitimacy as provincial government with its choice of the ultimately inadequate Fangyan. Patronizingly elitist toward the masses and finding their natural allies among county lineage elites, government officials endured the war years worried, bored, and grumbling (albeit with a stiff upper lip). The lineage elites, in their turn, with seeming eagerness took on the government's challenges of providing relief, enlisting local support, and providing various leadership functions—even as the presence of tens of thousands of outsiders exhausted their natural food and housing resources. The masses undoubtedly suffered. Whether their negative description by government officials suggests that they consciously exercised the "weapons of the weak" cannot be answered with certainty. It is important to note, however, that the dialog between the center and the periphery was not one-sided. The initial impact did come when the center entered the periphery; but wartime reality meant that the center and its representatives had to depend on the peripheral land and its people, its lineage elites, sedan chair porters, *dianxin* sellers, hotel

---

38. See the biography of Hu Qinmei, *YKX*: 748.

workers, village spinners. The story of the refugee mill illustrates what was surely the fact of life in these rear areas—relations between outsiders and locals were a process where each affected the other. Whether this process ultimately changed the appreciation and understanding of these particular Guomindang elites for the peripheries and their problems is yet to be studied.[39]

The history of the refugee textile mill raises the issue of wartime identity in several ways. The government's evident determination to provide relief and to solve problems faced by the mill reflects the government's pursuit of legitimacy. Crucial for the refugees was the question of social identity amid the chaos of wartime when old networks, relationships, and native place no longer anchored person, family, or group. The dramatic commitment of the refugees to the mill throughout their dangerous flight with mill machines and materials from Yongkang to Yunhe seems to underscore the point that in the mill the rootless grew new roots. The government's solution of work-relief was able to capitalize on the reality that the Potters found in rural Guangdong villages, that "work is the symbolic medium for the expression of social connection," that "work affirms relationship in the most fundamental terms" (Potter and Potter 1990: 195).

In *Seeds of Destruction* Lloyd Eastman noted that although the war did "buffet" the Guomindang regime, it survived another four years. Eastman explains this survival in negatives: "the low political consciousness of most Chinese" and the political repression of dissenters (1984: 222). The Yongkang economic experience suggests a more positive explanation which cautions against drawing any necessary direct line between the war and the Guomindang collapse. Yongkang's economic successes during the years 1938 to 1942 were indeed submerged under the Japanese military occupation from 1942 to 1945; but after this very bitter period, the economy revived, with flourishing cooperatives a hallmark of the recovery. It was not until 1948 and 1949 that economic collapse occurred and the Communist movement was victorious. In other words, in Yongkang at least, the period of civil war—the *immediate* context for the Communist victory—seems more critical than the anti-Japanese war. Certainly the war had an immense general impact on national Guomindang rule after the war. Some have claimed that the war so enervated the Guomindang that it could not deal effectively with the reconstruction (Levine 1992: xviii). The reality of reconstruction must be seen as well: the war's highly variable impact on localities produced an extraordinarily complex and unwieldy reconstruction task that would have been formidable even for a regime that functioned well. But Chen Yung-fa rightly reminds us that immediate rural

---

39. The experience of the Xiaoshan county government, which had to retreat in exile to South Township, brought the plight of that impoverished area to the attention of elites from more prosperous areas for the first time. In the end, however, after they returned to the core areas, they turned their backs on South Township. See Schoppa 1992.

tensions and proximate causes were more significant than any long-term trends, any change over time (1986: 134). In Yongkang the people seemed to overcome the harsh impact of the anti-Japanese war; the civil war was the chief agent of the Guomindang collapse.

Finally, this study raises questions about the efficacy of wartime Guomindang rule in central Zhejiang. The establishment, administration, and support of the refugee textile mill offer a good look at the nature of provincial government leadership in this region. The picture that emerges runs counter to the traditional view of Guomindang corruption, bureaucracy, and inefficiency (Ch'I 1982). It should be noted that this more positive interpretation is based not only on the writings of leaders whom we would expect to hold that viewpoint but on sources published in the People's Republic from which we would presumably not expect such a positive interpretation of Guomindang rule.[40] The refugee problem involved matters of public order as well as the image of the government, both of which the government was determined to address. In crisis decision-making, however, it was flexible; in the mill's establishment it was neither impeded by initial bureaucratic obstacles nor bound by centralizing tendencies. It turned quickly to local elites, arranged an immediate bank loan, and within a month had opened the work-relief facility. It gave local elites considerable rein in managing the mill's operation. When the mill faced a cotton and yarn supply crisis in 1941 and more bureaucratic difficulties threatened, the government circumvented the obstacles and approved the establishment of the seven branch factories and the spinning networks. When the Japanese invaded central Zhejiang in 1942, the government kept its commitment to refugees who had come to depend on it and moved the mill to Yunhe. In short, the Guomindang policy was rational and perhaps even enlightened; its decision-making was expeditious and concerned for the welfare of the refugees; its reliance on local elites and situations was a recognition of the kind of administration that would work most effectively. Whether this case is unique or indicative of a more general situation awaits further study; at the very least it calls for more analysis of actual local dynamics and conditions during the war— both for an understanding of the war years and what followed.

---

40. These sources include the lengthy 1991 gazetteer and the essays in the more than forty volumes of "historical materials" (*wenshi ziliao*) collections published in Zhejiang; several of these volumes of memoirs and historical accounts were published in the early 1960s, but most appeared in the 1980s and early 1990s.

References

Ch'i Hsi-sheng. 1982. *Nationalist China on War: Military Defeats and Political Collapse.* Ann Arbor: University of Michigan Press.

Ch'i, Hsi-sheng. 1992. "The Military Dimension, 1942–1945." In *China's Bitter Victory: The War with Japan 1937–1945*, edited by James C. Hsiung and Steven I. Levine. Armonk, NY: M. E. Sharpe.

Chen Li. 1975. "Zhanshi zhandi quanli tuixing difang zizhide Ruan Yicheng." *Zhejiang yuekan* 7, no. 3 (March).

Chen Yung-fa. 1986. *Making Revolution.* Berkeley: University of California Press.

Chi Jingde. 1987. *Zhongguo dui Riben kangzhan sunshi diaocha shishu.* Taibei.

Eastman, Lloyd. 1980. "Facets of an Ambivalent Relationship: Smuggling, Puppets, and Atrocities during the War, 1937–1945." In *The Chinese and the Japanese: Essays in Political and Cultural Interactions*, edited by Akira Iriye. Princeton: Princeton University Press.

————. 1984. *Seeds of Destruction.* Stanford: Stanford University Press.

Hsiung, James C., and Steven I. Levine, eds. 1992. *China's Bitter Victory: The War with Japan 1937–1945.* Armonk, NY: M.E. Sharpe.

Huang Shaohong. 1991. *Huang Shaohong huiyilu*, edited by Tang Yilin. Nanning: Guangxi renmin chubanshe.

Johnson, Chalmers. 1962. *Peasant Nationalism and Communist Power.* Stanford: Stanford University Press.

Journal of Studies of Japanese Aggression Against China. Carbondale, Illinois.

Levine, Steven I. 1992. "Introduction." In *China's Bitter Victory*, edited by James C. Hsiung and Steven I. Levine. Armonk, NY: M.E. Sharpe.

Lu Gongwang. 1991. "Zhejiang sheng zhenjihui nanmin ranzhi gongchang shimo ji." In *Yongkang xianzhi.* Hangzhou.

Naquin, Susan, and Chun-fang Yu. 1992. "Introduction: Pilgrimage in China." In *Pilgrims and Sacred Sites in China*, edited by Susan Naquin and Chun-fang Yu. Berkeley: University of California Press.

Nianpu. See Ruan Yicheng. 1976.

Potter, Sulamith Heins and Jack M. Potter. 1990. *China's Peasants: The Anthropology of Revolution.* New York: Cambridge University Press.

Ru Guanting. 1982. "Guomindang tongzhi shiqi Zhejiang sheng minzhengting jianwen." In *Zhejiang wenshi ziliao xuanji.* Volume 21. Hangzhou: Zhejiang renmin chubanshe.

Ruan Yicheng. 1972. "Ji Lu Gongwang xiansheng." *Zhejiang yuekan* 4, no. 11 (November).

————. 1976. *Yicheng zizhuan nianpu ji zishu*, juan 3. n.p. Cited in text as *Nianpu.*

————. 1978. "Fangyan yu Yunhe." In *Ruan Yicheng zixuanji.* Taibei.

————. 1980. "Kangzhan shiqi zai Zhejiang." *Zhejiang yuekan.* 12, no. 9

————. 1982a. "Kangzhan chuqi Zhejiang sheng zhengfu zai Yongkang Fangyan bangong ji." In *Yongkang zianzhi*. Taibei.

————. 1982b. "Panan xian chengli ji." *Yongkang zianzhi*. Taibei.

Schoppa, R. Keith. 1982. *Chinese Elites and Political Change*. Cambridge: Harvard University Press.

————. 1992. "Contours of Revolution in a Chinese County, 1900–1950." *Journal of Asian Studies* 51, no. 4 (November): 770–96.

Shen Bao. Shanghai. April 1920-June 1924.

Shibao. Shanghai. December 1923.

Skinner, G. William. 1977. "Introduction: Urban Development in Imperial China." In *The City in Late Imperial China*, edited by G. William Skinner, 3–31. Stanford: Stanford University Press.

Tao Yi. 1987. "Kangzhanqijiande Zhejiang sheng zhenjihui gaikuang." *Zhejiang yuekan* 19, no. 6 (June).

Tilly, Charles. 1975. "Reflections on the History of European State-Making." In *The Formation of National States in Europe*, edited by Charles Tilly. Princeton: Princeton University Press.

Wakeman, Jr., Frederic. n.d. "The Shanghai Badlands: Wartime Terrorism and Urban Crime, 1937–1941." unpublished manuscript.

Wang Huimin. 1981. "Dui Ri banian kangzhan shiling." *Zhejiang yuekan* 13, no. 6 (June).

Wang Ziliang. 1973. "Banian kangzhanzhong Zhejiang sheng sunshi diaocha." *Zhejiang yuekan* 5, no. 7 (July).

Wright, Quincy. 1942. *A Study of War*. Chicago: University of Chicago Press.

Wu, Odoric. 1994. *Mobilizing the Masses*. Stanford: Stanford University Press.

Wuyi xianzhi. 1990. Hangzhou: Zhejiang renmin chubanshe.

Xianju xianzhi. 1987. Hangzhou: Zhejiang renmin chubanshe.

Xinbian Zhejiang bainian dashiji, 1980–1949. 1989. Hangzhou: Zhejiang renmin chubanshe.

Xu Dequn. 1988. "Linshi shenghui zai Fangyan." In *Hangzhou wenshi ziliao*. Volume 10. Hangzhou: Zhejiang renmin chubanshe.

Yiwu xianzhi. 1987. Hangshou: Zhejiang renmin chubanshe.

YKX. See *Yongkang xianzhi*. 1991.

YXZ. See *Yongkang xianzhi*. 1982.

Yongkang xianzhi. 1991. Hangzhou. Cited in text as *YKX*.

Yongkang xianzhi. 1982. Taibei. Cited in text as *YXZ*.

Zhejiang fenxian jianzhi xia. 1984. Hangshou: Zhejiang renmin chubanshe.

Zhejiang xinzhi. 1936.

Zhejiang yuekan. 1972–1987.

Zheng Qinyin. 1984. "Huiyi 'Liyuzuo tanhui.'" In *Hangzhou wenshi ziliao*. Volume 4. Hangzhou: Zhejiang renmin chubanshe.

Doing Business with Strangers:
Guarantors as an Extension of
Personal Ties in Chinese Business

ANDREA McELDERRY
University of Louisville

Guarantors (*baozheng ren*) were and are a common feature of Chinese business practice, so common that they have largely been taken for granted. Their function in Chinese business arrangements is basically the same as in Western business. As anyone who has cosigned on a car loan for her child knows, guarantors are third parties to an contract who ensure the fulfillment of the specified terms. If there is a question about the guarantor's liability, one consults a lawyer, not an historian, anthropologist, economist, or philosopher. In China, however, the use of guarantors in the economic sphere was only one aspect of guarantorship. A concept of guarantees underlay the attempts of successive governments to maintain social order, as evidenced by the *baojia* or mutual responsibility system. Nor has the idea of guarantorship passed into oblivion. In regulations on the "management responsibility system" published in 1984, the Communist Party factory committee is designated as "guarantor and supervisor in regard to production and administrative management work . . ." (Changzhoushi 1984: 69; see also Chamberlain 1987). Thus examining the use of guarantors in Chinese business practice is one way to understand Chinese business in the context of Chinese society, and in this endeavor the perspectives of history, anthropology, economics, and philosophy as well as law are relevant.

From a modern Western perspective the practice of having a third-party guarantee a contract is not unusual. But the striking feature about guarantorship in the early twentieth-century Chinese economy was its use by employers in modern enterprises. More specifically, in Republican Shanghai (1911–1949), to gain employment in a bank, a department store, a factory, or other modern enterprise, an individual had to have a surety and the surety was normally another individual or a firm. This requirement does not fit neatly into the modern Western concept of free labor in an impersonal marketplace. It placed limits on the individual's ability to freely contract with another to dispose of his own person (Weber 1968: II, 729). Since the practice had roots in the particularistic ties characteristic of Chinese business organization in earlier periods, it can be viewed as a remnant of the past.

But this is not to say that it was a roadblock on the highway of economic change. From another perspective, employment sureties in modern Chinese enterprises can be seen as a means of adapting business practice to a more impersonal economy.

Guarantorship facilitated the transition from rural-based to urban-based enterprise and from small family-centered businesses to larger modern-style enterprises. In considering how and why guarantorship facilitated these transitions, two general premises inform the discussion. First, guarantorship was a form of risk reduction which was embedded in Chinese culture. It offered a readily available and well understood means of reducing risk as business transactions became more impersonal. Second, guarantorship evolved as the culture and economy evolved.

Risk Reduction in Chinese Business: a Model

The use of guarantors can be considered on a continuum with other forms of risk reduction in Chinese business practice, notably, the preference for dealing with kin and fellow regionals. It was also a legally enforceable contractual obligation in Qing and Republican customary law and in Republican statutory law. To appreciate how guarantorship fit into the pattern of Chinese business relations, I have devised a model of a "fiduciary community."

Seeking to minimize risk in market transactions is a universal goal. Exactly how risk is reduced will vary depending upon the political and legal context. Concepts from the economic theory of transaction cost are useful here. Whereas neoclassical economic theory takes price as the determinant of market behavior, transaction cost theory postulates other costs inherent in market exchanges. These transaction costs include information, negotiation, monitoring, and enforcement costs. Economic institutions or "governance structures" can be evaluated in terms of their ability to economize on these costs (Sigel 1992: 2; Williamson 1979: 243; Pollack 1985: 581–83). The nature of a given governance structure will depend on the institutional framework set by the state, that is, how property rights are defined and how the legal system operates (North 1980). In China the institutional framework differed from that of the West.

Chinese businessmen operated in a governance structure which I have labeled a fiduciary community and which can be visualized as a set of concentric circles with the inner circles being preferred in terms of risk reduction.[1] Historically, the

---

1. Robert Gardella suggested the term "fiduciary community" to describe this model. It has since been brought to my attention that Tu Wei-ming uses the terms in his analysis of *The Doctrine of the Mean* to designate a moral community based on Confucian concepts (1989: 33–66). The Chinese sociologist Fei Xiaotong uses an image of concentric circles with the individual in the center to describe Chinese society in the early twentieth century (1992: 62–63). Both Tu (1989: 53) and Fei (1992: 67) use the image of con-

innermost circle was the family and then, moving outward, were circles of lineage, place of origin, and guilds. The next two circles, *xinyong* (credit) and introductions (*jieshao*) were based on reputation. *Xinyong* was one's reputation in two English senses of the word credit: trustworthiness and solvency. An introducer loaned his *xinyong* to the one he recommended and could lose face but not money. The outermost circle was guarantees (*baozheng*). A guarantor, as I will discuss more fully below, could be, but was not always, legally liable for compensation in cases of default on a contract. These circles are analytically, but not functionally, distinct. For example, introductions and guarantees were likely to come from a kinsmen, a fellow regional, or a member of the same guild. Nor would preferences always follow the same order. For instance, a family head might prefer to form a partnership with a fellow regional rather than with certain lineage members. My emphasis will be on guarantors, but the other circles require some comment regarding their role in risk reduction.

The central role of the family in Chinese business enterprise has been well established, but the reason for its centrality needs more attention. With regard to contemporary Taiwan, Joseph Bosco has argued that the preference for family firms should be attributed to the legal and institutional context rather than to "a special family logic" (1992: 2). The same argument can be made for the historical importance of family enterprises. Since the state recognized the *jia* or family as the basic unit of property ownership, it was logically the basic unit of business ownership. The law as it pertained to the family economy, that is, property transactions, property division, inheritance, and marriage, was well developed. With regard to staffing a business, information about the character and skills of a family member was readily available, and both the government and Confucian ideology supported the authority which the head of a family had over its members. In addition the importance of the family to an individual's well-being could serve as a disincentive to take actions detrimental to an enterprise.

Lineage organizations, as David Faure has pointed out, were legally sanctioned institutions holding and managing assets in the form of land and should be "compared on a par with the business institutions of the mercantile firm" (1991: 2). In addition, the lineage organization lent support to the family-controlled businesses within it. For example, the lineage provided access to patronage networks, which were essential to business success (Faure 1989: 348–49; 360–66). At least in some cases, a family business could draw on lineage assets in times of crisis (Shiba 1977: 434, 438; Jones 1974: 77, 83). Lineages were also a source of additional staff for a family's business (Shiba 1977: 437).

---

centric circles to describe the concept of human relations contained in *The Doctrine of the Mean*.

As businesses expanded beyond the place of origin and beyond the capacity of the family's human and capital resources, transactions with fellow regionals played an important role in reducing risk. Regional ties are especially evident in partnership agreements and the hiring of staff. The nineteenth-century Ningbo merchants are a well-known example. According to Yoshinobu Shiba,

> It was said that a Ningpo man of power—whether a comprador, a bank manager, a shipping magnate, or simply a shopkeeper or ship's officer—never failed to employ fellow natives. In fact, preferences followed the usual concentric circles of particularistic loyalties that prevailed in Chinese society. Recruitment to Ningpo enterprises outside the region displayed a preference first for kinsmen (sons and nephews first, then other lineage mates), then for others from the same native place narrowly defined, then for those from the same county, and finally for persons native to other parts of the Ningpo region (1977: 437).

In terms of risk reduction, dealing with fellow regionals could economize on information and monitoring costs. Knowledge about the *xinyong* of a given family was more readily available, and opportunism on the part of a particular individual would affect his family's reputation in the locality of origin.

Guilds frequently institutionalized regional ties, and kinship ties remained important within guild leadership (Niida 1976: 2, 174; Jones 1972: 66; 1974: 80). In the cities and towns of late imperial China, guilds were more likely than the lineage to be the source of patronage (Faure 1989: 363–64). The Ningbo Guild (*Ningbo bang*) in Shanghai is an example. In the nineteenth century, Ningbo youths who did not have relatives in Shanghai gained employment through the Guild, which had "a close-knit and carefully controlled system for recruiting Ningpo youths into trade in Shanghai. . . ." (Jones 1974: 82). The Ningbo Guild also benefited from patronage based on regional ties. After the Small Sword Society rebellion was put down in 1853, a Zhejiang native succeeded a Cantonese as Shanghai *daotai* and pursued policies that supported Ningbo natives in challenging the Cantonese and Fujianese dominance in foreign trade (Leung 1990: 127; 150–51).

In more concrete ways guilds obviously reduced risk through monopolistic practices. But they also reduced transaction costs by specifying weights and measures and providing market information (Chen and Myers 1989: 322–24). They reduced enforcement costs by invoking sanctions against guild members who breached guild rules (Chen and Myers 1978: 22–25; Niida 1976: 323; McElderry 1992: 127–30). And membership in a prestigious guild could also enhance a businessman's *xinyong* (Chen and Myers 1989: 324–25).

Social scientists studying late twentieth-century Chinese business communities in Taiwan, Hong Kong, and Southeast Asia have documented the importance of *xinyong* in transactions among small businessmen (Barton 1983; DeGlopper 1972; Silin 1972). A man's *xinyong* "depended not only on his capital assets, liquidity and capacity for doing business, but even more upon his character, his investment in social relations and the amount of moral pressure which operated on him" (Barton 1983: 50). If two parties to an agreement knew and respected the other's *xinyong*, the transaction could be concluded without an introduction or a guarantee. As we shall see, the same was true in Republican Shanghai.

A person who did not have the necessary *xinyong* in a given transaction could borrow it from an introducer (*jieshao ren*). In his early 1970s study of a small port in Taiwan, Donald DeGlopper explained the attitude of a retail draper when introduced to a new wholesaler: "a lot depends on just who introduces [the wholesaler], and how well [the retailer] trusts [the introducer]. The introducer is in no narrow sense responsible for the wholesaler; he is definitely not a guarantor, but his recommendations do carry weight" (1972: 309). In early twentieth-century Shanghai introducers played a similar role. If the one introduced did not fulfill his obligations, the introducer was expected to mediate but was not legally liable (Shen Shiyi 190: 250). Unlike the introducer, a guarantor was legally liable, but his liability varied depending on the historical period, the place, and the contract.

Qing and Republican customary law recognized two types of guarantors, which Niida Noboru distinguishes as "ordinary" (*putong*) and "special" (*tebie*). Generally, the ordinary guarantor did not have responsibility to compensate, whereas the special guarantor did. In the latter case the guarantor's obligation to repay had to be stated in the contract (Niida 1980: 556). This customary legal distinction between ordinary and special guarantors was accepted by the Zongli Yamen, the agency of the Qing central government charged with foreign affairs. In 1868 Prince Gong, speaking for the Zongli Yamen, explained to the British representative, Rutherford B. Alcock, that a guarantor might merely agree to be a referee in case of dispute, or he might accept liability for recompense in case of default. In both cases there would be a signed agreement, and "in cases of reclamation against a guarantor the judge would first ascertain the precise terms of the obligation" (Jamieson 1970: 116–18). In 1886 a case involving a foreign firm and a Chinese guarantor was appealed from the Mixed Court in Shanghai to the Zongli Yamen. The latter agency ruled that the guarantor did not have to make restitution because the contract contained the words *sheli*, meaning "to be concerned with adjusting or regulation." The opinion also stated that when the parties to a contract intended the guarantor to be liable for repayment in case of default, then the contract should contain specific words to that effect (*Ibid.*: 118–19).

Early Republican customary law continued to recognize this distinction although the exact wording for designating a special guarantor varied from place to place. A county-by-county survey of customary law published in 1930 contains a number of examples. In Qingyuan, Hebei, the phrase was *daibao daihuan*; in Mengyin, Henan, *chenghuan baoren*; in Chengcheng, Shaanxi, *renyin liangbao* (*Minshang* 1930: II, 751, 804, 1213).

Statutes drafted during the Republican period deemed all guarantors as special and reversed the circumstances in which particular wording was required. The Civil Code (*Liufa quanshu*) first promulgated in 1930 and still the basis of Taiwan law, as well as a 1924 draft code, state that, unless otherwise specified, guarantors are responsible for paying the principal, interest, and compensation for damages (Yang 1930: 1198; Civil Code 1930: 189; Laws 1967: 216). The Civil Code also limited the circumstances in which a guarantor could be released from his obligation (Civil Code 1930: 189).[2]

From a legal perspective the trend was definitely toward making the guarantor's obligation stricter. The changes in the law were reflected in employment sureties or *baodan* from the 1930s and 1940s. They became more specific and often standardized, developments which paralleled the emergence of a more impersonal marketplace. In the twentieth century the growth of urban, regional, national, and international markets meant that businessmen were more likely to be making transactions outside of the inner circles of the fiduciary community. The outer circles became more prominent. Guarantors were particularly evident in the practice of employee bonding. Larger enterprises made it necessary to recruit staff from an expanded pool of applicants which in turn made it more difficult to monitor employees. Personal restraints on employee malfeasance were diluted as personal ties diminished. Guarantors were an accessible and well-understood way to reduce risk. They were not a static remnant from the past but a dynamic factor in the adaptation of traditional Chinese business practice to the economic changes of the late nineteenth and early twentieth centuries.

The Recent History of Guarantors

The extent to which guarantors were used to bond people in private business before the twentieth century is problematic. Judging from available sources, in the eighteenth century the government was more likely to require guarantors. Guarantors became more widespread in private business after the Treaty of Nanjing in 1842 stipulated the opening of five ports to foreign trade. From the 1850s to about 1900 the most obvious use of employee guarantees was by foreign firms, who

---

2. Article 745 of the Civil Code reads: "A surety can refuse to compensate a creditor if the creditor has not first filed proceedings against the property of the primary debtor in order to force execution [of the obligation] and without results." Article 746 limits this provision. A guarantor could not assert his right as stated in article 745 if (1) he had waived it, (2) claims against the principal debtor were complicated by his having changed his residential or business location, (3) the principal debtor had become bankrupt, or (4) the principal debtor's property was not sufficient to satisfy the creditor (SASS 1988: 258; *Civil Code* 1930: 189–90; *Laws* 1967: 217–18).

required their compradors to have guarantors. Although this observation may merely reflect the available sources, there is reason to attribute the spread of the practice in modern Chinese firms to foreign influence. This is because foreign firms in the treaty ports served as a models for modern Chinese enterprises and compradors were often involved in the development of these enterprises. Whatever the exact connection, by the early twentieth century both Chinese and foreign businesses required employees to have guarantors, and guarantor liability was becoming more specific.

During the Qing Dynasty (1644–1911) the government required guarantors in both the administrative and economic spheres. In the administrative sphere, for example, the government required a candidate for the position of yamen clerk to have a character guarantee. When seeking this office, the applicant had to present a signed guarantee from a neighbor vouching that he came from a good family (i.e., one that was not engaged in any of the "mean" occupations), that he had not committed any crime, that he was not a degree holder, and that he was not reentering the service under a different name. The magistrate then filed his own stamped guarantee with the Board of Civil Office (Ch'u 1969: 43; 229n). The *baojia* system, in which the government organized the population into groups responsible for each other's conduct, may be viewed as an administrative guarantee system and had its counterparts in the economic sphere. In the eighteenth century the government relied on officially dictated head-merchant systems to regulate certain areas of the economy, for example, salt, ginseng, and foreign trade. The designated head merchants had mutual responsibility for each other and, in turn, served as guarantors for the others in the trading system. After 1800 economic change, foreign pressure, and internal rebellion led the government to abolish the head-merchant system and rely more on brokers and guilds to regulate trade (McElderry 1992: 126–28). Brokers were used throughout the Qing period for the purpose of price control and tax collection. Technically all market transactions had to go through government licensed brokers (*yahang*), and be licensed, brokers needed guarantors. In the nineteenth century guilds often replaced brokers in government regulatory efforts, and in at least some cases the government required guild members to have guarantors (*Ibid.*: 130).

In private business guarantors are not so readily apparent. One might assume that apprentices needed guarantors, but whether this was the case in the eighteenth century is open to question. The sources documenting the requirement come from the twentieth century (see, for example, Burgess 1966: 156–58; Fong 1932: 73; Hershatter 1986: 145; Honig 1986: 7).[3] Available information on apprenticeship in

---

the eighteenth century does not mention guarantors (see, for example, Peng 1957: I, 181–92). When the apprentice was recruited from the inner circles of the fiduciary community, the guarantee may have been implicit in the obligations of a given relationship. Or, as was true in some cases in the twentieth century, the family may have had responsibility to compensate in cases of loss caused by the apprentice. Specific sureties may have been ordinary rather than special. Given the particularistic nature of employee recruitment, elaborate methods for employee monitoring were not necessarily indicated. If there were such arrangements, the records were more likely to have been filed in family and lineage records than with the yamen.

Significantly, in eighteenth-century Suzhou, where guarantors were used in private business, the situation was much like that of the late nineteenth- and early twentieth-century port cities. In both situations expanding enterprises needed to recruit employees from outside of the inner circles. According to a stele from 1720, over 10,000 craftsmen from outside of Suzhou were scattered among the 600 to 700 cloth-rolling workshops, averaging 14 to 17 per shop. In 1793 more than 800 paper workers were employed by 33 workshops, with an average of 24 workers per shop (Suzhou 1981: 68, 397). All of these workers came from outside of Suzhou and its environs (*Ibid.*: 68, 94). As wages fell behind inflation, strikes for higher wages became a major concern for employers and local authorities. In 1756 a stele prohibited paper workers from work stoppages to force up wages (*Ibid.*: 89). It was in this context that the local authorities instituted guarantee systems among paper workers and cloth-rollers (*chuaijiang*).

The rules for the paper workers, approved by the local authorities in 1793, specify responsibilities and liabilities for two types of guarantors, a *baojian* and a *baoren*. The *baojian* was a head artisan. He was to investigate workers whose backgrounds, i.e., native places, were not known and had liability to compensate if a worker stole goods. *Baoren* are mentioned only in connection with fraud. Specifically if a guilty worker who had been sent back to his native place changed his name and returned to work in another workshop and if the *baoren* knowingly permitted it, the *baoren* was equally liable for punishment. The *baojian* had the responsibility to investigate (*Ibid.*). Among the cloth rollers the government organized a mutual responsibility system (*Ibid.*: 68–71).

These examples suggest that the practice of requiring employees in private business to have guarantors was, at a minimum, influenced by government policies. In the nineteenth century, with the growth of the port cities, transactions among strangers became more common. At the same time the government's ability to maintain an orderly marketplace was weakening. Guarantors became evident in

---

fired for misconduct, but his research was done in the early twentieth century and originally published in 1928 (1966: 156–58).

private business arrangements and their liability became more specific. This process can be seen in the development of business arrangements between foreign and Chinese businessmen. Before the Treaty of Nanking in 1842 the Qing government limited foreign traders to Canton and regulated the trade through a head-merchant system. The government required foreign businessmen to trade with designated Chinese merchants, the so-called hong merchants. The hong merchants guaranteed transactions between foreign and Chinese merchants and government customs revenues.

The Treaty of Nanking privatized not only foreign-Chinese business dealings but risk reduction as well. The comprador system is an example. Before 1842 compradors had been licensed by the government and guaranteed under the hong merchant hierarchy (Hao 1970: 48). After 1842, compradors became private agents for foreign firms rather than government-mandated ones. At first a man seeking a comprador position with a foreign firm needed only a letter of recommendation from a well-known merchant (*Ibid.*: 157). This person was presumably a Cantonese with whom the foreign firm had developed personal ties before 1842. Beginning in the late 1850s, "almost every comprador had to be 'secured' (financially guaranteed). His surety might guarantee him fully or partially" (*Ibid.*: 159). As foreign firms expanded into more ports and risks to foreign firms increased, guarantor requirements became more stringent. Two early examples of comprador *baodan* (known in English as "security chop"), from 1859 and 1860 respectively, merely agree to compensate in case of loss caused by the comprador. In the 1860 contract the guarantor put up 1000 taels of "earnest money" (*Ibid.*: 156–59). By the turn of the twentieth century, security chops specified the circumstances under which a comprador was liable and set a monetary figure for the guarantor's liability.[4] Guarantors also had to post substantial bonds. Compradors paid a portion of their profits and interest on the security deposit to the guarantor (Hao 1970: 157; Arnold 1975: 255).

---

4. An 1895 surety contract for a comprador to a Japanese shipping company set the guarantor's liability at 10,000 British pounds, and it specified that all or part of it could be used "absolutely and without recourse" to cover deficits in the comprador's accounts, misappropriated funds, or any other such matters. The guarantor was not liable for freight and passenger fees not received by the accounting office (*Zhongguo* 1908: 288). Not surprisingly, foreign banks tended to have the most detailed comprador surety contracts and required the largest security deposits. Whereas a security deposit of Tls.10,000 was sufficient for most firms, banks demanded as much as Tls.200,000. Whereas surety contracts for most firms ran 70–100 Chinese characters, an 1899 surety contract for a comprador to the Tianjin branch of the Chartered Bank of India, Australia, and China ran over 700 Chinese characters detailing transactions in which the four jointly liable guarantors might have to compensate (*Zhongguo* 1908: 260; see also Hao 1970: 159–60). For other examples of comprador surety contracts, see *Zhongguo* 1908: 263, 292 and Hao 1970: 156–58.

In Yen-p'ing Hao's words, "While the foreign firm depended on the guarantee system to ensure a comprador's trustworthiness, the comprador himself, in recruiting his own staff, is known to have relied heavily on China's traditional values, especially familism and regionalism." This "stemmed partly from the weight of his responsibilities" (1970: 171). The comprador guaranteed the Chinese employees whom he hired and his transactions with Chinese businessmen on behalf of the foreign firm. Whether compradors normally required formal guarantee contracts from their employees is open to question. When such guarantees were required, they were apparently intended to reinforce China's traditional value system. Two examples of *baodan* for comprador's employees from around the turn of the twentieth century are brief ordinary guarantees, that is, the guarantor was not liable for compensation in case of loss. Both *baodan* were drawn up by relatives of the comprador's employee, and both contain the phrase "precedent dictates that a relative or friend stand as guarantor on his behalf" (*lixu jinyou dai wei zuo bao*) (*Zhongguo* 1908: 287–88). The question is what exactly was the precedent? Was it a written guarantee or simply a relative with a personal tie to the comprador orally vouching for the integrity of the employee? Likewise, did the comprador or the management of the foreign firm set the precedent?

Whatever the precedent, other evidence suggests that the demand for employment sureties increased in the late nineteenth and early twentieth centuries because China's traditional values were not deemed sufficient to reduce risk in an expanded urban economy. Nor were China's established institutions sufficient. As I have already mentioned, in the early nineteenth century the Ningbo Guild provided patronage for Ningbo youths who were seeking jobs in Shanghai. In the late nineteenth century newly prominent Ningbo business men challenged the guild by providing employee guarantees and thus creating their own patronage networks. According to Susan Mann, these businessmen, often compradors like Yu Xiaching,

> would contract with an apprentice from Ningpo seeking employment in any trade, and serve as bondsmen responsible for financial losses in his behalf. Or if a bond was not necessary, a simple introduction . . . was readily provided. Losses on the part of guarantors increased as this system became less particularistic, and finally a "mutual guarantee system" . . . was devised, whereby a candidate had to share equally in all losses he incurred (Jones 1974: 82).

Mann attributes the rise of the new networks to the fact that the extension of modern industry and foreign-style native enterprises opened up opportunities for newcomers to accumulate wealth outside of the established channels, that is, outside of the guild. It should also be noted that the spread of modern enterprises increased the demand for labor in a more impersonal marketplace, and hence increased the demand for employee guarantees. By the 1930s a prospective employee in a modern enterprise in Shanghai would almost certainly have to have a guarantor. But the efficacy of the practice depended upon the accountability of the guarantor.

Guarantors in Republican Shanghai

To find a job in Shanghai and other cities in the Republican period, an individual would almost certainly need an introduction and a guarantee. The introducer provided the personal connection. He had ties of kinship, region, or *xinyong* with both parties. The guarantor provided the legal recourse in case of employee malfeasance. The process of introduction and guarantee varied depending on the attractiveness of the job and the size of the enterprise. In small department stores and Chinese foreign-goods sundries shops, a new apprentice (*xuetu*) arrived for his first day of work accompanied by his introducer and carrying a *baodan* (written guarantee) as well as joss sticks, candles, a red felt rug, a red card requesting instruction, and host money, all of which, according to tradition, he presented to his "teacher," the shop head. The apprentice then kowtowed to the god of wealth and the store head, and after hearing words of encouragement from the store head and his introducer, he commenced his employment. The introducer, a friend or relative of the owner, might also serve as the guarantor (SASS 1988: 258).

In larger department stores the process was similar, but the ritual was different. For trainees (*lianxi sheng*) and prospective regular employees in large department stores, the introducer would be a friend or relative of a department head or higher-ranked employee, and the position of the introducer would affect one's chances of being hired (SASS 1988: 257–58; SASS 1981a: 91). The introduction might take the form of a letter of recommendation.[5] After being introduced, prospective Wing On Department Store employees had to take a qualifying test which included spoken English, commercial knowledge, abacus calculation, and arithmetic. Successful applicants had to furnish a guarantee from a business which accepted unlimited liability for any loss Wing On incurred because of the employee (SASS 1981a: 91–92). In addition, Wing On and some other department stores specified that the guarantor must waive his rights to contest his liability in court according to the provisions specified in the Civil Code, promulgated in 1930 (SASS 1988: 257).

From the perspective of management these procedures offered ways of monitoring employees in a less particularistic atmosphere. But the system also required ways to monitor the guarantors. As a Chinese folk saying went, "A go-between cannot guarantee the birth of a child; a guarantor cannot guarantee

---

5. Letters of recommendation for those seeking positions in Liu Hongsheng's enterprises not only commended the applicant's talents but usually identified his father or grandfather as well. They might also make reference to an applicant's financial position (Liu Hongsheng 12–064).

repayment" (Niida 1980: 555). Writing on insurance in the 1936 *China Yearbook*, S. H. Peek explained that in cases of embezzlement, employers found it difficult to collect from guarantors for a number of reasons: ambiguously worded agreements, the death of the guarantor, a change in his financial status, a change in the ownership or partners of a business, the closing of a business, "or for any one of a hundred other reasons. It is essential that a constant check be kept on the guarantors, if the protection intended to be afforded by the bonds is to be properly maintained, and few employers are in a position to see that this is done" (1936: 454).

To increase the efficacy of the employee bonding system, management took various approaches. One was to gain control of guarantor networks. A second was to stipulate who could stand as guarantor. A third was to require *baodan* which would stand up in court.

Management attempts to gain control of guarantor networks is particularly evident in the factories. Before World War II foremen controlled the hiring in the cotton mills of Shanghai and Tianjin and approved the guarantors. To get a job in a Shanghai mill, an individual had to be introduced to the foreman, and the introducers were almost always connected to "networks built on kinship relations or ties between people from the same native place" (Honig 1986: 83, 90; Fong 1932: 120). Usually these introducers were labor contractors, and both labor contractors and foremen had gangster connections. As Elizabeth Perry has shown, gangs were a powerful organizing force in the factory labor hierarchy. Unskilled immigrants from rural areas seeking work in Shanghai "quickly discovered that employment opportunities in the city were dependent upon criminal ties" (1993: 50, 25, 56). The importance of gangs among both foremen and unskilled workers in Shanghai factories meant that foreman-controlled guarantor networks were also gangster-controlled networks. According to one of Emily Honig's informants, "If you didn't know anyone to introduce you [to the foreman], you could find local hoodlums who had connections with the foremen in the mill. They would be your guarantor. They were in the neighborhood, and everyone knew who had the connections. You had to give them five dollars for this" (Honig 1986: 83).

One way in which managers sought to wrest control of guarantor networks from factory foremen was to set up training programs in which management could dictate guarantor requirements. In the 1920s and 1930s, however, the Shanghai mill managers who attempted to do so were stymied by the opposition of the foremen (*Ibid.*: 90).[6] Another way to control guarantor networks, or at least to limit their

6. In Tianjin, as the result of a strike in the 1910s, the Retail Grain Shops' Association agreed to accept and partially finance a worker-controlled recruitment and guarantee system. The arrangement took the process out of the hands of labor contractors (Fong 1934: 601). Arguably, the workers had more control over the worker-controlled system than the labor-contractor system.

influence, was to restrict the number of employees that one guarantor could bond. In 1939 the Rongchang Match Factory set up a regulation that a guarantor could not have more than five surety contracts for factory employees on file (Liu Hongsheng 02–046). The factory also wanted to ensure that a guarantor could compensate if the terms of the employment contract were not fulfilled.

Many enterprises insisted that employee guarantees come from a firm rather than an individual probably because they assumed that firms were more stable in terms of both assets and address and that they were less likely to take unnecessary risks. Firm owners were willing to stand as guarantors to increase their *xinyong* within the business community. After World War II, when Shanghai mill managers were able to set up training programs, guarantors had to be owners of a large store and make out a *baodan* assuming financial liability (Honig 1986: 91). A trainee in the Great China Dispensary in Shanghai had to furnish a guarantee from a prosperous shopkeeper or put up a relatively large security deposit (SASS 1990: 16). The Bank of China specified a guarantee with unlimited liability from a wealthy individual or prosperous business (*Zhongguo yinhang* 1971: 129–30; Yao 1967: 29). Banks also had the resources to investigate and approve a guarantor before a prospective employee could begin work.[7]

The preference for shop guarantees created problems for both employers and shop owners. An employer might not know who had the authority to use the firm's seal to stand surety, and owners or shareholders were liable for any surety with the company's seal. In 1934 the Chinese Chemical Industry Society asked the Shanghai Chamber of Commerce about a firm's liability when its manager made unauthorized use of the firm's seal to stand as guarantor. The Chamber of Commerce responded that "a firm's seal represents the firm and once used, the firm is completely liable.... Deciding who has responsibility for the seal is an internal decision. However, in external matters, people rely on the seal and don't ask who in the organization has responsibility for its use" (Yen 1936: 186–88; see also 183). Therefore it is no accident that contracts to form a company sometimes specified that the company's seal could not be used to guarantee others (Liu Hongsheng 12–001, #3, #10; Watson 1972: 27). Nor is it surprising that prohibitions against using the firm's seal to guarantee an individual were found in employee rules. If an employee broke company rules by misusing the firm's seal, then his guarantor would be liable. So the same firms which prohibited the use of the seal for sureties specified that employees had to have guarantors, thus increasing the temptation for unauthorized

---

7. Bank of Communications personnel records from the 1920s and 1930s at the Number Two National Archives in Nanjing (archive #397) contain numerous folios of correspondence relating to employee guarantors, including reports on investigations of employee guarantors, changes of guarantors, and guarantors' withdrawing their sureties. The Bank of China records (archive #397) contain less of the same sort of information.

use of the firm's seal for sureties. On the other hand, these clauses in contracts and company rules made it easier to seek legal recourse. The same considerations led employers to make surety requirements more specific.

Legal developments in the 1930s, notably the promulgation of the Civil Code and the establishment of a court hierarchy, led to more carefully worded and more detailed *baodan*. This is illustrated by an example from Wujin County in Jiangsu province. According to a source published in 1933,

> Formerly there was not a standard guarantor form for the employees and incoming apprentices of the Wuba Shop. The introducer simply wrote a letter stating that a certain person was honest. . . . The guarantor sent a written statement to the firm. . . . Recently since the movement to reform the selection of legal evidence, all companies and shops place importance on written documents, and suddenly there are printed forms and recorded regulations (Wu 1933: 2).

By the late 1930s attorneys' offices provided standard forms full of appropriate legal phrases to their customers (Shen Shiyi).

Whether standardized or not, employment sureties specified the guarantor's responsibilities, which almost certainly included a phrase establishing the guarantor's liability to make restitution.[8] In 1939 the Rongchang Match Factory changed its employment contract to read, "If there is loss caused by the employee, then the guarantor will compensate" (Liu Hongsheng 02–046). Wing On and some other Shanghai department stores required guarantors to assume unlimited liability and specified in the contract that the guarantor knowingly waive his rights contained in article 745 of the Civil Code (see note 1). Specifically, the guarantor could not insist that the employer first attempt to collect compensation from the employee. The standard contract specified that the trainee and guarantor or guarantors were jointly and severally (as opposed to sequentially) liable. This meant that the company could collect first from any one of the parties to the contract (SASS 1988: 258). Wing On also required detailed standard contracts from its concessionaires, accompanied by *baodan* in which the guarantor accepted full responsibility to compensate for any

---

8. A letter of guarantee from the 1930s written by a relative of a trainee at the one of the Rong family's factories read, "The guarantor, the manager of the Xiecheng Southern Goods Shop, today willingly guarantees Zhu Linjie as a trainee worker in the silk thread section of the Mengyi Factory. During his training period, the one guaranteed will undergo training with all his heart and obey factory regulations. Moreover, he will stay for the specified training period of two years and will not leave in the middle of the training period. If he has a disobedient attitude, I take full responsibility and will compensate the factory for any financial losses he may cause during the training period. These words are absolutely true. So that afterwards this may be relied on, it is put on file (Rong: #106).

losses the concessionaires caused to the company (*Shanghai Yong'an*: 225–00011, 225–00012).

The process of guarantees in its various manifestations represented management's concern with employee accountability. But it was not sufficient to simply require employees to have guarantors. Managers also sought to ensure the validity of the surety. They sought to control guarantor networks, specified acceptable guarantors, insisted on guarantor liability, and they availed themselves of new laws. In the final analysis, however, the most effective means of monitoring guarantors lay within the fiduciary community. Standing as a guarantor could enhance a businessman's *xinyong,* while defaulting on guarantor obligations could harm it. And having good *xinyong* played a significant role in the complex business environment of the early twentieth century.

Guarantors and *xinyong*

The use of guarantorship in employer-employee relations should not obscure the continued importance of other circles of the fiduciary community in business practice, but the relative balance among the circles during the early twentieth century is much more difficult to pinpoint because the marketing structure was so complex. Family management of individual firms, even joint-stock companies, remained the norm, and regional ties continued to delineate marketing niches in many trades. However, other types of personal ties, such as "same school" (*tongxue*) ties, became important with the development of new institutions. The marketplace had expanded in volume and products and now encompassed old and new forms of business organization, marketing techniques, and finance. Firms varied from small and medium-size single proprietorships and partnerships with unlimited liability to larger limited liability joint-stock companies. Goods might reach their final destination—a factory, an export firm, or a retailer—through middlemen, through a branch office, or on consignment. Means of payment ranged from cash in very small-scale operations to secured drafts from modern banks (*yinhang*).

How the fiduciary community fit into this more complex environment is the subject of current research. However, two facts are clear. Guarantors were not as uniformly employed in business-to-business relations as they were in employer-employee relations. And second, *xinyong* played a significant role. In older commodity markets, such as bulk tea and raw cotton, where credit operations were well established and readily available, having good *xinyong* could preclude the need for a guarantor. This is documented in studies published by the Shanghai Commercial and Savings Bank in the early 1930s. The research was not disinterested. The Shanghai Bank, a modern bank, which required security for its monetary advances, was competing with native banks (*qianzhuang*) and commodities dealers, which made unsecured loans. For example, Shanghai tea firms (*hang*) brought buyers and sellers together in the domestic market and loaned funds to sellers. Seventy to 80 percent of these loans were unsecured, "completely dependent on an individual's *xinyong* (*geren zhi xinyong*)." If a customer did not have *xinyong* "which inspired confidence," he had to find a guarantor (*baoren*), before the tea firm would loan him funds. The amount of interest native banks and tea firms charged on the unsecured loans varied, within limits, according to the customer's *xinyong* (SSXY 1931b: 63, 67).

Xinyong was not sufficient when the Huacheng Cigarette Company made arrangements to expand its sales in Shanghai's hinterland. Its consignment agents had to put up a security deposit (*baozheng jin*) and have a shop guarantor (*dianbao*), an individual guarantor (*renbao*), or a surety bond (*qiju bao*) (Fang 1989: 129). In this case significant risk was involved since Huacheng was challenging the already established cigarette distribution networks of the British-American Tobacco Company and the Nanyang Brothers Tobacco Company.

When *xinyong* was considered sufficient to reduce risk in business-to-business relations, one must ask if the word had the same meaning in early twentieth-century China as it has among small businessmen in contemporary Greater China. Isn't it likely that the Shanghai Bank researchers used the term *xinyong* to mean credit only in the sense of solvency and not necessarily in the sense of a reputation for sincerity and honest dealings? But if that is the case, what information did a potential creditor, a bank, or a firm have to determine a "credit rating"? Partnerships, which continued to be a preferred form of business organization, did not publicly trade their shares or publish information about dividends paid. Private businessmen were reticent about adopting the corporate form of business organization (Kirby 1995: 52). And the extent to which private corporations sold their stocks publicly is a question which needs to be researched.

Without "credit ratings" based on uniform criteria, judgments about *xinyong* were, by necessity, based partially on reputation. The reputation of an individual was likely to be more important than the creditworthiness of a particular firm. A 1934 Shanghai court case is instructive here. In 1934 the Ju Xing Cheng Bank sued the Tong Feng Silk Warehouse in the Jiangsu First District Court at Shanghai. The Ju Xing Cheng Bank, a native bank with unlimited liability owned by the Yang brothers, claimed that the Tong Feng Silk Warehouse and its partners owed the bank $41,455 from the sale of silk on the bank's account. The defendant, the Tong Feng Silk Warehouse, argued that it had withheld partial payment to the bank because another business, the Xian Silk Shop, owned by the Yang brothers and a Mr. Liu, owed the warehouse money. Since the Yang brothers had the larger interest in the Xian Silk Shop, the defendant's lawyer argued that it was a joint enterprise with the Yang brothers' bank. "Thus the trade between the defendant Tong Feng Warehouse and Qian Silk Shop completely depends on Mr. Yang's reputation." Reputation was linked to the question of liability. The defendant's lawyer concluded his argument with the statement: "The plaintiffs' bank and silk shops are both unlimited liability enterprises of the Yang brothers. Therefore Tong Feng's business is with the Yang brothers, and the Yang brothers have responsibility." The court, unlike the defendant's lawyer, distinguished between the two enterprises. It ruled against the warehouse saying that the silk shop's debt did not extend to the bank just because the Yang brothers had shares in both (Shen Shiyi Papers: 190:199).

The emphasis on individual assets over a specific firm was related to the fact that individuals with the best *xinyong* usually had interests in various enterprises. As the wealthy entrepreneur Liu Hongsheng told his son, "I don't put all of my birds in one cage, that is, my capital is dispersed. If one enterprise has a loss, another will have a profit so when the accounts are balanced, there can still be a profit (Zhong 1992: 282). Liu Hongsheng's cages tended to be limited liability joint stock companies which manufactured and marketed matches, coal, and coal products. Liu Hongsheng also kept control over his companies through a combination of old and new methods. The China Briquette Company was formed in 1919 as a joint stock limited liability company with Liu Hongsheng as general manager. A majority of the shares were held by Liu Hongsheng, his younger brother, Liu Jisheng, and four of Hongsheng's sons (Liu Hongsheng 05–002; 05–006). In 1929 the company committed its movable assets to Liu Hongsheng, a Ningbo native, who then, on behalf of the China Briquette Company, negotiated a fiduciary loan (*xinyong jiekuan*) of Tls.350,000 from the Ningbo Bank. In 1933, when the company was experiencing financial difficulties, the Ningbo Bank gave notice that it would not extend the loan. When Liu Hongsheng could not get a fiduciary loan from the Shanghai Industrial Bank, the company's board of directors agreed to commit assets, including land deeds, from its three factories to Liu Hongsheng, who used his personal assets, including his shares in China Briquette, to obtain a secured loan of $250,000 from the National Commercial Bank, another Ningbo enterprise. Part of this was used to pay off the balance of Tls.150,000 to the Ningbo Bank (Liu Hongsheng 05–004; 05–006; 06–002). These arrangements suggest that the company had a better credit rating through Liu Hongsheng's reputation and personal assets. On the other hand, these arrangements were really not board decisions, since Liu Hongsheng controlled the majority of shares in the company (SASS 1981b: 237). The loans increased his control but at the same time increased his liability for the company. In a sense Liu Hongsheng stood as guarantor for the China Briquette Company.

Liu Hongsheng's dealings bring us back to the innermost circle, the family. In spite of the changed economic and legal context, the central place of family survived in large Republican business undertakings. This is attested to by the Rong brothers cotton and flour mills, the Guo brothers Wing On Department Store, the Jian family's Nanyang Brother Tobacco Company, and Liu Hongsheng's close business relations with his brother. Family-centered enterprise survived as part of a governance structure, a fiduciary community, which allowed for the extension of business relations into less particularistic spheres. But large family-controlled enterprises needed to hire employees from other families and hometowns, people hose reputations were not known to them. Guarantorship facilitated the recruitment of such strangers into the family-controlled large enterprises.

Conclusion

Guarantorship as it existed in employment practices in early twentieth century China can be viewed from two perspectives. On one hand, it was rooted in the particularistic governance structure of an earlier period and was not a practice consistent with the concept of a free labor market. On the other hand, the process can be seen as supporting the development of a more impersonal labor market. The institutions which supported a free labor market in the West were only beginning to develop in early twentieth-century China. Chinese insurance companies were in their infancy. Legal codes were promulgated, only to be replaced by newer codes and complicated by administrative regulations.[9] Enforcement of the laws was curtailed by changes in the court hierarchy, imperfect central control, and by war. The Nanjing government law changing the structure of court system came into effect in 1935, two years before the Japanese invasion. At the end of the war in 1945 only 600 of the planned 1900 county-level courts had been established (Xu 1992: 260). Intrusive government made businessmen wary of taking advantage of new laws which in Western countries served to reduce risk. An example is the private sector's lukewarm response to the 1929 Company Law which provided for joint share limited liability companies. As William Kirby has shown, this Company Law of the Nationalist government was "one vehicle in promoting state ascendancy over all private enterprise" (1995:52).

The imperfect development of an institutional framework for risk reduction perpetuated reliance on the fiduciary community. But the fiduciary community had to adapt as the economic and political environment changed, and guarantorship offered one way. Unlike many of the commercial laws of the twentieth century, guarantorship was not an imported concept. The fact that it was recognized in customary law enhanced its appeal. As we have seen, in the 1930s, employment sureties were drawn up with new laws in mind. In a city like Shanghai where the new court system was operating, if a guarantor did not accept his liability, an

---

9. The two-volume compilation *Shangye* (1991) contains a plethora of draft laws, regulations, and other records from the Number Two National Archives and Jiangsu Provincial Archives which illustrate this statement. Subject headings include commercial law, business associations, taxes, and foreign trade. For information about the complicated history of company law, see Kirby 1995.

employer could bring suit in court. However, the guarantor might be beyond the reach of the court's jurisdiction, and the loss incurred might not justify the expense of a court case.

Nonetheless, the efficacy of guarantorship was not solely dependent upon its legal status. The fiduciary community provided checks on the behavior of both the guarantor and the one guaranteed. The preference for having firms or wealthy individuals stand as guarantors took into account the fact that they had a reputation to maintain. Having good *xinyong* was important to business success. Defaulting on a guarantor obligation could harm a guarantor's reputation for trustworthiness. Standing as guarantor could enhance *xinyong*. The more people that one could guarantee, the better for one's reputation. Since guarantorship was a form of patronage, standing as guarantor could also increase one's power. This is why the control of guarantor networks was an area of contention in the late nineteenth and early twentieth centuries. Of course, the system was not foolproof because a powerful patron could more easily risk defaulting on a guarantor obligation.

Misconduct on the part of the one guaranteed was checked by his ties within the fiduciary community. When an employee caused loss to his employer, he might go beyond the reach of his employer. He could not so easily go beyond his obligation to his kin and fellow regionals. Misconduct on his part could affect the reputation of those close to him. Likewise it could affect future access to patronage for himself and others in his inner circles, since a claim on a guarantor was also a claim on a patron.

While these considerations go a long way toward explaining the importance of guarantorship in Chinese business practice, there are other areas which need exploration. One is the relationship between government and business. Like the Qing government, Republican governments continued to rely on semi-official groups, such as brokers and guilds, and as a result, on their already established guarantor systems. This raises the question of how government policies influenced guarantor systems in the early twentieth century. Another area concerns the financial aspects of guarantorship. What kind of financial arrangements existed between the guarantor and the one guaranteed? Did guarantorship take on aspects of bonding insurance? Sketchy evidence suggests that on the assumption that only a certain percentage of people would default on their obligations, a store would guarantee a number of people in return for payment of a "premium" from each. Was undercapitalization a variable contributing to the preference for guarantors over security deposits and other forms of monetary transfer? Theoretically, a guarantor kept control of his funds unless the one guaranteed defaulted. The guarantor could have his funds invested elsewhere, and if he had sufficient *xinyong*, he could borrow funds when necessary, as in the example of Liu Hongsheng's China Briquette dealings.

Finally, what was the role of culture in perpetuating the role of guarantors? Although I have concentrated on the institutional reasons for the persistence of guarantorship in the Chinese economy, the role of culture has to be considered. For example, the concept of guarantees is evident in many aspects of the post-1978 economic reforms in the People's Republic of China. Guarantors are still prominent in many areas of the modern economies of Taiwan and Japan. The development of modern economic organizations may obviate a central role for guarantors, but the cultural concept of guarantees as an ordering principle in the economy may affect the institutional framework.

References

Arnold, Julean. 1975. *Commercial Handbook of China*, vol. 2. Washington DC: Government Printing Office, 1920; rpt. San Francisco: Chinese Materials Center.

Barton, Clifton A. 1983. "Trust and Credit: Some Observations regarding Business Strategies of Overseas Chinese Traders in South Vietnam." In *The Chinese in Southeast Asia*, edited by Linda Y. C. Lim and L. A. Peter Gosling. Vol. 1: *Ethnicity and Economic Activity*. Singapore: Maruzen Asia.

Bosco, Joseph. 1992. "The Role of Culture in Taiwanese Family Enterprises," *Chinese Business History* 3, no. 1 (November): 1–4.

Burgess, John S. 1966 [1928]. *The Guilds of Peking*. Taipei: Ch'eng-wen.

Chamberlain, Heath B. 1987. "Party-Management Relations in Chinese Industries. *China Quarterly* 112: 631–66.

Changzhoushi guoying qiye shixing changzhang fuzezhi de janxing guiding (Provisional regulations for implementation of the factory director responsibility system in Changzhou). 1984. *Jingji guanli* (Economic management) 13 (December): 37–41; English translation, JPRS-CEA-85-022 (March 5, 1985): 69–83.

Chen, Fu-mei Chang, and Ramon Myers. 1989. "Coping with Transaction Costs: The Case of Merchant Associations in the Ch'ing Period." In *The Second Conference on Modern Chinese Economic History*, 317–41. Taipei: Institute of Economics, Academia Sinica.

———. 1978. "Customary Law and the Economic Growth of China during the Ch'ing Period." *Ch'ing-shih Wen-t'i* 3, no. 10: 4–27.

Ch'u T'ung-tsu. 1969. *Local Government in China under the Ch'ing*, Stanford: Stanford University Press.

The Civil Code of the Republic of China. 1976. Trans. by Ching-lin Hsia, James L. E. Chow, Yukon Chang. Arlington, VA: University Publications of America.

DeGlopper, D. R. 1972. "Doing Business in Lukang." In W. E. Willmott, ed., *Economic Organization in Chinese Society*, 297–326. Stanford: Stanford University Press.

Fang Xiantang, ed. 1989. *Shanghai jindai minzu juanyan gongye* (Shanghai's modern indigenous cigarette industry). Shanghai: Shanghai shehui kexue yuan chubanshe.

Faure, David. 1989. "The Lineage as Business Company: Patronage vs. the Law in the Development of Chinese Business." In *The Second Conference on Modern Chinese History*, 347–76. Taipei: Academia Sinica, Institute of Economics.

———. 1991. "A Note on the Lineage in Business," *Chinese Business History* 1, no. 2 (April): 1–3.

Fei Xiaotong. 1992. *From the Soil*. Translated by Gary G. Hamilton and Wang Zheng. Berkeley: University of California Press.

Fong, H. D. [Fang Xianting]. 1932. *Cotton Industry and Trade in China*. Tianjin: Nankai University Committee on Social and Economic Research, Bulletin #4.

———. 1934. *Grain Trade and Milling in Tientsin*. Tianjin: Nankai University Committee on Social and Economic Research, Bulletin #6.

Hao, Yen-p'ing. 1970. *The Comprador in Nineteenth-Century China*. Cambridge: Harvard University Press.

Hershatter, Gail. 1986. *The Workers of Tianjin, 1900–1949*. Stanford: Stanford University Press.

Honig, Emily. 1986. *Sisters and Strangers, Women in the Shanghai Cotton Mills, 1919–1949*. Stanford: Stanford University Press.

Jamieson, George. 1970. *Chinese Family and Commercial Law*. Hong Kong: Vetch and Lee Ltd.

Jones, Susan Mann. 1972. "Finance in Ningpo: The 'Ch'ien Chuang,' 1750–1880." In *Economic Organization in Chinese Society*, edited by W. E. Willmott, 47–78. Stanford: Stanford University Press.

———. 1974. "The Ningpo Pang and Financial Power at Shanghai." In *The Chinese City between Two Worlds*, edited by Mark Elvin and G. W. Skinner, 73–96. Stanford: Stanford University Press.

Kirby, William C. 1995. "China Unincorporated: Company Law and Business Enterprise in Twentieth-Century China," *Journal of Asian Studies* 54, no. 1 (February): 43–63.

Laws of the Republic of China, Civil Code. 1967. Taipei.

Leung, Yuen-sang. 1990. *The Shanghai Taotai, Linkage Man in a Changing Society, 1843–1890*. Honolulu: University of Hawaii Press.

Liu Hongsheng. Papers. Shanghai: Qiye lishi yanjiu zhongxin, Jingji yanjiu so, Shanghai shehui kexue yuan. (Business History Research Center, Economics Institute, Shanghai Academy of Social Sciences).

McElderry, Andrea. 1992. "Guarantors and Guarantees in Qing Government-Business Relations." In Jane Kate Leonard, ed., *To Achieve Wealth and Security: the Qing State and Economy*. Ithaca: Cornell Center for Asian Studies.

Minshang shi xiguan diaocha baogao lu (A report on the investigation of customary civil and commercial law). 1930. N.p.: Sifa xingzheng bu.

Niida, Noburu, comp. 1976. *Pekin kosho girudo shiryōshū* (A collection of materials on Beijing trade and merchant guilds). Tokyo.

———. 1980 [1964]. *Chugoku hōsei-shi kenkyū: tochi-hō torihikiō ō* (A study of Chinese legal history—laws concerning land and transaction). Vol. 2. Tokyo.

North, Douglass C. 1980. *Structure and Change in Economic History*. New York: W. W. Norton and Company.

Peek, S. H. 1936. "Insurance in China." In *The China Yearbook*, edited by H. G. W. Woodhead, 447– 55. Shanghai: The North-China Daily News and Herald, Ltd.

Peng Ziyi. 1957. *Zhongguo jindai shougongye shi ziliao* (Materials on China's modern handicraft industry). Beijing: Sanlian shudian.

Perry, Elizabeth J. 1993. *Shanghai on Strike: the Politics of Chinese Labor*. Stanford: Stanford University Press.

Pollack, Robert A. 1985. "A Transaction Cost Approach to Families and Households," *Journal of Economic Literature* 23 (June): 581-608.

Rong Family. Papers. Shanghai: Qiye lishi yanjiu zhongxin, Jingji yanjiu suo, Shanghai shehui kexue yuan. (Business History Research Center, Economics Institute, Shanghai Academy of Social Sciences).

Rowe, William T. 1984. *Hankow: Commerce and Society in a Chinese City, 1796–1889*. Stanford: Stanford University Press.

[SASS] Shanghai shehui kexue yuan (The Shanghai Academy of Social Sciences), comp. 1981a. *Shanghai Yong'an gongsi di chansheng, fazhan, he gaizao* (The birth, development, and transformation of Shanghai's Wing On Company). Shanghai: Shanghai renmin chubanshe.

———. 1981b. *Liu Hongsheng qiye shiliao* (Historical materials on Liu Hongsheng's enterprises), 1911–1931, edited by Jingji suo. Vol. 1. Shanghai shehui kexue yuan, jingji yanjiu so, ed. Shanghai renmin chuban she.

———. 1988. *Shanghai jindai baihuo shangye shi* (A history of modern Shanghai department store business), edited by Jingji suo. Shanghai: Shanghai shehui kexue yuan.

——— and Zhongxi yaochang, comp. 1990. *Zhongxi yaochang bainian shi* (The "Great China Dispensary's" one hundred year history) Shanghai: Shanghai shehui kexue yuan.

Shanghai Yong'an gufen youxian gongsi dang'an (Archives of the Shanghai Wing On Company, Ltd.) at the Shanghai shi dang'an guan (Shanghai Municipal Archives), Shanghai, 1918–1966.

Shangye dang'an ziliao huibian, 1912–1928 (A collection of commercial archives). 1991. Edited by Zhao Dinglu. Nanjing: Dang'an chubanshe.

Shen Shiyi. Papers in the Shanghai shi dang'an guan (Shanghai Municipal Archives), Shanghai.

Shiba, Yoshinobu. 1977. "Ningpo and Its Hinterland." In *The City in Late Imperial China*, edited by G. W. Skinner, 391–440. Stanford: Stanford University Press.

Sigel, Louis T. 1992. "Transaction Cost Economics and Chinese Business History," *Chinese Business History* 2, no. 2 (March): 1–3.

Silin, Robert H. 1972. "Marketing and Credit in a Hong Kong Wholesale Market." In *Economic Organization in Chinese Society*, edited by W. E. Willmott, 327–52. Stanford: Stanford University Press.

[SSXY] Shanghai shangye xuwu yinhang (Shanghai Commercial and Savings Bank). 1931a. *Cotton*. Shanghai.

———. 1931b. *Tea*. Shanghai.

Suzhou lishi bowuguan, Jiangsu shufan xueyuan lishi xi, Nanjing daxue Ming Qing shi yanjiu shi, eds. 1981. *Ming Qing Suzhou gongshangye peike ji* (Records of steles related to Suzhou business during the Ming and Qing periods). Jiangsu renmin chubanshe.

Tu Wei-ming. 1989. *Centrality and Commonality*. Albany: State University of New York Press.

Watson, Andrew, trans. 1972. *Transport in Transition*. Ann Arbor: University of Michigan Center for Chinese Studies.

Weber, Max. 1968. *Economy and Society*. Edited by Guenther Roth and Claus Wittich. 3 vols. New York: Bedminister Press.

Williamson, Oliver E. 1979. "Transaction-Cost Economics: the Governance of Contractual Relations," *Journal of Law and Economics* 22 (October): 233–61.

Wu Guachen. 1933. *Zhongguo shangye xiguan daquan* (A compendium on Chinese commercial customs). Shanghai: Shijie shujia.

Xu Yuzhu. 1992. *Zhonghua minguo zhengzhi zhidu shi* (A history of the Chinese Republican political system). Shanghai: Renmin chubanshe.

Yang Honglie. 1930. *Zhongguo falu fada shi* (A history of Chinese law). Shanghai: Shangwu yinshu guan.

Yao Songling. 1967. "Zhonghang fuwu ji" (A record of service in the Bank of China). In *Zhuangji wenxue* (Biography and literature) 1, no. 6 (December).

Yan E'sheng. 1933, 1936. *Shanghai shangshi guanli* (Customary business practice in Shanghai). Shanghai: Xinsheng tongxing she chubanbu.

Zhong Xiangcai. 1992. *Zhongguo jindai minzu qiyejia jingji sixiang shi* (A history of the economic thought of modern Chinese industrialists). Shanghai: Shanghai shehui kexue yuan chubanshe.

Zhongguo jingji quanshu (An encyclopedia of Chinese Economics). 1908. Vol. 2. Tokyo: Lianghu zong jiandu canban.

Zhongguo yinhang zong guanli chu (Bank of China, Head Office), comp. 1971. *Zhongguo yinhang zhangze huibian* (Collected rules and regulations of the Bank of China).

Glossary

baodan	保單
baojia	保甲
baojian	保荐
baoren	保人
baozheng	保證
baozheng jin	保證金
baozheng ren	保證人
chenghuan baoren	承還保人
chuaijiang	踹匠
daibao daihuan	代保代還
dianbao	店保
geren zhi xinyong	個人之信用
hang	行
jia	家
jieshao	介紹
jieshao ren	介紹人
lianxi sheng	練習生
lixu qinyou dai wei zuobao	例須親友代爲作保
putong baoren	普通保人
qianzhuang	錢莊
qiju bao	契據保
renbao	人保
renyin liangbao	人銀兩保
sheli	設理
tebie baoren	特別保人
xinyong	信用
xinyong jie kuan	信用借款
xuetu	學徒
yahang	牙行
yinhang	銀行

Rethinking the Anthropology of China

NORMA DIAMOND
The University of Michigan

Over the past few decades there have been considerable shifts and changes in the way that Western social scientists have framed their interpretations of Chinese social organization, institutions, and cultural beliefs and practices. When I began graduate work at Cornell in the mid-1950s, anthropology had already begun to turn away from its long-time fascination with "primitive societies" toward a consideration of complex, stratified nation-states or segments thereof in what was referred to, for lack of better terminology, as "the Third World." In part, this resulted from the realization that the original objects of our affections were not true Edens untouched by civilization and its discontents. They were more like islands of survivors, long besieged by waves of intruders coming as traders, missionaries, soldiers, colonial officers, geological surveyors, settlers, beachcombers, tourists, and of course anthropologists. But perhaps the main reason for the change in focus was the awareness of the political significance of the emergent or struggling nations of the Indian subcontinent, Southeast Asia, Africa, and Latin and Central America. Foundation and government funding was suddenly available for any reasonably capable graduate student interested in studying an exotic language and willing to spend research time in places where these languages were actually spoken by the masses and written by the elites.

My interest in China was sparked in high school as news about the civil war in China filled the press. The interest further developed in my undergraduate days at the University of Wisconsin through courses on the cultures of East Asia, Chinese literature (in translation, at that stage), and particularly a course on social movements with sociologist Hans Gerth, who encouraged me to pursue a budding interest in something called the "May Fourth Movement." With acceptance into the graduate program in anthropology at Cornell, which offered me a scholarship and the added inducement of an intensive summer program in Chinese at Yale, I formally began my long march toward becoming a China scholar.

Anthropological inquiry on China had, by that time, moved beyond the old sinology, and was dominated by a British social-structural approach, to which had been added a Redfieldian concern with the relationship between the Great Tradition and the little traditions. For many, this still meant a focus on elites and elite-models for social organization and behavior. Beguiled by Confucian thought, the older generation of China anthropologists tended to describe pre-1949 China as a uniform, well-integrated, and stable society that allowed for upward mobility for the truly talented via an examination system that rewarded merit and ability. Similarly, hard work and frugality led to wealth. In this ideal world, social life was organized through complex lineages and adherence to the moral obligations attached to kinship. Families of all classes strove to meet the ideal of "five generations under one roof." Children were unquestioningly filial. Landlords were, for the most part, kindly patriarchs guided by Confucian ethics, linked to their tenants by ties of sentiment and obligation, who served as mediators of local conflicts and as role models.

The accepted model was elegant and static. It omitted or skimmed lightly over discussion of class, gender, ethnic variations, regional cultures, and social change. It shed no light on the roots of the recent revolution (or earlier popular uprisings) and had little to say about social change in the twentieth century. It could not even explain the genesis of the May Fourth Movement. What was being written in China itself was unavailable even in the wonderful Wason Collections at Cornell. It seemed to me and a few of my contemporaries that many questions remained unanswered and many avenues of research had not been seriously addressed.

The conservative and idealized approach was even more appealing to our academic counterparts in Taiwan. During my first fieldwork in Taiwan in 1959 I met small encouragement from the Taiwan academic establishment. They saw little point in doing fieldwork on Taiwanese society and culture, which they assumed was identical to an idealized construction of "traditional China." Their own interests were engaged with recording the dying customs and lifestyles of Taiwan's aboriginal populations. Anything one needed to know about the non-elites of China was already written, they told me, meaning that one should read the Confucian classics and the local gazetteers. My arrival in Taiwan had been preceded by that of anthropologists Bernard and Rita Gallin, and by Arthur and Margery Wolf, but the other American scholars doing research in Taiwan were mainly interested in pre-1949 Chinese history, literature, and philosophy, and they too thought of anthropology as a marginal field that dealt with exotica. There was little peer group support for what I was doing. Luckily my sponsoring unit was the Joint Commission on Rural Reconstruction, where people thought fieldwork might actually lead to better planning for economic development.

My fieldwork year was spent in a village setting that was unquestionably Han Chinese, but which had not produced scholars, officials, and wealthy landlords. I settled near Tainan in a fishing village, one of a long string of similar communities dotted along the western coast. It was a poor village, like many others in Taiwan or on the mainland of China, lacking formal corporate lineages (let alone segmented lineages) such as those described for the New Territories or the Pearl River Delta. It also lacked five-generation households, eminent male ancestors, and silent secluded women. Some of my mentors back home were unhappy with how little of the Great Tradition I found expressed through practice by ordinary, poor people and how pervasive were the local little traditions. One suggested that it was because I was a woman that I had not been apprised of the location of lineage halls, or invited to observe the complex lineage rituals and examine the lineage books. Fortunately, the swelling stream of scholars doing fieldwork elsewhere in Taiwan had similar problems locating the elite-model on the ground and like myself turned their attention to examination of what was of importance to people's lives: the territorial community, affinal kin ties, and friendship networks as well as ties of descent, local religious cults that united communities and forged links to other settlements, and variant marriage forms such as adopted daughters-in-law or love matches. And they wrote about women's lives, life in industrial and urban centers, the subcultures of class and occupational groups, and other issues that emerged in the course of their research.

One of the problems that hindered "understanding China" was that until 1979 the mainland remained closed to American scholars. For a long time Taiwan was the only China available, and it was understood that we ought not to offend the sensibilities of our hosts in future publications lest we cut off research access for ourselves and others. Alas, how easily the Taiwan gatekeepers of those times could be displeased. Those of us whose work reflected new approaches and developing theories in cultural ecology, the anthropology of religion, political economy, and gender studies made enemies without even realizing it. Issues of ethnicity or local culture were very sensitive: one was not supposed to suggest that Taiwanese local life varied from the ideal model, to refer to Taiwanese as a language, or to argue that the people who spoke it had any legitimate basis for seeing themselves as different from the Mainlanders who had joined them after 1948.

However, these above-mentioned approaches engaged successive waves of scholars, and research in Taiwan led to serious revisions of the ideal model of how Chinese society operated in the past and continues to operate in the present. The full restoration of diplomatic and trade relations with the People's Republic of China brought along with it opportunities for research in China itself, guided in great part by what we were able to learn in Taiwan. Relatively few anthropologists and sociologists are now researching Taiwan itself: increasing numbers are engaged in firsthand contact with the People's Republic, from Shandong to Xinjiang and from Inner Mongolia to Shenzhen. There is growing interest in the diversity of local cultures within the political boundaries of

China, both among the Han and the national minorities. Recent concerns within anthropology regarding issues such as personhood, agency, power relations, and cultural reinvention are reflected in the newer anthropology of China. Access to archival resources and to survey research materials collected in the 1950s is broadening and deepening our understanding, as well as revising and sharpening our view of pre-revolutionary China. Even those who remain fascinated by lineage organization in the New Territories and Guangzhou hinterland are now concerned with ethnic variations, class, the territorial community, and reinterpretation of earlier writings on the topic.

The following three essays are based on research done in China and are concerned in different ways with the issues of cultural diversity, class, social change, and the interactions of culture and economics. Two of the essays are by anthropologists (Hill Gates and Ann Anagnost) and one by a political scientist whose work reflects her interest in anthropology (Elizabeth Perry).

Hill Gates focuses on the question of footbinding , not as exotica or an expression of blind adherence to the model set by the gentry class but as a flexible practice reflecting available workroles for women at the local level and economic decisions made within families, before and after a woman's marriage. Her data come from extensive survey interviews with older women in rural and urban Sichuan and Fujian. Among other things they make clear that women's labor contributions to the household economy and regional commodity production have been underestimated, even by the socialist government of China in its usual presentation of the productive contributions of women prior to socialist reorganization of the workplace.

As Gates convincingly demonstrates, footbinding took many forms. Though a marker of respectability and higher social status, it was impractical for many households. Many met the problem by late binding and early unbinding so as not to lose the income that women's labor could provide. Only in areas where there was an increasingly commercialized market for yarns and textiles produced within the household was the gentry model of severe and permanent footbinding compatible with women's labor. When these commodities and the workforce that would produce them shifted to factories, the practice of footbinding rapidly disappeared. But elsewhere, spinning and weaving were a lesser part of "women's work." The labor of girls and women was often needed for a variety of tasks related to agriculture, livestock maintenance, processing of foodstuffs, and obtaining such needs of daily life as water, firewood, grass for the pigs. These tasks were rendered almost impossible by severe footbinding. Gates's Sichuan data suggest that a third or more of the older women had never undergone any kind of footbinding, and most of the others unbound their feet after marriage. Her discussion is tied to an analysis of the household mode of production and to political and economic changes within the larger society.

Yet, as Gates also argues, footbinding could in some cases be viewed as a protection for one's daughters against the increasing work demands of the petty capitalist mode of production that intensified from Ming times on. It could protect them also against being deployed into unpleasant heavy labor. It might enhance their chances for an upwardly mobile marriage, though conversely it might only open the doors to concubinage or sale as prostitutes. What Gates accomplishes here is a deconstruction of the term "footbinding" into its various meanings and practice. She presents a view of the common people as rational decision makers rather than blind adherents to tradition.

Ann Anagnost's contribution also deals with multiple and interrelated issues, one of which is the changing understanding that the educated elites of China have about the kind of childhood socialization now necessary for future survival and success. She provides as an example the variety of activities that a preschool child of a certain class may be exposed to in order to assure entry into the best schools and to uncover whatever talents the child may have. Emergent (or perhaps reemergent) here is the idea of the child as an individual whose potential must be given full play rather than as an extension of self who continues along traditional lines set by family needs. The ideas of self and personal identity are important again, after several collective decades in which the ideal person was immersed in the collective and individual expression was highly suspect. Since 1979 China's nation-building has shifted from the egalitarian ideals of the socialist, all-encompassing paternalistic State to an acceptance of a visible hierarchy of wealth and power in which educated talent may possibly enter the elite strata.

As Anagnost explores the issue, she brings out its links to the one-child family policy and the recent campaigns for improving the "quality" of the population and building a more spiritual civilization as part of the process of modernization. Little Dandan is much more than simply an overindulged child of overly optimistic parents who hope to uncover a tiny genius in their midst. She is also an indicator of the new class lines that are being drawn, and her regimen of improvement reflects a wider concern with demonstrating the superiority of Chinese culture and the socialist society. The production and enhancement of superior children is part of the current nationalist agenda, though at first glance this seems improbable given the decline of the schools system in the rural areas and the absence of formal schooling for the hundreds of thousands of children whose parents have joined the floating population seeking work in the towns and cities. It resonates also with the revived interest in eugenics and current writings that link poverty and underdevelopment in some areas with hereditary inferiority. Dandan stands in contrast to the still backward masses, a model for an imagined nation of the future.

Elizabeth Perry's essay on the Cultural Revolution gives us a picture of the events from the bottom up, concentrating on the working class and their interpretation of goals and events during that turbulent era. In contrast to the picture of the Cultural Revolution as a movement powered by mindless factionalism or the ultra-leftist excesses of the Gang of Four, Perry brings us into the minds of some ordinary citizens who thought this was their opportunity to resolve workplace injustices. Her article is a corrective to our own overemphasis on political rhetoric: there were, as she clearly demonstrates, legitimate economic grievances within the Shanghai workforce, particularly among those who were contract workers or temporary workers. Demands for job security, for the right to remain in the cities, and for a living wage drew many into the ranks of the organizations that emerged in Shanghai, and undoubtedly elsewhere. "Rebels" challenged the Party's authority. "Conservatives" defended the Party but looked for reform. And a third, large faction addressed the economic issues that directly affected their lives, in many instances locating the sources of injustice within the socialist system itself.

The interviews and life histories in Perry's essay bring the individuals into focus through examination of the origins, the life experiences, and the political engagements of those allied with different factions. They have their flaws and hidden agendas, but that is beside the point. What is more important here is the opportunity she gives us to hear the multiple discourses of the Chinese working class and to speculate on what they may demand in future.

These three essays address the subculture of class and individual choice or family agendas that are responses to changing economic and political situations.

Footbinding and Handspinning in Sichuan

HILL GATES

Stanford University

Imagine we are sitting in the foggy, bamboo-girt courtyard of a timber farmhouse in the Sichuan hills, two hundred kilometers southwest of Chengdu. With us are a cadre from the Sichuan Provincial Women's Federation, a local Women's Federation representative, and our 62-year-old hostess, a tiny woman born here in Minshan county. We ask her why her parents had bound her feet for only a few months. She replies:

> When I was four or five, Mother bound my feet so I wouldn't have to do outdoor work, which was very heavy in our area—carrying stones for pathways, carrying firewood to market, cutting pig food in the mountains. I cried a lot, but Mother said I would have a better marriage, so she was going to do it even if I cried. But one day, I walked with Mother to the market [it was about 5 km.—H.G.] and I cried all the way from the pain. When I came home, Father felt sorry for me. He said, "If we unbind you, you'll have to cut weeds for the pig." I said I didn't care, I would feed the pigs. I was really happy to have my feet let out of the bindings.

This answer, and the rest of her responses during the hour or so we talked, epitomizes the themes around which my data on footbinding group themselves. We hear about the harsh labor regime rural life might require of women. We hear family conflict: between the parents and their child, who is in real and constant pain; and between mother and father, who want the best for their child, but do not agree on how to define what is best. We hear the weighing of a trade-off extremely important to the parents of Chinese daughters: between giving girls a higher future status by binding their feet, and using natural-footed labor power to the fullest for the family's benefit.

Because of an unbalanced sex ratio, virtually all Sichuan women married, but not all men. Typically, women married into families with slightly more property than their natal families possessed: hypergamy was the norm. Although most brides thus married "up," the social distance they traveled generally was not great. Especially desirable brides, however, might leap from the hard life of a farm woman into luxury. Prosperous families wanted respectable, hard-working daughters-in-law, but they could afford to demand beauty as well. Footbinding constructed attractions that transcended a girl's natural endowment. Through footbinding, a plain daughter could be improved, and a pretty one made beautiful. Achieving a grand marriage for herself, she could also link her family to powerful relations. Footbinding was a gamble, a long shot, for there were more poor pretty girls than rich families to marry them. Yet it was a gamble open to anyone, and nearly cost-free. All her family lost was a girl's ability to do hard labor. The frequency of footbinding suggests that many parents were willing to forego that labor.

Such a conclusion appears to support the widely held notion Chinese women "watched the children and did the housework," living as economic dependents on their men. Based on the large body of evidence to be described below, that conclusion is wrong.

During the first half of this century, and doubtless for generations before that, one of the best ways for producer-class households to earn cash was the work of women and girls. Careful interviewing has convinced me that in many of China's densely populated agricultural regions, work that elites, and even rural women themselves describe as "agricultural" or "housework" was often the manufacture of labor-intensive goods both for home consumption and for sale. In large Sichuan and Fujian samples, men did most of the heavy outdoor labor that produced a family's food, and, in consequence, were seen as a household's main supports. Women's less strenuous work usually produced commodities that were marketed by their husbands and fathers. Women produced silk, cotton, ramie, hemp, and other textile products; tea, opium, and tobacco; meat and eggs; and extracted such exotic substances as white wax. Most, if not all, of these things vanished from women's hands through the prestidigitation of the market into debt repayment, hidden money hoards, or purchased products. Women's contributions to domestic economy were thus classically alienated: less visible, though perhaps just as essential, as the bowl of rice grown with menfolks' sweat.

In many parts of China, women's products, or earnings from the sale of their products, made the difference between family comfort and family privation. Adele Fielde, a sensitive, long-term observer of women in the Chaozhou area in the late nineteenth century, collected household budgets. She determined that the value of the family's home-spun, home-woven, and home-sewn clothing was roughly equivalent to the entire value of the household's agricultural means of production—not including land, but including draft animals and tools (Jamieson 1888: 114). One-half of the women in my 5,000 Sichuan sample regularly earned cash incomes in the years before their marriages. These cash-in-hand earnings were over and above the labor they contributed to their households as they worked in family fields, made cloth and clothing for family members, helped raise the family pig, and pursued the other unremunerated occupations of domestic life. By my best estimation two-thirds of Sichuan women, even as quite young girls, contributed enough by their own labor to provide their own food, clothing, and daily needs. Women who produced high-value commodities generated surpluses for family coffers.

The Sichuan Sample[1]

For untold generations footbinding was a sensitive indicator of gender, household, and economic dynamics. But empirical evidence for its existence, its variations, and its context is extremely limited. Through 1991 and 1992, in collaboration with the Sichuan Provincial Women's Federation, I set up, tested, and supervised a survey of nearly 5,000 women of sixty-five and older. We interviewed in ten widely spaced counties, chosen to illustrate varied regional economic and ecological features. The first of our two survey questionnaires elicited unambiguous facts about each woman's background, footbound status, work done before and after marriage, and a few other matters. This was administered by local Women's Federation workers supervised by Provincial Women's Federation cadres with whom I had worked previously. From the 5,000, we selected 10 percent for a longer additional interview which inquired into the area's history of footbinding, documented the subject's circle of female kin, and investigated the local economic background; I interviewed 140 of these women myself. From these and other sources,[2] I am beginning to fill in a picture of footbinding practices, the economic role of women's work in the first four decades of this century, and how changes in that work affected—indeed, I hope eventually to argue, *caused*—the decline of footbinding.

Transparently, this research program aims to gather and interpret empirical data on a scale beyond the capacity (or probably the interest) of the people who lived with footbinding. I find what people of both genders and all classes have said about footbinding fascinating. These ideas, and the actions they rationalize, were a part of the process of history. But they were a small part. On the issue of whether to bind or not to bind a girl's feet, Chinese families responded to forces driven by powerful, distant people whose very existence was largely unknown to my subjects. Social analysts must be optimistically alert to the possibility and the power of resistance among the oppressed; they will be merely foolish,

---

1. The Sichuan and Fujian surveys were accomplished with funds from the Harry Frank Guggenheim Foundation's program on the causes and consequences of violence and aggression; other Fujian data were gathered with funding from the Luce Foundation; Taiwan household registry materials were collected with the help of Taiwan's National Science Council and Chiang Ching-kuo Foundation, and of Arthur Wolf. Thanks are due, too, to the reliable and cooperative members of the Sichuan Women's Federation; to the Xiamen City Women's Federation; to Dr. Zheng Ling, formerly of Xiamen University, to Professor Shih Yi-long, of Xiamen University, and to China and Taiwan associates too numerous to list here.

2. During the same period, with the Xiamen City Women's Federation, I did a parallel survey of 770 Fujian women, interviewing 60 key informants with the help of several Women's Federation cadres. In addition, I shared in the information collected through a project funded by the Luce Foundation and headed by Arthur Wolf. This provided basic information on footbinding for about 10,000 Fujianese women.

however, if they assume that a little Chinese girl stood on an equal playing field with Jardine, Matheson and Company.

My goal in undertaking this work was twofold. First, I wanted to explore a custom which was both a key element in Chinese women's lives and a strongly distinguishing feature of Han culture. And second, I wanted to test some arguments which I have developed elsewhere (Gates 1989, 1995) about the nature of the Chinese kinship/gender system, and the role it played in later imperial political economy.

A Cultureless Custom

Part of my goal in this research was to add to the bare facts of footbinding. One of the most energetically pursued tasks in contemporary anthropology is the assembly and analysis of information about the way the world appears to women, the strategies they use to gain their gendered ends, and the influence their actions have on society. Footbinding, I thought, would have generated intense women's traditions.

We know something of the complex of sexual/erotic ideas surrounding the bound foot from the writings of many literate Chinese men: Feng Jicai's 1986 novel *Sancun Jinlian*, translated by David Wakefield as *The Three-Inch Golden Lotus* (1994), elaborates these as a pornography of mingled sexuality and dissent. Howard Levy (1967) wrote a resolutely masculinist study summarizing past literary explorations of the topic. Chinese erotic pictures offer insight as well (e.g., Van Gulik 1951). A great many ideals, ideas, values, images, metaphors, and other "cultural" matters accompanied the physicality of footbinding for elite men. China scholars recently have shown much interest in what these men wrote: Dorothy Ko organized a symposium on the topic at the 1994 Association for Asian Studies meetings. The postmodern focus on the body (e.g., Elvin 1989; Zito and Barlow, eds. 1994) has drawn new attention to the literature of a custom now long in desuetude.

However, when I began to talk to women—ordinary, rural and urban women—about the culture of footbinding, I listened in vain for traces of the invaginated discourse of a Li Yu or a Foucault. Footbinding, which girls and their mothers had endured for centuries, was extraordinarily unelaborated.

"Did your mother do anything special on the day that she bound your feet?" we asked.

"No."

"Did she choose a good day, or burn incense and pray to ask for success, or make special food, or put medicine on your feet?"

"No."

"Where did she bind your feet, and who was there?"

"In the house, no one was around. It wasn't anything special."

"Were there any customs [*fengsu*]?"

"No."

The local Sichuan Women's Federation women suggested that we ask, "Were there any *guiding* [rules and regulations]?" So we asked that, and the answer to that, too, was "No."

The problem was not poor interviewing or lack of responsiveness. From our informants, we collected *ku jia ge*—bridal laments. Some of these, in Sichuan, are clever and counterhegemonic, leaning on wittily ambiguous criticism of the stinginess of the bride's agnates over dowry. We also got spinning songs, tea-picking songs (though not the naughty parts), but never a song about footbinding. "Who would sing about that?" a woman retorted.

"Did differences in style of shoe show differences between women?" we asked. "Could you tell if a woman was married or unmarried, or where she was from by her shoes?"

"No. Brides wore red shoes when they married. Otherwise, you just made shoes however you wanted to."

"If a woman came from a distant village, would she bring different styles of shoe?"

"No. Everybody's shoes were different, because everybody's feet were different."

By contrast with all this negativity, when we asked about marriage customs, or birth customs, or how people worshipped "in the old society," we got the usual range of unresponsiveness and voluble answers: some people like to talk about these things and some do not. But everyone knew *something*. We even got information about indigenous methods of contraception and abortion. ("But none of them worked!" they told me.) So the problem in asking about footbinding customs was not lack of rapport or embarrassment about questions that might slip into erogenous zones. In one Sichuan county jolly grandpas told Arthur Wolf that men did not want to sleep with natural-footed women "Because it would be like sleeping in your grave"—that is, the woman's big feet would loom up like tombstones above the recumbent couple. Nor do I think the absence of cultural elaboration was due to ignorance on the part of little girls of what their mothers had been doing. Some of our informants were old enough to have bound their own daughters' feet.

In a few villages in Lezhi County, Sichuan, three women told us that before binding, their feet were washed in water from the paddy field "so it wouldn't hurt so much;" two were first bound in the cowshed, "so my feet would be small like a cow's feet;" and two said that their fathers had done the first binding. These were the only "customs" I have found so far in this wideranging survey. Even in the same part of Lezhi county, many women had never heard of these ideas, and thought they were inappropriate, meaningless. The usual elaboration of symbolism that is so richly present at other Chinese life ceremonies, and which has often proved so resistant to erosion, was simply not there. The pain of footbinding was not cushioned in a comforting cocoon of myth, rationalization, and magical assistance. "Mother just sat me down one day when I was seven, washed my feet, wrapped them as tight as she could, and made me stand on them. That was all."

What I heard instead was the constant repetition of two anxious phrases in answer to my questions about why a woman's family had bound her feet. Over and over, women said to me: *"bu bao jiao, jiabuchuqu;"* and *"bao jiao dang xinniang; bu bao jiao, jiu dang binu."* That is: an unbound girl would be unmarriageable; footbound girls become brides while the unbound become bondservants. These statements, stereotyped as they were, were clearly important, but they were also uninformative if taken literally. Footbound or not, only 2 of 5,000 Sichuan women had never married (this because of physical defects). I must therefore explore this custom with much less help from my informants' own often sharp perceptions than is usually the case with the anthropologist's task.

Footbinding proved to be a cultureless custom in another sense as well. It is widely believed by the educated that antifootbinding political and social movements were responsible for the abolition of footbinding (Pao Tao 1992). Indeed, such movements affected elite and urban people directly and rapidly. But their reach into the countryside was slight—unsurprisingly, in view of the fact that fewer than one out of ten of these women had received any education whatsoever. Only a handful of the rural, and even the urban working-class, women I have interviewed had ever heard any direct antifootbinding information, teaching, or propaganda—even in Chengdu and the "westernized" Xiamen. Nor, to their knowledge, had the members of their families. Traveling villagers, usually men, sometimes returned from an urban sojourn with the news that footbinding was no longer "necessary" or "required" by authorities, though not that it was forbidden. The implementation of that idea, however, depended on other factors.

The abandonment of footbinding in an area, once begun, was often quite rapid, and clearly had a political significance which I will not discuss here. But in the continental areas I have researched, authorities transmitted no anti-footbinding imperative to commoners. As I will argue below, footbinding disappeared for much more material reasons; we hardly need invoke explicit, self-conscious "culture" at all in understanding either its practice or its abandonment.

Variations in Footbinding

Why did Chinese mothers maintain this brutal custom over so many generations? Footbinding has been explained in a number of ways: sado-masochistic erotic appeal based on exaggerated gendering for strength/weakness oppositions; management of ethnic distinctions; historical origin among the elite, spread by social emulation; the maintenance of gender hierarchy;

maintenance of social hierarchy generally, especially parental authority; varying need for agricultural labor. The issue of labor, recently raised by Fred Blake (1993), has never been empirically studied.

What place did footbinding have in Chinese culture and economy? Our sample revealed regional variation in intensity of the practice. This took two principal forms: differing proportions of women who were ever footbound, and differing duration of footbinding as fractions of women's lives.

The mass of anecdotal evidence drawn from written sources suggests considerable regional differences in the proportion of footbound women throughout China. In the late nineteenth century footbinding was near universal on many parts of the North China Plain and in north Taiwan; observers believed it to be highly class-dependent in the Guangdong region and the Jiangnan; accounts for Yunnan and the far northwest show it varying, with some precision, as a Han/non-Han boundary marker; for many areas we simply have no idea how many girls were bound and under what circumstances.

In our Sichuan survey—see Table 1—the percentage of boundfootedness (women whose feet had *ever* been bound) ranged from 43.2 percent (in remote, hilly Min Shan) to 82.8 (in equally remote Lezhi), and 82.5 percent in Longquan, a suburb of Chengdu, with an average of 66.4 percent for all women.

Table 1. Sichuan Sample:
Ever Bound and Permanently Bound Women by Site

Site	N	Number Ever Bound	Percent Ever Bound	Number Permanently Bound	Percent Permanently Bound
Total	4987	3309	66.4	747	15.0
Longquan	500	411	82.5	134	26.8
Minshan	491	212	43.2	34	7.0
Zigong	500	303	60.6	70	14.0
Suining	499	343	68.7	149	30.0
Nancheng	500	306	61.2	89	17.8
Neijiang	499	282	56.5	18	3.6
Ba	500	307	61.4	85	17.0
Dazhu	500	350	70.0	81	16.2
Emei Shan	500	381	76.2	19	3.8
Lezhi	500	414	82.8	68	13.6

In some parts of China, footbinding as a marker of Han identity is a powerful predictor of some of this variation. Han (though not Hakka) women tended to be footbound in high ratios in regions where Han and non-Han coexisted. As Norma Diamond has shown in a brilliant paper (1988), those boundaries were fraught with life-threatening tension even when they were not literally zones of war. North Taiwan at the turn of the century was just such a Han-Aborigine frontier; Hokkien women there were bound at the rate of 95 percent. In our Sichuan Emei Shan sites 76.2 percent of girls were footbound, though only 3.8

percent persisted in footbinding throughout life. This pattern reflects ethnic tensions between immigrant and indigenous people that were highly salient up to the age of marriage. Further complexities would surely be observed in populations including the ambiguous Han but nonfootbound Hakka people; our 5,000 sample, however, contained virtually no Hakka, who are not common in Sichuan.

Closely associated with footbinding as a Han identity marker is its use after the Taiping rebellion to demonstrate that a family had not allied itself with the natural-foot-favoring rebels; bound feet signed political loyalty, a key element of normative Han-ness. Similarly, but on a much smaller scale, the rebellious ancestors of a community near the Western Hills had been punished by being officially forbidden to bind feet. After the fall of the dynasty in 1911, they re-implemented the practice (Morrison 1987: 75–7, 90). I will examine the political symbolism of footbinding in another publication.

Knowing that a woman had once had her feet bound elides many issues and adds to the difficulty of establishing tidy correlations of footbinding with types of work common for girls in different regions. Average age at binding, tendency to unbind, and average age at unbinding all differ regionally. Sichuan girls, for example, were bound at an average of six years of age, while the average Fujian girl in our 770 sample was not bound until she was almost twelve. The number of women who, once bound, never *un*bound their feet looks very different in our Sichuan subsamples. These range from 30 percent in Suining to 3.6 percent in Neijiang, with a Sichuan average of 15.0 percent. While in some regions, once bound, women remained bound throughout life, in others, virtually all married women unbound shortly after marriage. Controlling for age, family property-ownership, and education in regional footbinding patterns, and establishing differential duration-of-footbinding "exposure" norms are important aspects of this on-going analysis.

Families, Labor, and Modes of Production

Recent analysis has focused on the significance of a major form of women's work in protoindustrial China, the making of textiles. In the late empire, cloth rivaled grain in importance. The work of Wu Chengming and others, summarized by Philip Huang, reveals that "the exchange of cotton cloth for grain accounted for two-thirds (69.9 percent) of the total volume of trade on the eve of the Opium War" (Huang 1990: 90). Unlike luxury goods such as tea, opium, white wax, and fine handicrafts, textiles were an item of mass consumption as necessary to life as food. Textiles were made in many parts of China, following the well-known peasant strategy of self-sufficiency, often from fibers the family grew or gathered. Where cotton and silk did poorly, other fibers, such as hemp, ramie, "wild" silk, wool, and less well-known materials substituted in part or in whole. Yet some areas lacked appropriate fibers or had more rewarding work (such as tea- or opium-picking) for girls to do; even the poor in such regions bought their textiles on China's centuries' old market for such products.

Huang stresses the role that family production has continuously played from the Ming until the present, with only brief interruption between the later 1950s and the late 1970s. He insists—and I believe quite correctly—that during the Ming and Qing, commercialization in China grew ever more elaborated without leading in the direction of capitalism. Rather, he says, it brought growth without development—"involution" in the sense in which Clifford Geertz (1963) applied it to Indonesian agriculture. In this, of course, Huang is restating, in a highly focused way, a position first enunciated by Mark Elvin, who described the involutional relationship of commerce, labor intensification, and population growth as a "high-level equilibrium trap" (1972). Huang also agrees with Chao Kang, whose appositely named *Man and Land in Chinese History: An Economic Analysis* (1987) makes very much the same points: an increasing population forced more intensive use of land; handicrafts grew up as ways to earn extra income; families needed all the labor they could produce for peak agricultural use and for handicraft production; families were the indigenous "firms" or production units of the economic system; and, because the workers were kinfolk, not hired laborers, large numbers of sometimes unnecessary workers had to be supported even when it was not rational in capitalist terms to maintain them.

Both Huang and Chao argue for the kinship corporation—the *jia*—as *the* characteristic Chinese production unit, and for the cumulative significance of the small-scale exchanges that enmeshed these many households in a highly commercialized—but *not* capitalist—political economy.

Huang, however, makes a further point of extreme importance. He shows that during the Ming and Qing in the Yangzi delta, a time and place of early and expansive commercialization, handicraft cotton and silk production brought heavier and heavier workloads for women and children. Huang says:

What happened was an increasing switch to more labor-intensive commercial crops, especially cotton and mulberries (for silk). We have not in the past understood properly the nature of this switch. I will show that those cash crops were produced by a greater use of labor for higher total values of output per unit land, but lower average returns per labor day. The growth of commercialized "sideline" household handicrafts based on those commercial crops was a part of this process. The sideline activities generally brought lower returns per workday than "mainline" farming. They were pursued to some extent by adult males in their spare time, but to a far greater extent by women, children, and the elderly for whose labor there was little or no market outlet (p. 14).

Even under early industrialization, low-paying work came to be absorbed by household auxiliary labor, especially of women. That economic involution, in turn, acted as a counterincentive to labor-saving capitalization (p. 129).

Huang, then, would agree with what I have argued elsewhere (Gates 1989), that historical shifts to family-based commodity production, especially of textiles, brought marked changes to women's lives—and to those of children as well. Indeed, he makes a major point of this expanded use of female labor. Curiously, however, he fails to absorb some of the implications of his own research. In a footnote on what Alexandr Chayanov may or may not have meant by "self-exploitation" in such peasant households, Huang declares that a family cannot exploit itself in the technical Marxist sense of extracting surplus value from labor. "It simply makes no sense . . . to speak of a family extracting the surplus value of its own labor" (Huang 1990: 6 fn.) This approach is based on the same assumptions which move him to observe repeatedly that Chinese family production differs from capitalist production in an important way. "[F]amily farms were often burdened with surplus labor that they could not 'fire'" (70). This idea has been a central tenet in the analysis of Chinese economies at least since Max Weber; it remains the principal obstacle to a clear view of Chinese political economies.

Feminist scholars see the kind of petty commodity producer households Huang describes rather differently. About contemporary French wine-growing households, Winnie Lem writes:

> The male household head's control over [family] labor is mediated through a variety of ideological devices, especially those associated with the sanctity of the family. But, this control over labor gains real force through the head's control over property. Men also tend to control the products of labor: the income generated . . . is paid to the male head of the household who ultimately controls its distribution. . . . The dependent status of other members of the domestic unit underlines the authority of the male head, who may withdraw, apportion and appropriate goods, services, and labor.
>
> In these respects, it becomes possible to speak of a "class-like" relationship prevailing in the domestic domain. Property and labor are not united in the "peasant enterprise" as is so often asserted but rather are separated by gender and generation. ... This means the intensification of female labor in subsistence plots, clothes-making, animal rearing, and processing farm and animal products. Thus the domestic arena in [petty commodity production] is an assemblage of contradictions which act as the context for the mobilization of labor. The site of cooperation and shared consumption is also the site of domination, exploitation and conflict over the control and allocation of resources, including labor (1991: 110–11).

Parallel observations have been made recently about Taiwan and Shandong household production (Greenhalgh 1994; Judd 1994). Women and girls were not only controlled by male household heads, but received less from the common pool of resources than males. Norms of filiality, backed by the imperial state, stretched this control to its extreme.

Kinship, feminist analysts point out, perhaps the principal social mechanism for the reproduction of the gendered division of labor, is necessarily productive of contradiction, mystification, and ambiguity. Chinese households, like all others, are arenas for the power struggles between women and men that create a hegemonic, patriarchal "harmony." A key goal in these struggles is control of labor and earnings.

In China not only women's labor, but their persons, were at the disposal of kin seniors; females and junior males were not as secure in their household membership as Huang and Chao have assumed them to be. Although they could not be "fired" exactly, they could be disposed of through infanticide, out-adoption, selling into local forms of bondage (known as *muijai* in Cantonese, *cabo kana* in Minnanhua, or *yatou* in Mandarin), and infant ("minor") marriage (Wolf and Huang 1980; Gronewold 1985; Jaschok 1988; Jaschok and Miers 1994). The possibility of divorce threatened even legitimate wives and mothers of children. By the twenty-fifth year of marriage, Arthur Wolf has discovered, the cumulative probability of childless north Taiwan women being legally divorced was 0.230 for those in major marriages, and .557 for those in minor marriages. If they bore two children, their probability of divorce fell to 0.074 and 0.185 respectively—between 7 and 19 percent of all marriages (Wolf 1995: 156–57). The practice of family heads disposing of unnecessary females is known to have been especially common in highly commercialized areas like turn-of-the-century Taiwan and Guangzhou and may well have been common in the protoindustrial Yangzi delta as well.

While Chinese kinship behavior is organized around powerful consistencies, most of these involve men, their agnatic relations to each other, and their relations with their common property (A. Wolf 1985). Kinship behavior that involves women is much more likely to vary from place to place and from time to time. This, I argue, is largely a function of regional differences in demand for women both as workers and as wives.

Secular Trends in Footbinding: A Historical Scenario

Let me present a historical scenario in two parts: first, footbinding spreads along with petty capitalist commercialization; then it is abandoned as China encounters capitalist-industrialism. The first of these shifts happens as a largely subsistence economy experiences market expansion. Such transitions are frequent in Chinese history, as regional pressures to commoditize rise and fall. This is a "natural" economy, firmly controlled by a state-centered ("tributary" [E. Wolf 1982]) mode of production that extracts and circulates goods on non-market principles.

Boys and men grow crops, girls spin, and women—probably—weave.[3] In small, local markets, households sell an extra piglet now and then or a few

---

3. Weaving was sometimes done by men. This was particularly true for high-quality fabrics made on elaborate looms—the kinds that are most likely to be documented in

baskets of eggs or vegetables to pay for things they must buy; they exchange some of their grain to pay for rent and taxes, and they eat the rest. People do not produce principally for sale. As in all classic agrarian states, markets do not alter the fundamental self-subsistence of the region. Nor do they have they have the dynamism to undermine the hierarchical political-economic processes of the dominant mode.

Let us also imagine that footbinding has been established here for a very long time as an elite custom both expressing and reproducing hierarchy. It has spread through China's tiny ruling class as official families move about in response to governmental duties, but it penetrates only slowly, if at all, into the lives of commoners. Elite families bind feet to emphasize their high social standing, to discourage girls from going about independently, and to teach them obedience. Bound feet do not hinder girls and women from the spinning and weaving which are their primary jobs in such households, where servants do the heavy work. Girls from more ordinary families—the great majority—are not bound, as bound feet would make it difficult for them to grind grain, walk on wet ground, or carry loads of water, firewood, grass, and harvested crops.

Let us imagine further that we can observe an important historical shift toward an intensified and increasingly commoditized economy. Local people, pressed by growing families and fragmented land plots, are drawn into the kind of protoindustrialization—petty capitalism—that Huang has described for the Jiangnan.

Formerly, if everyone was warmly dressed, and there was adequate bedding, a woman might rest from weaving for a while and stop her daughters' spinning. Now, not to spin in every spare moment is to waste the possibility of taking two or three *liang* of yarn to market every few days. The spinning of cotton and the twisting of hemp or ramie forms a critical bottleneck in making cloth: between six and forty spinners are needed to keep up with one handweaver, depending on the fineness of the thread. Spinning is an easily learned, tedious task that requires little strength but much discipline. The work sops up much labor for small reward. It is deadly dull. It is the ideal job for those at the bottom of the hierarchy. It is girls' work.

A girl's former duties remain, of course: she collects pig food and cooks it over fuel she has gathered from hillsides; she husks and grinds grain; she carries water and babies; she makes clothes and shoes; she tends the old; she washes and cooks. When agricultural demands are heavy, she ignores the cultural ideal that women stay indoors and plants, weeds, and harvests.

The better the market for her salable products, the harder she must work to sustain the double burden of income-earning and subsistence household duties.

---

written records. My Sichuan interviews track weaving of everyday cloth by women back to the late 1800s—as far as human memory can take us; I suspect it has always been the work of married women, as it was in my sample. Handspinning, however, seems always to have been girls' work. I know of no evidence that suggests otherwise.

In that black-magic transformation that petty capitalism shares with capitalism, Time becomes Money—and a woman's work is never done.

What women and girls do is of calculable value. Making yarn or cloth for sale brings in a direct, tangible income. Women in Lezhi Xian sent two or three *liang* of yarn to every three-day market one hundred and more times each year—and knew exactly how much their work had earned. The daughter who spun, the wife who wove, commanded some respect for her labors. Women from cotton-producing areas, fourth or fifth daughters in a household where the women provided all the family's income, were proud of their work and worth. Several showed me particularly fine pieces of their own or their mothers' weaving which they had kept as family heirlooms.

The better the market for their product, the more women are likely to claim credit for what they contribute to the household. The more commodity production, the greater the possibility that women may get "out of control." The problem of preserving a daughter's virginity becomes intensified at the same time as the problem of keeping her working harder than ever grows more troublesome. Parents have a right to the income of all their kin subordinates and a duty to amass resources for their male heirs. It is only proper that a daughter should contribute to her natal household's wealth before marriage transfers her labor elsewhere. At the same time parents bear heavy legal and customary responsibilities for upright behavior in their households. Under market pressures daughters should work, but not at tasks that endanger their good name and marriageability. A crisis in relationships between the genders and the generations looms.

We see here the infiltration, through commodity production, of a complex of political-economic, kinship, and ideological relationships of petty capitalism. This involves not only, or even primarily, the productive techniques and equipment for making concrete commodities. It includes as well both patterns of social relations—relations of production which are also those of kinship—and customary practices and their ideological justifications. A mode of production is a total system through which surpluses are transferred from less powerful to more powerful people—categorized here as classes, generations, and genders. In China's petty capitalist mode, women faced both new opportunities and new threats in their household negotiations over resources—including their own labor. But they were not thereby relieved of the burdens imposed by the nonmarket, gender-specific transfers of the tributary mode of production. These, in the final analysis, were backed by the state in the persons of scholar-officials and kin elders.

As commodity production becomes more and more indigenized in a specific region, and people become more and more accustomed to market transactions, commoditization spreads from things to persons. It becomes easier to fire surplus family labor through direct selling, adoption, and the manipulation of marriage forms. Under such conditions new ways of dealing with daughters are likely to emerge or to spread. Footbinding creeps from elite to commoner classes, simultaneously solving both the persistent problem of maintaining maidenly chastity and the newly urgent one of keeping an important wage-earner busy at her task. Binding a daughter's feet will teach a young girl that she must submit to even extreme control by her parents, but at the same time it will not interfere with her spinning. We see here, then, a coincidence, not a contradiction, between the need to control a daughter's activities and the need for her labor.

If the bound feet become an impediment to something the family wants the girl to do—should she have to go out to work as a servant or porter, for example—her feet can be unbound. Binding is not an absolute commitment, at least for a few years. The girl herself is encouraged to bear her pain because it may help her make a more advantageous marriage; her bound feet will identify herself and her family as disciplined and thus eminently marriageable. When moneymaking light work is available for young women, there are many reasons to bind a daughter's feet and only a few not to.

One powerful and persistent obstacle to the spread of footbinding was the resistance of children to pain and their mothers to causing that pain. What outside observers often remarked, my informants emphatically insisted on: footbinding was a curse, a cruelty, that robbed little girls of their childhood through months and years of suffering. They showed me their scars to prove it. Why was such an extreme solution necessary to the problems of controlling daughters and having them work efficiently?

One possible answer—mother love—makes sense only in the context of a commercializing political economy. The combination of tributary parental power with the pressures of a voracious market put girls at risk of extreme exploitation. Under the ever-increasing squeeze that a commodity economy places on women—the "labor class" of the family—footbinding may have spread as a form of female resistance to women's increasing labor burden. Mothers, and sometimes little girls themselves, accepted footbinding as a protection from further exploitation of their labor and also from the direct commoditization of their persons. Sometimes even very young girls could see the logic of this argument: an 85-year-old woman from Lezhi Xian endured a great deal of pain during her footbinding, which began when she was five. She knew, however, that if she let out her feet, she would be sent as a hired girl to grind grain, so she put up with it. *"Tui mo shi women zhe'rli zui xingkude"* (Pushing a mill was the worst work around here), she commented. Other women spoke of the harsh labor demands of rice-growing, with its costs in heatstroke, back injuries, snakebite, and waterborne disease. Footbinding exempted women from such labor.

Where the pressures on women were especially great—during a commercial boom in the products they produced—footbinding offered a painful but acceptable defense against yet more painful possibilities: being sent to work at some of the backbreaking jobs so common in any preindustrial economy or being sold into some inferior form of sexual servitude. This, I think, is what women were saying when they insisted that if you could tolerate footbinding, you had the right to be a *xinniang*—a properly married woman—but if you were left unbound, you might become a *binu*—a concubine, bondservant, or prostitute.

I think—and this is the conclusion of my speculative scenario—that footbinding spread widely among China's common people principally where and when there was abundant, income-earning, light work for women—of which textile production is the most obvious example. From the time it became diffused among the elite, footbinding probably always tempted parents who wished to control their daughters strictly and to demonstrate their respectability to the world. But parents who needed their daughters to do work incompatible with footbinding—portering, finding pigfood, pushing mills—did not bind them. The family's immediate need for labor took precedence over their long-term hopes for her marital future. Commodity production of textiles, which boomed in the Song and expanded further in the late Ming and Qing, made it possible to exercise control without losing economic efficiency. When such work for girls was readily available, parents found that footbinding produced too many advantages to ignore. Mothers especially, who did almost all of the actual binding, chose immediate pain for their daughters in a desperate bid to save them from life-long misery of more complex kinds.

The Abandonment of Footbinding

Historical sources display little interest in either everyday production, or the lives of commoner women. It is unlikely that much information on these subjects will ever be found. In consequence, the scenario outlined above cannot be shown to be the only explanation for where and when footbinding was common. Our only real chance to support the explanation will come from the data such as those the Women's Federation and I have collected—and these catch the custom in decline.

From systematic information about abandonment, however, we can infer a great deal. As machine-made yarn spun by young women in Lancashire, Calcutta, or Shanghai insinuated itself into their lives, handspinners began to find their traditional occupation redundant. Families lost a source of cash income that had long been taken for granted in their budgets. Daughters were seen as increasingly worthless. A decline in footbinding follows closely the arrival of foreign yarn in a region, which we ascertain by asking women about fabrics in their dowries.[4] Sichuanese in textile-producing communities did not

---

4. The complex correlations that support this contention must be the subject of another paper.

use machine yarn or leave off binding until the mid-1930s, despite the much-vaunted efforts of indigenous and foreign antifootbinding activists in the late nineteenth century.

My Sichuan field notes are raucous with remembered family disputes as footbinding went into decline. Older informants, women of 70 and up, complained bitterly about their suffering, but said they were given no escape from its torture. Their kin seniors enforced footbinding with a combination of beatings and optimistic promises, supplemented sometimes with edible treats and especially pretty shoes. A soft-hearted, dilatory mother was usually overruled by a household head or tough-minded granny.

Younger women, however, report many disagreements from the years between the late 1920s and the late 1930s. Fathers usually took the position that a daughter need not be footbound, because "society had changed." Often they voiced a purely economic accusation: mothers bound their daughters, and daughters accepted the binding, in order to evade the hardest work. A Zhejiang migrant, too young for our survey at 61, but an interested participant in a group discussion, told us that she bound her own feet at age 10, with the agreement of her mother. Her father was strongly opposed because, he said, "You just want to have small feet so you don't have to work."

Mothers, by contrast, were likely to insist on binding long past the time when word was in the air that city girls were going natural. Women were acutely aware that mothers-in-law had special problems with new brides, and they saw filial obedience—which footbinding was thought to instill—as highly desirable. Once the new wife had been properly controlled, however, Sichuan mothers-in-law often demanded that their daughters-in-law unbind if the household had no light, indoor work for them. The economic significance of bound feet lay largely in the division of female labor between unmarried girls, who must work but must also stay close to home, and married women who, by and large, graduated at marriage to more demanding tasks.

Once capitalist industry began to supply its endless flows of yarn and cloth throughout China, most parental arguments over footbinding were settled in favor of unbound feet. When the conditions for the abandonment of footbinding had emerged clearly enough for all to see, fathers often responded directly to the issue of their daughters' labor contributions, while mothers manifested concern for their daughters' status and marriageability. But both were dealing with girls whose lives, like their feet, were to be shaped by the pressures of markets for both their persons and their labor, and by the presence in those markets of more or less cotton yarn.

In the twentieth century capitalist (and later socialist) industrialization both "modernized" and dispossessed little girls. Fossil-fuel industrialism threw onto the market a new abundance of labor power, superadded to that which had already been demographically accumulated by the patterns of the Chinese past. More than ever, only petty capitalism—commodity production by households—

offered Chinese families some sort of short-term hope. The economic history of this century must largely be glossed as attempts to transcend the limits of petty capitalism without abandoning the fixed tributary obligations that give households a degree of accumulative power. In that history even little girls are actors.

References

Chao Kang. 1987. *Man and Land in Chinese History An Economic Analysis.* Stanford: Stanford University Press.

Diamond, Norma. 1988. "The Miao and Poison: Interactions on China's Southwest Frontier." *Ethnology* 27, no. 1: 1–23.

Elvin, Mark. 1972. *The Pattern of the Chinese Past.* Stanford: Stanford University Press.

————. 1989. "Tales of *Shen* and *Xin*: Body-Person and Heart-Mind in China during the Last 150 Years." In *Fragments for a History of the Human Body*, Part Two, edited by Michael Feher, 236–49. New York: *Zone* [magazine].

Feng Jicai. 1994. *The Three-Inch Golden Lotus.* Honolulu: University of Hawaii Press.

Gates, Hill. 1989. "The Commoditization of Chinese Women." *Signs* 14, no. 4: 799–832.

————. 1995. *China's Motor: A Thousand Years of Petty Capitalism.* Ithaca: Cornell University Press.

Geertz, Clifford. 1963. *Agricultural Involution: The Processes of Ecological Change in Indonesia.* Berkeley: University of California Press.

Gronewold, Sue. 1985. *Beautiful Merchandise: Prostitution in China, 1860–1936.* New York: Harrington Park Press.

Huang, Philip C. C. 1990. *The Peasant Family and Rural Development in the Yangzi Delta, 1350–1988.* Stanford: Stanford University Press.

Jamieson, George. 1888. "Tenure of Land in China and the Condition of the Rural Population." *Journal of the China Branch of the Royal Asiatic Society*, n.s. vol. 23: 57–174.

Jaschok, Maria H. A. 1988. *Concubines and Bondservants: The Social History of a Chinese Custom.* London: Zed Books.

Jaschok, Maria, and Suzanne Miers, eds. 1994. *Women and Chinese Patriarchy.* London: Zed Books.

Judd, Ellen R. 1994. *Gender and Power in Rural North China.* Stanford: Stanford University Press.

Lem, Winnie. 1991. "Gender, Ideology and Petty Commodity Production: Social Reproduction in Languedoc, France." In *Marxist Approaches in Economic Anthropology*, edited by Alice Littlefield and Hill Gates, 103–18. Society for Economic Anthropology Monograph No. 9.

Levy, Howard. 1948. *Chinese Footbinding: The History of a Curious Erotic Custom*. New York: Bell Publishing.

Morrison, Hedda. 1987. *Travels of a Photographer in China, 1933–1946*. Oxford: Oxford University Press.

Pao Tao, Chia-lin. 1992. "The Anti-footbinding Movement in Late Ch'ing China: Indigenous Development or Western Influence?" Delivered at the 44th Annual Meeting of the Association for Asian Studies, Washington, D.C.

Van Gulik, R. H. 1951. *Erotic Colour Prints of the Ming Period*. Tokyo: n.p.

Wolf, Arthur P. 1985. "Chinese Family Size: A Myth Revitalized." In *The Chinese Family and Its Ritual Behavior*, edited by Hsieh Jih-chang and Chuang Ying-chang, 241–60. Nankang, Taiwan: Institute of Ethnology, Academia Sinica.

——. 1995. *Sexual Attraction and Childhood Association: A Chinese Brief for Edward Westermarck*. Stanford: Stanford University Press.

Wolf, Arthur P., and Huang Chieh-shan. 1980. *Marriage and Adoption in China, 1845–1945*. Stanford: Stanford University Press.

Wolf, Eric. 1982. *Europe and the Peoples without History*. Berkeley: University of California Press.

Zito, Angela, and Tani E. Barlow, eds. 1994. *Body, Subject and Power in China*. Chicago: University of Chicago Press.

Children and National Transcendence in China

ANN ANAGNOST
University of Washington

Early in our stay in Nanjing in 1991 my four-year-old daughter tearfully conveyed the news that her best friend had transferred to another preschool. As this little girl lived in a dormitory not far from our own, we went for a visit to discover why she had been moved. "Ta zuobuzhu" (meaning literally she was unable to sit still) was all her mother would say. I was surprised as I felt that the discipline in the classroom was already quite strict, although the teachers were patient and loving. But the child's mother had not been satisfied, expending considerable time and effort to secure a place for her daughter in what she considered to be a "superior" preschool.

Despite this setback I confidently told my daughter that she would be able to play with her friend after school. However, when I tried to arrange a visit, I was dismayed to discover that there seemed to be no time left in this child's busy schedule. She was awakened every morning at 5:30, marched by her father to the basketball court for an hour's exercise before breakfast, and then school, after which she was scheduled for an impressive array of extracurricular classes in music, dance, painting, and calligraphy. If my daughter wished to play with her, there was one half hour free before dinner every Friday afternoon. It became quickly apparent that the child's inability to "sit still" signified for her parents an intolerable degree of indiscipline that could only be redressed in this relentless regimentation of her schedule. In the next several weeks we visited back and forth, but after a while both my daughter and I had apparently decided, without a word being spoken, that we no longer wished to continue the relationship as other friends began to fill her social needs.

What had made our visits so painful was that we had both become aware of our new role as a passive audience to what had become the transubstantiation of this little girl from an ordinary child to child prodigy (*shentong*). Transubstantiation is a word that I use advisedly here to refer to the multiple dimensions of bodily and intellectual transformations that this regimentation of childhood promises to deliver, as if the very substance of the child were to be transformed into something other than its inherent form. As witnesses to this process, our role was to sit politely and watch the child sing, dance, practice her

195

196

Ann Anagnost

English, and present her artistic production for that week. No reciprocal performance was demanded of my daughter, and I began to get the uncomfortable feeling that a special dispensation had been made in the child's schedule to utilize us, not for play, as we had intended, but as a special resource to acquire an "international" experience, so necessary to the construction of imagined futures for children of an urbanized educated class. Indeed, as I later became more aware, her after-school activities were chosen not so much for enrichment, but as arenas widely recognized as appropriate for the development and display of superior intelligence in early childhood (see Champagne 1992).

Although this child may represent an extreme case, we saw signs of this performance pressure on almost all of the children we knew with any degree of familiarity, most of whom were children of intellectuals or bureaucrats. Moreover, the emphasis on child performance seemed to be echoed widely in the rapidly expanding consumer economy of the early 1990s, which began to offer an ever-expanding variety of goods and services devoted to the project of developing the bodily quality and the intellectual capacities of the very young. This attention to the child's body and its enhancement through the commodity form must be placed in the context of a more generalized culture of consumption that is focused on the body and its well being (Farquhar 1994). However, the child's body is enhanced not only by the input of new commodity forms into its developing "substance," but also with an increased attentiveness to the exhaustive use of time, resulting in a regimentation of childhood that seemed to challenge the very notion of childhood itself.

While this trend appears to echo the experience of childhood in other modern East Asian societies (notably Japan, Taiwan, Singapore, and Hong Kong), I feel cautious about labeling it as a pan-Asian phenomenon. Indeed I would argue that it is part of a transnational transformation of childhood in the rapidly changing conditions of late-twentieth-century capitalism. We see this played out when critics in the U.S. cast envious glances at Japan's schooling system as part of the "recipe" for economic success. The reform of schooling and the role of education in preparing students for the workplace have become increasingly contentious issues in U.S. politics, suggesting that the regimentation of schooling as a strategy for "self-strengthening" has undergone an about-face in the global circulation of models for school reform.

Therefore the issues I raise here beg a comparative discussion of late twentieth-century childhoods interlinked across national boundaries in the transformations of the global economy, a project well beyond the scope of this essay. I focus here more narrowly on the question of how the increased parental investment in the child articulates with the specificities of a post-Mao Chinese politics of culture and how this set of child-rearing practices might relate to a longer history of seizing upon the child as a site of national salvation. In particular, I am interested in how these practices may be the expression of a class anxiety among educated urban parents within the context of rapidly changing social and economic mobilities of the post-Mao period and how these class anxieties articulate with late-twentieth-century Chinese nationalism.

While the category of class is a vexed issue in the post-Mao years, the class anxiety I refer to here is indicative of a subjective (as well as objective) positioning of oneself as a member of an educated, urbanized elite in contradistinction to the mass of rural peasantry. To some extent these positions are a legacy of the spatial politics of Maoism, with its rigid division between city and country. However, the increasing economic and geographical mobilities of the post-Mao years are dissolving the rigid boundaries between classes as the established pathways for social mobility through education no longer ensure elite status in the entrepreneurial culture of the 1990s.

Finally, a discussion of intensified parental investment in the child can not fail to mention China's population policy, which since the late 1970s has attempted to limit births, especially among its better-educated urban populations, to one per family. This policy has done much more than merely limit population growth; it imposes a newly defined normative family form with all its attendant power effects in reorganizing familial relationships and strategies for socioeconomic mobility. While some attention has been paid to the ways in which fertility limitation produces its power effects on the bodies of women, via technologies of surveillance and control, what has gone less recognized is the way in which children's bodies also provide a site upon which new modes of power and knowledge are produced.

Within this changed context of the family, the child becomes a fetishized object, not only of parental investment, but also of an intensified societal absorption with mental and bodily quality. By fetishism I mean what Emily Apter has called "a site of displaced lack" which becomes fixed upon a material object (Apter 1993: 2). For my present argument I wish to draw upon the multi-vocality of this concept, as one central to both Freud and Marx, by making it refer both to the child (and its body) as the concentrated focus of societal desire and to the commodities which provide the necessary supplement for what is lacking in the child. Through this intense psychic and material investment, the child becomes a repository of stored value against the uncertainties of rapid economic development. Even as China appears to be approaching its long-awaited "historical destiny" as a modern world power, it also brings great uncertainties about family security and political stability that become focused on the child.

I hope to demonstrate that, far from being merely a household strategy to guarantee family futures, investment in the child is complexly linked to concerns about the future of the Chinese nation and its ability to transcend its status as inferior, whether in terms of the quality of its population, its living standards, or its political power on the world stage.[1] The birth policy has shaped the present conditions for the household regimentation of childhood, and the economic reforms have set up new ways in which the population can be disciplined by way of consumer desire. The national culture can be renovated via consuming practices that promise to enhance the competitiveness of one's child in a global marketplace.

What is critical here is the way in which ideologies of modern subject formation become imbricated with those of Chinese nationalism. In her geneology of "individualism" as a category of intellectual debate in early republican China, Lydia Liu has suggested that it is impossible "to treat the self as an isolated site of unique personal identity" because the "violence of China's encounter with the West forces nationhood upon selfhood, and vice versa." And yet she refuses to reduce conceptions of modern self to national identity, noting in detail how the relationship between the two is marked by "incongruities, tensions, and struggles, as well as their mutual implication and complicity" (1993, 169). Moreover, although we can see the figure of the child as a recurring site for expressing concerns about the reform of the national culture in modern Chinese history, each recurrence must be carefully situated within a wider politics of culture that is historically specific. Therefore, the following discussion presumes to compare images of the child from the republican and post-Mao periods by noting the historical discontinuities that mark the very different conditions of China's integration into a global economy at two widely spaced moments in its modern history.

In particular the figure of the child does not stand alone in national preoccupations but bears a complex relationship to its shadowy complement— the image of the rural poor who dwell in the hinterlands or who throng the centers of rapid development as a migratory source of cheap labor. The child's singularity stands in marked contrast to these thronging masses. The frame that links these two figures together is the discourse on "population quality" (*renmin suzhi*). For the past decade, as the pace of economic growth has accelerated, population policy in China has increasingly emphasized issues of quality alongside those of quantity. This discourse focuses obsessively on the two figures of the backward peasant and the child.

As Rey Chow has recently noted in her discussion of director Chen Kaige's film "The King of the Children" (*Haizi wang*), these two figures have long been objects of fascination for Chinese intellectuals as twin sites for the regeneration

---

1. See Jing Wang's discussion of how the equation of "wealth and prosperity" (*fuqiang*) with "modernization" (*xiandai hua*) in post-Mao intellectual debates restores the hegemonic power of Chinese nationalism (1991).

of the national culture. The indeterminacy of the child offers the possibility of disrupting the blind reproduction of culture in the creation of something new. "By training them to read and write *from scratch*, ... it might be possible to regenerate national culture in a positive manner" (1991: 15). Indeed this indeterminacy of children mirrors that of the "people" as a reservoir of untapped national vitality. Together they form the ground for any contemporary discussion of a national pedagogy. And yet they both share an indeterminacy that inspires fear as well as hope. What would happen if the masses actually exercised their political agency to counter their own fetishized presence in the representational economy of the state? (What lurks in this question is the spectre of a mass insurgency against the Party's legitimacy to rule.) What would happen if children were to become other than the predictable products of the mechanical reproduction of Chinese cultural tradition? (What lurks here is the spectre of single children who grow to be self-centered, unregenerate individualists who fail to fulfill the requirements of a modern citizenry.)

Therefore both the child and the backward rural masses promise a performativity difficult to rein in, threatening the authoritarian structures of the state and domestic orders. Together they form a chiasmatic figure, a crossing over of images in the history of Chinese nationalism: where one appears, the other recedes from view, or, as I will argue for the 1990s, they reappear at either side of a great divide, a chasm.[2] For despite the persistent linkage of these two figures as merely ambivalent, it is perhaps more than ambivalence that holds them in tension in the 1990s. Therefore I would like to explore how they presently mark a disjuncture in the body of the people-nation. Whereas it was possible for intellectuals in the 1920s and 1930s to identify with an oppressed rural peasantry as the mirror image of their own suffering, today the (single) child becomes the narcissistic object of desire onto which anxieties about an eroding class position in a society undergoing rapid economic transformation are increasingly displaced. The quality of the child is what assures an urban elite their distance from the mass of China's rural backward hinterland, whereas the mass exemplifies the lack for which the child becomes the supplement. The child becomes the means by which urban educated parents can replicate their class position in a moment when the future presents both heady visions of a national emergence as an economic superpower and terrors of political disintegration and economic instability.

---

2. Rey Chow's suggests that in Chen Kaige's film, "The King of the Children" it is woman who disappears as the child appears in the narcissistic absorption of male intellectuals. I do not dispute her analysis, but merely want to foreground issues of class as opposed to gender.

The reform-era focus on population quality is reminiscent of concerns first expressed early in this century about the need to refashion the Chinese people into a modern citizenry. Intrinsic to this notion is an internalized critique of an essentialized Chinese national character that has been (re)articulated at critical moments in China's modern history. Part of my current project is to explore the apparent resonances of present-day concerns about population with social Darwinist and eugenics discourses of the early twentieth century to determine how China's integration into global economic systems at two very different moments of its history produce parallel concerns about the cultural renovation of the masses. While both moments are obsessed with the problem of constituting a modern citizenry out of the undisciplined mass, the earlier moment attempted to do so under the conditions of semicolonialism in which the emergent nation-space became defined in reaction to the highly localized physical presence of a multinational imperialism (France, Germany, Britain, Japan, and the U.S.). The problem can be simply stated: How do we theorize the project of modernity in the context of the semicolony in which the powerful influence of modern ideas spills over from the physical space of the foreign concessions to affect the emergence of a modern national identity and an anti-colonial politics? The presence of the treaty ports represented simultaneously the conditions of possibility for the emergence of a modern national consciousness and the conditions of impossibility for China to constitute a national sovereignty, a paradox that continues to beg for more nuanced exploration in current theoretical debates on colonialism and culture.

In contrast, China's opening out to the world, following a protracted period of relative political and economic isolation under Mao, offers a welcoming embrace to foreign investment, which has concentrated in the coastal provinces while making tentative incursions into the hinterlands of the interior. The localization of enterprise zones is in a sense a sign of the controlled insertion of foreign capital governed by a Chinese national sovereignty (unlike the imposition of foreign concessions under imperialism). However, what both moments share is a radical disjuncture in the nation-space between enclaves, which come to represent modernity and civility, and the rest of the nation, which becomes defined in contrast as backward and ignorant. This disjuncture perhaps explains why the student movement of 1989 chose to forego the strategy of linking with their potential allies among workers and peasants. A closer examination of intellectual strategies for defining their elite status in conditions of rapid dislocation and change might illuminate the ways in which China's incorporation into late twentieth-century capitalism has perhaps intensified the sense of the nation as a paradoxical unity. But to explore these issues requires us to first take a detour into the history of Chinese nationalism.

Children's Bodies and the Search for Natural Spirit

I would like to begin with a passage from a brief essay entitled "Shanghai Children," written by Lu Xun in 1933, when he was himself the father of a four-year-old son.

> On the main roads ... your eyes are caught by the splendid, lively foreign children playing or walking—you see scarcely any Chinese children at all. Not that there are none, but with their tattered clothes and lack-lustre expression they pale into insignificance beside the others (1980, 3: 334).

What is striking here is how much Lu Xun's concern over the differences among children was expressed in national terms. Later in the essay he describes Chinese children as split between "hooligans" and "'good children' with bent heads, round shoulders, downcast eyes, and completely blank expressions." They were either "savage or stupid" in accordance with the two dominant methods of Chinese childrearing: children were either left to "run wild" or they were beaten into submission to become "slaves or marionettes." In any case, Lu Xun notes, neither of these methods produces subjects capable of meaningful action outside the hierarchical confines of family and kin. They are incapable of constituting a modern citizenry, in contrast to the "well-behaved" English, the "proud" Germans, or the "intelligent" Japanese. This portrait of Chinese children reflected unfavorably on the national character by comparison with children from modern nations whose very bodies, as illustrated in children's books, Lu Xun notes, display the indelible marks of civic discipline, national pride, and modern educational training. In relation to foreign children, Chinese children paled to the extent they apparently disappeared from sight.

What a curious play of presence and absence! The bodies of foreign children were visible because they possessed a certain indwelling spirit that endowed them with a special postural quality. Chinese children disappeared through its lack; they were rendered mere ghostly presences. Lu Xun warned that the agenda of social reform had paid too little attention to the education of children. "Stupidity and lethargy are enough to make men decadent" (1980, 3: 335).

Lu Xun's brief essay inscribed a comparative history of uneven national development upon the bodies of children, so that children's bodies became a privileged site for envisioning a national pedagogy that can transform "savage" and "stupid" bodies into "lively" and "splendid" ones. He attributed the failure of a modern citizenry to emerge in China to a mindless cultural reproduction of hooligans and slaves incapable of comprehending what Benedict Anderson has called the "deep horizontal comradeship" peculiar to a national sensibility

(1991: 7). This concern with the absence of a national "self-consciousness" (*zijue*) among the masses did not originate with Lu Xun, but was central to the emergence of a nationalist discourse in China, beginning perhaps with Liang Qichao's call for a "new citizen" (*xinmin*) in the first years of the century. Indeed, Liang's formulation of the modern citizen, the antithesis of both hooligan and slave, loves liberty but also possesses a highly developed sense of civic responsibility and concern for the public welfare, and is not a passive subject of despotic rule but the active citizen of a national community (Huang 1972: 66).

Implicit in this notion of popular renovation is a concern with national character, a curious introjection of European discourse on Chinese difference that comes to enframe the nation by marking the very factors that ensure its absence as a freestanding subject.[3] This lack of awareness implies a lack of agency and assertiveness that Liang Qichao invidiously compared to the national spirit of Japan which embodied, for non-Western nations, the possible attainment of the Hegelian idea of the nation as the subject of history.[4] The lack of spirit signified an exclusion from the stage of history in which all the major players have already attained their (modern) national form. Therefore discussions among Chinese intellectuals at the turn of the century mark a significant shift in the discourse of reform in which the "national essence" (*guocui*) no longer marked a domain inviolable to the imperative of reform.[5]

The crisis generated by the Sino-Japanese War of 1894–95 forced a recognition that modernization had to be confronted at both the levels of the seen and the unseen, the material and spiritual. Liang Qichao focused on the manifestations of spirit, variously translated as *jingshen* ("spirit"), *qi* ("vital energy"), *hun* ("soul"), and even *yanshipilichun* (a transliteration of the English "inspiration"), of which Japanese *bushidô* (Chinese: *wushi dao*, the way of the warrior, the samurai spirit) was the most immediate model (see Pusey 1983). Indeed, contemporary Japanese constructions of *bushidô* to express the strength of their national essence were perhaps linked to Hegelian

---

3. For a discussion of European fetishizing constructions of Chinese national character, see James Hevia 1995.

4. Timothy Mitchell reminds us that the influence of the Japanese model figured importantly in places beyond the compass of East Asia (1991: 109–10).

5. The *tiyong* reformers of the 1860s attempted to preserve Chinese culture by limiting reform to the level of technology. Zhang Zhidong pleaded to retain the Chinese classics to inculcate spiritual values but to apply Western learning at the level of technology, a program encapsulated by his phrase "Chinese learning as the substance and Western learning for application" (zhong wei ti, xi wei yong). See, for example, Frank Dikötter 1992: 127–28.

notions of the nation as expressing most fully the unfolding of spirit, a conception made available through the recent translations of Enlightenment historiography into Japanese. This self-enframing of a Japanese national spirit as *bushidô* was enormously influential with Chinese intellectuals in the first decade of the century (Anagnost 1997: 82–83). *Bushidô* represented a Japanese spirit that was indwelling but which had to be made explicitly available to the project of constructing a national identity. With this model before them, Chinese intellectuals engaged in a concerted search within their own tradition for the presence of an indwelling spirit that was active, not passive. *Bushidô* encapsulated all the characteristics that Chinese intellectuals found lacking in their own national character. Most importantly, *bushidô* signified an East Asian referent for a national assertiveness that, if absent now in the Chinese national character, could be developed, indeed, had to be developed, if China was ever to attain the status of nation.

Lu Xun's comments to the contrary, the modernizing project in China from its very beginnings in the late Qing had seized upon education as a primary site for instituting a national pedagogy. Indeed under the influence of Samual Smiles's *Self Help*, that late Victorian exhortation to industry so useful in Great Britain for instructing the laboring classes, as well as in the colonies, it was the regimentation of education and its use to promote industry and discipline among the people that later became the object of critique by more radical educational reformers in the 1920s, who saw the regimentation of modern schooling as stifling creativity.[6]

The literary revolution that began in 1917 refocused the debate from the renovation of the people in general toward the reform of the written culture to transmit modern modes of knowledge to the young, and to encourage mass literacy. The New Culture Movement (1915–1921) was imagined in terms of a youth rebellion, in which the term *qingnian* (youth) became a sign in cultural debates as important as other like terms, such as *funü* ("woman") and *gongren* ("worker"), that defined both the agents and beneficiaries of social revolution.[7]

The literary revolution launched an even more radical critique of Chinese tradition, which focused on issues of pedagogy as the site of cultural transmission and renovation, hence its emphasis on youth as the hopeful space for cultural transformation. The literary conventions of China's written culture were attacked as impediments to accessing the "Real." Written language was to

---

6. Smiles's *Self Help* came to China by way of Japanese translation (see Bailey 1990: 78).

7. See Tani E. Barlow (1991) for a discussion of how "woman" as a generic category is constructed for the project of social transformation.

be brought closer to spoken language, so that it could offer a more transparent conveyance of reality, using European nineteenth-century literary realism as a model. This valuing of speech over writing extended to theories of education as well. Progressive schools designed their curricula around Dewey's "learning by doing." They removed their students from the "smell of ink" and placed them in the midsts of garden plots to learn scientific principles through a direct engagement with the material world.[8]

In relation to this new notion of a national pedagogy, let us return then to Lu Xun's commentary on Shanghai children, where we see not just a commentary on the invisibility of Chinese children in Lu Xun's own act of looking at them, but a critique of how Chinese children are in fact represented. Lu Xun is comparing not just physical children, but cultural constructions of the child and childhood in national traditions of children's literature. The way in which the child is looked at in China is what he finds deficient, contributing to China's failure to achieve political modernity. Why this sudden intense absorption with the act of looking at the child? It suggests a certain fetishism of the gaze, in which the object of that gaze becomes the repository for a displaced desire, in this case, for a national transcendence of China's semicolonial status. It is interesting to note that Lu Xun's essay is entitled "Shanghai Children," not "Chinese Children." An international community in which children of different nationalities co-resided in the Foreign Concessions, Shanghai compelled this invidious comparison. Foreign children were the Shanghai children who became visible while Chinese children paled into insignificance. One was "forcibly" present to the other's absence. It is here that we can see most clearly the intensely paradoxical subjectivity of the semicolony, in which the intrusion of a foreign culture into the national body provides both the imperative and the model to constitute a national subjectivity.

However, having made his critique, Lu Xun notes hopefully that China also has begun to produce a modern children's literature which represents Chinese children in a way that compares more favorably with its foreign counterparts.[9] These new images suggest the figure of prolepsis in which an image of a thing anticipates its actual emergence into reality, as if by way of represention the upright and spirited character of imagined children could magically effect the emergence of a national self consciousness.

---

8. See, for instance, Marston Anderson's 1989 discussion of Ye Shaojun's novel, *Ni Huanzhi*. The first half of Ye's novel is a detailed portrait of how schemes of national salvation were projected onto new theories of children's education.

9. This development was of course heavily influenced by Lu Xun's brother, Zhou Zuoren, who saw an important linkage between children's literature and education (see Chang-tai Hung 1985).

In looking for images of spirited children from the period, one is almost inevitably drawn to the paintings of Feng Zikai, most of which were produced in the late 1920s and early 1930s. His images of children fall into the category of *manhua* ("random sketches"), a genre originally derived from the Japanese *manga*, which may be comic, but which might also be the vehicle for social satire or commentary. In 1921 Feng Zikai had traveled to Japan for ten months of study, where he had been exposed to Western art, as well as to *manga* (Chinese: *manhua*).[10] In Feng Zikai's hands *manhua* exhibited a spontaneous brushlike quality that captured all the more powerfully a breathless sense of a sketch done quickly from life. In his pictures of children especially we see a compelling encounter between "modern" constructions of the child (as another order of being, closer to nature, artless and spontaneous) and the older tradition of *zenga* ("zen pictures") through which the spontaneous act of painting itself was a mode of attaining enlightenment, here transmuted into the trope of capturing the "truth" of the child. Feng's lifelong fascination with Buddhism also plays a role here, but his use of the brush also represents his desire to devise a popular art that could comment on contemporary social issues that would also be intrinsically Chinese (Harbsmeier 1984). In his pictures of children, his brush appears to capture something essential about the nature of childhood and the spontaneity of children's play. All of these factors together point towards the hybrid quality of the paintings as an object in which identifications are sought simultaneously with an essentialized Chinese culture *and* with the universalizing claims of modernity. In these images Chinese children participate in a universalizing construction of what a child is, in a genre that constructs itself as both modern and Chinese.

What seems modern about these paintings is how they represent children in a way that was strikingly new. They fetishize children as objects of desire in the very intensity of their gaze, a gaze that sets the child up as a spectacle, illuminating it as the central focus, in what is almost a photographic framing.[11] Indeed, the child sometimes seems to fill the space, so that the figure suggests a repleteness of the image, not much else being required or desired. Traditional Chinese New Year's paintings were also often filled with a child image, but one that was stereotypical in keeping with its magical function for effecting fertility and wealth. In contrast, Feng's sketches have a freshness and

---

10. By the end of the Tokugawa period the *manga* had become a highly hybridized form, having been influenced by the British political cartoon (see Frederik L. Schodt, 1983: 38 and passim).

11. Here I am closely paraphrasing Jacqueline Rose (1993: 29). This suggestion begs for a better understanding of the history of photography in China, especially in the area of family portraiture.

immediacy that suggest that they were taken from life. His are not imagined or idealized children, but very real ones (the models often being Feng's own six children), operating in a world that almost seems to transcend culture. These images capture a sense of what is natural to the child; they express a certain universalizing construction of childhood that seems readily familiar. We must find these images charming! I confess to finding myself becoming inordinately fond of them, having given myself unlimited license to indulge my own love of looking at them (not to mention my pleasure in offering them to your gaze, which magnifies my pleasure many times over). And yet, putting the question of my own pleasure to one side to look at these images critically, I am not trying to question whether these images capture a certain "truth" of childhood (in which my own subjectivity as a parent and as a bourgeois subject is heavily invested), but rather how, at this particular moment in history, these images suggest a certain set of metaphysical premises about the necesssity to reform Chinese culture. Why do these particular aspects of childhood suddenly become imaginable as suitable topics for pictorial representation? If these images are so immediately legible to our gaze, does this suggest merely the influence of "Western" conventions of the pictorial representation exemplified, for instance, by the late Victorian passion for photographing children (see Mavor 1995)? Or is there something much more profound taking place?

Jacqueline Rose, in a recent discussion of children's literature in Britain, suggests that the modern adult subject's psychic investment in the child is the displacement of a desire unobtainable to the self. In the context of post-Enlightenment metaphysics, the child represents "a lost pure point of origin in relation to language, sexuality, and the state." The child presumably still preserves "a direct and unproblematic access to objects of the real world." The "innocence of the child" is equated with a "primary state of language" (1993: 8–9). Indeed, Rose suggests that the genre of children's literature in English remained the last bastion of realist literature following the more general literary turn to modernism. This commitment to realism was more than just incidental but was invested with the project of national salvation. The so-called "golden age" of English children's literature is precisely contemporaneous with the peaking and decline of British colonial power (1880–1930), suggesting an eerie simultaneity with the seizing of literary realism to create a national literature by Chinese intellectuals.[12] What is fascinating here is how the child becomes fetishized simultaneously at the center of empire as well in the colonial periphery. The child is set up as the site of a lost truth and/or moment of

---

12. For a discussion of how literary realism came to signify modernity to Chinese writers, see Theodore Huters 1994.

history, a missed opportunity, that still contains the possibility of transcending a rotten and decaying culture (Rose 1993: 43; Steedman 1995). The child, then, becomes for the adult a means of nostalgic retrieval of an innocence lost through the corruption of culture and the mediation of writing between the child and the real world. The figure of the child is thus closely tied with the emergence of notions about civilization, modernity, and national identity at a moment that is fully contemporaneous in both metropolitan cultures and the colonial periphery. This exemplifies for us the problem of colonial modernity which must move away from merely noting how colonialism frames the project of modernity for colonized peoples (China's "response" to the West) to one which looks at the project of modernity as itself an emergent product of the colonial encounter for both sides, colonizer and colonized!

2-29

Figure 1

Lu Xun's attention to the problem of representing children has already suggested the links these images must have with the project of modernity as it was articulated in the 1920s and 1930s. How exactly should we read them in relation to the specificities of China's semicolonial status and emergent national culture? To start, we see evidence in these pictures for a special attentiveness to the child's "different" relationship to objects of the real world. In Figure 1 we see a child putting shoes on the four legs of a stool. In Chinese, as in English, the word for the leg of a stool is the same as the one denoting a human limb. The child notes a difference in number but not in quality, displaying an artless literalness about language that expresses itself in play. The charm of this image lies in its depiction of the natural curiosity and wonder of the child who, in the spirit of play, rearranges the rules which govern the combination of objects according to a logic of metaphoric extension rather than grammatical rule, a playfulness that embodies a liberating sense of freedom and spontaneous innovation not bound by the rules of culture. Such ideas go all the way back to Rousseau's *Emile* and his praise of Defoe's *Robinson Crusoe* as the only literature fit for children because of the hero's ability to display the same innovative logic.

See, for example, the series of four images entitled "Research" (*Yanjiu*) (Figure 2), which exemplify the way in which a modern pedagogy should seize upon the child's unmediated relationship to the objects of the real world by designing a hands-on, experiential education in the tradition of Dewey. In Figure 3, entitled "Early Reading" (*Chu du*), we see the child in rapt absorption, not with the traditional "Thousand-Character Classic" (*Qianzi wen*), but with a modern picture book, which conveys images without the supplement of writing. Here we see a turning away from the idea of the rote memorization of Chinese ideographs to embrace a more direct relationship with the object world in the child's first encounter with a "written" language. This image fully occupies its frame, suggesting a rapt absorption in the child's obvious delight in its relationship to the book-object. These paintings relate closely to other paintings by Feng, such as "Associations on the Cutting of Hedges" (Figure 4), which critique more pointedly the stultifying regimentation of schooling in China as institutionalized by the educational reforms in the late nineteenth century. Although this particular painting was made in the 1940s, the stunting of individual creativity through schooling was a frequent topic of Feng's, inspired by his own unhappy observations as a teacher. Indeed, his critique of education explains why he took such special delight in depicting, as he himself put it, the antics of "naughty children" (see Harbsmeier 1984: 63).

Figure 2

初讀

前夕冬青
瞬想

Associations
on the cutting
of hedges
(1949)

Figure 3   **Figure 4**

As suggestive as these images are, they pale in comparison to "Self-recognition" (*Ziji renshi*) (Figure 5), which offers to our gaze the child's contemplation of its own mirrored image. This sketch, which dates approximately from 1931, eerily anticipates the psychoanalytic model of the "mirror stage," first introduced by Jacques Lacan in 1936, as a founding moment in the constitution of the ego (Lacan 1977: 1–7). Once again it is not so much the child's act of looking at itself in a mirror that makes this image so compelling; rather, it is the act of looking intently at this act of looking. Why does this process of mirroring the self suddenly become marked with so much significance at this moment in China's history? In Lacan's formulation of the mirror stage, the child, as yet unable to walk or stand, nevertheless overcomes his nursling dependency in a "jubilant flutter of activity" that inclines him toward his mirrored image as if about to merge with it in the pleasure of his identification with it as a bounded and autonomous ego. But what Lacan describes as a sudden and punctual event, others, such as Laplanche, have suggested is better understood metaphorically in terms of the child's relationship to the representational economy itself, a relational process that takes place over time, in which the child has reflected back to it more complex mirrorings of who and what it is, that do not always cohere unproblematically (Silverman 1995). This act of recognition constitutes for Lacan the domain of the imaginary, in which the child (mis)recognizes the image in the mirror as a bounded and coherent self, a process that Lacan suggests is a necessary precondition to the child's entry into the symbolic orders of language and society of which it is a part. However, as a universal construction of the emergence of the ego, one wonders to what extent this obsession with boundedness might not be a preoccupation specific to the formation of the bourgeois individual whose imaginary coherence becomes the foundation for the project of modernity. To properly read this image, I suggest we need to put it into the context of the debates on the concept of individualism taking place in China during this period.

Figure 5

What is immediately striking about Feng's image is its very recursivity. The child sits in a huge, overstuffed armchair, a *shafa*, itself a powerful signifier of a cosmopolitan bourgeois domesticity, and peers fascinated at its own reflection in a hand-held mirror, no other social gaze being represented (as in Lacan's image, one imagines the mother holding the child and thrilling to the child's delighted shock of recognition). And yet this image ties together a complex exchange of gazes, in which the one who consumes the image takes over the position of the absent parental gaze to attain a certain specular pleasure, as if the child's absorbed look succeeded in filling in something painfully absent.

Our analysis of this circulation of gazes cannot stop here, however, given the sociohistorical provenance of the image. As Lu Xun has already demonstrated for us, the gaze of the cosmopolitan Chinese subject upon the child is informed by the absent presence of cultural others, so that the look is always juxtaposed with looks at others. Our reading of Feng's picture must speak to its context in a semicolonial setting, and in so doing we can subject the universalizing assumptions of Lacanian psychoanalytic theory on the birth of the subject to a critique which demonstrates its sociohistorical specificity. If we amend Lacan's formulation to become a theory of the modern bourgeois subject in formation, then we can begin to recognize why that momentary feeling of fullness and identification becomes so endlessly fascinating for us as adults to observe in children. The mirror stage effectively becomes a screen image which obsessively disavows, in its endless replay, our anxiety about (not) being a coherent and autonomous ego. As John Cascardi has argued, "The culture of modernity is given shape as a divided whole that can only be unified through the powers of an abstract subject, or its political analogue, the autonomous state. Indeed ... the state ... provides the means through which the divided subjects of modernity can be made whole." Lydia Liu (1993) cites this passage to point out these interlinkages between bourgeois individualism and the modern state as her strategy for disrupting discourses about "Chinese collectivism versus Western individualism." In other words the emergence of the individual is embedded in the problem of modernity itself; it constitutes both a liberation and a loss that must be compensated for in the illusion of the coherent ego and the unified nation-state. However, the critical apprehension of Chinese intellectual debates on an individualism "proper" to China is reflected in the use of *ziji* as denoting "the self" in the painting's caption. As Liu has documented for us, *ziji* was only one of the many contested translations of the notion of "self" or "individual" in 1920s debates on individualism among Chinese intellectuals. Moreover, as a new binomial expression, *ziji* incorporated the ideograph *ji*, which opens a set of connotative linkages to the Neo-Confucian concept of *daji*, "the greater self," which in this new context becomes a figure for the nation (*guojia*) or the new concept of society (*shehui*)

(*Ibid.*: 177–78). Hence, *ziji* gestures toward the embeddedness of the individual within the larger social collectivity.

If the illusory coherence of the subject is a source of obsessive anxiety for persons in societies that have already gone through the "passive revolution" of capitalist transformation, how much more anxious for those whose societies have suffered the tumultuous upheaval of colonial fragmentation that hinders its attempts to obtain a modern political form. Feng's image of the birth of the free-standing subject must be viewed within its historical context in which this birth is seen as fundamental to the birth of a modern national sovereignty. The picture is iconic of contemporary obsessions with the emergence of a new kind of subjectivity, one whose apparent alienation is counterbalanced by an elaborated "interiority" signifying a psychological complexity and depth which carries the meanings of nation-ness into the very soul of the subject (*Ibid.*: 182).

If the emergence of the freestanding subject was a necessary precondition for national self-awareness, nevertheless it was not sufficient for constituting the nation as a freestanding sovereignty. After the bloody split between the Communists and the Nationalists in 1927, increasingly the mass of China's peasantry became the focus of desire for leftist intellectuals as a potential source of revolutionary agency. The rural masses displaced the child as the principle object of a revolutionary pedagogy. In a process somewhat parallel to the idealization of children's unmediated relation to the phenomenal world, peasants were idealized as having a more direct connection to the Real, the brute forces of necessity which powered the course of history itself. This connection to the Real became the imaginary completion of an elite sense of their own lack of agency.[13] And yet there is always a certain ambivalence built into the idea of the masses as the embodiment of the nation. The "people" embody the nation; national representation is possible only in their name, and yet they are objectified as the "other" of modernity, a radical disjuncture in the time of the nation.[14] During the Maoist era the struggle of peasant bodies with the forces of nature continued to be of central importance to the signifying economy of the political culture. Under Maoism peasant deprivations, embodying a model of self-sacrifice instructive to the young, came to express the strength of a national will. This spirit of self-sacrifice was integral to the tactical play against time intended to hurry China along its modernizing path. A socialist pedagogy revolved around the recalling of past bitterness and

---

13. This relationship was most eloquently stated by Marston Anderson (1991) again in his discussion of *Ni Huanzhi*. I follow his practice of referring to the Real as the abstract referent for the material forces that constitute brute necessity.

14. This theme is elaborated in Prasenjit Duara (1995).

present sacrifice to educate the revolutionary successors about the historical inevitability of revolution and the hegemonic leadership of the socialist state. This sacrifice is now recognized as having been cavalierly wasted by the excesses of Maoist development policies, leaving in their wake, a sense of lost time, marking Chinese bodies as unmodern, undisciplined, and incivil (Anagnost 1997). It is against this narrative of historical devolution under Maoism that the problem of population quality now attains its distinct articulation with a post-Mao politics of culture.

Neo-Malthusian Fantasy and the Commodity Form

In the post-Mao era the figure of the child and that of the rural masses once again connect in a chiasmatic figure, a crossing over that marks a discontinuity within the body of the nation. The masses are objectified in political discourse as requiring a diverse array of orthopractic measures and disciplinizing orders because of their low quality, their lack of education, their lack of modern ways of knowing and acting, their otherness to the modern. The state and its educated elites thus refract the evaluative gaze of global capital that sees Chinese labor as cheap but undisciplined by modern standards of labor quality.[15] In the subjective "chronotope" (time-space) of modern China we see a radical reterritorialization of the national body. The cosmpolitan subject situated in the areas identified as *fuyu* (prosperous), *fada* (developed), *wenming* (civilized) (the coastal provinces well on their way, in their tumultuous boom and bust fashion, to the "molecular transformation" of capital) looks with dismay at those areas of the interior that are identified as *pinkun* (poverty-ridden), *luohou* (backward), and *pianpi* (isolated). The discourse of the state addresses the rural masses as essentially inert until aroused by the state's own disciplinary schemes and the inspiriting kiss of enterprise capital. Or they are perceived as "dangerously active" in rebellions against state authority (Kung 1994: 11, 2).

But in the last half dozen years we see that the child too has become subject to an intensified surveillance and discipline that completely restructures the urban family in response to the state's call "to reproduce less in order to nurture better" (*yousheng youyu*). These discourses impose a newly defined normative family form, promoted by China's population policies, that focuses the attention of many adults upon the single child. Grandparents may be adjunct caretakers but they are not authorities of a newly valorized "science" of child rearing

---

15. It is, of course, a classic strategy of capitalism to construct different kinds of labor, according to race, gender, and ethnicity, as a way of lowering its cost.

which addresses the subjectivities of "modern parents" who are, in turn, themselves disciplined to consume knowledge and commodities appropriately.[16] Indeed, an intensified application of commodities in the raising of one's only child appears to be perceived as a possible means of ensuring a secure class position in a society that is rapidly differentiating economically. Early childhood has become an active site of intervention on the part of parents whose new responsibility is now to nurture better to produce a better product. Indeed, for parents to delay in their active intervention in their child's early development is to reproduce the anxious awareness of time lost in their own childhoods during the Maoist era, a deficit that can never be made good. Much could be said here on the experience of temporality under socialism and its reform. The sense of lost time is also a sense of things being in a state of stasis for which it is now time to play the game of catch up. The expanded responsibility of parents thereby becomes their desire, filling in a gap that they locate as indelibly a part of themselves. At the same time, however, parents of a certain age are often nostalgic about the "tempering" they acquired from their experience in Maoist mobilizations that they feel continues to mark their bodies and their character with strengths and virtues they find themselves unable to replicate in their children.

Parents feel tremendous pressure to know what is necessary to turn the ordinary substance of their child into a superior product. Their interventions work to displace anxieties about rapid development, as well to permit the envisioning of child and its intellectual promise as a potential escape route in dreams of emigration. Education still works as a strategy of status enhancement if it encompasses the valued experience of study abroad. There has been an explosion of popular literature on childrearing (on the order of *Fumu bidu* "What all parents should read") which focuses specifically on the varied causal factors in childhood development. What is interesting about this literature is the degree to which it focuses on successful techniques for producing a superior child, whereas less attention is focused on the actual accomplishments of children. The premise is that given the proper inputs of parental attention and resources, a superior product will be the result even with an unexceptionable raw material (Champagne 1992).

---

16. Although the grandparental generation once saw themselves as modern parents, they have quite a different relationship to the commodity form that sets them apart as a generation with its own distinct culture and modes of nostalgia, as exemplified in recent years by the emergence of a generational discourse configured in a series of four distinct cohorts beginning with Mao (*si dai ren lilun*). See Wang Luxiang's characterization of all four in Wan 1991: 74–75.

Perhaps because I had very young children with me in 1991, I was exposed daily to this set of concerns in ways that vividly recall to mind Lu Xun's comments on Shanghai children. My infant son, especially, became the medium through which people would elaborate at length about the differing qualities of bodies East and West. I found myself caught up in a complex mirroring process expressed in strikingly concrete ways, through the material body of my son. People would squeeze his arm or leg and comment appreciatively about the hardness of his flesh, the pallor of his skin, his size, the depth of his cranium. The appearance of my children in public places would invite the occasional person to deliver impromptu lectures on the differences of children's bodies East and West to anyone willing to listen. The conclusion would be that "the quality of body" (*shenti suzhi*) of Western children was higher. They were larger, more supple, and had a glow of health presumably lacking in Chinese children.[17]

This focused attention to my child's body was directed to his intellectual development as well. People would comment on his responsiveness to others, his eagerness to explore things, his strong will. These traits were praised as indicators of superior intelligence and creativity, but the subtext here was clearly that they also produce a less controllable child. This ambivalence is heavily inscribed in the word *pi*, used to describe naughtiness in children. When parents complain that their children are *pi*, one detects a secret satisfaction mixed into their irritation, an ambivalence that comes from being caught between the opposing fears of social disorder and cultural stasis. It shows itself both in the subtle critique of the Chinese tradition of paternal authority as constraining creativity and intellectual freedom, and in the concern often expressed that the next generation of single children will be overindulged, self-centered, and difficult to control. This conflicted response is perhaps not far removed from Feng's delight in depicting the antics of naughty children. The larger societal implications of *pi* were brought home to me in an especially vivid way when, on the afternoon of June 4, 1989, as I talked to a university professor about the bloody crackdown in Beijing, he said, pointing to his spirited and sometimes headstrong nine-year-old daughter, "Her generation will not stand for this. And that, too, will be a kind of progress."

In the rapidly expanding consumer economy of the 1990s everyday practices of consumption mark out certain commodities as contributing to the improved mental and bodily quality of the child: chocolate, dairy products, even potato

---

17. This attention reflects a deep and abiding concern that relates bodily quality to national strength in twentieth-century China.

chips.[18] Indeed, my son's Chinese caretaker, a retired children's nurse, became convinced that the oatmeal I served my children every morning was an important causal factor in their "superior" bodily quality, converting her into an avid propagandist for the virtues of this humble commodity which was being newly repackaged as a "children's nutritional supplement" (*ertong liangshi*). The concern here is with the malleability of the child's body, its responsiveness to capital inputs in enhancing its quality. This concern extends even to the period prior to birth in the uncanny reappearance of a "premodern" practice of "fetal education" (*taijiao*), in which the fetus is imagined as already receptive to commodified inputs, scientifically applied.[19]

The child's body becomes the repository of stored value, presumably justified by its heightened quality which compensates for the loss of more reproduction. By means of the very practices intended to enhance its development, the child's body comes to express not only concerns for the national future, but also fears about the loss of class position on the part of urban parents, who experience an intense anxiety about their ability to maintain a foothold in an elite class. In the highly volatile atmosphere of reform-era China, which has witnessed the mercurial rise and fall of fortunes and the possibility of undreamed-of wealth, none of the old strategies for status enhancement remain secure. One's single child must be prepared for heightened competition not just in China, but on a global stage. The concern with children's bodies reflects the fears of urban parents about falling into the mass. The incredible elaboration of modern childrearing practices among this class is an urgent project of maintaining a critical distance between themselves and those others. Superior intelligence is considered the *sine qua non* for future economic mobility. Explaining her rigorous regime of fetal education, one expectant mother confided that "society has changed, and competition is much

---

18. Hu Yaobang was a booster for chocolate and dairy products; potato chip packaging sometimes has a pitch suggesting that it can "open up [childhood] intelligence" (*kai zhili*). One must note the preponderance of highly processed cereals and snack foods in this category of "children's food" (*ertong shipin*). A problem with some of these nutritional supplements and tonics lies in their use of hormonal additives leading to untimely sexual development in even small children.

19. See, for instance, a *Wall Street Journal* report on the use of English language tapes applied *ex utero* to give the fetus a head start on *second* language acquisition. The late Qing reformer, Liang Qichao, was also a believer in fetal education. He held this time to be a period when the forces of education and heredity were working together to produce effects that could be passed down to improve the race (see Pusey 1983: 102–3). For descriptions of premodern beliefs in prenatal education, see Guo 1979, and Van Straten 1983.

tougher that it was when I was growing up" (*Wall Street Journal* 1994). The net effect for many families is a regimentation of childhood that transcends what could be accomplished by schooling alone to include every detail of the child's life. And these concerns are also transforming the structure of access to education with the establishment of private schools for the children of the *nouveaux riches* (*Zhenming* 1993: 38–39).

These anxieties are expressed in terms of transforming the child's body into a modern body. The national body can thereby be transubstantiated in the materiality of children's bodies via the commodity form, a form of fetishism which endows material things with magical powers to effect miraculous changes. However, the issue of transforming the mental capacity of the child is fraught with far deeper ambivalence, especially in the debate over what is necessary for the production of modern cultural agency. Naughtiness or *pi* is ambivalently connected to notions about the creative development of the child. "Creativity" (*chuangzao xing*) is posed as the antithesis to traditional Chinese literary culture, which is seen as a mere mechanical reproduction no longer linked to the Real. Yet many of the after-school activities assigned to my daughter's little friend acted as a theater to exhibit the child's ability to carefully model her work on that of adults. My daughter discovered to her shame the importance of following the model at school when she gratuitously added black flags atop her carefully reproduced image of Tiananmen Square, an act that could have been construed as a counterrevolutionary act in the months immediately following the crackdown in 1989. Creativity is both admired and suspect for it is aligned with the characteristics of willfulness and independence which are much more ambivalently regarded. If Feng Zikai's *manhua* represent a radical reframing of children's naughtiness and creativity as liberating, giving birth to a modern subjectivity that could stand alone and become the strength of the nation, nevertheless they must be contextualized along with the military regimentation of education during the Republican era despite scattered attempts at reform. In the post-Mao period this struggle between regimentation and playful creativity continues. The spectre of a new generation that is over-indulged, self-centered, and difficult to control frequently appears in newspaper accounts of children, referred to as "little emperors" (*xiao huangdi*), whose uncontrolled temper may lead to murderous rage.[20]

---

20. In Guangdong Province a fourteen-year-old boy flew into a rage when his mother failed to serve his dinner on time due to a power outage. He killed her with a meat cleaver and then hanged himself. Police blamed the murder on the parents' over-indulgence of their son, characterizing him as a "little emperor." See the news briefs in *China News Digest* on internet for 17 April 1994.

And yet I am haunted by the face of one of my Chinese colleagues who, with her ten-year-old daughter, accompanied me on a research trip. When our interview with a local propaganda cadre had concluded, the child engaged in a saucy banter in response to his questions and to his obvious delight. As her mother quietly watched, I observed on her face a look of eloquent sternness struggling to repress a smile of wondrous delight in the cleverness and quick wit of her offspring. The play of conflicting emotions across her face was the very picture of ambivalence caught in some indeterminate place between pleasure and alarm.

Conclusion

The figure of the child gathers into itself anxieties about national futures as well as personal ones. The single child represents stunningly the demographic implosion of the social into the body of the child, an unavoidable consequence of the state's stringent birth limitation policy in urban areas. So many futures hinge on the fate of this one being, in a society where long-term economic security is perceived as increasingly fragile and uncertain.[21]

We see in China a new articulation of power between an authoritarian government that styles itself a "socialism with *Chinese* characteristics" and the logic of global capitalism, an unholy alliance that radically reterritorializes the body of the nation between a backward hinterland and the advanced littoral, at the same time it makes possible the marking out of class positions through participation in modern modes of labor and consumption. Both of these processes figure importantly in the discourse of bodily quality which focuses most obsessively on the bodies of backward peasants and children.

List of Figures and Their Sources

Figure 1: "Ah Bao has two legs, the stool has four" (*An Bao liangzhi jiao, dengzi sizhi jiao*). Feng 1983, plate 2–29.
Figure 2: "Research" (*Yanjiu* 1–4). Feng 1983, plates 2–42–2–45.
Figure 3: "Early Reading" (*Chu du*). Feng 1948, plate 1.
Figure 4: "Associations on the Cutting of Hedges." Harbsmeier 1984.
Figure 5: "Self-recognition" (*Ziji renshi*). Feng 1948, plate 2.

---

21. And with good reason, given the rate of inflation during the 1990s and the increasing privatization of what was once part of the socialist redistribution system, such as housing, health care, and pensions.

References

Anagnost, Ann. 1997. *National Past-Times: Narrative, Writing, and History in Modern China*. Durham: Duke University Press.

Anderson, Benedict. 1991. *Imagined Communities: Reflections on the Origin and Spread of Nationalism*. Second Edition. London: Verso.

Anderson, Marston. 1989. *The Limits of Realism: Chinese Fiction in the Revolutionary Period*. Berkeley: University of California Press.

Apter, Emily and William Pietz, eds. 1993. *Fetishism as Cultural Discourse*. Ithaca: Cornell University Press.

Bailey, Paul. 1990. *Reform the People: Changing Attitudes Towards Popular Education in Early Twentieth-Century China*. Edinburgh: Edinburgh University Press.

Barlow, Tani E. 1991. "Theorizing Woman: *Funu, Guojia, Jiating* [Chinese Woman, Chinese State, Chinese Family]," *Genders* 10 (Spring): 132–60.

Champagne, Susan. 1992. "Producing the Intelligent Child: Intelligence and the Child Rearing Discourse in the People's Republic of China." Ph.D. diss., Stanford University.

Chow, Rey. 1991. "Male Narcissism and National Culture: Subjectivity in Chen Kaige's *King of the Children*." *Camera Obscura* 25/26: 9–39.

Dikötter, Frank. 1992. *The Concept of Race in Modern China*. Stanford: Stanford University Press.

Duara, Prasenjit. 1995. *Rescuing History from the Nation: Questioning the Narratives of Modern China*. Chicago: University of Chicago Press.

Farquhar, Judith. 1994. "Eating Chinese Medicine," *Cultural Anthropology* 9 (4): 471–97.

Feng Zikai. 1948. *Ertong shenghuo manhua* [Sketches from the lives of children]. Shanghai: Ertong shuju.

—————. 1983. *Zikai manhua quanji* [The complete sketches of Feng Zikai]. Amoy: Shulin chubanshe.

Guo Licheng. 1979. *Zhongguo shengyu lisu kao* [Studies in Chinese birth rituals and customs]. Taipei: Wenshizhe Publishers.

Harbsmeier, Christoph. 1984. *The Cartoonist Feng Zikai: Social Realism with a Buddhist Face*. Oslo: Universitetsforlaget.

Hevia, James. 1995. "The Scandal of Inequality: *Koutou* as Signifier," *Positions: East Asia Cultures Critique* 3, no. 1 (Spring): 97–118.

Huang, Philip. 1972. *Liang Ch'i-ch'ao and Modern Chinese Liberalism*. Seattle: University of Washington Press.

Hung, Chang-tai . 1985. *Going to the People: Chinese Intellectuals and Folk Literature, 1918–1937*. Cambridge: Harvard University Press.

Huters, Theodore. 1994. "Ideologies of Realism in Modern China: The Hard Imperatives of Imported Theory." In *Politics, Ideology and Literary Discourse in Modern China*, edited by Liu Kang and Xiaobing Tang, 147–73. Durham: Duke University Press.

Kung, James Kaising. 1994. "Peasants in a 'Hot Pot': Pushing the Limits of a Biased Strategy against Agriculture?" In *China Review 1994*. Hong Kong: Chinese University Press.

Lacan, Jacques. 1977. "The Mirror State as Formative of the Function of the I." In *Ecrits: A Selection*, translated by Alan Sheridan, 1–7. New York: W. W. Norton.

Liu, Lydia. 1993."Translingual Practice: The Discourse of Individualism between China and the West." *Positions: East Asia Cultures Critique* 1: 160–93.

Lu Xun. 1980. "Shanghai Children." *Selected Works of Lu Xun*. 3rd ed. Vol. III, 334–35. Beijing: Foreign Languages Press.

Mavor, Carol. 1995. *Pleasures Taken: Performances of Sexuality and Loss in Victorian Photographs*. Durham: Duke University Press.

Mitchell, Timothy. 1991. *Colonizing Egypt*. Berkeley: University of California Press.

Pusey, James. 1983. *China and Charles Darwin*. Cambridge: Harvard University Press.

Rose, Jacqueline. 1993. *The Case of Peter Pan: or The Impossibility of Children's Fiction*. Philadelphia: University of Pennsylvania Press.

Schodt, Frederik L. 1983. *Manga! Manga! The World of Japanese Comics*. Tokyo: Kodansha.

Steedman, Carolyn. 1995. *Strange Dislocations: Childhood and the Idea of Human Interiority, 1780–1930*. Cambridge: Harvard University Press.

Van Straten, N. H. 1983. *Concepts of Health, Disease and Vitality in Traditional Chinese Society*. Wiesbaden: Steiner.

Wall Street Journal. 1994. "Study This Baby: Chinese Fetuses Bear Heavy Course Loads." February 8.

Wan, Pin P. 1991. "A Second Wave of Enlightenment? Or an Illusory Nirvana? *Heshang* and the Intellectual Movements of the 1980s." In *Deathsong of the River: A Reader's Guide to the Chinese TV Series 'Heshang'*, edited by Richard Bodman and Pin P. Wan, 63–89. Ithaca: Cornell East Asia Program.

Wang, Jing. 1991. "*Heshang* and the Paradoxes of Chinese Enlightenment." *Bulletin of Concerned Asian Scholars* 23, no. 3: 23–32.

Ye Shaojun (Ye Shengtao). 1958. *Ni Huanzhi*. In English translation as Yeh Sheng-tao. *Schoolmaster Ni Huan-chih*, translated by A. C. Barnes. Peking: Foreign Languages Press.

Zhengming. 1993. "Beijing guizu xuexiao de jueqi" (The rise of Beijing's aristocrat schools). September, 38–39.

Glossary

bushidô (Chinese: *wushi dao*)	武士道	*si dai ren lilun*	四代人理論
		ta zuobuzhu	她坐不住
"Chu du"	初讀	*taijiao*	胎教
chuangzao xing	創造性	*wenming*	文明
ertong liangshi	兒童糧食	*xiandai hua*	現代化
ertong shipin	兒童食品	*xiao huangdi*	小皇帝
fada	發達	*xinmin*	新民
Fumu bidu	父母必讀	"*Yanjiu*"	研究
funü	婦女	*yousheng youyu*	优生优育
fuqiang	富強	*zenga* (Chinese: *chanhua*)	禪畫
fuyu	富餘		
gongren	工人	*ziji*	自己
guocui	國翠	"*Ziji renshi*"	自己認識
guojia	國家	*zijue*	自覺
Haizi wang	孩子王		
hun	魂		
ji	己		
jingshen	精神		
kai zhili	開智力		
luohou	落後		
manga (Chinese: *manhua*)	漫畫		
pi	皮		
pianpi	偏僻		
pinkun	貧困		
qi	氣		
Qianzi wen	千字文		
qingnian	青年		
renmin suzhi	人民素質		
shafa	沙發		
shehui	社會		
shenti suzhi	身體素質		
shentong	神童		

Working at Cross Purposes:
Shanghai Labor in the Cultural Revolution

ELIZABETH J. PERRY
Harvard University
and
LI XUN
University of California, Berkeley

The Cultural Revolution looms as one of the most important, yet least understood, milestones of the twentieth century. Having built an enormously powerful system of state domination, Chairman Mao in 1966 called upon the masses of China to "bombard the headquarters"—to attack the Party-state apparatus itself. In responding to Mao's clarion call, Chinese citizens evidenced a capacity for political improvisation that startled even the most seasoned observers of Communist systems, reliant as they had been upon a totalitarian model that downplayed the influence of social forces.[1]

Thanks in part to an explosion of new sources, especially the Red Guard press and refugee interviews, a number of sophisticated analyses of student activism during the Cultural Revolution has appeared (Lee 1978; Chan, Rosen, and Unger 1980; Rosen 1982). Worker participation was also a critical ingredient in the social unrest of this decade, but the relative dearth of source materials makes it difficult to address labor's involvement with anything approaching the degree of refinement attained in studies of the student movement.[2] We have tried to fill the gap by utilizing a variety of heretofore unavailable sources: factory surveys, confidential reports, handbills, public security bureau confessions, and other documents held by the Shanghai Municipal Archives, as well as first-hand interviews with key participants.[3] The result, we hope, not only puts a more human

---

1. For a discussion of this interpretive change, see Schurmann 1968: vii, 504.

2. Pioneering studies of labor in Shanghai include White 1976; Walder 1978; and Wylie 1981.

3. This essay is drawn from a co-authored book (Perry and Li 1997). The sources we have relied upon have their own limitations of course. Our study is restricted to the case of Shanghai. Although Shanghai was undoubtedly the most important center of worker activism during the Cultural Revolution, it was also atypical in a number of respects. The close links between worker rebels in Shanghai and top leaders in Beijing and the relatively nonviolent character of factional strife in Shanghai both distinguish the Shanghai experience from the situation in other Chinese cities.

face on the workers' movement but also facilitates a more comprehensive analysis of the bases of labor activism. The sources permit us to explore a number of questions: Why were workers motivated to join the Cultural Revolution? What divided the ranks of "rebels," "conservatives," and apolitical members of the workforce? Did workers separate along lines of class background, ideological inclination, political networks, or other criteria? And what do such divisions imply about the sources of dissatisfaction and potential for change within the Chinese socialist system?

Scholarly explanations of mass activism during the Cultural Revolution have fallen into three basic camps. The dominant approach, developed by Hong Yung Lee, Stanley Rosen, and others emphasizes the importance of *socioeconomic groups*—especially classes, but also age cohorts, skill levels, and the like—in inclining different categories of students and workers to enlist in rival mass organizations.[4] By this account rebel mass organizations recruited their constituents from those groups with a grudge against the socialist system: people with bad class labels, contract and temporary workers, young apprentices, and so forth. Conservative outfits, by contrast, were generally composed of those from good family backgrounds, older, skilled workers, model workers and the like. A second interpretation, elaborated by Andrew Walder in particular, stresses the role of *political networks* in mobilizing workers along competing lines of patronage and allegiance. According to Walder, Party-sponsored networks (which cut across other bases of group affiliation) generated much of the strife that gripped Chinese factories during the Cultural Revolution (1986; forthcoming). A third explanation highlights the centrality of *psycho-cultural orientation* in giving rise to the factions. As formulated by Lucian Pye and Richard Solomon, it is the extreme psychological dependence of ordinary Chinese upon higher political authorities that produces periodic outbursts of "chaos" (or *luan*), of which the Cultural Revolution was the supreme example. Factionalism was but one expression of a larger psychocultural complex (Pye 1981; 1968; Soloman 1971; Liu 1976; Chan 1985; Dittmer 1977; 1987).

Although socioeconomic, political, and psychocultural approaches have sometimes been posed as competing interpretations, they might better be seen as complementary. Group characteristics, party networks, and personality traits all played a role in shaping the militancy of the day. Moreover, labor unrest during the Cultural Revolution was not all of a piece; three distinctive forms can be identified: rebellion, conservatism, and economism. Each type of activism, we suggest, is best explained by a different analytical tradition. While psychocultural orientation (albeit a substantially modified version of the Pye-Solomon argument) has much to tell us about the *rebel movement*, party networks are essential for understanding the *conservative reaction*. And in explaining the *"wind of*

---

4. See Lee 1978; Chan, Rosen, and Unger 1980; Rosen 1982. On the importance of class categories in Communist China, see especially Kraus 1981.

economism" that swept the Chinese workforce in the winter of 1966–67, we seem best served by an emphasis on group characteristics. Let us now examine how each variety of labor protest unfolded in the Shanghai context.

Rebels: The Workers' General Headquarters

The Workers' General Headquarters, commanded by Wang Hongwen (later designated one of the "Gang of Four"), was an umbrella organization of rebel worker outfits founded on 9 November 1966, whose activities were aimed at toppling party authorities from the factory level right up to the Shanghai Party Committee. Buttressed by support from Zhang Chunqiao and other members of the "Cultural Revolution Small Group" of radical intellectuals in Beijing, the Workers' General Headquarters became a major vehicle for seizing power from the Shanghai Party Committee in the January Revolution of 1967 and remained a factor in Shanghai politics (albeit under new names) until the close of the Cultural Revolution decade in 1976.

Chairman Mao's endorsement of the January power seizure encouraged workers to rush to join the rebel ranks and by late 1967 the Workers' General Headquarters was the majority force in most Shanghai factories. Prior to that point, however, rebel groups could claim but a small percentage of the industrial workforce. The sudden influx of new members in January 1967 (many of whom had earlier been associated with conservative factions) propelled to top posts within the Headquarters those who had stood bravely by Wang Hongwen's side from the very start. Known as "old rebels" (*lao zaofan*), these stalwarts became the core leadership.

Who were the old rebels and how do we explain their bold challenge to the Party authorities? Fortunately we are aided in this inquiry by a comprehensive registration drive conducted by the Workers' General Headquarters of all the leaders of its subordinate liaison posts and rebel brigades.[5] The investigation revealed a demographic profile of rebel leaders that was not greatly at variance with the characteristics of the workforce as a whole. For example, the overwhelming majority of rebel leaders (both old rebels and post-January recruits) came from good class backgrounds. Nearly 88 percent of the old rebels (and 85 per cent of the rebel leaders as a whole) listed worker, cadre, poor peasant, or urban poor as their inherited class label.

The rebel leadership was fairly young, with more than 55 percent falling into the 26–35 year age cohort. Since this was the largest age group in the Shanghai

---

5. Surveyed units included the twenty municipal bureaus and their subordinate companies and factories as well as the liaison posts of the ten city districts and ten suburban counties. Survey forms asked of each rebel leader: name, sex, age, work experience, family background, personal status, educational level, political affiliation, pre-Cultural Revolution occupation, time of joining the rebels, and current position in the rebel organization. See *Xin ganbu tongjibiao* (Statistical tables on new cadres) 1969.

workforce, it is not surprising that it generated a substantial proportion of rebels—yet it was represented among the old rebel leadership at a rate almost double what we might expect from the age structure of the workforce as a whole.[6] In view of the fact that protest movements usually do recruit disproportionately from among the young, however, this statistic is not unexpected.

Most of the old rebels had graduated from middle school or high school, giving them a somewhat higher educational standing than the average for Shanghai workers at the time. Whereas nearly half the general workforce could claim at best an elementary school education, less than a fifth of the rebel leaders fell into this poorly educated category. In part no doubt because the Cultural Revolution began as a rather esoteric ideological debate fought out via the medium of big-character posters, it attracted the better educated stratum of the workforce.[7]

Perhaps the most interesting finding to emerge from the registration data concerns Communist Party and Youth League affiliation. Although it is often asserted that Party and League members were rare among the rebels, this was not actually the case. As Table 1 shows, at this time about 12 percent of the Shanghai workforce belonged to the Communist Party—a figure which included units like schools and government agencies where Party members were especially numerous. If we take factories alone, the percentage drops to under 10 percent (*1965nian* 1965). Among old rebels, however, the proportion of Party members was considerably higher. Furthermore, Youth League membership was nearly double that of the general workforce.

Table 1.
Party and League Membership

TYPE	Members among Shanghai Workforce		Members Among Old Rebel Leaders	
	Number	Percentage	Number	Percentage
Communist Party	186,510	12.1	269	18.2
Communist Youth League	115,425	7.5	196	13.3
Masses	1,237,990	80.4	1,012	68.5
TOTAL	1,539,925	100.0	1,477	100.0

Source: *Shanghai gongren geming zaofan zongsilingbu zaofandui zuzhi qingkuang tongji biao* (Statistical tables on the rebel organizations of the Shanghai worker revolutionary rebels general headquarters) Workers' General Headquarters edition (Shanghai: November 1967).

These high levels of Party and League membership (together accounting for about one-third of the rebel leaders) suggest that old rebels tended to be more politically inclined than the general populace. Yet since few of these rebels had

---

6. Workers aged 26–35 comprised 30.8 percent of the Shanghai workforce at that time.

7. Had many rebel groups not explicitly excluded anyone with university credentials from their ranks, the proportion of this most highly educated segment (5.9 percent of the old rebels) would surely have been much higher.

attained cadre or managerial status prior to the Cultural Revolution, we can presume a gap between their ambitions and their achievements.[8] Unlike those who enlisted on the conservative side, rebel workers included a number of Party and League activists who had been passed over for higher leadership posts. The Cultural Revolution, with its call to rebel against "unjust" authority, offered a golden opportunity to settle scores. The sociopolitical profile of the rebel leaders which emerges from this investigation offers some limited support for the importance of both social groups and political networks. Although class background does not appear to have been a deciding factor, rebel leaders did tend to be younger, better educated, and more politically active than the workforce at large. On the other hand, none of these attributes distinguishes them definitively from their conservative rivals.

To appreciate the key distinctions among different types of labor leaders during the Cultural Revolution (rebel, conservative, and economistic), we must move beyond summary statistics to probe individual biographies. The most influential old rebels in the early days were nine individuals: Wang Hongwen, Wang Xiuzhen, Geng Jinzhang, Pan Guoping, Huang Jinhai, Chen Ada, Ye Changming, Dai Liqing and Ma Zhenlong. Three were Party members; three had been designated as "backward elements" by their work units; and three were ordinary workers prior to the Cultural Revolution. A review of their personal histories suggests that neither group attributes nor political networks can adequately capture their commonalities. (In the interests of space, we will consider here only five of the nine—two party members, two backward elements, and one ordinary worker.)

The commander of the Workers' General Headquarters, Wang Hongwen, hailed originally from Manchuria. While serving in the military, Wang entered the Communist Party. After five years of military duty, he was demobilized and sent to the Shanghai #17 cotton mill as a machine operator (*Fandang* 1977). Workers who knew Wang Hongwen at the #17 mill remember him as an affable and loyal friend who enjoyed a certain standing among the workers. But he was also said to be afflicted with "office addiction" (*guanyin*)—a longing for political position. Wang was known to have remarked to the master craftsman who taught him his workplace skills: "I don't want to eat skilled rice; I want to eat political rice" (Chen 1987). His ambition was to escape the ranks of the ordinary workers and serve as a leading cadre.

Wang Hongwen's upward trajectory was not quite as smooth as he apparently anticipated, however. According to an account written by the Shanghai Party Committee small group to investigate the Gang of Four,

---

8. More than 80 percent of the old rebels had been ordinary workers before the Cultural Revolution began; approximately 1 percent had been leading managers, 1 percent had served as Party cadres, and less than half a percent as union cadres.

In 1958 Wang Hongwen was chosen as Party committee member of the day shift in the #2 spinning room, but was not made branch Party secretary. He believed that he had received the most votes but that higher levels had decided the original branch secretary would continue to serve in that position while Wang remained at his work post. As a consequence Wang Hongwen frequently refused to participate in branch committee meetings (*Fandang* 1977).

Despite this early disappointment Wang continued to move upward. In March 1960 he was loaned to the factory security department to handle militia work. Not long after he was formally transferred to the security department as a cadre in charge of militia work for the entire factory. From this point Wang left behind the blue-collar ranks of productive laborer and gained the status of white-collar cadre.

Between September 1960 and October 1962, during the terrible famine that followed the Great Leap Forward, Wang Hongwen was sent to Chongming Island to participate in reclamation and flood-prevention work (*Ibid.*).[9] Despite his position as a party member and a political cadre, he is reported to have been an outspoken critic of the policies of the day:

In 1960, during the economic retrenchment . . . Wang Hongwen exclaimed, "Damn it! What kind of socialism forces people to go to work on an empty stomach? What kind of policy makes people starve to death?"

Wang Hongwen observed, "My fellow villagers in the Northeast haven't eaten and in Anhui tens of thousands of people have starved. We workers should be working in the factory. What are we doing going to Chongming to reclaim land? In my view the natural calamities were mostly a man-made disaster" (*Ibid.*).

Wang evidently was not an obedient apparatchik, ready to champion whatever policies the Party dictated, but a feisty individual willing to think and speak for himself. He read the newspapers carefully so as to stay on top of the latest domestic developments and even listened regularly to forbidden short-wave radio broadcasts to keep abreast of international events (*Ibid.*). When the Cultural Revolution began, Wang Hongwen was a savvy thirty-one-year-old security cadre who had been working in a factory for nearly a decade. Undoubtedly his independent spirit contributed to his rebelliousness during the Cultural Revolution.

The beginning of Wang Hongwen's "rebellion" can be dated to 12 June 1966, when he announced his open opposition to the factory authorities by posting a big-character poster at the #17 mill. Wang and several of his co-workers accused authorities at his work unit—in particular Deputy Director Zhang Heming—of failing to grasp class struggle, practicing revisionism, and ignoring mass opinions. The poster went up at 10:00 a.m. Less than an hour later the Party committee

---

9. Because of a cutback in industrial production, the Shanghai Party Committee decided to send 100,000 people to Chongming. Each factory assigned workers and cadres to participate.

secretary of the company [*gongsi*] in charge of the #17 mill arrived at the factory to convene an emergency meeting. The factory Party committee then proceeded to seek out the signatories to Wang Hongwen's poster to admonish them for their insolent act (*Shanghai 17chang* 1975).

In this heated atmosphere the Textile Bureau dispatched a Cultural Revolution work team to the #17 cotton mill to direct the ongoing struggle. Wang's rebel action received the instant blessing of the work team. But soon this first work team was recalled and replaced by another team sent from the Shanghai Party Committee itself and headed by Shanghai Federation of Trade Unions vice chair, Shi Huizhen. Shi was an older cadre who had entered the Party back in 1938 and had been active in the underground Shanghai labor movement before the founding of the People's Republic. She did not support Wang Hongwen's precipitous attack on Deputy Director Zhang Heming; instead, Shi selected the other Deputy Director, Zhang Yuanqi, as the proper target of criticism (*Ibid.*).

A conflict between the two Zhangs had developed over who would assume the directorship of the #17 mill. Zhang Yuanqi had relatively little formal education, but substantial work experience. Charged with overall responsibility for security matters at the mill, he had developed a close working relationship with security cadre Wang Hongwen. Like Wang, Zhang Yuanqi was a demobilized soldier from North China. Originally from Shandong province, he spoke with an accent unintelligible to the southern workers. By contrast, Zhang Heming had been promoted to his cadre position from among the ranks of the workers themselves, spoke with a familiar Ningbo accent, and enjoyed closer relations with the ordinary workers (Tang 1992).

Before the Cultural Revolution, Zhang Yuanqi's portfolio at the factory included personnel as well as security matters. Wang Hongwen's support of Zhang Yuanqi apparently stemmed not only from their previous cooperation on security issues, but also from Wang's calculation that Zhang's control of personnel appointments might facilitate his own promotion in future (Ma 1989). In any event Wang's refusal to denounce Zhang Yuanqi created substantial friction with Shi's work team. The differences surfaced in early August when the #17 cotton mill made plans to establish a "Cultural Revolution committee" to direct the struggle at the factory. Although the rebel faction among the workers nominated Wang Hongwen to serve as chair of this committee, the work team refused to consider him. At this time the rebels were still a tiny minority at the factory and Wang Hongwen was not chosen.[10] Having been the favorite of the first work team posted at his factory, Wang had come to expect a position of leadership during the Cultural Revolution. Thus when the second work team of Shi Huizhen blocked his

---

10. Wang Hongwen's followers at the #17 mill numbered at most 100–200 workers—out of a workforce of some 10,000—in August-September 1966. By contrast, the conservative organization that formed in opposition to Wang's rebel initiatives enlisted between 4,000–5,000 workers almost overnight (Ma 1989).

appointment, he was bitterly disappointed. Wang admitted on more than one occasion: "In the beginning if I had been permitted to serve as Cultural Revolution chair I would not have rebelled" (Wang 1967).

In early October Wang Hongwen put up a second big-character poster which attacked the work team at his factory. A few days later he and his followers founded a rebel group. Unable to prevail at their own factory, the rebels decided to venture north to plead their case directly to Party Central. The next day Wang Hongwen led fifteen followers off to Beijing (*Shanghai 17chang* 1975).[11] Wang's trip to the capital was a bold move that won him the lasting admiration of other rebels among the Shanghai work force. Prior to his foray, the "exchange of experiences" had been the exclusive prerogative of student Red Guards. Now workers too were performing on a national stage. When Wang returned to Shanghai, he was lionized by rebels at nearby factories who invited him to their workplaces to discuss the situation in the capital. Later Workers' activist Huang Jinhai admitted, "I worshipped Wang Hongwen." When Huang Jinhai received a telephone message on 6 November from student Red Guards inviting him to a planning meeting for the founding of an all-city rebel labor organization, he immediately informed Wang Hongwen so that he too could participate. That afternoon Wang Hongwen led two others from his factory to the historic meeting that would seal his fate as a worker rebel (Huang 1976).

Wang Hongwen's story does indeed highlight the significance of competing Party networks in structuring the factionalism of the Cultural Revolution era. The longstanding conflict in which Wang's patron, Zhang Yuanqi, was embroiled became Wang's battle as well. These networks, moreover, developed at least to some extent out of shared social backgrounds: both Wang and Zhang Yuanqi were demobilized soldiers from North China working on security matters at the mill. However, when we survey the biographies of other rebel leaders it becomes clear that neither political networks nor social characteristics were as important as Wang Hongwen's own restless temperament and frustrated ambition—his longing to eat political rice as he put it so aptly—in explaining the urge to rebel.

Geng Jinzhang was a very different sort of Party member from Wang Hongwen. Geng had been in the Party for longer than any of the other rebel leaders, having joined in 1949. He was also one of the oldest rebels: 41 years of age at the onset of the Cultural Revolution. But Geng had always been an ordinary worker who never held any managerial position in the factory. His educational level was also extremely low; he was functionally illiterate.

---

11. When Zhang Chunqiao learned of the arrival of rebellious workers from Shanghai, he welcomed them to the capital and arranged for them to meet directly with Chairman Mao and Defense Minister Lin Biao. The result was a substantial increase in personal prestige for Wang Hongwen as well as a lasting connection to the Cultural Revolution radicals in Beijing (Chang 1981: 78).

Like Wang Hongwen (as well as Wang Xiuzhen, the third Party member among the top Workers' Headquarters leadership), Geng hailed originally from North China. The child of poor peasants in Shandong, he lost his father at the age of six and his mother a year later. At age eight he went to live with his paternal uncle, who could not afford to keep him so put him up for sale. In desperation Geng fled to a nearby temple, pleading to be taken in as a novice. When the monks refused to accept him, he went off to live with his maternal aunt. At the age of ten Geng began a seven-year term working for a landlord. After his dismissal from that job, he was forced to resort to short-term stints as a hired hand interspersed with periods of begging. In January 1945 Geng enlisted in the Japanese "puppet" forces in his home county of Ningyang. The following year he again entered the military under the command of Guomindang general Wu Huawen. In 1948 General Wu joined the Communist forces and Geng was incorporated into the People's Liberation Army. In May 1949, as his battalion was fighting its way south, Geng joined the Communist Party (*Guanyu* 1967).

Demobilized in 1957, Geng was assigned a job at the Shanghai paper pulp factory. Ordinarily a longstanding Party member like Geng would at the very least have become a foreman at his factory. Yet he remained an ordinary worker—thanks to his reputation as a womanizer and a troublemaker. While serving in the Japanese military, Geng had been accused of rape and as a PLA soldier had received a stern intra-Party warning for illicit sexual relations. Then in 1963, after one of his neighbors inadvertently burned Geng's son with boiling water, he delivered a sound thrashing to the neighbor and his wife, ripping their clothing to shreds and destroying much of their furniture—a transgression for which he was dealt a second Party warning (Geng 1979: 11/27).

Later Geng Jinzhang's workmates at the Shanghai paper pulp mill offered the following evaluations of their erstwhile colleague:

This person is an uncouth blockhead."

He often beat up people at the factory."

He's simpleminded, uneducated, yet ambitious. Because he was never made a foreman at the factory, he wanted to create a stir."

This guy was always barbarous. He was obsessed by a lust for office. He always wanted to be an official and the Cultural Revolution gave him a chance to rush forth. In the past he had beaten and cursed people (Transcript 1979).

Like so many of the rebel leaders, Geng Jinzhang's rebellion followed upon retribution for having posted criticisms of his factory management (Geng 1979: 3/6). These rebel initiatives rendered Geng a natural candidate for inclusion in the Workers' General Headquarters. On 9 November he was resting at home—having worked the middle shift the day before—when a fellow worker from his factory stopped by to say that he had seen a poster announcing the inauguration of the Workers' General Headquarters later that day. The two men ate an early lunch and hastened to the founding ceremonies (*Ibid.*).

Different as Wang Hongwen and Geng Jinzhang most assuredly were, both (along with Wang Xiuzhen) were members of the Communist Party. This was not the case with the rest of the top rebel leadership. After the founding of the Workers' General Headquarters, conservative opponents charged that the new rebel organization harbored a surfeit of ruffians, gangsters, and riffraff. Later Zhang Chunqiao noted that those under greatest suspicion were Pan Guoping, Chen Ada, and Huang Jinhai. We turn now to the latter two individuals.

Huang Jinhai was known colloquially as a "dandy" (*afei fenzi*) because of his penchant for fancy attire. His fashionable clothing rendered him a conspicuous figure in the drab atmosphere of Maoist China, where simplicity of dress was near universal. At the start of the Cultural Revolution in 1966 Huang was thirty-one years old. Like so many of the rebel leaders, his childhood had been less than idyllic. Within a month after his birth, Huang's mother died of illness. His father was an opium addict who put his children up for adoption. When Huang was only seven or eight, his foster father also died of illness. His foster mother took in laundry and managed to pay for three years of schooling for him. But in 1947, with prices skyrocketing in the postwar environment, she could no longer afford to keep him. Huang was packed off to a shantytown in Shanghai to rejoin his natural father. Living with his still addicted and abusive father, he completed his elementary school education.

In 1952, at the age of seventeen, Huang was assigned to the Shenxin #5 factory (later the #31 cotton mill) to learn to operate a lathe (Huang 1977: 4/5). At first Huang was diligent in his work and energetic in pursuits outside of work:

> After entering the factory, I applied to join the Youth League. In my spare time I helped write the blackboard newspaper in my workshop, led the aerobics in step to the broadcast, and later joined the company chorus, dance troupe, and basketball team. I slept at the workers' bachelor dorm. Every week on my day off I worked overtime for no pay. In addition I studied at night school three nights a week. My work skills also improved rapidly (*Ibid.*: 1/2).

In spite of Huang's success on the job, his opium-addicted father continued to present a problem. To support his drug dependence, Huang's father embezzled public funds—a crime for which he was sentenced to five years in prison. Huang Jinhai recalled, "When I heard this news I was devastated; I felt that I would never be able to cast off this terrible burden" (*Ibid.*: 4/5). Indeed, his father's impropriety became Huang Jinhai's Achilles' heel in the years ahead, blocking the recognition he felt he deserved. In 1958 Huang and several of his fellow workers discovered a method of reusing discarded parts that resulted in a major savings in time and materials for the factory. However, when their innovation was appropriated by the workshop League secretary to make a name for himself, Huang's efforts at protest proved in vain. His father's unsavory record was an insurmountable obstacle to his own advancement. Robbed of his just due by the dishonesty of his League secretary, Huang sought solace in "dissolute" pursuits:

> I knew that my application to enter the League had been in limbo for many years and now the prospects looked even dimmer. So I became depressed and no longer participated in extracurricular activities. . . . The more I shouldered my political burden, the more despondent I became. For a time I grew a beard and spent most of my nonworking hours playing cards in the club. On Sundays I went to the suburbs to fish instead of engaging in proper duties. I even bought a necktie and then went to a shop that sold exotica to buy a used western suit. Sometimes I ventured to the city center in coat and tie. When I saw people wearing leather jackets, I spent more than 40 yuan to buy one. I was totally preoccupied with my playboy lifestyle. My frivolous habits gave the older workers a very bad impression. I organized dances and the like, which the older workers didn't appreciate (*Ibid.*).

Although we now know that Chairman Mao himself was enjoying dance parties—and more—within the protective walls of Zhongnanhai at this very time, such frivolity was not sanctioned for the populace at large (Li 1994: 93–94, 280, 345–46, 356, 479). In any event, family responsibilities eventually revived Huang Jinhai's interest in political activism:

> In 1964, I felt that to continue in this way wasn't right. I already had a child and my personality was undergoing a major change. At that time I studied a copy of Chairman Mao's works and had a conversion. I was a small group leader of my union and I once again actively threw myself into social activities: family visits, political study, technical assistance. In 1965 our group was named a "five-good small group" for the entire factory. I was also named a "five-good worker." I felt that this the only meaningful kind of existence (Huang 1977: 4/5).

When the Cultural Revolution began, Huang Jinhai plunged into the movement. However, his bold big-character poster elicited a harsh reaction from the Party authorities at his factory. Huang's opprobrious family history and his own penchant for flashy apparel made him an easy target. Fueled by resentment over this counterattack, Huang attached himself to the growing rebel movement. On 6 November he attended the preparatory meeting for the Workers' General Headquarters and was chosen as a member of its leadership group. Soon he joined the Workers' Headquarters first standing committee.

Chen Ada was another worker rebel with a somewhat unsavory reputation. Known in Shanghai dialect as "*awu*" (a dishonest good-for-nothing), he was widely regarded as a petty gangster—prone to profanity and coarse behavior. As a common saying put it during the Cultural Revolution, "wherever there's an armed battle, you'll find Chen Ada."

At the start of the Cultural Revolution, Chen was a twenty-four-year-old blacksmith employed at the Shanghai valve factory who had risen above difficult family circumstances. He was born into a poor family in rural Shaoxing. His mother worked as a servant and his father as a peddler in Shanghai. When he was twelve Chen broke his leg and his mother—unable to care for him at home—took him to the big city to join his father. At first Chen lived with his father in the "poor people's district" (*pinmin qu*) in the western part of the city. They rented a space to sleep—father and son sharing a bed. In the same room more than a dozen other sleeping spaces went to other peddlers. During the day these men ventured forth to sell their wares; at night they had nothing but time on their hands. Their chief recreation was to play cards for money and tell crude jokes. Chen Ada lived in this environment for a year. The next year his father brought Chen's younger brother to Shanghai from the countryside. Unable to survive three-to-a-bed, father and sons moved to another "shantytown district" (*penghu qu*) and rented a small room in a hut made of straw and mud. Chen Ada followed the older boys to various disreputable places of recreation (dance halls, ice-skating rinks, and the like) where he learned to speak with bravado and harass girls (Chen 1977: 8/10).

In 1958, as part of the Great Leap Forward, an urban commune was briefly set up in Shanghai. To rid the city of its unproductive residents, petty gangsters and others seen as local troublemakers were rounded up and packed off for labor reform. Many of Chen Ada's friends were seized in this initiative. Chen himself was assigned to the Zhonghua shipyard that year as a temporary worker. At first he labored as a loader; then as a fitter. At that time the factory's evaluation of him was quite favorable: "Chen Ada's work style is proper, his life style frugal, his food and clothing economical, and his family background impoverished" (Ye 1989).

Three years later Chen joined the army. Upon his discharge, he was assigned to the valve factory. Chen Ada's experiences in the military seem to have exacerbated his earlier wayward tendencies, however. At the valve factory, he did not achieve "activist" status and after work he spent much of his time gambling—an activity which was strictly prohibited at the time (Chen 1977). Considered a backward element among the workers, Chen had often been subjected to criticism by the cadres. The Cultural Revolution presented an opportunity to wreak revenge.

Chen Ada was basically uneducated and his early motivations for involvement in the Cultural Revolution did not imply much political sophistication: "As for the bunch of jerks in the factory, I wanted to settle accounts with all of them" (*Jiefang* 1977). The jerks (*chilao* in Shanghai dialect) were the factory cadres.

It was his participation in the preparatory meeting of the Workers' General Headquarters that propelled Chen Ada to its leadership ranks. On 6 November a rebel worker who happened to pass by the foundry of the valve factory at noontime spotted a large number of big-character posters hanging inside. He decided to go in to make contact with the authors of the posters and inform them about the meeting to be convened that afternoon. Chen Ada happened to be loitering in a corner of the workshop and, hearing about the upcoming get-together, took it upon himself to attend.

Dai Liqing was an unknown ordinary worker—neither activist nor backward element—before the Cultural Revolution. Like so many of the worker rebel leaders, Dai came originally from North China. Born into a poor urban family in Shandong, his father had served as a policeman under the Guomindang. As a youngster in his teens Dai moved with his family to Shanghai; soon thereafter he began an apprenticeship at a textile mill in the western part of the city. In 1956 Dai was sent to Gansu to help in the building of Lanzhou. Six years later, his father having been hospitalized with a terminal illness, Dai returned to Shanghai. After his father's death Dai resigned from the factory in Gansu where he had been working to help out at home. Thus began a three-year period of joblessness during which Dai operated first a cigarette stand, then a tea stand, and finally a plumbing and electronics repair stand. In late 1963 his household registration was officially transferred to Shanghai, and the following year he began a brief stint at the Shanghai #10 steel mill as a temporary worker. The next year Dai was introduced by his district labor office to the Jiangnan metallurgical factory (later renamed the #1 standard materials factory) as an outside contract worker (*wai baogong*). Soon thereafter his classification was changed to that of a temporary worker (*linshi gong*) (*Qingkuang* 1977).

Dai Liqing's personal history as well as his status as a temporary worker became grounds for suspicion once the Cultural Revolution began. He was criticized for having returned from the interior during the period of economic difficulties following the Great Leap Forward "because he feared hardship." His efforts at petty entrepreneurship during his years of unemployment were now portrayed as "engaging in speculation and profiteering" (*Ibid.*). Even the other worker rebels looked down on Dai because he was not a permanent worker. Dai Liqing's troubles were made worse by his own indiscretions. Forced to abandon his wife in Lanzhou when he returned to Shanghai, Dai took up with a young woman apprentice soon after he entered the metallurgical factory. Charges and counter-charges surrounding Dai's peccadillos fueled the unfolding of the Cultural Revolution struggle at his factory:

An investigator dispatched by the Party branch discovered Dai's improper liaison with apprentice Du at his factory. So the branch called Dai in for a talk, asking him to make a written statement. Dai wrote a self-criticism, but he was quite enraged and felt a deep animosity toward Party Secretary Fu. Later Dai learned from apprentice Du that although Fu was thirty-seven years old he hadn't yet married and had previously pursued Du himself. This information delighted Dai; in the name of criticizing the bourgeois reactionary line of the Party branch, he goaded Du into writing a big-character poster exposing Fu (*Ibid.*).

Apprentice Du's big-character poster, entitled "My accusations," galvanized the entire factory and Dai was able to force Secretary Fu to hand over the keys to the Party branch office and the archive room (which held the personnel dossiers on all factory employees). But this power seizure was soon repudiated by the district work team. Dai responded by going first to the company, then to the bureau, and finally all the way to Beijing to lodge a complaint (Dai 1979).

The capsule biographies of these individuals offer a revealing view of the tensions brewing within the Chinese socialist system in its first seventeen years of operation. Although the official rhetoric of the Cultural Revolution would portray such contradictions as rooted in class differences, most had a more mundane basis: regional rivalries, personal ambitions, family problems, individual indiscretions, resentment against factory authorities, and the like. Interestingly, five of the nine top rebel leaders (and four of the seven who remained active after the January Revolution) were northerners. As the situation at Wang Hongwen's #17 mill indicates, regional allegiances could play a significant role in shaping loyalties that later translated into Cultural Revolution factionalism. Cooperation along lines of native-place origin was certainly not a new feature of the Shanghai labor scene. Linguistic affinities and feelings of alienation vis-à-vis the dominant Shanghai culture had long acted to forge a sense of separateness and solidarity among recent arrivals from North China (Perry 1993).

Workplace grievances played an important role in triggering rebellion. Sometimes these problems were structural in nature; sometimes (as in Dai Liqing's affair with an apprentice at his factory) they were basically personal.[12] Virtually all of the old rebels harbored resentment against their factory leadership, but most workers in China, and elsewhere for that matter, routinely encounter a host of workplace disappointments. For these to translate into overt protest requires an additional stimulus.

Like previous campaigns of the People's Pepublic, the Cultural Revolution offered an opportunity for heretofore frustrated or obscure workers to rise on the basis of political activism. In contrast to previous campaigns, however, the Cultural Revolution opened the door to criticism of the Party authorities themselves. Yet the boundaries of criticism were never entirely clear and the possibilities for retribution ever present. Those willing to hazard the immense risks inherent in confronting Party officials were unusually bold individuals.

To understand such personalities seems to call for an excursion into the murky realm of political psychology. The Pye-Solomon approach has been roundly, and rightly, attacked for its caricature of Chinese personality formation (Kagan and Diamond 1973). But it would be unfortunate if such criticism were to discourage other investigations into the popular culture of the Cultural Revolution era. Mass violence was a distinctive feature of this period. Although it is now fashionable to compare its excesses to the state-sponsored terror of Stalin's USSR or Hitler's Germany (Walder 1991; Chirot 1994), there is a crucial difference: in the case of the Cultural Revolution, social forces were called upon to play a central role. To

---

12. Liu Guande, a writer who undertook a lengthy interview with Pan Guoping after the latter's release from prison in 1987, said Pan Guoping was incensed by the unfair wage scale at the glass machinery factory where he worked (Liu 1987).

understand why ordinary citizens accepted Mao's invitation with such alacrity does seem to demand a foray into popular mentalities. While we will barely scratch the surface of this still largely unexplored terrain, we will venture a few preliminary thoughts on the psychology of the old rebels.

The one striking point of commonality among these very diverse rebel leaders was their forceful personalities. A certain audacity was a prerequisite for the high-risk strategy of challenging Party committees and work teams. The sources of this boldness were various, but they point to subcultures of opposition that were both more pervasive and more powerful than previous studies have led us to anticipate. Whereas scholarship on the political culture of Communist China has tended to portray it as an essentially static and homogeneous entity, in fact there was significant diversity (Perry 1994a). The interstices of the dominant Maoist system offered some space for creative resistance. Alien native-place origins, difficult family circumstances, dissident peer groups, and even military service provided breeding grounds for rebel leaders.

For Party members strictly disciplined in obedience to higher authorities, outsider status as recent immigrants to the city evidently facilitated a willingness to challenge the powers-that-be. Wang Hongwen, Wang Xiuzhen, and Geng Jinzhang—the three Party members among the top nine rebel leaders—all hailed from North China. For Party and non-Party members alike, arduous family circumstances seem to have helped mold venturesome personalities. Among those from the North, combatting poverty was a constant trial. Among Southerners, the shame of parental indiscretions (such as the opium addiction of Huang Jinhai's father) may have provided a similar challenge. Many of the rebel leaders were demobilized soldiers—individuals whose horizons had been broadened by the opportunities for travel and job mobility that came with military experience. (A number of these ex-soldiers served as militia captains at their factories.) Such personal experiences encouraged some of those who felt disadvantaged by the system to thumb their noses at Party authorities. Chen Ada's youthful years in the shantytowns of Shanghai exposed him to the dissolute pursuits of itinerant peddlers as well as the rowdy ways of local toughs. His later penchant for gambling and fighting was an outgrowth of these earlier exploits. Playboy Pan Guoping's reputation as a *xiao doulou* (hoodlum) and foppish Huang Jinhai's designation as an *afei fenzi* (dandy) were further signs of the colorful subcultures that bubbled just beneath the drab surface of Maoist China. Although we know very little about such countercultural trends, it seems clear that they helped to arm workers with weapons of resistance.

Despite differences in individual backgrounds and dispositions, we can detect a common audacity in the eagerness with which all these old rebels seized the initiative in denouncing Party authorities. Just the opposite was true in the case of their conservative opponents, for whom networks of Party patronage had fostered a play-it-safe strategy of defending Party traditions.

Conservatives: The Scarlet Guards

On 23 November 1966—exactly two weeks after the rebels had inaugurated their Workers' General Headquarters—representatives from twenty-three Shanghai factories met to establish an umbrella organization for conservative workers to counter the Workers' General Headquarters. The group decided to adopt the historic name of Scarlet Guards (*chiwei dui*), the term for armed militia units in the Communist base areas during the 1927–37 period. The next day another group of Shanghai conservatives—the "Workers' Pickets to Defend Mao Zedong Thought"—held an inaugural meeting at a theater in the western part of the city. In designating themselves "workers' pickets" (*gongren jiuchadui*), this organization asserted a historical linkage to the Three Workers' Uprisings of 1926–27 when armed unionists had formed pickets to welcome the Northern Expeditionary forces to the city.

On 25 November the Workers' Pickets sent ten representatives to the Scarlet Guards to make inquiries about a possible merger.[13] Satisfied with their mutual interrogation, the two groups decided to unite. Soon they were joined by the "February 7 Warriors," a conservative outfit from the Shanghai Railway Bureau named in commemoration of the famous Communist-inspired strike on the Jinghan Railroad of 7 February 1923. These three groups—all of which had chosen names intended to link themselves explicitly to the historic traditions of the Chinese Communist Party and all of which enjoyed tacit sponsorship by municipal Party authorities—comprised the mainstay of a new organization called the "Shanghai General Command Provisional Committee of Scarlet Guards to Defend Mao Zedong Thought." Known as the Scarlet Guards, the organization was formally inaugurated on 6 December (Zhongcheng 1983).

In contrast to the countless rebel organizations that sprang up across the city, representing differing points of view and rival leadership ambitions, Shanghai's conservative movement exhibited a striking feature: only one conservative organization emerged in each work unit. Virtually all leaders of these conservative outfits had been Party activists in the years preceding the Cultural Revolution. Influenced by the norm of Party unity, conservatives were quick to link up with other organizations which shared their basic political outlook.

If the rebels represented countercultural undercurrents in Maoist China, the conservatives embodied the mainstream reaction. Rank-and-file Scarlet Guards claimed a large representation of pre-Cultural Revolution activists, especially Communist Party and Youth League members, labor models, and advanced producers (*Qingkuang* 1968). But they also included a number of individuals with

---

13. The chief of the Organization Department of the Shanghai Party Committee, Yang Shifa, noticed that the manifesto of the workers' pickets was much like that of the Scarlet Guards which had formed the day before and took it upon himself to introduce leaders of the two conservative organizations to each other (Zhongcheng 1983).

questionable dossiers for whom enlisting on the conservative side was a calculated attempt to minimize risk. Before Chairman Mao intervened to make clear his preference for the rebel faction, the conservatives grew to rapidly outnumber their rivals in virtually every factory in Shanghai.[14]

Unlike the old rebels, who initially enjoyed very little backing from higher-level Party authorities, the conservative leaders were well plugged into local Party networks and could count on substantial behind-the-scenes support for their activities. Even so there does seem to have been a genuine element of spontaneity in their initiatives. Much of their activism was sparked by a visceral distaste for the personalities and methods of the rebels. Li Jianyu, a Scarlet Guard leader at the #31 cotton mill, recalled of the earliest rebel leaders at his factory:

> Those who put up big-character posters all belonged to a group of people whose performance (*biaoxian*) was usually pretty poor. Some of them were not diligent workers who even after the Cultural Revolution didn't change their ways. They were careless and irresponsible. . . . There were also some people who suffered from problems that today we wouldn't consider problematic. For example, if one's father had been a Guomindang officer it was said that one's family background was bad [*chushen buhao*]. But even by today's standards many of these people were of shoddy character: adulterers, extortionists, embezzlers—people who would be shunned in any era.

> So at that time I was really dismayed. I felt that these people's basic character was bad and yet here they were, issuing commands and criticisms of the Shanghai Party Committee. Their own ass wasn't clean but they were collecting "black materials" on others. Today they would attack this factory cadre; tomorrow they would attack that Party Committee member. Whenever they got off work they went wild (Li 1992).

Or as Ma Ji, Scarlet Guard commander at the #17 cotton mill, reported:

> I didn't oppose the idea of criticizing the leadership since the Cultural Revolution was calling on everybody to rise up and criticize. But I did oppose the idea of doubting everything and destroying everything. . . . Wang Hongwen and his followers took quotations from Chairman Mao that had been meant for criticism of landlords and used them against cadres and Party members. I couldn't stand that.... Thus as soon as Wang established his "Forever Loyal" group, we established our "Warriors to Defend Mao Zedong Thought" to counter Wang and his followers. When Wang Hongwen seized the materials of the work team, we protected them. We believed that since the work team had been sent by the Party, it wasn't right to wantonly criticize them (Ma 1989).

The conservatives formed as an indignant reaction against what they perceived as rebel excesses. Consequently they were especially numerous in those industrial

---

14. Only two weeks after the formal inauguration of the Scarlet Guards, they already numbered 400,000; at their height they claimed twice that following (*Zhongcheng* 1983).

sectors which had suffered the most deleterious effects of rebel initiatives and in those factories where rebel outfits were most militant.[15]

To a person, the top Scarlet Guard leaders were trusted Party members— serving as political cadres at their factories—whose promotions from the ranks of ordinary workers had come as a reward for active participation in previous Party-sponsored campaigns. Although they were lower staff (*ganshi*) paid according to the wage scale for regular workers, they enjoyed close relations with leading cadres and they wielded some discretionary power over the other workers.

Take the case of Ma Ji, a cadre in the security department of the #17 cotton mill who rose to the challenge of countering Wang Hongwen. Thirty-three years of age at the outset of the Cultural Revolution, Ma Ji had been born into an impoverished Shanghai family. His father worked at a beancurd shop while his mother gave birth to ten children, of whom only Ma Ji and a younger brother survived. Ma began factory work at age seventeen as an apprentice. He studied at night school where after 1949 he joined the Communist Youth League and chaired the student association. During the 6 February 1950 bombing of Shanghai Ma participated in rescue teams, gaining a reputation as an activist. Soon he was assigned to the Yufeng spinning mill, the precursor of the #17 cotton mill. Initially he worked as an oiler and then as an accountant. At the same time Ma Ji continued to accumulate political credentials, advancing from secretary of the Youth League branch in his workshop to the factory Youth League committee. After joining the Communist Party, he was made Party secretary of his workshop. In 1955 Ma's factory sent him to a cadre school for training. Upon his return he requested a transfer to the factory security department. There he took an active part in the Anti-Rightist campaign and remained involved in the supervision of cadres until the start of the Cultural Revolution (Ma 1989).

Li Jianyu, Scarlet Guard opponent of rebel Huang Jinhai at the #31 cotton mill, had entered the mill in the last group of managerial trainees (*lianxisheng*). After completing the initial training period, Li became an accountant in the dye room. Like Ma Ji, he was sent away for special education at the expense of his factory. In March 1957 Li was dispatched to a cadre school of the East China Textile Bureau (later renamed the Shanghai Textile Bureau) for further training in statistics. In 1958, when Chairman Mao called on urban cadres to go down to the rural villages, Li went with other members of his factory Party committee to an agricultural

---

15. With the railway system disrupted by the Anting Incident and the movement to "exchange experiences," many conductors, train service attendants, and workers in the control room joined the Scarlet Guards. After the Shanghai postal system was interrupted by the *Liberation Daily* Incident in which the rebels insisted upon having their tabloid delivered to newspaper subscribers, numerous postal carriers joined the ranks of the Scarlet Guards. Similarly, those factories which generated the top leaders of the Workers' General Headquarters were the same factories which produced the commanders of the Scarlet Guards, as well: the #17 cotton mill, the #31 cotton mill, the glass machinery factory, the Lianggong valve factory, etc.

cooperative in the suburbs of Shanghai. After half a year in the countryside he enlisted in the military and was sent to the Number Two Aviation Institute in Qingdao (Shandong) to study mechanics. Half a year later Li was retained at the Institute as a district captain (*qu duizhang*). In December 1962 he joined the Communist Party. Demobilized the following year, Li returned to his original factory as a cadre in the Party committee's Organization Department. In the latter half of 1964, as the Socialist Education Movement turned into the Four-Cleans campaign, Li was assigned to a Four-Cleans work team at the Textile Bureau (Li 1992).

The Scarlet Guard commanders were all basic-level cadres (*jiceng ganbu*) charged with serving as links between the Party and the ordinary masses. As such, they wielded considerable power over the rank-and-file workers. Ma Ji, as secretary in charge of security, had the authority to detain for interrogation any suspicious worker. Li Jianyu, as secretary of the Organization Department, was in a position to investigate the personal, family, and political conditions of cadres as well as workers. Because many cadres became targets of struggle during the Cultural Revolution, basic-level Scarlet Guard organizations often explicitly excluded cadres above the level of department chief (*kezhang*) and even lower staff (*ganshi*) who were not on the ordinary workers' pay scale from recruitment (*Ibid.*). This precaution was taken in order to avoid being upstaged by rebels, who accused them of "loyalist" tendencies. Had such limitations not been imposed, the proportion of cadres among the Scarlet Guard ranks would have been even higher. The conservatives insisted that their organizations were independently established entities, rather than an artifact of higher-level cadre manipulation. Even so, gaining the approval of higher authorities was considered a crucial step. Li Jianyu recalled,

> The establishment of the Scarlet Guards at our factory was our own idea. The rebels had their organization. Without our own organization we had no power to constrain or challenge them. The Party Committee and the Municipal Committee were in favor of our establishing an organization. They didn't directly instruct us, but they did give us covert encouragement (*Ibid.*).

The formation of the February 7 Warriors, precursor to the Scarlet Guards at the Shanghai Railway Bureau, illustrates the general pattern. The Warriors were founded during the Anting Incident as a reaction against the disruption in rail traffic. When the deputy director of the control room, Wang Yuxi (who was on duty at the time of the Anting Incident), suggested making a public appeal to the citizens of Shanghai to put a stop to the rebels' actions, the majority of workers in the control room applauded his proposal. One worker penned a supportive handbill on the spot. Thus far the process was spontaneous. But Wang Yuxi, as an obedient Party man, quickly sought out the director of the political department and the Party secretary of the railway bureau as well as the vicemayor of Shanghai in charge of transportation. Only after all these officials had indicated their approval did Wang proceed to formally establish the February 7 Warriors and distribute handbills in the name of the new organization (*Zhongcheng* 1983).

Once the Scarlet Guards were formed, the Shanghai Party Committee provided substantial material assistance. A deputy sent to make contact with the fledgling conservative organization later remembered,

> The Shanghai Party Committee wanted the Shanghai Federation of Trade Unions to contact the Scarlet Guards, so the higher levels sent me as a liaison officer. When I asked how to handle the Scarlet Guards' finances, Zhang Qi [member of the Shanghai Party Committee standing committee and chair of the Federation] said meaningfully, "The union has so much money, now is the time to use a little." And within ten days we had provided 125,000 armbands for the Scarlet Guards.
>
> After the Scarlet Guards emerged, they were greatly praised by cadres at all levels, who provided covert and overt support, helping them with tactical planning and offering all sorts of material assistance. Some factory-level unions, following the lead of the Federation, also provided offices for the Scarlet Guards (*Chouming* 1968).

Former Scarlet Guard Jin Ruizhang acknowledged that the Shanghai Party Committee was a source of significant aid:

> The day after Mayor Cao Diqiu approved the formation of the Scarlet Guards, he arranged for us to have an office in the Shanghai Federation of Trade Unions. Immediately we were allocated pens and paper, typewriters, printing presses, bicycles, and many other supplies. Later we also used Federation jeeps to procure fifty bolts of red cloth and commissioned six workers to sew Scarlet Guard armbands (*Ibid.*).

Scarlet Guard commander Wang Yuxi had a similar recollection concerning the Party Committee's interest in his organization's activities:

> Over the space of five months they sent five liaison officers to us, to help us with strategy and tactics, to assist us with "manifestos," to revise our proclamations and some criticism materials (*Ibid.*).

Just as higher-level sponsorship was helpful in launching the Scarlet Guards, so the withdrawal of such support signalled the imminent demise of the conservative movement. When Chairman Mao on 11 January instructed Party Central, the State Council, the Military Affairs Committee, and the Cultural Revolution Small Group to send a joint congratulatory telegram to Wang Hongwen's Workers' General Headquarters—recognizing it as the sole legitimate representative of the Shanghai working class—the conservatives lost any semblance of credibility. Thanks to a decision by Wang Hongwen to welcome former conservatives to his rebel organization, most Scarlet Guards hastily jumped ship to the side of their erstwhile enemies. Wang's policy of reconciliation spelled the organizational destruction of the conservatives and spared Shanghai the sort of bloody factional fighting that wracked many other parts of the country.

The Wind of Economism

In the winter of 1966–67 a new type of labor association—neither rebel nor conservative in orientation—appeared on the Cultural Revolution scene. Dubbed "economistic" because of their relative disinterest in the political debates of the day, these organizations were not centrally concerned with the issue of attacking or defending Party leaders. They focused instead on improving their own material lot. We have records of 354 such organizations in Shanghai alone.[16] The earliest type of economistic organization was composed of temporary workers (*linshi gong*), contract workers (*hetong gong*), and outside contract laborers (*waibao gong*). Use of temporary and contract labor had been a standard means of supplementing the work force since 1949. During the economic recovery of the early 1960s State Chairman Liu Shaoqi advocated expanding the temporary and contract system so that labor might be allocated more flexibly. The system had obvious advantages for the Chinese state in terms of both efficiency and cost. Unlike permanent workers, temporary and contract laborers were employed on an ad hoc basis and received no lifetime securities, pensions, disability coverage, health insurance for their dependents, etc. Often they were paid not by the month, but by the day or by piecework rates.

The cries of these downtrodden members of the Chinese workforce introduced a socioeconomic note to the otherwise relentlessly political discourse of the Cultural Revolution. As an eye witness to the inaugural ceremonies of the Workers' General Headquarters remembered the distinctive contribution of the temporary workers to the convocation,

> Those up on the platform were criticizing the capitalist reactionary line of the Shanghai Party Committee, but down below the platform were a group of women workers between thirty and forty years of age wearing tattered work clothes and hats. These women didn't look like factory workers, but like temporary workers who pulled carts. They weren't paying any attention to the speeches on the platform, but periodically shouted out "We want to become permanent workers!" "We want a pay raise!" (Shen 1989).

The exact nature of the relationship between organizations of temporary and contract workers and the Workers' General Headquarters remains obscure. The largest and most influential such organization in Shanghai—with branches in other cities as well—was the "Revolutionary Rebel General Headquarters of Red Workers," known simply as the Red Workers (*hongse gongren*). It was widely rumored that Wang Hongwen's wife had joined the Red Workers and that Wang's

---

16. In some cases these groups were extremely small and engaged in rather suspect activities. For example, a "rebel headquarters" which specialized in robbery actually comprised a three-person family!

own lack of enthusiasm for opposing economism was related to his wife's protest activities (Huang 1980).

A second type of economistic organization was composed of employees who had been mobilized to return to their native places as a result of the retrenchment campaign of the early 1960s. The largest of this type of organization was the "Revolutionary Rebel General Headquarters of Shanghai Workers Supporting Agriculture who Returned to Shanghai," known as Support Agriculture Headquarters [*Zhinong si*]. Their chief slogans were: "We want to return to work!" and "We want to eat!" (*Wuchanjieji* 1967).

In 1960–62, during the severe economic crisis after the Great Leap Forward, many factories had been forced to halt or severely curtail production. In view of the surplus labor problem the government had asked overstaffed urban factories to relocate those workers who had relatives back in the countryside or other means of resettling outside the city. This was a kind of mass layoff, with the implicit promise that as soon as the national economy improved most of the repatriated workers would have first option on returning to their old jobs (*Xin* 1990). After 1963, the Chinese economy began to improve. However, the demographic explosion put pressure on urban employment that made it impossible for factories to make good on their previous promise to reinstate repatriated workers. The resentment of displaced workers was heightened when they discovered that the city of Shanghai had taken liberties with central guidelines in implementing the layoffs in the first place. In an apparent attempt to save money Shanghai had violated central policy by targeting more experienced workers (who of course garnered higher paychecks) for the relocation effort (*Jixu* 1967).

Now these repatriated workers were converging on Shanghai from every direction, involving cadres at all levels in their demand to return to the city. According to a report of the Shanghai Labor and Wage Committee on 15 December 1966:

> The repatriated workers have established two rebel commands and have raised demands for being made permanent workers, changing the method of income allocation, and improving work benefits. We have learned that a "revolutionary committee of repatriated employees" with more than 10,000 registered members has been established in Wuxi (Jiangsu) and has disseminated numerous handbills. They are requesting either a return to work or an official retirement settlement. At present a number of other places have also seen groups of repatriated employees demanding an immediate return to Shanghai (*Guanyu* 1966).

A third type of economistic organization was made up of workers helping out with construction in the interior. As the premier industrial city in China, Shanghai for many years had sent a large number of people to assist with development projects in other parts of the country. In some cases whole factories had been relocated to the interior. Some of these assistance programs were carried out according to central directives, while others were direct transfers from Shanghai to the interior. Quite a few of the relocated workers were apprentices in the middle of their training periods. After the Cultural Revolution began, many of them rushed back to Shanghai to protest the disruption in their training schedule and demand immediate reassignment to their old jobs (*Jixu* 1967).

A fourth type of economistic organization comprised young people who had been relocated in the "up to the mountains, down to the countryside" and "support agriculture, support the frontiers" campaigns of the 1960s. To reduce the unemployment problem Shanghai had mobilized a large number of "social youths" (*shehui qingnian*), who were unemployed or just graduated from middle school, to go down to the suburbs of Shanghai or to more distant locales to work on state farms. During the Cultural Revolution these workers also took advantage of the general disruption to hurry home. As a report of February 1967 indicated:

> At present the great majority of intellectual youths sent to neighboring state farms, as well as some of those sent to the military farms in Xinjiang, have already returned to Shanghai. They claim that "mobilizing city youths to go up to the mountains and down to the countryside to support agriculture and support the frontiers is a giant plot." They demand to return to Shanghai and reclaim their household registrations (*Ibid.*).

Yet a fifth type of economistic organization—and one which quickly succumbed to repression by the Public Security Bureau—was formed by private entrepreneurs. The city's largest such association, the "Shanghai Private Entrepreneur Laborers' Revolutionary Rebel Headquarters," was deemed "capitalist and antirevolutionary" and its leaders apprehended by the authorities. As a rebel handbill reported unsympathetically on its operations:

> This organization was founded in December 1966. In addition to a general headquarters, it established branches in ten districts and four counties. To entice recruits it promised that "those who join our organization in future can enter state enterprises with labor insurance, permanent jobs, and old age welfare and disability."
> Its members claimed that in seventeen years of liberation the working people have "turned over" and become masters, but the private entrepreneurs are still oppressed by the powerholders. More than thirty criticism sessions were held in every district to attack the taxation policy. They charged that three big mountains rest on the heads of the peddlers: the taxation bureau, the industrial-commercial department, and the market management office.
> In the name of striving for a state enterprise, they engaged in economism. They demanded that "private merchants and peddlers must be state employees," and they rejected the current system of cooperatives.

> They even hoped to seize power from the Shanghai industrial and commercial administrative management bureau and the industrial-commercial bureaus in each district. As a result, they were chased out by the rebel faction at these units (*Jianjue* n.d.).

Although the private entrepreneurs appear to have been better organized than other economistic groups, their association with capitalist tendencies rendered them an easy target for repression.

The so-called "wind of economism" first gained momentum among those who lacked secure jobs or household registrations in Shanghai.[17] Denied the privileges that came with permanent employment at state enterprises or fixed residency in a major city, the have-nots demanded access. But even those more favored by the system were not entirely free from dissatisfactions; eventually they too raised materialistic demands. Indeed, the wind of economism can be read as a kind of weathervane measuring the level of deprivation among the Shanghai workforce, shifting direction over time from the most disadvantaged elements toward more privileged sectors: from contract and temporary workers to repatriated workers to apprentices, and finally to permanent state employees with Shanghai residency.

Apprentices, who occupied a kind of intermediate position on the employment roster (promised permanent employment and secure benefits in future yet still laboring under harsh treatment), were instrumental in redirecting the wind of economism from the streets into the factories. As the Shanghai Revolutionary Committee noted in its chronology published in March 1967:

> On 27 December 1966 some apprentices in the ninth district of the Port Authority, while searching for black materials, discovered documents concerning the official wage scale for apprentices. Realizing that their wages did not match what was stipulated in the documents, they went to the district bureau to demand a supplement. Li Guang, Party secretary of the Maritime Transport Bureau of the northern district, agreed to issue a year's wages as recompense (*Wuchanjieji* 1967).

News of the apprentices' success spread like wildfire and soon not a single enterprise in the city was unaffected by monetary requests from its workers. Insisting that previous wage hikes had not kept pace with official directives, employees demanded subsidies to compensate for years of substandard treatment. Even newly hired workers rushed forward to press wage claims; for example, a group known as the "58 Regiment"—the membership of which was primarily young workers who had entered the factories in 1958—insisted that new hires had been subjected to wage discrimination for which restitution was due (*Wenge* 1982).

Another strategy for raising wages was to change the ownership form of an enterprise, thereby altering the employees' status. In a number of instances insistent workers convinced Shanghai Party Committee secretary and vicesecretary Chen Pixian and Cao Diqiu to sign agreements that converted formerly private and collective enterprises into new state-owned units. A group known as the "Elementary Teachers' Headquarters," claiming at its height some

---

17. On the importance of the household registration system in creating stratification in socialist China, see Cheng and Selden 1994.

30,000 members, was established to demand that private schools be redesignated as publicly owned institutions (*Ibid.*). In the case of one privately run elementary school, the conversion to state ownership resulted in a 70 percent wage increase for teachers (Zhu 1969).

Wages constituted only a fraction of an urban employee's total income—much of which was in the form of subsidies. Workers at state enterprises received cash allowances for transportation, baths, meals, nutritional supplements, uniforms, towels, soap, shoes, gloves, and the like. The wind of economism stirred up a concern over subsidies that was almost as feverish as that over wages. In some cases workers at collective enterprises demanded treatment equivalent to that enjoyed by workers at state enterprises; in others workers at state enterprises asked for the restoration of benefits which had been lost during the economic troubles of 1960–62.

Along with wage and subsidy increases workers raised a demand for various Cultural Revolution "living expenses." Fees to exchange revolutionary experiences, spread propaganda, produce armbands, purchase broadcasting equipment, procure vehicles for transportation, and so forth were demanded (*Ibid.*). A particularly costly manifestation of the economistic wind was a call to divide up various pots of money—such as union operating expenses, year-end production accumulation funds, shares of coops, etc. In Yimiao district one cooperative disbursed the entire ¥50,000 it had accumulated since 1963; similarly, the Huaihai Weaving Factory completely divided up its union's ¥16,000 cash surplus account (Telegram 1967).

In addition to claims for monetary compensation—whether in the form of higher wages, subsidies, Cultural Revolution expenses, or shares of accumulated funds—workers demanded the right to unionize. Behind the quest for unionization lay a desire for medical benefits and welfare provisions (*laobao* or labor insurance) accessible only to union members. China's trade union regulations stipulated that neither private entrepreneurs nor workers at collective enterprises were eligible to join unions. This meant that such people were denied the medical and retirement benefits obtainable only through union membership. In late August of 1966 hundreds of workers from street factories, private schools, local hospitals, and trade, government, and construction industries marched with symbols and drums to the Shanghai Federation of Trade Unions to demand unions (Shen 1989). But soon the Federation itself came under attack as part of the Cultural Revolution assault on bureaucratism, rendering unionization an infeasible option.

One of the more violent manifestations of the economistic wind was the seizure and occupation of housing. Population pressure had created a severe housing shortage in the city. The Cultural Revolution offered a convenient opportunity to appropriate housing in the name of "rebellion." Acts of confiscation were carried out by individuals or groups of individuals, but usually in the name of the rebel faction at their work unit. Under the pretext of expelling "capitalist roaders," "four pests," and "reactionary authorities," workers took possession of housing that they coveted for themselves and their families. In the space of five days between 30 December 1966 and 3 January 1967, "all the housing in the city that was awaiting allocation was forcibly occupied" (Zhu 1969).

After the wind of economism spread from the streets into the factories, the basic ranks of rebel and conservative workers alike became especially vociferous in pressing materialistic demands. Some of the rebels were affiliated with Wang Hongwen's Workers' General Headquarters, others with splinter groups like the Second Regiment or the Workers' Third Headquarters. As far as we can determine, however, the rebel organizations themselves did not raise economistic demands—aside from asking for subventions of expenses associated with Cultural Revolution activities. Their handbills indicate that their actions as well as their slogans were "political" attacks on powerholders, rather than "economistic" requests for increased income. Thus although rank-and-file rebels were deeply involved with economistic activities (which Wang Hongwen initially refused to condemn), the rebel forces were relatively free organizationally of such entanglements. As a consequence when Party Central issued a directive opposing the economistic wind, the Workers' General Headquarters was quick to place the blame entirely on the shoulders of those cadres whom their ordinary followers had forced into signing disbursement agreements—charging that these cadres had used money to corrupt the rebel ranks. The alleged criminality of the cadres in fanning the winds of economism became a pretext for the rebel seizure of power from the Shanghai Party Committee.

Conclusion

Important as social forces were in the unfolding of the Cultural Revolution, they pulled in contrary directions. Within the working class of Shanghai, we have identified three distinctive tendencies. *Rebels* challenged Party authorities and *conservatives* defended them, while *economistic* groups clamored for material improvements. Labor was working at crosspurposes: rebellion, conservatism, and economism were promoted by different sorts of leaders acting on the basis of dissimilar motivations. These distinctions, we suggest, are best captured by different analytical traditions.

The socioeconomic approach stresses the influence of favored versus disfavored backgrounds in generating a kind of "interest group" behavior that translated into rebel and conservative factionalism during the Cultural Revolution. Hong Yung Lee concludes that the rebel mass organizations recruited mainly among groups with grievances against the establishment: "among the workers, they were those from the smaller, poorer factories, the contract and temporary workers, the apprentices and unskilled workers in the larger factories, and the individual laborers" (1978: 34). This is an accurate characterization of workers who were active in the wind of economism. Although previous scholarship has erred in conflating economism with the rebel movement, the materialistic upsurge is indeed well explained by a socio-economic approach. Economism was in essence a protest against the inequities of the command economy. Groups of workers criticized the administrative methods that arbitrarily divided them into different categories with differential access to benefits. Those least favored by the system—contract and temporary workers, relocated workers, apprentices, collective and private sector employees—raised the most strident complaints. The wind of economism pointed the finger of blame at the many flagrant injustices inherent in the operations of China's socialist system. In this respect economism presented a more fundamental criticism than did the rebel movement.

Rebel leaders, like their conservative opponents, were playing a political game whose rules had been laid down by higher levels. As was true in previous campaigns, the *rewards* of the game remained the promise of political office—yet the *rules* of the game changed dramatically during the Cultural Revolution. Uncertainties over proper targets of struggle permitted those outside or on the edges of established Party networks to seize the initiative in a manner unthinkable in earlier political campaigns.

Unlike those who participated most vocally in the wind of economism, the old rebels are not easily explained in terms of group analysis; some were Party members, others were ordinary workers, and yet others were considered "backward elements." Those who rose to the challenge of criticizing Party committees and work teams were audacious individuals whose feisty personalities had often been born out of difficult family circumstances and nurtured in rowdy subcultures that operated on the margins of orthodox Party life. Northern origins, shantytown childhoods, and youth gangs all seem to have played a role in fostering rebel leadership in Shanghai. Unfortunately we know very little about such dissonant currents in Communist China.[18] But it is certainly clear—Pye and Solomon notwithstanding—that not all Chinese exhibited a "dependent" orientation in the face of higher authority.[19] Even one of Wang Hongwen's most

---

18. Emily Honig's pioneering work on native-place divisions in Shanghai is an important contribution to our understanding of "ethnic" influences among the working class even after the establishment of the People's Republic (1992: esp. chap. 7). On the culture of the shantytowns of Shanghai, see Nai 1982.

19. In his more recent writings, Lucian Pye has acknowledged the existence of two political cultures in Communist China—a Maoist rebel culture which he identifies with the heterodoxy of Daoism, Buddhism, and folk religion in imperial days and a Dengist restraint which he identifies with the orthodoxy of Confucianism (see 1988: esp. chap. 2). Unfortunately Pye does not provide a convincing explanation for the origins and operations of these competing cultural tendencies in the contemporary context. Anita Chan's (1985) use of the "authoritarian personality" concept to explain student rebels during the Cultural Revolution also offers little help in understanding rebel leadership among workers. Her interviews with student Red Guards led Chan to highlight the centrality of the school

faithful rebel colleagues, a Party member himself, criticized many of the other rebel leaders for their unrestrained temperaments:

> Wang Hongwen never forgot those who rose in rebellion with him and was always looking out for them. . . . However, I couldn't stand those other Workers' General Headquarters leaders like Huang Jinhai, Chen Ada, or Dai Liqing. They were rascals. We were after all party members and were used to strict demands on ourselves. During the Cultural Revolution I never could get along with those other people (Tang 1992).

If a rebel could express such distaste for his fellow rebel leaders, we can appreciate the feelings of revulsion that gripped those on the conservative side. The disgust with which conservative leaders regarded their radical adversaries reflected the cultural gulf that distanced the persons and actions of the rebels from accepted Party practice.

While rebels and conservatives were both embroiled in a high-stakes political contest, conservatives drew upon the resources of established Party-state networks in mounting their offensive. As Andrew Walder has noted, "the party reaches out to the citizenry through constantly cultivated patronage relationships, in which active support and loyalty are exchanged for mobility opportunities, material advantages, and social status" (1993: 246–47). Although rebel condemnation forced the conservative Scarlet Guards to disavow any intimate connection to higher-level patrons, Party backers did in fact play a crucial role in promoting their activities.

Such political networks are sometimes seen as having been created *de novo* by the Communist state during the 1950s, but they had important roots in the pre-1949 Communist labor movement—as the conservatives' preference for historical nomenclature borrowed from the revolutionary struggles of the past suggested. At the start of the Cultural Revolution the Shanghai Party Committee and the Shanghai Federation of Trade Unions were replete with old cadres from the Jiangnan region who had been active in the pre-1949 labor movement. Both Federation Vice Chair Shi Huizhen (who led the work team that condemned the rebellion of Wang Hongwen at the #17 mill), and Federation Chair Zhang Qi (who authorized the provision of material aid to the Scarlet Guards) were former activists in the underground Shanghai labor movement whose initiatives during the Cultural Revolution offered clear encouragement to the conservative forces. Long accustomed to a modus operandi that favored reliance upon fellow Party loyalists from Jiangnan, they continued this familiar tactic during the early months of the Cultural Revolution. Had Chairman Mao not intervened to indicate his personal support for the rebels' assault on established Party networks in Shanghai, the Scarlet Guards would undoubtedly have emerged victorious.

---

socialization process—a factor that does not figure significantly in workers' accounts of their turn to rebellion.

Mao's preference for the rebel challengers unleashed many of the disruptive consequences of the Cultural Revolution decade. Eventually Party networks in work units were reestablished, but not without a marked deterioration in discipline. The irreverent style of the rebels was fertile soil for the growth of a general disrespect for Party authority—with serious implications for the future of Chinese politics.[20]

The variety of ways in which workers responded to the Cultural Revolution cautions against too facile a portrait of working-class politics in Maoist China. The Communist workunit [*danwei*] induced not only dependency, but also defiance—both toward individual workplace authorities (on the part of the rebels) and toward structural features of the system itself (when those with the fewest privileges under the *danwei* system demanded a redress of grievances during the wind of economism.)[21]

In part because of source limitations and in part because of the prevailing image of Chinese workers as basically quiescent, studies of protest in the People's Republic until recently have focused almost exclusively upon students and intellectuals. This has been the case not only for the Cultural Revolution, but for the Hundred Flowers Campaign, Democracy Wall, and the Tiananmen incidents of 1976 and 1989 as well. Increasingly, however, we are discovering that workers played a key role in all these movements.[22] Indeed, one might well propose that the draconian fashion in which each of these upsurges was eventually suppressed was due above all to the Beijing regime's deep-seated anxieties about a restive workforce. Moreover, as Poland's Solidarity dramatically demonstrated and as new theories of democratization underscore, the Chinese leadership was hardly being irrational in harboring such fears. In the industrial age, regime transitions are often closely associated with labor movements (Rueschemeyer, Stephens, and Stephens 1992; Collier 1992; Collier and Collier 1991).

Upcoming transformations of the Chinese polity will surely bear more than a casual relationship to worker unrest. And yet, as in the past, labor activists are likely to continue to work at crosspurposes. Only by uncovering the divergent political, psychocultural, and socioeconomic strains within the Chinese labor movement can we hope for a reliable guide to its future bearings.

---

20. On rebel culture, see Perry and Li 1993. For the influence of this cultural style on the uprising of 1989, see Schwarcz 1994.

21. The issue of defiance is developed in Perry, forthcoming.

22. For a case study of worker activism during the Hundred Flowers, see Perry 1994b. On the Tiananmen Incident of 1976, see Heilmann (1994). And on the 1989 uprising see Walder and Gong 1993. An elaboration of this argument can be found in Perry 1995.

References

1965nian Shanghai shigong jiben qingkuang tongji (Statistics on the basic
conditions of the Shanghai workforce in 1965). 1965. Shanghai: Shanghai
Statistical Bureau. In Shanghai Municipal Archives [SMA].

Chan, Anita. 1985. *Children of Mao: Personality Development and Political
Activism in the Red Guard Generation*. Seattle: University of Washington
Press.

Chan, Anita, Stanley Rosen, and Jonathan Unger. 1980. "Students and Class
Warfare: The Social Roots of the Red Guard Conflict in Guangzhou
(Canton)." *China Quarterly* 83 (September): 397–446.

Chang, Parris. 1981. "Shanghai and Chinese Politics: Before and After the
Cultural Revolution." In *Shanghai: Revolution & Development in an Asian
Metropolis*, edited by Christopher Howe. Cambridge: Cambridge University
Press.

Chen. 1987. [Former #17 cotton mill rebel]. Interview with Li Xun.

Chen Ada. 1977. Testimony August 10. In SMA.

Cheng, T. J., and Mark Selden. 1994. "The Origins and Social Consequences of
China's Hukou System." *China Quarterly* (September).

Chirot, Daniel. 1994. *Modern Tyrants*. New York: The Free Press.

Chouming zhaozhu de Shanghai chiweidui (Notorious Shanghai Scarlet Guards).
1968. Shanghai: Workers' General Headquarters, October.

Collier, Ruth Berins. 1992. *The Contradictory Alliance: State-Labor Relations
and Regime Change in Mexico*. Berkeley: International and Area Studies,
University of California.

Collier, Ruth Berins and David Collier. 1991. *Shaping the Political Arena:
Critical Junctures, the Labor Movement, and Regime Dynamics in Latin
America*. Princeton: Princeton University Press.

Dai Liqing. 1979. Testimony, October 18. In SMA.

Dittmer, Lowell. 1977. "Political Culture and Political Symbolism." *World
Politics* 29, no. 4 (July): 552–84.

Dittmer, Lowell. 1987. *China's Continuous Revolution*. Berkeley: University of
California Press.

Fandang fenzi Wang Hongwen zuixing nianbiao (Chronology of criminal
activities of anti-Party element Wang Hongwen). 1977. Shanghai Party
Committee small group to investigate the Gang of Four case. March. In
SMA.

Geng Jinzhang. 1979. Testimony, November 27, March 6. In SMA.

Guanyu erbingtuan fuzeren Geng Jinzhang juliu shencha de qingkuang baogao
(Situation report on the detention and interrogation of Second Regiment
leader Geng Jinzhang). 1967. April 11. In Shanghai Public Security Bureau,
Yangpu district office.

Guanyu xianzai nongcun de jingjian zhigong de anzhi yijian (Opinions concerning the settlement of streamlined workers now in the villages). 1966. Shanghai Labor Wage Committee Report to the Shanghai Party Committee, with copies to Party Central and the East China Bureau. December 15.

Heilmann, Sebastian. 1994. "The Social Context of Mobilization in China: Factions, Work Units and Activists during the April Fifth Movement in 1976." *China Information.*

Honig, Emily. 1992. *Creating Chinese Ethnicity.* New Haven: Yale University Press.

Huang Jinhai. 1976. Testimony, October 28. In SMA.

———. 1977. Testimony, January 2, April 5. In SMA.

———. 1980. Testimony, July 16. In SMA.

Jianjue fencui zibenzhuyi fubi niliu, chedi jiefa pipan "gelaosi" yixiaocuo bie you yongxin de toutou de zuixing (Resolutely smash the capitalist restoration countercurrent; thoroughly expose and criticize the crimes of the ambitious heads of the "private entrepreneurs headquarters"). n.d. Handbill. In SMA.

Jiefang Ribao (Liberation Daily). 1977. November 20.

Jixu qingshi de jige wenti (Several issues in urgent need of instructions). 1967. Shanghai: Shanghai People's Commune, February 15.

Kagan, Richard, and Norma Diamond. 1973. "Father, Son and Holy Ghost: Pye, Solomon and the 'Spirit of Chinese Politics." *Bulletin of Concerned Asian Scholars* 5, no. 1 (July): 62–68.

Kraus, Richard. 1981. *Class Conflict in Chinese Socialism.* New York: Columbia University Press.

Lee, Hong Yung. 1978. *The Politics of the Chinese Cultural Revolution: A Case Study.* Berkeley: University of California Press.

Li Jianyu. 1992. Interview with Li Xun, July 3.

Li Zhisui. 1994. *The Private Life of Chairman Mao.* New York: Random House.

Liu, Alan P.L. 1976. *Political Culture and Group Conflict in Community China.* Santa Barbara: Clio Press.

Liu Guande. 1987. Interview with Li Xun.

Liu Xiaobo. 1994. "That Holy Word, 'Revolution.'" In *Popular Protest and Political Culture in Modern China,* edited by Jeffrey N. Wasserstrom and Elizabeth J. Perry, 309–24. Boulder: Westview Press.

Ma Ji, 1989. Interview with Li Xun 6 July.

Nai Peichun. 1982. *Dushili cunzhuang* (Village within a city). Film.

Perry, Elizabeth J. 1993. *Shanghai on Strike: The Politics of Chinese Labor.* Stanford: Stanford University Press.

———. 1994a. "Chinese Political Culture Revisited." In *Popular Protest and Political Culture in Modern China,* edited by Jeffrey N. Wasserstrom and Elizabeth J. Perry. Boulder: Westview Press.

———. 1994b. "Shanghai's Strike Wave of 1957." *China Quarterly* (March).

————. 1995. "Labor's Battle for Political Space: The Role of Worker Associations in Contemporary China." In *Urban Spaces in Contemporary China: The Potential for Autonomy and Community in Post-Mao China*, edited by Deborah Davis et al. New York: Cambridge University Press.

————. Forthcoming. "From Native-place to Workplace: Labor Origins and Outcomes of China's *Danwei* System." In *China's Mid-Century Transitions*, edited by William Kirby. Cambridge: Harvard University Press.

Perry, Elizabeth J., and Li Xun. 1993. "Revolutionary Rudeness: The Language of Red Guards and Rebel Workers in China's Cultural Revolution." *Indiana East Asian Working Paper Series on Language and Politics in Modern China*, no. 2 (July).

————. 1997. *Proletarian Power: Shanghai in the Cultural Revolution*. Boulder: Westview Press.

Pye, Lucian W. 1968. *The Spirit of Chinese Politics: A Psychocultural Study of Authority Crisis in Political Development*. Cambridge: MIT Press.

————. 1981. *The Dynamics of Chinese Politics*. Cambridge, MA: Oelgeschlager, Gunn, and Hain.

————. 1988. *The Mandarin and the Cadre: China's Political Cultures*. Ann Arbor: University of Michigan Center for Chinese Studies.

Qingkuang huibao (Situation report). 1977. Shanghai Revolutionary Committee. April 18. In SMA.

Qingkuang huibian (Situation bulletin). 1968. Shanghai: Workers' General Headquarters, April 22.

Rosen, Stanley. 1982. *Red Guard Factionalism and the Cultural Revolution in Guangzhou (Canton)*. Boulder: Westview Press.

Rueschemeyer, Dietrich, Evelyne Huber Stephens, and John D. Stephens. 1992. *Capitalist Development and Democracy*. Chicago: University of Chicago Press.

Schurmann, Franz. 1968. *Ideology and Organization in Communist China*. Berkeley: University of California Press.

Schwarcz, Vera. 1994. "Memory and Commemoration: The Chinese Search for a Livable Past." In *Popular Protest and Political Culture in Modern China*, edited by Jeffrey N. Wasserstrom and Elizabeth J. Perry, 170–83. Boulder: Westview Press.

Shanghai 17chang wenhua geming shiji (Annals of the Cultural Revolution at Shanghai's #17 factory). 1975. Shanghai: Shanghai #17 cotton mill. In the archives of Shanghai #17 cotton mill.

Shen Jingbo. 1989. August.

Solomon, Richard H. 1971. *Mao's Revolution and the Chinese Political Culture*. Berkeley: University of California Press.

Tang Wenlan. 1992. Interview with Li Xun, May 17.

Telegram to Party Central. 1967. January 6.

Transcript of roundtable concerning Geng Jinzhang at the Shanghai paper pulp mill. 1979. December 1. In Shanghai Middle-Level Court archives.

Walder, Andrew G. 1986. *Communist Neo-Traditionalism: Work and Authority in Chinese Industry.* Berkeley: University of California Press.

————. 1991. "Cultural Revolution Radicalism: Variations on a Stalinist Theme." In *New Perspectives on the Cultural Revolution,* edited by William A. Joseph, Christine P. W. Wong, and David Zweig, 41–61. Cambridge: Harvard University Press.

————. forthcoming. "The Chinese Cultural Revolution in the Factories: Party State Structures and Patterns of Conflict." In *Worker Identities in East Asia,* edited by Elizabeth J. Perry. Berkeley: Institute of East Asian Studies.

Walder, Andrew G., and Gong Xiaoxia. 1993. "Workers in the Tiananmen Protests: The Politics of the Beijing Workers Autonomous Federation." *Australian Journal of Chinese Affairs* 29 (January).

Wang Hongwen. 1967. Speech to the Workers' General Headquarters standing committee. In SMA.

Wenge chuqi Shanghai gelei qunzhong zuchi jiankuan (Overview of various types of Shanghai mass organizations in the early period of the Cultural Revolution). 1982. Shanghai Office to "Expose and Criticize the Gang of Four and Their Remnant Forces in Shanghai.

Wuchanjieji wenhua dageming zhong Shanghai fandui jingizhayi da shiji (Annals of Shanghai's opposition to economism during the Great Proletarian Cultural Revolution). 1967. Shanghai Revolutionary Committee, March 17. In SMA.

Xin ganbu tongjibiao (Statistical tables on new cadres). 1969. Edited by Workers' General Federation. December. In SMA.

Xin Shanghai 40 nian (40 years of new Shanghai). 1990. Edited by the Shanghai Statistical Bureau. Beijing: China Statistics Publishing House.

Ye Yonglie. 1989. *Wang Hongwen xingshuai lu* (A record of the rise and fall of Wang Hongwen). Changchun: Shidai wenyi chubanshe.

Zhongcheng yu dang de Shanghai gongren chiweidui (Scarlet Guards: Loyal to the Party). 1983. Shanghai Federation of Trade Unions. September.

Zhu Yongjia. 1969. *Shanghai yiyue geming dashiji* (Annals of the January Revolution in Shanghai).

The Interaction of Culture and Economics: Does Culture Count?

ROBERT F. DERNBERGER
The University of Michigan

For the past twenty-seven years that I have been teaching, most textbooks on comparative economic systems assert that economic outcomes or an economy's performance depends upon a great variety of factors: purely economic variables, social organizations and behavioral values, historical forces, geographical endowments, political organizations and decisions, and so forth. To simplify this complex nexus, these interdependent factors are organized under three categories of variables: the society's economic system, its environment, and economic policy choices.

Over this same period of time most of my colleagues in economics were developing sophisticated and complex theoretical models that imposed restrictive definitions on economics as a discipline within the social sciences. They assumed or defined rational behavior to mean efficient and maximization behavior (i.e., maximum real income, profit, or output). Assuming that individuals are rational, they declared the only rational economic system to be a free-market one.[1] This solves the problem of the variables in the category of economic systems. Furthermore the only rational economic policies are those marketizing and privatizing enhancing policies that work to best facilitate a free-market economic system. While they admitted that governments can adopt irrational policies, an analysis of these policies would show them to be inefficient—irrational—or second best to the preferred policies of privatization and marketization.

Where do the variables in the environment category come into the analysis? The economists' theoretical models can be used to analyze *changes* in the environment, but the economists usually assume the *variables* in that category as

---

1. Frank Knight, father of the Chicago School of Economics, is said to have argued that economics was defined as, and limited to, the study of a free-market, capitalist economic system. There were other economic systems (traditional, religious, cooperative, etc.), but they were irrational and therefore not the subject of economists' attention.

givens; they do not play a part in the analysis of cause and effect.[2] Inasmuch as the analyses of these economists worked fairly well in predicting the outcome of policy regimes and policy changes for most economies in the developed world, it did appear reasonable to believe that culture and institutions were not very important. At most cultural and institutional differences caused "white noise" in the analysis, but the power of rational behavior and purely economic forces overcame these minor irritants. In other words, culture and institutions may matter, but not enough to make any significant difference in the economists' first approximation of the truth.

As a student of China's economy I found it hard to accept the assumption that culture and institutions—along with all the other variables in the environment category—were not significant. As a consequence in my own work over the past decade I have focused on trying to bring culture and institutions back into the analysis of economic developments in China as important if still secondary variables. As director of the East Asian Modernization Project at the East West Center in Hawaii during the 1980s, I commissioned a review of the literature on modernization under the direction of Gilbert Wong at the University of Hong Kong. His research group collected an extensive bibliography, and in his final report evaluating the literature, Wong asserts that although non-economists frequently highlight the relationship between culture and modernization, "few attempt to establish the nature of any causal relationship between culture and modernization." When we get to economists writing on economic developments in East Asia, however, "few authors offer more than passing comment on the role of non-economic variables in the economic success of the East Asian nations" (1990: 8, 15). The East Asian Modernization Project also sponsored workshops on such topics as the source of entrepreneurship, the role of the government, the savings-investment mechanism, and the economic policy process in Asian economic development to highlight how and why culture and institutions must be included in the analysis.[3]

---

2. This failure to include institutions as part of the analysis, of course, was one of Marx's major criticisms of classical economics: he held that classical economics was limited to one particular institutional stage in the evolution of economic history.

3. After the demise of the Modernization in East Asia Project at the East-West Center, several associated with it secured financial support from the Tokyo Group in Japan to continue the work to show that culture and institutions were significant in explaining the East Asian "miracle." The Japanese had put considerable pressure on the World Bank to accept that an Asian model of successful development was different, due to cultural and historical factors, from the traditional Western model. For the project I wrote an as-yet-unpublished paper, "Culture and Economics: Back to The Future" which argues that the creators of economics as a discipline, i.e., Smith, Ricardo, Malthus, and

Over the past few decades several new fields have blossomed within economics—economic history, which studies the evolution in a society's economic institutions and outcomes; institutional economics, which studies the impact of the environment in determining the evolution of a society's economic institutions; and game theory, which allows for different institutional organizations, principal-agent relationships, incentives, and strategies, and allows for different results as a result of these differences. Yet despite these developments the core of neoclassical economics has strengthened its position of dominance as the defining methodology. Within the last decade the fields of comparative economic systems and economic development, two fields that often did rely explicitly on cultural and institutional differences as possible explanations for observed economic results, have declined in importance. The downfall of communism and the rejection of the Soviet-type economy by many former members of the Soviet bloc permitted economic system reforms that were widely assumed to have as their objective the creation of a free-market, capitalist system. In addition, a very aggressive corps of economists from Cambridge, Massachusetts, the World Bank, and elsewhere have been advising the former Communist countries to "privatize" and "marketize," which after a brief period of bitter adjustment, will solve their economic troubles.

In a very important and perceptive review Peter Murrell argues that the advice these economists give and conclusions they promote reflect their general agreement on the paradigm of the transition process: an idealized market (1995). They ignore "the crucial question of how the reforms engage existing society," with all its historical legacies and cultural values (*Ibid.*: 177). While Murrell does not expect economists to delve deeply into history and society, he argues that they "barely scratch the surface" of the environmental variables. Obviously, to learn why some reform policies based on their paradigm work and some do not, "the historical legacy, in politics and society, as well as in economics, has to be an important factor" (*Ibid.*).[4]

John Stuart Mill, explicitly recognized the importance of culture and institutions and included these variables in their analyses.

4. With regard to the simple, uniform advice given former members of the Soviet bloc, I argue that "capitalism" is only an ideal and not an operational policy variable. In reality there are many different varieties of capitalism. Capitalism may be thought of as a *family* name within the *order* economic systems. Each individual economy may represent a *species* within the family "capitalism," and our task is to better define the characteristics of those different species so that they will be operational when implemented by a borrower. The point is that culture and other institutional and historical variables will play a significant role in explaining how those operational models become a subset of the higher-order ideal, which is by definition culture-free. See Dernberger 1997.

While economic models based on ideal types may work fine as first approximations for predicting economic outcomes for a specific economy, that is not all we are interested in as social scientists. We would also like to better understand why and how things *actually* happen and for this we need both purely economic variables and environmental variables. The residual of econometric estimations or the white noise in any general theory has great interest to us in the study of a particular economy.

Unfortunately our real problem is not to convince people that culture matters, but to prove that it does—to show exactly why and how it affects economic results.

The contributions that follow in this volume address the question explicitly and, I believe, convincingly. "China's Gradual Approach to Reforming its State-Owned Enterprises," is by Lili Liu, who works at the World Bank. Despite the many successes the Chinese have had with their program of economic reforms, they have encountered difficulty in reforming the state enterprise sector. Unlike the former Communist countries that have abandoned socialism and are trying to transform their economies into a free-market, capitalist economy, China has not rejected Communism or a socialist economy, with state-owned and operated enterprises. Instead, the Chinese hope to reform the enterprises and make them more efficient. They have, however, encountered serious problems in doing so, and this remains a major obstacle to the success of their economic reform program.

Liu describes four stages in the Chinese efforts at reforming the state enterprises between 1979 and 1993. She then evaluates the impact of the reforms in terms of their objectives, which were the transformation of managerial objectives from fulfilling output targets to making profits, increasing their productivity and efficiency, and removing the soft-budget constraint. Liu also assesses the latest stage in the attempts to transform state enterprises—the creation of stockholding corporation with the state as the largest stockholder—and draws the reader's attention to the problem of state asset erosion and the debates over divestiture. She concludes by revealing the extent to which the environment of the state enterprises has changed over the past decade and arguing that future reform of the state enterprises will also be incremental and gradual. Liu's reliance on contemporary literature in Chinese clearly illustrates the extent to which our knowledge can be informed by the work of our Chinese colleagues, surely one of the greatest benefits to outside observers of the post-Mao reforms.

How does Liu's detailed analysis highlight the role of culture? To account for the many arguments concerning optimum reform packages or necessary sequences of reforms and to address the question of gradual versus immediate comprehensive reform measures. Liu makes her position clear. "The historical context in which Chinese economic reform unfolds not only defines the extent of difficulties which reform has to tackle, but also helps shape the very path of the reform process." And, therefore, "[t]he Chinese reform path has been characterized by evolutionary change rather than revolutionary Big Bang. This experience seems to be consistent with a basic premise of institutional economics, namely, that changes in institutions (i.e., the rules of the game) typically are path dependent and incremental. This is because it is difficult for society to dissolve its collective past." Her argument and discussion clearly support this statement as to why culture matters.

"Technology, Innovation, and Institutional Identity in Modern China," by Jonathan D. Pollack of the RAND Corporation, makes the path-determined nature of the reforms and culture an important explanatory variable and of direct concern throughout the analysis. Obviously no economic activity in a modern economy is possible without an entrepreneur or manager to organize and direct it and no sustained growth is possible without technological change. It should be equally obvious, but not always appreciated, that both entrepreneurial activity and technological innovation are significantly influenced and even framed within cultural and institutional legacies. It is the process of technological change—the attempts of Chinese leaders to adapt China's cultural and social traditions and economic organizations to provide for necessary technological innovation over the past century and a half, that Pollack tries to explain or understand.

Pollack surveys four approaches that have been used to explain the role of an economy's traditional culture and economic organization in the process of technological innovation. The first level he calls "cook-book" methods, which rely on highly aggregated variables and tautological arguments, describing the ingredients of growth, but not explaining them. The complex and often difficult-to-understand workings of culture and institutions are left out. At the next level, culture and institutions may be brought into an explanation of specific cases, but within a general explanation provided by the cookbook method. The third level emphasizes sociocultural factors, which allows for a richer and deeper explanation for the sources of economic growth. Finally, on a fourth level, which Pollack prefers, economic institutions and the political decision-making process also figure prominently in the search for an explanation of why and how economies grow.

After explaining why we might want to study a single country to find this explanation and why China is an excellent choice to be that single country, Pollack traces the evolution of growth policy since 1949. The major theme is that the Communist leaders under Mao adopted a strategy and institutions that remain very influential to this day. Although China's present leaders and people may have different objectives, such as efficiency and technological advancement, their ability to achieve these goals remains constrained by the cultural values and institutions of the past: the present reforms are indeed path dependent and we must know and appreciate that past if we are to understand the present. Yet the present does not repeat the past. Economic growth itself helps create a new material environment, while the decentralized political system has significantly changed the political process. As a result the historical, cultural, and institutional constraints upon successful technological innovation may not succeed in frustrating the most recent attempts to meet China's external threats.

Liu argues that the Chinese reform program is path dependent—constrained and determined by the institutions and policies of the past. Pollack argues that the policymaking process within the political system is an important determinant of the success of the economic reform program and that success will depend of the ability of the present policymaking system to escape from the legacies of its past. In "Rice, Culture, and Growth in East Asia" Bruce Reynolds of Cornell University looks for an explanation of the East Asian economic miracle in fundamental characteristics or original environmental endowments, variables well removed from economic-system ones or economic-policy ones.

The World Bank has argued that in addition to having the correct fundamentals in place—the basic elements of a free market system—the East Asian governments were able to "get their economic policies right" as they played a more active or interventionist role in the economy than was prescribed in the traditional model of a free-market economy (World Bank 1993). The World Bank warns other economies, however, that they should be wary of adopting similar interventionist policies in their attempts to replicate the East Asian miracle because they are unlikely to get the policies right. Reynolds raises the necessary prior question: why were the East Asians so lucky as to get the policies right and to implement those policies so successfully? He looks at the very size and location of China's geological land mass, a given if there ever was one, and offers a most interesting string of hypotheses as to why this given may explain part of the East Asian economic miracle.

Rice is highly productive both in producing seeds per head for the next crop and in calories per unit of land for human consumption. Wet-rice cultivation is one reason why there are one billion Chinese alive today. Wet-rice cultivation, however, requires a monsoon climate and the East Asian land mass is the only location in the world that generates a monsoon climate. Wet-rice cultivation, furthermore, is labor-intensive, requiring focused, time-consuming, and knowledgeable effort and management. It has few economies of scale. Ownership or at least a share in harvest profits is a necessary incentive for obtaining the patient and exhausting devotion that wet-rice cultivation requires. Over the centuries this small-scale activity carried out by entrepreneurial, frugal, hardworking people produced in East Asians a work ethic combined with managerial and entrepreneurial talents that made them ready to take advantage of any policy regime that would "get the policies right."

By going beyond the narrow focus of neoclassical economic models, the following essays yield a richer, more meaningful explanation of economic developments in China and East Asia. Adam Smith and the other founders of economics as a social science had no trouble involving political, geographical, historical, and institutional variables in their analyses. While the neoclassical approach does provide a useful first approximation, a more interdisciplinary approach or one that recognizes the importance of a broader range of variables may get us even closer to the truth. A broader approach certainly does pay off in the study of China's economic evolution.

References

Dernberger, Robert F. 1990. "Culture and Economics: Back to the Future." Unpublished paper.

————. 1997. "Capitalism and the East Asian Miracle." In *Asia's New World Order*, edited by George T. Wu, 43–75. London: Macmillan.

Murrell, Peter. 1995. "The Transition According to Cambridge, Mass." *Journal of Economic Literature* 11 (March): 164–78.

Wong, Gilbert. 1990. Final draft report on "Modernization in Asia." East-West Center, Hawaii. Photocopy.

World Bank. 1993. *The East Asian Miracle: Economic Growth and Public Policy.* New York: Oxford University Press.

China's Gradual Approach to Reforming Its State-Owned Enterprises

LILI LIU

The World Bank

Introduction

After the Cultural Revolution ended in 1978, China put reform of its state-owned enterprises (SOEs) at the core of its ambitious economic reform program. The reform objectives were clear, and enjoyed considerable consensus among reform proponents: to eliminate state bureaucratic control of management, instill accountability for profits and losses, and improve efficiency. Guided by these objectives, reform has focused on redefining the relationship between the state and SOEs and on development of appropriate incentives.[1]

Reform of SOEs, as with other aspects of the reform, has been a gradual and incremental process.[2] The reform began with the delegation of limited

---

1. Problems that troubled SOEs were subjected to extensive criticism by reform proponents after the Cultural Revolution ended. Following the historical Third Plenum of the Eleventh Congress of the Chinese Communist Party in 1978, which marked the start of economic reform, reformers called for significant restructuring of the enterprises. See, for example, Dong 1979, Liu Shibai 1979, Liu Suinian 1980, Lin 1980, Ma Hong 1981, Xu 1981, and Huang 1982.

2. The gradual strategy is best summarized by Deng Xiaoping's famous saying: "groping for stones while crossing the river," which has been echoed by Chinese intellectuals and policymakers. A lead article in the influential official *Jingji yanjiu* (Economic research journal) asked "How to ensure the success of the economic reforms?" and suggested four steps (Liu Suinian 1980). First, due to the complexity and difficulty of the reforms, there was a need to place leaders at various levels who were both authoritative and favored reform; second, it was important to use all media to reveal the problems of China's economic regulatory system, to educate people on the urgency of reforms, to encourage debate for building consensus on the direction of reform, and to use success stories of reform to convince those who opposed it; third, it was necessary to prepare for reform. It was not sufficient to understand the need for reform; the more important question was "how to reform," Thus, various concrete and coordinated policy measures, legislation, and training were prerequisite to economic reforms. Otherwise reforms were

management autonomy and financial benefits to the managers of SOEs while maintaining the central planning framework. It then gradually expanded to the dismantling of central planning and the development of output and some input markets. Parallel to the reform of SOEs, from the beginning, Chinese government policy has greatly encouraged the growth and expansion of the non-SOE sector, including collectives, township and village enterprises (TVEs), private and foreign-owned enterprises, and various mixed-ownership enterprises. However, privatization has been delayed. In November 1993, fifteen years after the reform started, China announced an ambitious plan to fundamentally restructure its SOEs by turning them into shareholding companies. This plan is being supported by a series of measures aimed at moving toward full marketization.

In reviewing China's reform process, I will focusing on reform of SOEs in the industrial sector,[3] with particular interest in the following questions: How have existing institutions affected the process of moving toward new institutional arrangements? Has the reform simply evolved out of ad hoc experiments or has it been guided in a particular direction? Why has the reform taken its particular pattern of sequencing and timing? How have the dynamics of reform affected the objectives of SOE managers and SOE performance? And, finally, what are the prospects for future reform of SOEs, in light of the changing interplay between the residual problems of central planning and the new institutional elements that have been brought forth?

The historical context in which Chinese economic reform unfolds not only defines the extent of the difficulties which reform has to tackle, but also helps shape the very path of the reform process. Decades of central planning, with state control of major production activities, left China with a gigantic and deeply troubled SOE sector. In 1978, SOEs (with the exception of collectives) accounted for close to 80 percent of industrial output and 80 percent of urban and town employment. Various government agencies controlled SOE investment and production through a highly hierarchical and complex organization and a mandatory plan. Since central planners could not acquire full knowledge of the opportunities of supply and demand, the principal-agent problem manifested itself through a bargaining process among various government agencies and managers, leading to rent-seeking, high transaction costs, and inefficiency, which was further augmented by the lack of linkage

---

intentions at best. Finally, emphasis was given to the importance of carrying out experiments before the reforms were expanded to a large scale.

3. Other sectors, such as housing and social insurance, will be brought into the discussion only when they have a direct bearing on reform in the industrial sector.

between efforts and rewards. Enterprises were eating from the same big pot (*daguo fan*), regardless of how much they put in, which is the extreme case of a soft budget constraint.

The Chinese reform path has been characterized by evolutionary change rather than a revolutionary Big Bang. This experience seems to be consistent with a basic premise of institutional economics, namely, that changes in institutions (i.e., the rules of the game) typically are path dependent and incremental. This is because it is difficult for society to dissolve its collective past. "The formal rules may change overnight, but the informal constraints do not. Inconsistency between the formal rules and the informal constraints (which may be the result of a deep-seated cultural inheritance because they have traditionally resolved basic exchange problems) results in tensions that typically get resolved by some restructuring of the overall constraints—in both directions—to produce a new equilibrium that is far less revolutionary" (North 1991: 7).

While gradual, changes do occur. The accumulated effects of China's sustained efforts to reform the existing system have been significant, inserting one by one new institutional elements into the existing framework, thus changing the dynamics of the institutional matrix. Change has been gradually induced by a demand-driven process. Problems that were not resolved by ongoing experiments led to a new set of experiments, through which a learning process occurred, which in turn further expanded the reform process. Phases of reversal have occurred, but political commitment to the ultimate goal of productivity growth has pushed the reform forward again.

The major experiments and policy changes from 1979 to 1993 have two closely related components: redefining the role of the state with its enterprise, and dismantling central planning and creating markets. The central objectives have been to separate management from state bureaucratic control, to ensure enterprise accountability, and to increase efficiency. The impact of this reform on managerial incentives, autonomy, and efficiency was less satisfactory than originally expected. Although reforms have greatly enhanced their profit motive, managers still must weigh expected payoffs from seeking maximum profit against conflicting pressures from government supervisory agencies, particularly local governments, and from workers, whose objectives may differ from profit maximization. Management autonomy has increased substantially, but critical areas of decision making—particularly investment—largely remain at government discretion. Managers also are constrained in labor decisions and in mergers and acquisitions. The gradual reform strategy recognizes the necessity of developing labor markets, social security schemes, and banking reforms, all of which take time to complete. This in turn constrains the process of privatization. Limited experiments with a shareholding system began in the mid-1980s and gained momentum in the early 1990s. The remarkable progress in other areas of reform has changed the dynamics of the institutional matrix. The prospect for SOE reform should not be viewed in isolation, but in the context of China's newly emerging institutional structure, which is characterized by a growing non-SOE sector and increased market competition.

Major Experiments in Reforming State-Owned Enterprises (1979–1993)

The problem of ensuring accountability and efficiency under public ownership and central planning has troubled the socialist experience since Karl Marx. Marx's vision of communism, with public assets owned directly by the people, without state organs, has never existed in reality. As argued by Chinese intellectuals at the beginning of reform, the challenge for socialism (the intermediate stage between capitalism and communism) is to find a modality to truly exercise public ownership. Public ownership of assets (in reality state ownership) should be understood in terms of economic relationships, including asset management and operation. Unless enterprises and workers can directly manage and operate assets, public ownership is not truly exercised and state ownership masquerades as public ownership.[4] The reform thus attempted to search for modalities to assure accountability and efficiency of SOEs, while gradually recognizing the necessity of creating competitive markets for such assurance.

Initial reform attempts, which began in 1979, decentralized certain decision making and granted limited financial benefits—including profit retention—to SOEs. Beginning in 1983 reform expanded to include the areas of taxation, pricing, and planning, which aimed at creating a competitive environment for all SOEs. In the mid to late 1980s, reform struggled to find management and incentive structures between the state and firm management so that the new autonomy of SOEs would be directed toward improving efficiency, rather than rent-seeking activities.[5]

---

4. Dong Furen, a prominent economist, was the first since the end of the Cultural Revolution to redefine the role of the state in its relation with enterprises (1979). Dong's article was followed by a series of policy papers calling for giving more autonomous power to state enterprises. See, for example, Liu Shibai 1979, Liu Suinian 1980, Lin 1980, Ma Hong 1981, Xu 1981, and Huang 1982. In the early debates, managers and workers were perceived to have common objectives.

5. There was overlap between these phases, due to the gradual and experimental nature of the reform process.

Limited Management Autonomy and Profit Retention (1979–1983)

The initial reform efforts that began in 1978 aimed at granting limited management autonomy and financial incentives to state-owned enterprises within the framework of central planning, while introducing some market elements. Sichuan Province was the first to experiment, followed by trial efforts elsewhere. By the late 1980s experiments had been expanded to about 6,000 firms which were under central budgetary allocations, accounting for 16 percent of SOEs in China and 60 percent of industrial output.[6]

Key provisions of these experiments included allowing firms, after they met plan targets, to share profits with the state and to enjoy some freedom in marketing and production. The profit retained by the firms could be used for investment, wages, and bonuses, according to specified ratios. Formulas for profit retention varied across firms within the same industry, across industries, and across regions.[7]

Three notable problems soon developed from these early experiments. First, profit differentials across firms did not necessarily relate to managerial effort. This was partly due to the distorted price structure, which contributed to differences in shadow and book values of profitability. Plan targets and input

---

6. For the experiment in Sichuan, see, for example, a report by the Ministry of Light Industry Research Group for Economic Systems (1980) covering 21 firms in light industry out of 100 firms being experimented in the province, and Tian et al. 1981 covering 149 firms in Chongqing, of which 31 were SOEs. For the experiment in Shanghai, see Zhu and Cao 1981, and in Ji'nan and Qingdao, see Ma Quanshan et al. 1982.

7. The "industrial responsibility system" was a variation of profit retention—the firm is responsible for fulfilling a certain quota of profit remission, then the extra quota portion is divided between the firm and the state. Share formulae vary across firms. By the summer of 1981 65 percent of all state-owned enterprises (county level and above) had implemented the industrial responsibility system. For variants of the industrial responsibility system, see Xu 1981. Zhu and Cao 1981 detailed the profit retention experiment in Shanghai. Profit retention was divided into two parts: base-profit retention and extra-profit retention. Base profit was the firm's profit level in the previous year. For a firm that achieved its base-year profit, a percentage of the base profit could be retained. Base-profit retention ratios varied across firms and averaged 4.2 percent. They were fixed for three years for firms joining the experiment in 1979 and were adjusted yearly for firms joining the experiment in 1980. Extra-profit retention applied to the firm's profit in excess of its base-profit level. The extra-profit retention ratio did not vary across firms, with 10 percent for firms joining the experiment in 1979 and 20 percent for firms joining the experiment in 1980. Different variations of the above formula could be found in experiments in other provinces and cities.

allocations also constrained the manager's freedom in making production decisions. Further, since the formulas for determining profit retention were based on the prior year's performance, the typical base-year approach under central planning, firms with higher past productivity were often at a disadvantage.

Second, conflicts arose between the small part of the system that was being reformed and the rest of the unreformed institutional structure. For example, even if managers were theoretically allowed to fire redundant workers, in reality the managers often had to accept workers assigned from government labor bureaus. Firms also had difficulty marketing products themselves after fulfilling plan targets, because marketing channels were still controlled by the state marketing monopolies. Although it was argued in the beginning of the reform (Dong 1979) that a firm should be allowed to decide optimum capital assets (i.e., dispose of unproductive capital assets), this did not occur in practice, due in part to the difficulty of defining property rights between the firm and the various government entities that represent the state.

Third, giving more autonomous power to the enterprises added new dimensions to the bargaining between firms, their direct government supervisory agencies, and other state agencies, such as material suppliers. Pre-existing principal-agent problems appeared to multiply as decentralization of power turned into a struggle to gain maximum benefits. Almost every aspect of production could be bargained for—base profit, fixed capital asset depreciation fees, bonuses as percentage of total wage funds, and profit retention ratios. Constraints on managerial freedom imposed by the central planning system led to opportunities for bargaining and reduced transparency. As the experiment was expanded to include more firms, the base-year concept became a disincentive. Since a higher profit level meant a higher base figure, firms tended to reduce their profit levels in the year prior to joining the experiment so as to lower their base profits and leave room for larger extra profits in subsequent years.

As the experiments were monitored, optimism was replaced by a realization of the difficulty of decentralizing decision-making power while ensuring an "equitable" environment for SOEs. Early proposals for solution reflected a limited understanding of the role of the state. For example, it was argued that instead of taking the base-year profit as a given in determining retention ratios, the government should carefully evaluate the base-year profit case by case, taking into account factors such as price distortion that are outside of a manager's control but that affect the profitability of a firm.[8] This, it was hoped,

8. See, for example, Zhu and Cao 1981 and the Ministry of Light Industry Research Group 1980.

would result in a more rational formula that would truly reflect a firm's efforts. The argument implicitly assumes that the state can possess perfect information about a firm's internal and external environment. Paradoxically, uniformity and transparency tended to punish managerial efforts. Discretionary rules were thus called on to resolve problems, further complicating bargaining and increasing transaction costs.

Ligaishui, Reducing the Mandatory Plan, and Dual Pricing (1983–1993)

Recognizing these problems, China launched a major experiment to change the profit retention system into an income and product taxation system (*ligaishui*). At the same time debate increasingly focused on the need to increase the role of the market, so that state-owned enterprises would face the discipline of a more competitive environment. In 1984 the Party called for significant reforms that moved away from a mandatory plan toward a guidance plan, so that the market would play a greater role in resource allocation.[9] This was supported by policies to further increase the role of the non-SOE sector, such as collectives, TVEs, and foreign investment and to expand partnerships between SOEs and private entities.

By instituting more uniform tax rates in lieu of profit-sharing, *ligaishui* attempted to minimize the bargaining and the arbitrariness that accompanied profit retention and help break down the control state agencies had over SOEs. In profit retention the supervisory agencies of SOEs, whether local governments or central ministries, negotiated with the firms on retention ratios. Further, *ligaishui* was intended to correct the impact of the distorted price structure on divergence of a firm's shadow value of profitability from its book value. The new system also was motivated by the pressure of declining central fiscal revenue, which had come about largely as a result of the profits retained by local governments and enterprises.[10]

Ligaishui was implemented in two stages. The first began in June 1983, when income taxes were levied on SOEs, with the after-tax profit split between

---

9. Prominent economist Liu Guoguang in the earlier reform phase proposed a change from the mandatory plan to a guidance plan, while letting the market play a greater role in resource allocation (Liu Guoguang 1980, 1986). Although resisted by conservatives, his idea was finally reflected by the major 1984 Party decision on economic reforms.

10. See, for example, Liu Zhicheng 1983, Dai 1984, and Wei 1984.

the firm and the state.[11] The second stage, begun in late 1984, was aimed at the gradual introduction of a complete tax system. Of particular importance to SOEs were the product tax and the adjustment tax. Profits differed across state enterprises partly because of the distorted price structure. For example, depending on their use of low-priced energy and raw materials, some state enterprises enjoyed greater profits than others. This posed a problem for the government. If price reform were carried out at one stroke, adjustment costs would be large for many SOEs. To reduce price-distortion-induced profit differentials, a product tax with differential rates was levied on different industrial product groups. Products viewed as having higher profits due to distorted output/input prices were taxed more heavily than products viewed as having lower profits. The appropriate levels of the tax were debated, as was the need for other taxes to further narrow price-distortion-induced profit differentials.[12] A high product tax, after the 55 percent income tax, was viewed as inappropriate, partly because it would leave many firms in the red. Instead, a fixed asset utilization tax was proposed to account for differentials across firms in fixed capital asset utilization. However, the idea was abandoned because it would be too difficult for the government to determine the shadow values of capital stocks. Many firms would also not be able to pay extra taxes after income and product taxes. As a result, an adjustment tax was imposed on about a quarter of the SOEs with higher profitability in an effort to reduce further price-distortion-induced profit differentials.

Using discretionary administrative intervention to put all SOEs on an equal footing proved inherently unworkable. In reality, the adjustment tax became firm-specific, leaving settlements to negotiations conducted on a case-by-case basis.[13] Loss-making firms generally were able to avoid paying taxes, while profit-making firms were taxed heavily. Although the deficiencies of the adjustment tax were recognized, and it was regarded as a compromise step between what was possible at that time and a broader reform program.[14] It was also recognized later that without an efficient capital market, capital asset

---

11. Income tax was levied on large and medium SOEs at the rate of 55 percent, and progressive income tax with eight brackets was levied on smaller enterprises, with the marginal tax rate at 55 percent.

12. For a brief summary of this debate, see Wei 1984.

13. The base year originally was meant to adjust yearly. Later it was fixed for seven years, due to the incentive problem.

14. See, for example, Dai 1984.

valuation and the resulting capital asset utilization tax would be arbitrary and would not reflect shadow values of capital stock.[15]

Ligaishui was not an isolated experiment, but one element within the broader reforms aimed at reducing the mandatory plan and increasing reliance on market forces. Agricultural reforms found early success, and in 1984 attention shifted to urban reforms, with reforming SOEs as the main focus. Discussions on reducing the mandatory plan had started in the early 1980s.[16] By 1984 experiments had expanded to allow enterprises to market products themselves after fulfilling plan targets and supply contracts. Markets for producer goods were tried in Shanghai and Sichuan.

"The Decisions by the CCP on Economic Reforms" in 1984 formally began the reform which reduced command control and introduced market forces. Progress since then in reducing plan targets and input quotas has been substantial. By 1993 only 5 percent of total industrial output was subject to mandatory planning. The coverage of goods by the material allocation plan has been substantially reduced, from 837 goods in 1980 to only 16 goods in 1993 (including primarily steel, timber, rubber, coal, and some metal ores and products).

Meanwhile, a series of proclamations issued since the mid-1980s was aimed at further expanding management autonomy of enterprises, to include authority over marketing, pricing, input purchasing, and the use of retained earnings, wages, and bonuses. Firms could also opt to form joint ventures with other firms and choose production technologies.[17] These were codified into the Enterprise Law of 1988. In 1992 the State Council issued the implementing regulations of the Enterprise Law of 1988. These explicitly provided for noninterference by the government in the operations of the enterprises, which were granted a set of fourteen rights over their operations.[18]

Price adjustments and reforms, an integral part of the move to greater marketization, began in 1978 with the state adjusting prices for those goods in

---

15. This was recognized by some economists. See, for example, Hua et al. 1988.

16. See, for example, Ma Hong 1981, Liu Guoguang 1980, 1986.

17. In 1984 the government issued the "Provisional Regulations on the Enlargement of Autonomy of State Industrial Enterprises." In 1985 the State Economic Reform Commission issued its "Transitional Decision to Revitalize Large and Medium Size Public Enterprises," which explicitly allowed public enterprises to determine their production operations in terms of output mix after fulfilling plan targets.

18. These fourteen rights are: control of production operation, pricing, marketing, material purchasing, internal organizational structure, wages and bonuses, use of retained earnings, investment, mergers and acquisitions, refusal of outside demand for expenditures, foreign trade, disposal of assets, labor, and personnel management.

particularly short supply, including agricultural products, raw materials, and energy. By 1984 prices for producer goods outside the mandatory plan were allowed to float within a 20 percent margin. Although in the mid-1980s there was no disagreement on the necessity of pricing reforms, there was disagreement on how to proceed. Should the reform continue with price adjustment or take a more decisive turn towards a market-based price-setting mechanism? Recognizing that sudden price shocks across the market would prove disastrous, most economists favored a midway reform known as the dual pricing system, and the government adopted this in 1985.[19]

Dual pricing would prove to be a hallmark of the Chinese reform. The change in the price-setting mechanism worked in sequence with the reduction of the mandatory plan. Products within the plan had a dual pricing structure: output within plan targets was sold at planned prices, but firms that fulfilled their plan target could sell excess products at market prices. Gradually plan targets were reduced and the scope of market-determined prices expanded. By 1993 market-determined prices accounted for 95 percent of total retail sales, 85 percent of capital goods and materials, and 90 percent of agricultural products.

Separating State Control from Management—Revisited (1986–1993)

In the mid-1980s the earlier reform strategy to revitalize state-owned enterprises, via greater decision-making power and financial incentives, underwent serious debates and criticism. Problems that emerged in the reform ignited new and deeper discussion on the issue of separation of the state from management. By this time the problems of the partial reforms were evident. Dual pricing and reduction of the mandatory plan had pushed the economy into "dual disequilibrium." There were serious concerns that China's reform might fail to mature, repeating the fate of Hungary's reform experience. Profit retention, *ligaishui*, and the emerging contract responsibility system had simply turned into a bargaining process again, in which SOEs competed for financial benefits and concessions from the state. Despite the reduction of the plan, bureaucratic control had nevertheless crept into enterprises.[20] Moreover, beginning in 1984 investment, wage funds, and consumption expanded rapidly,

---

19. For details of the debates, see Hua et al. 1988.

20. For example, although by mid-1987 the State Planning Commission's mandatory plan for industrial production covered only 20 percent of output, many lower levels of government continued to increase mandatory targets. In Shanghai, central government targets accounted for 18 percent of industrial output, but in steel, textile, and many machinery products, close to 100 percent of output was subject to the local mandatory plan. *Renmin ribao* (People's Daily), 14 May 1987.

pushing up price levels, which stimulated administrative intervention to halt price hikes.[21]

Economists started to link macroeconomic imbalances with enterprise behavior. Wu Jinlian seriously questioned the earlier reform strategy, which in his view aggravated competition among enterprises for financial benefits, thus increasing aggregate demand (1987). The rapid expansion of investment and consumption was viewed as mainly due to soft budget constraints, which in turn resulted from poorly defined property rights and the economic interests associated with such rights. As a result, the relationship between the move toward a market-based economy and a property rights structure for SOEs was seen as the fundamental issue to be resolved (Hua Sheng et al. 1986). According to Bian Yongzhuang (1987: 5), "property rights are not clearly defined for a state-owned enterprise in terms of its internal structure and external relationship, which is the fundamental reason for restricting the role of the market."

The search intensified for a management and incentive structure that would ensure that the enterprises' new freedom would be directed toward improved efficiency rather than into rent-seeking activities and short-term behavior.[22] The country experimented with various models, including the capital asset management responsibility system (CAMRS) and the contract responsibility system (CRS).[23] While CAMRS enjoyed greater theoretical popularity, it was tested in only a small number of firms and was quickly overtaken in the late 1980s by much larger-scale "spontaneous" experiments with CRS.

The capital asset management responsibility system, developed in the mid-1980s by a group of influential young economists, attempted to reconcile state ownership with an increasingly market-oriented environment by developing a modality for restructuring the property rights of SOEs to ensure a hard budget constraint.[24] The principal mechanism of CAMRS is competitive bidding for evaluation of capital assets: a pool of potential managers are invited to bid for projected returns on capital assets for an SOE in the future year T+N. These

---

21. Retail prices (year-end) increased to 4.7 percent in 1984 and 10.7 percent in 1985, compared with annual average of 2.1 percent in the period 1981–83.

22. See, for example, Hua et al. 1986, Song and Wang 1986, Lu 1987, Shi 1987, Zhou 1987, and Dong 1988 on the capital asset management responsibility system and the contract responsibility system.

23. Variations of each model also existed. One example was a leasing system, which was most used in small retails and services.

24. For discussion of the theory and practice of CAMRS, see, for example, Hua et al. 1986; the Chinese Academy of Social Sciences (CASS) 1987a, 1987b; and Bian 1987.

projected returns are then used to estimate shadow values of existing capital assets at the base year T.[25] An evaluation committee selects the highest bidder. A contract is then signed between the committee and the bidder, who becomes the firm's manager. At the end of the contract (year T+N), a new bidding process starts. Financial reward or punishment would then be applied to the manager depending on performance, as measured by the difference between the imputed value of capital assets in year T and year T+N, both of which would have been determined by a bidding process.

The bidding process was designed to mimic the role of the then nonexistent capital market; equalize external constraints facing a manager, such as planned targets, designated material supplier, and dual pricing; develop a market for a professional managerial class; and rationalize the firm's short-term behavior, since the actual value of capital assets in year T+N would be used for reward or punishment.

Proponents of CAMRS argued that the CRS system would further exacerbate the bargaining process and could not put an end to the soft budget constraint and bureaucratic interference. They also pointed out that CAMRS would pave the way for establishing shareholding corporations, since the system's essence is a competitive valuation of capital assets.

Despite its innovative design, CAMRS did not solve the problems of inadequate incentive structures and the lack of accountability of the various government agencies with jurisdiction over SOEs. CAMRS implicitly assumed that government representatives shared the common objective of increasing the aggregate value of state assets, which was not so in reality.

We can see this by analyzing the evaluation committee—a key institutional arrangement. The evaluation committee, which selects the winning bidder, consists of the supervisory agency of the enterprise, which holds 40 percent of the voting power; other government agencies (such as the banking and the reform agency and the planning, finance, and taxation bureaus) with 20 percent of the voting power;[26] and the firm's workers' representatives, with 40 percent of the voting power. The evaluation committee functions as the owner of the state assets. However, since these representatives have different objectives, the implicitly assumed common objective of increasing the value of the assets vanishes in the heat of bargaining. For example, before signing the contract between the government supervisory agency and the manager, the government

---

25. Other factors used in the estimation include interest rates on bank loans and an industry-specific profit/capital ratio.

26. Because the state assets function is diffused among various government agencies, the participation of these agencies was envisioned to reflect complete representation of the state assets.

supervisory agency would on the one hand bargain with other government agencies on issues such as whether debt service would be exempt from taxation and the rate of the profit tax and on the other hand bargain with the manager, as every contract item is negotiable.[27] According to the model design, the direct supervisory agency of the enterprise should estimate a preliminary figure for the value of existing capital assets before inviting bidding. However, the incentive was to set this value at a low level in order to ensure comfortable future returns. In the bidding those whose prices were consistent with the estimated base were often given higher evaluation marks. Another problem concerned monopolization of the bidding process, in which "outsiders" (i.e., bidders from other regions and areas, managers from other firms under different government judiciaries) were prevented from competing or were not given accounting information.

Another key institution in the operation of CAMRS is the state assets management agency, which establishes subsidiary investment firms. These firms, as principal players in capital markets, were envisioned to be responsible for maximizing the value of state assets, for example by transferring state assets across enterprises.[28] The sole criteria used by the highest state assets management agency are the safety and return of capital and increase in the value of capital assets. The highest agency would use these criteria to judge the performance of the managers of competing investment firms, and the subsidiary investment firms would follow these criteria to maximize returns on state assets. However, certain major issues were not resolved. What system would the state assets management agency use to monitor the investment firms? What mechanisms would it use to ensure that the objective of the state representatives was solely that of maximizing returns on capital assets, and how would this be measured in the absence of market pricing? Moreover, CAMRS requires a two-thirds vote of the executive council (the decision-making agency inside the SOE which consists of representatives of the investment firm, the managers, and the workers) to transfer assets, merge with other firms, or declare bankruptcy. Managers and workers, each with 30 percent voting power, would be unlikely to favor maximizing the value of state assets if that meant either closing the plant or accepting a change in management.

---

27. See CASS 1987a, a report which documented the bargaining problem.

28. The structure of the state asset management system varies (see CASS 1987b), but the basic idea is similar, i.e., under the highest state assets management agency, there are numerous competing investment firms.

Proponents of CAMRS were not unaware of some of these problems. While some problems were due partly to an inadequate understanding of the system, they also noted

> a deeper systematic factor, the unresolved ownership issue. For example, the direct supervisory agency acts as the owner of assets when bargaining with the managers, but acts as the manager when bargaining with government tax and finance bureaus. The duality of behavior profoundly reflects the positions of the direct supervisory agency as both representative of the state and as representative of management. . . . When a manager even uses the projected profit return that is the basis of his bidding selection as an object of bargaining, the principle of CAMRS has been violated and even denied in reality (CASS 1987a: 9).

The basic principle of the contract responsibility system[29] was a contract between a state-owned enterprise and the government for delivery of a lump sum tax payment for a set time period. Once the contract was signed, the government was to separate itself from the firm's management decisions concerning production, and the enterprise managers were to be held responsible for fulfilling the contract. Profit in excess of the tax payment would become discretionary income for the firm.

The CRS expanded rapidly in 1986, and by 1988 it covered the majority of SOEs. This rapid expansion was largely due to three factors. First, its adoption was inspired by the visible success of the family responsibility system in rural areas. It was thought that the CRS would eliminate state agency interference in managerial decisions. Second, unlike CAMRS, the system gave managers some freedom without substantially changing the existing institutional structure. Third, it was hoped that tax revenue would be stabilized through fixed-term contracts with firms, thus reducing the increasing fiscal imbalances of the central and local governments.

But CRS quickly encountered a number of problems, many of which were already familiar. First, reaching agreement on a contract generated heavy bargaining over the firm's tax base, subsequent tax increases, and other contract terms. Since the tax payment in the previous period provided the basis for determining the incremental increase of future tax obligations, the firm negotiated with the government on both the tax base and the rate of incremental increase. Contracts varied across firms as to the rate of increase for

29. Unless otherwise indicated, this discussion is largely based on the author's field mission to China in the summer of 1988 to research the reform of large- and medium-sized Chinese public enterprises. The project was jointly conducted by the Chinese Academy of Social Sciences and the University of Michigan's Center for Chinese Studies.

future tax obligations, how the base-year tax would be decided, and the number of years it covered.[30] Parties to the negotiations might include the enterprise's direct supervisory agency, tax and finance bureaus, banks, and others, as well as the enterprise itself. The interests of the parties differed. The firm was interested in decreasing its taxable base; the finance bureau wanted to maximize tax payments and reduce debt service, which was tax deductible; and the bank wanted its loans repaid. Since investment credit was rationed, bank loans often became an item for negotiation. The results of the contract negotiation depended on the dynamics of the bargaining in each case.

Second, managers' motivations tend to be short term, since contracts usually range from one to five years. The incentive to engage in long-term risky investment was weak, because such investment might not generate profits in the contract period. Amply documented and observed were the inventive devices enterprise managers used to include various welfare benefits allocated to workers in cost accounting so as to decrease the taxable base. Because of the short-term orientation, attempts were made to modify the CRS, for example by increasing the period of the contract to three or even five years to establish some incentives for investment. The government also enforced investment, research, and development by specific regulations for some firms, such as requiring the firm to invest a certain percentage of retained earnings and putting a ceiling on wage payments. By 1991 over 90 percent of firms with prior contracts had negotiated and signed new contracts containing a more comprehensive index which replaced the simpler tax obligations.[31]

Third, contract monitoring and enforcement were weak. The contract tended to be enforced primarily with profitable firms, while little was done to discipline firms which failed to fulfill their contract. Usually contracts were negotiated hard but ended up soft.[32]

Initially it was hoped that the CRS would generate positive results similar to those brought about by the family responsibility system in agriculture. But

---

30. For example, in one form of contract the firm and the government set profit and tax remission targets. For profit exceeding the agreed target, the firm and the government share the extra profit according to prenegotiated progressive ratios; the higher the extra profit, the higher the share the firm retains. In another form the firm could get all profit after paying the government a lump sum. Another variation allowed the total wage payment of a firm to grow in proportion to the rate of increase of the contracted tax payments. For a loss-making firm, the contract set how a firm's loss would be reduced over time.

31. For 1991 data, see World Bank, 1992: 104.

32. See Du 1987.

problems emerged in implementation.[33] It is easier to define property rights in labor-intensive, land-related agriculture activities. Land, the most important capital asset, can be divided into pieces, and the family responsibility system essentially contracts return on the land. But industrial activities require complex capital assets. In the late 1980s and early 1990s the Chinese regarded CRS as a temporary compromise, not as the final answer to the problems of SOEs.

The Impact of Reform

The accumulated effects of reform have substantially altered the environment in which the managers of state-owned enterprises operate. Consequently their objectives have changed, and they have more autonomy. However, empirical evidence tends to show that these enterprises are performing far less satisfactorily than expected. Political and social concerns have generally precluded bankruptcy for a large number of loss-making SOEs. While labor markets and social security are being developed to prepare for bankruptcy, soft budget constraints still continue.

Managerial Objectives

Prior to reform the chief objective of state enterprise managers was to fulfill plan targets comfortably. Reform has greatly increased the manager's profit motive, particularly since the non-SOE sector and foreign imports have created competitive pressures.

Although one study suggests a primary profit-seeking motive by SOE managers (Jefferson and Rawski 1994), there is no conclusive evidence that in China that is their chief objective. Empirical evidence seems to support a generally held hypothesis that these managers pursue a variety of objectives.[34] Dismantling central planning and granting management autonomy to SOEs do not automatically make managers drive for maximum profitability. Managerial incentives are complicated by the reform process, which has changed the rules and the major institutional players. A manager now faces the competing demands of various players: workers, government agencies (particularly local governments), and non-SOE competition. The perceived payoffs for meeting each player's demands carry different weight with the manager. The final result

---

33. See for example, Wu 1987, Hua et al. 1986, and CASS 1987b.

34. For a summary of the general theoretical discussions, not specifically on China, see Galal et al. 1994.

depends on the balance of power among the players, which varies across SOEs in terms of the jurisdiction of government agencies overseeing the firm, how the manager is selected (appointed by government or elected), and the *de facto* contract time. The strong influence of local governments over firms under their jurisdiction is commonly recognized, particularly over investment decisions. The interrelationship of interests can be quite complex. For example, it has been observed that a loss-making SOE under local government jurisdiction can become a reimbursement bank for such local government expenditures as banquets. The local government may subsidize the firm's losses to sustain the firm's production, which in turn adds to the total value of output and the turnover tax paid to the local government; subsidies can be made by returning the turnover tax to the firm.[35] Further, it has been amply documented that one objective, sometimes the main objective, of enterprise managers is to improve workers' welfare. This has caused inefficient investment decisions, such as using retained earnings to finance wage increases and resorting to borrowing to finance investment, because of the availability of low-interest tax deductible loans.[36] According to 1990 statistics covering 842 industrial firms in the city of Chongqing, labor productivity was ¥21,037 for profitmaking firms compared with ¥9,322 for loss-making firms; profitmaking firms also compared favorably with loss-making firms in other statistics such as material costs. But average wage and share of bonus over total wages were the same for both types of firms.[37]

Managerial Autonomy

As product markets have been progressively liberalized, the autonomy of state-owned enterprises in making production decisions has increased significantly in areas such as pricing, production, marketing, and materials purchasing. However, some critical areas of decision making, such as investment priorities and disposal of capital assets, remained largely at the government's discretion in the early 1990s. In addition, managers were still constrained in labor decisions.[38]

---

35. See Wang 1994.

36. See, for example, Hua et al. 1986, Bian 1987, and Wu 1987. Evidence gathered during my 1988 field mission in China support this view.

37. Zhang 1994. Of these 842 firms, 830 were state-owned and 12 were not.

38. The first national survey of enterprise managers conducted in 1993 (Zhongguo qiyejia diaocha xitong [China's Enterprise Managers Survey Group] 1994) found the percentage of surveyed managers who had autonomy in: production operation (89 percent); price setting (76 percent); marketing (89 percent); material purchasing (91

Because the banking system has only recently come under reform, banks have had little incentive to ensure that lending is profit-driven. And until the banking system is reformed, decentralized investment decisions will be inherently expansionary, as banks do not screen competing investment projects according to profitability. This is regardless of whether the investment decisions are made by local governments with jurisdiction over the enterprises or by the enterprises themselves. Efforts to rationalize production through mergers and acquisitions face constraints from government agencies which, as the owners of assets, often resist the acquisition of firms within their jurisdiction by firms outside their jurisdiction. Labor decisions are politically sensitive. Under central planning, SOEs had high expenditures on housing, pensions, and social services. Until labor markets are reformed and a social security system and basic social services are developed, SOE management autonomy in labor decisions will be constrained. Finally, managers may also consider expected returns from diverting their activities into the non-SOE sector. SOE managers may set up a subsidiary under different ownership to transfer profits and to avoid taxes, while at the same time enjoying the easy access to credit and cheap inputs that the government provides to SOEs.

Performance of State-Owned Enterprises

Empirical work on the impact of reforms on state-owned enterprise performance has generally focused on total factor productivity growth, which measures technical efficiency, i.e., maximum physical output obtained given real inputs. Work on total factor productivity up to the mid-1980s rejected the hypothesis that reforms since 1978 had improved the total factor productivity of SOEs.[39] For performance after 1984 Jefferson et al. (1992) estimated that total factor productivity of SOE grew at 2.4 percent on average from 1984 to 1987, and in a recent study they suggest that competition from the non-SOE sector and liberalized trade has pressured SOEs to cut costs, improve efficiency, and increase the pace of product development (Jefferson and Rawski 1994). However, a recent work paints a less optimistic picture. Using a sample of 300

---

percent); internal organizational structure (79 percent); wages and bonuses (70 percent); use of retained earnings (64 percent); investment (39 percent); disposal of capital assets (29 percent); merger and acquisition (23 percent); personnel (54 precent); and hiring/firing labor (44 percent). It should be noted that the survey includes managers in non-SOEs. It appears to be the consensus that reforms have significantly increased management autonomy, particularly in large SOEs.

39. See Hu et al. (1994) for a brief summary of total factor productivity estimates by Chow 1985, World Bank 1985, Dernberger 1988, and Perkins 1988.

large and medium SOEs, Hu Yongtai et al. (1994) estimated that total factor productivity growth of SOEs during the period 1984–88 was zero at best. Their findings appear to be more consistent with observations and anecdotal evidence on the performance of SOEs.

Evidence comparing the performance of SOEs and non-SOEs is more conclusive; indicates that SOE productivity growth is lower than that of TVEs or collectives, which do not enjoy preferential treatment given to SOEs such as government subsidies, soft loans, and guaranteed cheap materials. They must survive or perish on their own in the market.[40]

A firm can be technically efficient, but allocatively inefficient, i.e., its input mix is inefficient in the sense that the marginal value of an input deviates from its marginal cost. Evidence on allocative inefficiency of SOEs is scant. Recently Murakami et al. (1994) made an attempt to compare the performance of SOEs and TVEs by estimating both technical and allocative efficiencies. Their estimates, using firm-level data in the garment industry, conclude that the TVEs are far more efficient technically and allocatively.

An argument often heard in Chinese policy circles, and sometimes in the West, attributes the poor performance of SOEs to an unfavorable policy environment. Compared with the non-SOE sector, SOEs have high expenditures on housing, pensions, and social services. However, Hu Yongtai et al. (1994) estimated that even after excluding their capital and labor expenditures on social services, the total factor productivity of SOEs grew at zero percent at best from 1984 to 1988, compared with their estimated negative growth for the period if one does not exclude those expenditures. Empirical work is generally lacking on how the performance of SOEs is affected by their access to soft loans, subsidies, tax exemptions, and other preferential treatment, and their ability to extract monopoly rents.[41] A new study by Ma and Kim

---

40. According to Jefferson, Rawski, and Zheng (1992), from 1984 to 1987, collectives' total factor productivity grew at a 4.6 percent annual average compared with 2.4 percent for SOEs. Svejnar (1990) estimated that the total factor productivity of TVEs grew at a 13 percent annual average from 1981 to 1986. Hu et al. (1994)'s findings support the conclusion of more rapid growth of collectives' total factor productivity. Woo et al. (1993) found negligible annual total factor productivity growth for a sample of 300 SOEs, compared with 8–10 percent growth for a sample of 200 TVEs during the period 1985 to 1988.

41. For example, SOEs have easier access to credit and often pay less than market prices for inputs. In the sample (Hu et al. 1994), 300 large and medium SOEs purchased 80 percent of their coal, electricity, and fuel at planned prices in 1987, which were lower than market prices. In the same year, 200 TVEs in the sample bought less than 20 percent of their coal and fuel, and half of their electricity at planned prices.

(1995) finds that SOEs have had a more favorable environment than TVEs when environment is measured by the cost of investment adjustment. They applied a model of investment adjustment cost which measures the difficulties that a firm faces when it attempts to achieve its desired level of investment. By comparing the estimated adjustment cost for SOEs and for TVEs, their finding implies that once all enterprises have equivalent external environments in the sense of equal adjustment cost, the SOEs will be even poorer performers than they are at present.

The dynamic emerging non-SOE sector in China (collectives, TVEs, joint or solely foreign-owned firms and others) has outperformed the SOE sector. For the period 1980–1992 in the industrial sector, the annual growth rate of real output averaged 7.8 percent for SOEs, 18.4 percent for collectives, 64.9 percent for private firms, and 37.2 percent for others.[42] This growth rate differential has substantially reduced the relative share of SOE contribution to industrial output from about 80 percent in 1978 to less than 40 percent in 1994.

Soft Budget Constraint

Even in the early phase of the reforms many in China shared the view that firms should be accountable for their own losses.[43] The proclamation of the Bankruptcy Law in 1986 was the result of an emerging consensus that SOEs must be allowed to fail in the market-oriented environment toward which China was heading. However, bankruptcy of SOEs has proceded slowly, and the government has only recently provided implementing regulations to the law. Of 1,417 firms declared bankrupt by the courts from 1988, when the Bankruptcy Law became effective, to 1993, most were small non-SOEs and only 10 percent were SOEs (Wang 1994). Under the old planning system SOEs were responsible for providing their workers with pension plans, and many also provided free housing, school, and health services. Therefore, one critical concern in China has been to weigh the costs of bankruptcy (loss of jobs and associated political pressure) carefully against efficiency gains. Other reforms, including labor markets, housing, and social insurance schemes, need to be established before bankruptcy can proceed more broadly. Bankruptcy of SOEs also has met with resistance from local governments, which are unwilling to relinquish power and control over the enterprises under their jurisdiction.[44]

---

42. "Private firms" employ eight or fewer workers. "Others" include private firms employing eight or more workers, joint ventures, foreign-owned firms, and other mixed ownership arrangements (Jefferson and Rawski, 1994).

43. See, for example, Liu 1979, Ma 1981, and Xu 1981.

44. For a good summary, see Wang 1994.

Due to the difficulties of implementing bankruptcy, budgetary subsidies have continued to cover the financial losses of SOEs in contrast to the experience of collectives and TVEs, which are not protected by the government. An often-cited statistic indicates that about one third of SOEs make "explicit losses," and another third make "hidden losses." The aggregate explicit losses of SOEs have steadily increased from ¥14.1 billion in 1980 to ¥75.7 billion in 1992, while the explicit loss of industrial SOEs has increased from ¥3.2 billion to ¥30 billion during the same period. Budgetary subsidies to cover operating losses have ranged from ¥8.5 billion in 1984 to ¥60 billion in 1989 and about ¥51 billion in 1991 (International Monetary Fund 1994: 42, 27). Soft loans are another form of subsidy, and SOEs are given priority access to bank loans. There are also indirect subsidies—preferential access to foreign exchange, noncollection of tax arrears, and cheap inputs. Moreover, the SOEs are locked in a tangle of debt ("triangular debts") they owe to each other and to the state-owned banking system, estimated to be roughly US $100 million. The central bank estimates that no payments are being made on about a third of these debts. Many will never be repaid and thus amount to hidden subsidies (*Washington Post* 7 March 1995).

Deepening Reform

In November 1993 the Party decided to accelerate economic reforms, with fundamental restructuring of SOEs as a priority. This was to be achieved through their "corporatization," that is, their conversion into shareholding companies. The reform was to be supported by increased moves toward full marketization.

Experiments with shareholding corporations began on a limited scale in the mid-1980s. Shareholding was viewed as a positive option—where the interests of the state, the enterprises, and the workers could be genuinely united through joint ownership of shares of stock in the enterprise. The state would translate its existing assets into shares, and the enterprise's retained earnings would be divided between the enterprise share and the workers' share. Shareholding was believed to give the general public direct ownership of public assets. However, some felt that, given the partial reform, spreading the shareholding among several different state institutions would intensify state control. Some feared that firm managers would use the shares issued to workers to increase the workers' benefits.[45]

---

45. See Yan 1984, Shi 1986, Fan et al. 1986, Bian 1987, Hua et al. 1988, and Zhong 1989.

Experiments with the shareholding system gained new momentum in the early 1990s. The stock exchanges set up in Shanghai and Shenzhen in 1990 helped pave the way, along with the establishment of the China Securities Regulatory Commission in 1992 and the adoption of the new Company Law in 1993. The central government has issued a series of policy papers to implement the shareholding system. The Company Law provided a legal framework for converting SOEs into shareholding enterprises. They would become either limited liability companies or limited liability stock companies. Both would have corporate governance structures in line with international practice. Specifically, the state-owned enterprises would be established as legal entities with rights to make decisions concerning assets entrusted to them by owners and investors. One hundred SOEs were selected to experiment with modern corporate structure.

While hopes were initially high, once again experiments with the shareholding system have demonstrated the path-dependency of reform.[46] Problems, both old and new, already have begun to surface. Wage pressures and in-kind benefits, for example, may divert earnings away from much-needed long-term investment. Government supervisory agencies continue to interfere with firms' management. And it is still too early for shareholders to gauge the firms' performance through the two stock markets, which have had their share of insider trading and stock manipulation. Moreover, most SOEs will be restructured, at least in the medium term, into limited liability companies rather than limited liability stock companies. Bank credit, therefore, rather than share issues, likely will be the dominant source of financing. However, the deeply troubled state banking sector is not yet capable of imposing financial discipline on SOEs.

How to manage state assets efficiently is still a major problem. The leadership is committed to state dominance in certain industries. The structure of state asset management has recently been debated in China. Recognizing that the State Asset Management Commission (which represents the government as the owner of the state assets) and an SOE have asymmetrical information, one popular view argues for establishing intermediate institutions to represent the state by holding shares in the SOEs. Such intermediaries, whether commercial banks, asset management firms, shareholding firms, or investment firms, would seek to maximize the value of state assets. Some of these arguments have been influenced by the role of financial institutions in

---

46. Problems with the shareholding system have been widely documented and discussed in China. For the 1980s, see Yan 1984, Shi 1986, Fan et al. 1986, Bian 1987, Hua et al. 1988, and Zhong 1989. For recent discussion, see, for example, Ma 1994 and Yu 1992.

Japan and some Western European countries in monitoring enterprises.[47] One may also discern some similarities between these arguments and the capital asset management responsibility system.

However, the notion of maximizing the value of state assets could result in new problems. These state players might have a vested interest in the continuation of an SOE that performed poorly. At the heart of the problem is the inconsistency between the objective of maximizing the value of state assets and the market principle of resource allocation, where winners and losers are not predetermined by their status as state or non-state. For example, a financial institution invested in an SOE which turns out to be failing might push for the merger of that firm with another SOE in which it holds shares, even though a private firm might be more efficient and thus a more rational merger partner. It might also prove difficult to close down a financially troubled SOE in which state financial institutions hold majority shares.

It is also far from clear that this scheme would avoid the bargaining process that occurred during the earlier reform efforts. Nor has it been determined what type of incentive and monitoring system the State Asset Management Commission would adopt to hold these financial institutions accountable for their investment decisions. If, as is likely to be the case, the state financial institutions have their local branches hold shares in local SOEs or the local subsidiary of a parent SOE, strong local political influence will likely persist over decisions such as lending, merger, bankruptcy, and asset transfer across firms.[48] Another worry is that local financial institutions would monopolize local financial markets, thus diverting credit from the non-SOE sector and leaving SOEs no closer to full accountability for their profits and losses. In addition, no institutional mechanisms are in place to resolve potential conflicts among an SOE's managers, workers, and the institutional shareholders. Conflicts could arise, for instance, when maximizing the value of state assets comes at the expense of closing the plant.

---

47. For a brief review of this discussion, see Qian 1995.

48. To make the State Asset Management Commission and its financial institutions accountable, it is proposed that they be placed directly under the National People's Congress. See, for example, Ma 1994 and Qian 1995. Local branches would be subject to the direction of the local people's congress. Since the people's congresses are elected by vote, it is hoped that state asset management would be indirectly monitored by constituents. But political reforms would be necessary to empower the People's Congress.

The Context of Reform

Overall, China's economic reform has been evolutionary rather than a revolutionary Big Bang, in large part because it is difficult for a society to dissolve its collective past. The SOE sector is still undergoing reform, even as significant progress on other fronts continues to change the dynamics of the Chinese economy. The prospect of reforming SOEs cannot be viewed in isolation, but must be seen in the context of China's growing non-SOE sector and increased market competition. China's sustained efforts to reform its system have introduced, step by step, new institutional elements, which have in turn changed the dynamics of SOE reform.

Continued expansion of the non-SOE sector likely will prove the most important stimulus for future reform. The vibrant non-SOE sector has provided growth and employment, thus sustaining popular support for reform over the last fifteen years. It also has accelerated the learning process through which policymakers, the public, and growing numbers of enterprises recognize the payoffs from competition. This has helped build demand for further change and reforms. Moreover, a managerial and entrepreneurial market is gradually developing in the non-SOE sector that has increasingly attracted the more experienced and educated managers away from SOEs.[49]

Other recent government moves suggest some firm footholds are being established in the reform effort. New tax reforms initiated in 1994, for example, are moving China toward a modern taxation regime.[50] Compared with the

---

49. According to a survey report on Shanghai private firms (Shanghai geting siying jingji fazhan keti zu [Shanghai Research Group on Private Sector Development] 1994), a majority of managers and owners of the surveyed firms who previously worked for SOEs left them to develop their potential, to utilize their professional skills, or to respond to market challenges in their chosen industries. In 437 private firms engaging in science and engineering consulting services, 71 percent of 762 partners have college or advanced degrees. In the past they would have been assigned to SOEs. Comparing these figures with previous surveys in Shanghai and Zhejiang, the report concludes that the education level of managers in private firms has substantially increased compared with that in the late 1980s: the share of managers and owners with only elementary or middle-school education has rapidly declined, in contrast to a rapid increase in the share of managers and owners with high school education and particularly with college and advanced degrees.

50. The reforms include replacing the contract responsibility system, broadening the tax base, improving the efficiency of tax instruments, eliminating the product tax and profit adjustment tax, equalizing corporate income tax rates across all domestic firms, and the use of value-added tax as a major revenue source.

difficulty of implementing *ligaishui* in the mid-1980s, a modern tax system has become a realistic goal, given China's increasing reliance on markets today.

China's external trade is integrating the country with the world economy—and making SOEs aware of the potential export opportunities for efficient producers. A more open trade regime creates more competition for SOEs. In addition, the abolition of the mandatory exports/imports plan, unification of the official and market exchange rates, and the elimination of the retention system leave SOEs freer to pursue profits competitively. Foreign investment, meanwhile, continues to pour into China at unprecedented levels, bringing new technology and new management expertise, as well as access to new markets.[51]

Crucial progress, necessary to minimuze the political and social risks of SOE overhaul, has also been made toward reforming social security and the wage and employment system. Reform of unemployment benefits, pensions, and health care already has started. In many cities the housing markets are being commercialized, taking this burden away from the SOEs also.

More difficult tasks essential for success are being tackled. These include the areas of banking reforms, bankruptcy, and exchange of property rights. However, changes will probably not come quickly: banking reforms, for example, though identified as a priority, will be particularly difficult to implement. Bank loans continue to be used to subsidize SOE losses. Some economists feel a huge recapitalization may be necessary, at the cost of perhaps 15 percent of gross domestic product. The success of banking reform, in turn, will be affected by the pace of reform in productive sectors, as loss-making SOEs will continue to demand soft loans.

One important step in the restructuring of SOEs will be the continued development of property rights exchange centers, of which about 180 existed nationwide in 1994. Set up to facilitate the transfer of idle equipment across firms, the property rights exchange centers now cover a wider range of activities including the auction of firms and management contracts. Acquisitions and mergers are beginning to extend to medium-sized and even large firms. Private and foreign firms also have participated in transactions.[52] Further development of such centers needs to tackle the problem of the segmentation of markets caused not only by lack of information and lack of professional capacity in accounting and finance but also by the resistance of

---

51. Foreign direct investment in China has increased substantially, with actual flows to China increasing from an annual average of US $3 billion during 1985–91 to US $11 billion in 1992, US $25 billion in 1993, and more than US $30 billion in 1994.

52. On property exchange centers, see, for example, Zhu and Ni 1994.

government institutions, including local governments, to the exchange of property rights across jurisdictions.

Over the next few years the government's mission is clear, even if the actual steps are not yet fully charted. According to the State Economic and Trade Commission, a pilot project now under way in eighteen cities will invest heavily in the technological renovation of some SOEs, but will allow others to go bankrupt. In March 1996 State Economic and Trade Commission Minister Wang Zhongyu reported that the project had resulted in 366 mergers and 103 bankruptcies by December 1995—the loss of 1.4 million SOE jobs. Both bankruptcies and mergers will face increasing social pressure resulting from massive layoffs and the unwillingness of government agencies to relinquish jurisdictional power over their SOEs.

Under the Ninth Five-Year Plan, which commenced in January 1996, SOE reforms will focus on transforming the top 1,000 firms into "the pillars of the national economy." According to the plan, these 1,000 large and medium-sized SOEs account for 66 percent of total SOE earned profits and 51 percent of net SOE assets. Certain industries, including banking, communications, transportation, energy, and mining, will remain firmly under government control. Others, including light industry and textiles, will probably see a gradual withdrawal of state support. The eighteen-city experiment will expand to fifty cities in 1996, with medium-sized and small SOEs encouraged to merge or reorganize as joint-stock corporations.

Further SOE reforms, thus, are likely to be gradual. It is vitally important for the leadership to maintain the growth momentum of the non-SOE sector to sustain not only output and employment growth but also popular support for the reforms. To do this it will have to enforce fair competition between SOEs and non-SOEs. Fair competition will affect the learning process of various players, which in turn will affect the direction of economic change. If the players perceive higher payoffs in corruption and rent-seeking activities, then they will divert resources away from productive activities, thereby hindering China's future economic growth.

Prospects for future SOE reform depend on the interplay between the existing and the emerging institutional structures. Those organizations and interest groups that owe their existence to the existing institutional arrangements will "strive to assure the perpetuation of that institutional structure—thus assuring path dependence" (de Capitani and North 1994). Since the inception of economic reform in China, political commitment to productivity growth and careful balancing of the costs and benefits of reform have been critical to breaking many ideological barriers and effecting institutional change within the existing structure. Thus, political commitment to SOE reform, including eventual divestiture, and careful balancing of the benefits and costs of each step are more than ever crucial.

References

Bian Yongzhuang. 1987. "Zichan jingying zerenzhi de lilun gouxiang" (Theory of the capital asset management responsibility system). In *Zhongguo shehui kexueyuan Jingji yanjiusuo, qiye tizhi gaige yanjiuban jiaocai* (Chinese Academy of Social Sciences, Institute of Economic Research, enterprise reform research materials). Volume 3, *Zichan jingying zerenzhi gaige de lilun yu shijian* (The theory and practice of the reform of the capital asset management responsibility system). Beijing, China.

Chinese Academy of Social Sciences, Institute of Economic Research. 1987a. "Gongyouzhi qiye gaige zai renshi: Qibu, shenhua, shenghua—Zichan jingying zerenzhi shidian kaocha baogao" (Understanding anew reform of public enterprises: Beginning, deepening, and accelerating—A report on an experiment in the capital asset management responsibility system). *Jingji yanjiu* (Economic research journal), no. 5.

————. 1987b. *Theory and Practice of a Capital Asset Management Responsibility System.* Lecture series. Enterprise Reform Research Group. Vol. 3. Beijing.

Chow, Gregory. 1985. *The Chinese Economy.* New York: Harper and Row.

Dai Yuanchen. 1984. "Ligaishui shi jingji tizhi gaige de guanjian yibu" (*Ligaishui* is one critical step in economic reform). *Jingji yanjiu* (Economic research journal), no. 9.

de Capitani, Alberto, and Douglass North. 1994. "Institutional Development in Third World Countries and the Role of the World Bank." World Bank working paper, October.

Dernberger, Robert F. 1986. "Economic Policy and Performance." In U. S. Congress. *China's Economy Looks Toward the Year 2000.* Vol. 1. Washington, DC: U. S. Government Printing Office.

————. 1988. "Financing China's Development: Needs, Sources and Prospects." In *Financing Asian Development 2: China and India,* edited by Robert F. Dernberger and Richard Eckaus. Washington, D.C.: University Press of America.

Dong Furen. 1979. "On the modalities of Chinese socialist ownership". *Jingji yanjiu* (Economic research journal), no. 1.

————. 1988. "Jingji yunxing jizhi de gaige he suoyouzhi de gaige" (Reforms of the economic system and ownership structure). *Jingji yanjiu* (Economic research journal), no. 7.

Du Haiyan. 1987. "Jingji diaocha chengbaozhi: Guoyouqiye tizhi gaige de chushi xuanze" (Contract responsibility system: Initial option for restructuring state enterprises). *Jingji yanjiu* (Economic research journal), no. 10.

Fan Maofa et al. 1986. "Gufenzhi bu shi quanmin suoyouzhi qiye de fangxiang" (Stock shareholding is not the direction of public ownership). *Jingji yanjiu* (Economic research journal), no. 1.

Galal, Ahmed, et al. 1994. *Welfare Consequences of Selling Public Enterprises: An Empirical Analysis.* New York: Oxford University Press.

Hayek, Friedrich A. 1995. "The Use of Knowledge in Society." *American Economic Review* 35, no. 4.

Hu Yongtai et al. 1994. "Zhongguo qiye gaige jiujing huode le duoda chenggong?" (How much success has the reform of Chinese enterprise achieved?) *Jingji yanjiu* (Economic research journal), no. 6.

Hua Sheng et al. 1986. "Weiguan jingji jichu de zhongxin gouzao—Zai lun Zhongguo jinyibu gaige de wenti he silu" (Reconstruction of the microeconomic foundation—Problems and options for furthering Chinese economic reforms). *Jingji yanjiu* (Economic research journal), no. 3.

———— et al. 1988. "Zhongguo gaige shinian: Huigu, fansi, he qianjing" (Ten years of Chinese reforms: Looking back, rethinking, and viewing the future). *Jingji yanjiu* (Economic research journal), no. 9.

Huang Zhenqi. 1982. "Dui guoying qiye kuoda jingying guanli zizhuquan ji ge wenti de tantao" (Exploring a few issues on expanding the autonomous power of state-owned enterprises). *Jingji yanjiu* (Economic research journal), no. 3.

International Monetary Fund. 1994. *Economic Reform in China, A New Phase.* Washington, DC: International Monetary Fund.

Jefferson, Gary, and Thomas Rawski. 1994. "How Industrial Reform Worked in China: The Role of Innovation, Competition, and Property Rights." Prepared for the World Bank's Annual Conference on Development Economics.

Jefferson, Gary, Thomas Rawski and Yuxin Zheng. 1992. "Growth, Efficiency, and Convergency in China's State and Collective Industry." *Economic Development and Cultural Change* 40, no. 2.

Kornai, János. 1980. *Economics of Shortage.* New York: Oxford University Press.

Lin Qinsong. 1980. "Ruhe zhengque de renshi qiye zizhuquan de keguan yiju" (An objective rationale for the correct understanding of the autonomous power of enterprises). *Jingji yanjiu* (Economic research journal), no. 12.

Liu Guoguang. 1980. "Luelun jihua tiaojie yu shichang tiaojie de jige wenti" (Several issues on plan and market adjustment). *Jingji yanjiu* (Economic research journal), no. 10.

———. 1986. *Collected Works of Liu Guoguang*. Taiyuan: Shanxi People's Publishing Company.

Liu Shibai. 1979. "Shilun jingji gaige yu shehui zhuyi quanmin suoyouzhi de wanshan" (On economic reform and socialist public ownership improvement). *Jingji yanjiu* (Economic research journal), no. 2.

Liu Suinian. 1980. "Guanyu woguo jingji tizhi gaige fangxiang de tantao" (Exploring directions for reforming our economic system). *Jingji yanjiu* (Economic research journal), no. 1.

Liu Zhicheng. 1983. "Guoyingqiye shixing ligaishui de jige wenti" (Several issues on implementing *li-gai-shui* in state-owned enterprises). *Jingji yanjiu* (Economic research journal), no. 7.

Lu Hongwei. 1987. "Suoyouzhi he jingji yunxing jizhi: Niu bu kai de lianhuan tao" (Ownership reform and economic mechanism: Inseparable linkages). *Jingji yanjiu* (Economic research journal), no. 8.

Ma Hong. 1981. "Guanyu jingji guanli tizhi gaige de jige wenti" (Several issues on reforming the economic management system). *Jingji yanjiu* (Economic research journal), no. 7.

Ma Jun. 1994. "Gufenzhi de guoji jingyan ji qi dui Zhongguo de jiejian yiyi" (International experience of shareholding systems and its relevance to China). *Jingji yanjiu* (Economic research journal), no. 4.

Ma Jun and Hyung-ki Kim. 1995. "Does Government Policy Help or Hinder China's State-Owned Enterprises? An Adjustment Approach." World Bank, draft.

Ma Quanshan et al. 1982. "Ji'nan, Qingdao liangshi shixing gongye jingji zerenzhi de diaocha" (Report on experiments on the implementation of the industrial economic responsibility system in the cities of Ji'nan and Qingdao). *Jingji yanjiu* (Economic research journal), no. 2.

Ministry of Light Industry, Research Group for Economic Systems. 1980. "Sichuansheng qinggongye qiye kuoda zizhuquan shidian qingkuang de diaocha baogao" (Report on the experiment to grant more autonomous power to enterprises in light industry in Sichuan province). *Jingji yanjiu* (Economic research journal), no. 4.

Murakami, Naoki, Deqiang Liu and Keijiro Otsuka. 1994. "Technical and Allocative Efficiency among 'Socialist' Enterprises: The Case of the Garment Industry in China." *Journal of Comparative Economies* 19 (December).

North, Douglass. 1991. "Towards a Theory of Institutional Change." *Quarterly Review of Economics and Business* 31, no. 4.

Perkins, Dwight. 1988. "Reforming China's Economic System." *Journal of Economic Literature* 76, no. 2 (June).

Qian Yingyi. 1995. "Qiye de zhili jiegou gaige he rongzi jiegou gaige" (Reform of the governance and finance structure of enterprises). *Jingji yanjiu* (Economic research journal), no. 1.

Renmin ribao (People's Daily). 1987. Beijing. May 14.

Shanghai geti siying jingji fazhan keti zu (Shanghai Research Group on Private Sector Development). 1994. "Shanghai siying qiye wenjuan diaocha fenxi baogao" (Report on a sample survey of Shanghai private firms). Draft report.

Shi Zhengfu. 1987. "Chanye zuzhi de zhuanhuan yu chanquanzhidu de gaige" (Transformation of the industrial structure and reform of property rights). *Jingji yanjiu* (Economic research journal), no. 10.

Shi Zuosheng. 1986. "Guanyu sheji woguo gufen zhidu moshi de tantao" (Exploring modalities for a Chinese shareholding system). *Jingji yanjiu* (Economic research journal), no. 1.

Song Yangtan and Wang Haidong. 1986. "Suoyouzhi: Jingji gaige de kunnan yu chulu" (Ownership structure: Difficulties and options of the economic reforms). *Jingji yanjiu* (Economic research journal), no. 9.

Svejnar, Jan. 1990. "Productive Efficiency and Employment." In *China's Rural Industry: Structure, Development, and Reform*, edited by William Byrd and Lin Qingsong. New York: Oxford University Press.

Tian Fang et al. 1981. "Chongqingshi kuoda qiye zizhuquan shidian de chubu diaocha" (Preliminary report on the experiment of granting more autonomous power in the city of Chongqing). *Jingji yanjiu* (Economic research journal), no. 3.

Wang Wuyi. 1994. "Guanyu woguo guoying qiye pochan qingkuang de yinsu fenxi" (On factors related to the bankruptcy of China's state-owned enterprises). *Jingji yanjiu* (Economic research journal), no. 6.

Wei Liqun. 1984. "Ligaishui he qiye kuoquan yu jihua tizhi gaige" (*Li-gai-shui* and expanding enterprises' autonomous power and reforming the planning system). *Jingji yanjiu* (Economic research journal), no. 9.

Woo, Wing Thye, Gang Fan, Wen Hai, and Yibiao Jin. 1993. "The Efficiency and Macroeconomic Consequences of Chinese Enterprise Reform." *China Economic Review* 4, no. 2.

World Bank. 1985. "China: Long-Term Development Issues and Options." Washington, D.C.: World Bank.

―――. 1992. "China: Reform and the Role of Plan in the 1990s." Washington, D.C.: World Bank.

Wu Jinglian. 1987. "Guanyu gaige zhanlue xuanze de ruogan sikao" (On choices of reform strategy). *Jingji yanjiu* (Economic research journal), no. 2.

Xu Dixin. 1981. "Guoying qiye shixing jingji zerenzhi de jingji wenti" (Several issues on implementing the economic responsibility system in state-owned enterprises). *Jingji yanjiu* (Economic research journal), no. 12.

Yan Simao. 1984. "Shehui zhuyi gufen gongsi chutan" (Tentative ideas on a socialist shareholding company). *Jingji yanjiu* (Economic research journal), no. 12.

Yu Genqian. 1992. "Gufenzhi zouyang de yuanyin ji qi zheng fu xiaoying" (Problems with a shareholding system and the impacts). *Jingji yanjiu* (Economic research journal), no. 9.

Zhang Qizi. 1994. "Qiye de zhineng zhuanhuan he gongsihua" (The transformation of the enterprise function and corporatization). *Jingji yanjiu* (Economic research journal), no. 4.

Zhong Dong. 1989. "Chanquan zhidu de xuanze he woguo zouxiang gufenzhi de daolu" (Choice for property rights and the Chinese path to a shareholding system). *Jingji yanjiu* (Economic research journal), no. 2.

Zhongguo qiyejia diaocha xitong (China's Enterprise Managers Survey Group). 1994. "Gufenzhi: Zhongguo qiye zhidu gaige zhi lu—Gufenzhi qiye diaocha baogao" (Shareholding system: A path to the reform of Chinese enterprises—Report on a survey of shareholding enterprises). Draft report. Beijing.

Zhou Xiaochuang. 1987. "Qiye jingying tizhi ji qi duiying de zhengti jingji moshi" (The enterprise management system and overall economic model). *Jingji yanjiu* (Economic research journal), no. 4.

Zhu Yan and Cao Yifeng. 1981. "Dui Shanghai shi kuoquan qiye lirun liucheng de fenxi" (Analysis of profit retention for enterprises in Shanghai which have been granted more autonomous power). *Jingji yanjiu* (Economic research journal), no. 9.

Zhu Zhigang and Ni Jiexiang. 1994. "Guoyou qiye chanquan jiaoyi wenti yanjiu" (On the transaction of property rights of state-owned enterprises). *Jingji yanjiu* (Economic research journal), no. 10.

Technology, Innovation, and Institutional Identity in Modern China

JONATHAN D. POLLACK

RAND

The sources and implications of economic growth and technological innovation are themes of enduring interest to scholars and decision makers alike. A wide range of academic disciplines have staked claims in this realm, with various theories and methods affecting in significant ways how political elites, industrial managers, entrepreneurs, and international institutions view their choices and calculate their interests.

Modern Chinese history presents an unusually fertile ground for testing various explanations and hypotheses about economic change. Over the past century and a half Chinese leaders have grappled with the forces that seemed to explain China's shifting economic and technological fortunes, all in the context of the challenges posed by external powers whose industrial and military capabilities had surpassed those of the Chinese state. At various turns Chinese elites have sought to deny, defy, deflect, co-opt, replicate, or surpass the power of the outside world. In its most elemental sense this challenge reflected the capacity of the state to harness social, technological, and economic resources for its own purposes. To the degree that the country's incapacities enabled the outside world to exact a price from Chinese leaders, this has been a challenge that even weak regimes and weak leaders have been unable to ignore.

China's responses to these external challenges have depended on the organization of Chinese society, the capability of ruling elites to mobilize economic and technological power in purposeful fashion, and the consequences of both considerations for China's political and military prowess. Even more fundamentally, these issues concerned the malleability of Chinese cultural and social traditions and the organization of economic activity in China. Yet internal rivalries, social and economic upheaval, military threats, and civil war have repeatedly disadvantaged Chinese leaders in their quest to counter the power of the outside world. The fact that the West and subsequently Japan were able to extend their reach into China meant that physical distance would no longer keep the outside world at bay. Whether through war, alliance, or economic competition, the struggle to come to terms with the power of the outside world has defined much of China's political and institutional identity for the past century and a half. In addition this process has altered how Chinese have viewed their relationship to the political and economic power of the state. It has also helped define the character of China's political institutions and the capacity of China to adapt to external forces that China could no longer dominate.

The economic and technological challenges confronted by China over the past century and a half thus constitute some of the defining dimensions of modern Chinese history. They shed particular light on the efforts of leadership to shape the country's economic processes, the allocation of power within China, and the attitudes and expectations of Chinese toward their ruling elites. These concerns continue to influence beliefs and policies today, as China grapples with its unprecedented economic interdependence with the outside world and as China's citizens again redefine their possibilities for economic and technical advancement.

Explaining Economic Change

There is a broad spectrum of explanations on why and how some societies innovate successfully and others do not. The Chinese case presents a wealth of data against which various frameworks and methods can be tested. At the risk of oversimplification, four broad interpretations have predominated in this debate. Each school of thought reveals a good deal about the assumptions underlying different academic disciplines and their relevance to understanding recent patterns in Chinese history, as well as the country's future prospects.

The first approach treats the economic performance of societies in broadly comparative terms.[1] Interpretation at this level focuses on the contributions of labor, capital, and technology as explanatory variables, all within the context of the management of macroeconomic policy. To the degree that these inputs are available on favorable terms and can be applied in reasonably rational fashion, then economic growth will occur. A country's factor endowment and the success with which it encourages investment, savings, and productivity growth largely explain economic performance and the capacity to innovate. We have termed this approach the "cookbook method." It does not delve very deeply inside any economic system, but instead examines change in highly aggregated if comparative terms. As a result it does not fully address how and why some societies are more able than others to innovate and advance. Indeed, such explanation runs the risk of tautological wisdom: particular systems achieve more

---

1. For a recent example of this literature applied to East Asia's rapid development, see World Bank 1993. Although Taiwan's development is one of the book's case studies whereas China's is not, the framework of analysis could readily be extended to China's economic growth.

economically because they are "better" at economic performance than others. This school of thought may describe the ingredients underlying economic success, without satisfactorily explaining them.

The second approach, though focusing on a similar set of variables, addresses specific historical factors and circumstances that shape individual cases (Perkins 1975). For example, analysis at this level examines patterns of land distribution and utilization, education and literacy levels, savings rates, demographic patterns, market structures, geographic or locational patterns of economic activity, and other considerations affecting economic transactions. Such an approach also analyzes the relative autonomy of various economic units: to what extent are they self-sufficient, or do they depend on other levels of the political or institutional system for critical inputs? What are the outlets for entrepreneurial activity? How much does the state exploit the products and resources of a specific sector or locality? What is the character of the market system within which economic agents operate? Are there appropriate channels for international commerce? A contextual approach is by definition more differentiated: it postulates that the whole *does* consist of more than the sum of its parts. But to the degree that contextual explanations focus on factors that change appreciably only over time, analysis may not always be able to explain how and why economies grow and decay and the high degree of variability often observed within a given economic system.

A third category of explanation focuses on sociocultural factors (for example, Fukuyama 1995). In essence, economic activity is embedded in a broader set of social and interpersonal patterns that condition how individuals, families, and enterprises function as economic units. These relationships shape the character of economic exchanges at all levels. At the same time motivation, risk taking, and innovation all derive from broader habits and beliefs. Cultural norms impart a clearer sense of the underpinnings and logic of economic transactions within a given social and political setting. How do individuals conceptualize their opportunities for economic activity and their incentives for introducing new tools and technologies into their economic behavior? Is there a preferred pattern of behavior that an economically rational actor is likely to pursue? How much latitude is possible in relation to expectations and strictures imposed by formal authority?

A fourth level of explanation focuses on the political and institutional context within which economic transactions take place (for example, Perry and Wong 1985; Shirk 1993). This approach assumes that economic change and technological innovation are determined in significant measure by specific decisions, processes, and structures. The power of the state can either be direct or indirect, but it has the capability to appropriate or distribute resources and to constrain or broaden the range of economic possibilities. By implication, higher-level authority can reward, facilitate, or subsidize the activities of different economic units. The choices of political leaders may sometimes entail specific economic criteria, but the basis for decisions will frequently reflect nonrational considerations. Thus the role of systemic factors will be conditioned and shaped by decision-making and resource-allocation considerations made for reasons having little to do with economic rationality *per se* (Lieberthal and Lampton 1992). Other goals may be maximized as a consequence of such decisions—e.g., political loyalty, social stability, or national-level goals to which leaders attach particular value quite independent of more "rational" economic ends. In essence, systems and structures matter, but leadership beliefs and bureaucratic practices are likely to matter even more.

Why Study One Country?

Although this review of alternative explanations is necessarily oversimplified, it highlights the wide range of attitudes, norms, relationships, and behavior that shed light on China's economic history and future prospects. Once analysis shifts from a highly aggregated level, explanation and description become denser, more complex, and less susceptible to treatment according to a limited number of variables. These considerations help explain why scholars study individual countries: the big picture frequently does not provide a satisfactory rendering of the variation encountered across a range of cases. The cookbook method may be necessary for a first order approximation of the way the economic world works, but it often leaves a good deal of societal and economic behavior unexamined and unexplored.

So construed, scholars study individual countries for reasons that are defensible both in descriptive and explanatory terms. The fundamental challenge is to understand the complex social, cultural, institutional, and political realms in which economic behavior is embedded. The diverse sources of economic change highlight the role of mediating factors between larger forces and structures and economic outcomes. Detailed knowledge, moreover, affords a sanity check against grand theory paying insufficient heed to real world considerations.

Comprehensive explanation, therefore, requires understanding at numerous levels, including systemic attributes, the character of economic activity within a particular social system, the rate and directions of technological diffusion, the calculations of individual economic actors, and the role of political elites in shaping economic policy. There is an unavoidable tradeoff in intensive examination of an individual system, as opposed to gathering data across a larger number of cases. In the end, however, analysis seeks insight not only into economic growth, but into the forces underlying it. This represents an area of continued scholarly debate. For example, in a controversial recent essay, Paul Krugman disputes the widely held belief that Asia's rapid economic growth of recent decades (including that of China's since the onset of Deng Xiaoping's reforms) is attributable to increases in economic efficiency. Krugman contends instead that huge increases in capital inputs—a variant on the extensive growth strategies pursued by centrally planned economies in the 1950s—explain most (if not all) of these gains. To posit a single model of Asian economic development, Krugman further asserts, misrepresents the process of economic development (1994).[2]

Underlying Krugman's argument is the pivotal issue of measurement: how do we determine that societies have become more productive and efficient in their use of human and physical resources? In particular, how do we measure the rate at which technological change is taking place, and the efficiency with which it diffuses within a society? These are very complex issues that take us well beyond this essay, but they highlight how highly aggregated assessments can limit our understanding. To measure what societies produce and the rate at which this may be changing relative to other socioeconomic systems, scholars clearly require a means to compare relative economic performance. But such comparison provides incomplete insight into why and how economic systems undergo change. In essence, Krugman's critique of existing theories of Asian economic growth poses a challenge as well as opportunity to the country specialists—the need to identify how innovation takes place within a given society.

But study of a country does not necessarily require elaborate theoretical explanations. Textured analysis enables scholars to do more than force a country into a preconceived model of how the world is supposed to work: understanding and theory can be built from the bottom up as well as from the top down. So construed, "thick description" is a legitimate and appropriate tool of economic analysis. Intuitively, for example, we know that culture and social structure matter, and that they both find expression in the organization of economic life. Moreover, outcomes can be distinctive without presuming uniqueness or an ability to generalize to other historical, social, or cultural contexts. More important, focusing on the single case is intuitively satisfying to many scholars and analysts—in essence, part detective work, part archaeology, and part psychology.

In the case of contemporary China the increasing opportunities for direct observation and measurement have profoundly altered the study of the Chinese economy. From the late 1950s until the early 1980s, analysts of Chinese economic development were exceptionally data poor. Observations and measure-

---

2. Krugman's argument, while very provocative, seems to overreach. It nevertheless highlights fundamental issues for scholars and policymakers.

ment were undertaken largely from a distance; for the most part China had to be studied in highly aggregated terms, though with some attention to the effect of political and institutional factors.

Three principal considerations have radically reconfigured scholarly analysis over the past decade. The first has been East Asia's larger economic successes, of which China has increasingly been a part. Weberian explanations presumed that Confucian cultures would be profoundly disadvantaged in the process of modernization. But the demonstrable success of Asia's rapid developers suggested a need to revisit the relevance and logic of Confucian precepts. It also underscored the deep cultural roots of economic behavior that are often slighted or ignored in economic analysis (see Krieger and Trauzettel 1991). Second, the increasingly sclerotic performance of socialist economies cast growing doubt on the relevance of models based principally on central planning and extensive growth. China's rural and urban reforms and the collapse of the Soviet Union inexorably focused attention on marketization and internationalization as driving forces behind economic advancement. Third, since the 1980s it has been increasingly feasible to observe and understand China directly. This has permitted a richness in detail and attention to the human dimension of economic behavior, with clear regard to historical factors as well.

China's economic evolution, therefore, is not a bloodless, disembodied search for ever higher levels of abstraction. Intuitively, we know that leaders, culture, institutions, and social systems all matter in explaining innovation and economic growth. But how do they matter? To address this question, this essay will briefly explore some of the economic history of China under Communist rule. This history sheds light on the interaction of development strategies, institutional and social change, and the attitudes and habits of China's citizenry, all through the prism of beliefs and policies pursued by China's leaders. I make no attempt at grand synthesis or reconciling divergent approaches. My intention is to illustrate the value of hybrid explanation, in particular the interrelationship between economic change and the political and institutional transitions China has confronted, as well as those the country could face in the future.

The Evolution of China's Industrial Development Strategy

When the Chinese Communist Party came to power in 1949, it quickly sought to consolidate control over the full territory of China. It extended its reach into China's social and economic structures at all levels, displacing traditional local elites and effecting an economic reorganization befitting collectivist goals (see Schurmann 1968). It endeavored to launch a process of industrial growth and military development premised principally on models and know-how imported from the Soviet Union. Though the Party sought to build on a preexisting indigenous industrial base, the scale of technology transfer and industrial development in the country's early years was extraordinary. A strategy of extensive growth enabled the mobilization of resources in service of national goals, but it also introduced patterns of economic and industrial organization that (at least in the major state-owned enterprises) remains remarkably undisturbed to the present day.

Did this pattern of economic organization make sense? Mao early on sought to demonstrate his fealty to Marxist-Leninist principles and his personal loyalty to Stalin; this dictated the extensive adaptation of Soviet organizational models and methods in the industrial and military sectors. These were the areas where Mao believed that China most urgently needed to counter the West's technical superiority. The pervasive introduction of central planning indicated the leadership's determination to eradicate Western influence and to sharply erode the economic dominance of the major urban centers in China's coastal regions.

The early decades of Communist rule thus reflected the deep rural roots of the Chinese revolution, entailing an inward orientation and a deep antipathy toward the cosmopolitanism of the treaty ports. China's experience was comparable to those of other Asian nationalist movements. As observed by Thomas Rohlen:

> Anti-colonialist revolutions and the formation of new nation-states [in Asia] have generally been followed by initial tendencies toward isolation and consolidation. . . . Nationalist revolutions brought the military to the forefront of state building . . . and they gave rise to political preoccupations with ideology and with physical borders.... Efforts to make "modern" nations meant forcefully transforming traditional social structures, and this focused on largely agricultural populations. . . . An ideology that was anti-commercial and anti-foreign was notable in the emergent nationalism of Asia. Former colonial cities were not in favor. . . . Nationalism, in sum, stood in opposition to the cosmopolitanism of commercial cities oriented toward the outside world (1995: 9).

By turning prevailing economic patterns inward rather than outward, the Party leadership made decisions of genuine strategic consequence. This autarkic industrialization strategy severely limited Chinese interactions with the capitalist world, denying China's industrial managers information, know-how, and understanding of the then gestational economic forces that in subsequent decades transformed the economic landscape of East Asia. Chinese policies reflected a primary commitment to regime consolidation, rather than technological innovation or modernization as such. Even though there was rapid economic growth in the early years of Communist rule, regime goals came at the expense of broader societal development or of a meaningful capacity to compare and evaluate China's economic performance outside the confines of the socialist world. The prospective benefits of a more diversified economic strategy posed far too great a potential threat to the Party's efforts at consolidation and social control: political logic overruled economic logic.

Many observers, however, argue that China's autarkic strategy was imposed by the capitalist world, given that the West implemented a policy of economic denial and containment virtually from the onset of Communist rule. There is undoubtedly some validity to this proposition. But Chinese policies reinforced these policies at virtually every turn, denying economic actors within China any reasonable prospect for maintaining (let alone enhancing) economic linkages with capitalist societies. At the same time, the Chinese Communist Party was clearly intent on a process of regime consolidation that would have severely limited commercial and institutional linkages with the outside world, even assuming there had not been a denial and containment strategy.

The social and institutional arrangements devised by Mao and other leaders had lasting consequences. Even allowing for the upheaval from the late 1950s to the late 1970s, an extraordinarily durable set of institutional patterns was introduced in the industrial sector. China was able to generate appreciable economic growth in systemic terms; more than that, an entire way of life was spawned (Walder 1986). These policies, in turn, conditioned the expectations of Chinese workers. Organizational units became full-service institutions that employed, fed, housed, and educated tens of millions of urban Chinese. The durability of these arrangements cannot be explained by economies of scale alone; indeed, conceived in terms of strict economic efficiency it is doubtful that such large, vertically integrated structures made sense. Alternatively, they may have been justified by the dictates of Soviet-style industrial strategy in China's earliest years. However, other than keeping large numbers of Chinese employed and housed, such large enterprises failed to provide for sustained economic growth or meaningful technical innovation.

This judgment, however, assumes that Chinese leaders and China's citizenry attached primary importance to economic efficiency and technological advancement. It is at least as likely that economic institutions were valued for reasons very different than profit or technical advancement. Work units provided assurance of lifetime employment and built a safety net that guaranteed a modicum of social stability, thereby strengthening political support for the regime. This arrangement entailed an implicit contract between the Chinese state and the organizations and enterprises in which Chinese workers were employed. Indeed, though this process required widespread compliance on the part of individual Chinese, managers and workers alike secured benefits from these transactions.

Mao's subsequent decision to break with the Soviet Union, though premised on ideological differences with Moscow, paradoxically reinforced many of the prevailing characteristics of previous industrial policies. For example, the industrial and defense relocation programs of the early 1960s replicated the cradle-to-grave security provided by other state-owned enterprises (Naughton 1988). Mao's "third line" strategy introduced these institutional arrangements to some of China's most backward areas, bringing relative prosperity to extremely impoverished locales. The self-sufficiency, localism, and geographic remoteness of these enterprises, while nominally justified on national security grounds, provided a compliant labor pool for China's industrial and defense needs. Measured against standard economic criteria, the third line program was monumentally inefficient and dislocative. But it enabled the political leadership to extend its political and institutional reach to distant locations, all in the service of larger security and industrial goals, however ill-conceived and costly they may have been.

The ability of the Party to impose these policies, and the extraordinary durability of these arrangements in the industrial sector, cannot be explained by conventional economic logic alone. The predominant cultural and interpersonal characteristics in Chinese society provide one possible explanation. For example, Francis Fukuyama argues that Chinese society has a limited capacity for spontaneous association at the intermediate levels seemingly crucial to economic advancement, especially as societies undergo rapid development (1975, esp. Part II). Fukuyama characterizes China as a "low trust" society, rooted heavily in familistic associations that do not readily transfer loyalties either to larger institutions or to economic activities premised on high degrees of professionalism and technical competence. In his judgment it is only through pervasive state intervention that societies like China have been able to build large-scale industries or mobilize the requisite resources for high-priority leadership undertakings. Hierarchy and rules are thus necessary to induce the behavior sought by political leaders, and they can then frequently ensure a reasonable degree of compliance on the part of China's workers. But these arrangements exact a definite cost. The incentives for risk-taking are virtually nonexistent under such a system, generally resulting in low production rates and minimal innovation. The expectations under such a system are for predictability, not productivity. These liabilities extend to the scientific area as well. With scientific labors restricted to sequestered, highly protected laboratories, the possibilities for the diffusion and application of specialized knowledge within the society as a whole are greatly reduced.

Familism, however, does not preclude appreciable economic growth, especially in smaller-scale industrial and commercial activity. The experiences of Taiwan and Hong Kong compellingly demonstrate how family-oriented and operated enterprises can be highly adaptive and innovative as market opportunities develop. We therefore need to distinguish between the generation of commercial activity and the prosperity it creates, from larger-scale innovation and industrial advancement. Thus a society can be entrepreneurially inclined, but this does not always translate into widespread or sustainable technological dynamism, especially in product areas that require the mobilization of capital on a larger scale.

But extensive growth can generate enormous resources for priorities deemed vital by leaders and central planners. In the Chinese case some of the most telling examples are found in the defense sector, especially the nuclear weapons program. Mao spared no expense in ensuring that China could achieve at least symbolic equivalence in nuclear weapons with the Soviet Union and the United States. Whether out of patriotic conviction or scientific motivation, those involved in the program understood the significance Mao attached to it and were deeply determined to succeed. There was a definable purpose for this activity, unambiguously identified as the highest of national priorities (Lewis and Xue 1988).

The nuclear program was also the beneficiary of largesse from the Soviet Union on an extraordinary scale. Soviet nuclear assistance to China in the 1950s is without precedent or repetition in the history of defense technology transfer. Moscow's June 1959 decision to abrogate its nuclear weapons assistance to China no doubt was a huge setback to China, and the fact that Chinese scientists were able to overcome extraordinary deprivation and hardship to complete the program represented a monumental accomplishment. But Chinese accounts of the history of this program pointedly downplay or ignore the exceptional array of technologies transferred by Moscow prior to the severing of the agreement (see Pollack 1988: 161–92). Mao's readiness to proffer whatever resources were needed to complete the project and the existence of a substantial coterie of Chinese scientists and engineers trained at elite institutions in the United States and Soviet Union were also major contributory factors to the ultimate success of the program. Finally, and perhaps most important, building a nuclear weapon is more a science and engineering challenge that a manufacturing problem. Though it entails a significant measure of precision in design and in experimentation, the ultimate output (i.e., a limited number of nuclear weapons and associated delivery systems) can be almost individually tailored; it does not require large-scale manufacture. Production is concentrated, highly specialized, and not readily transferable to other sectors.

But the evident success of the nuclear weapons program was not replicated elsewhere in China's defense industries. The shortcomings of Chinese military aviation afford a relevant example of the larger challenges of technical and industrial innovation (Allen, Krumel, and Pollack 1995: esp. Chap. 8 and App. E, F). Modern combat aircraft derive from a complex array of technologies and systems that are integrated into a single product and then manufactured in se-rial production. In the 1950s the Soviets (through weaponry transfer and co-production agreements) enabled China to assemble one of the world's largest air forces in a remarkably brief period of time. Despite a major commitment of resources in subsequent decades, however, China's indigenous production capabilities continued to lag well behind the advanced industrial states. China's aviation industry today is able to produce only limited numbers of aircraft that push appreciably beyond Soviet design technology of the late 1950s, and only after prodigious, long-term development efforts. The record of indigenous design and production over the past two decades is extraordinarily slim, and the ability to adapt advanced Western components to existing Chinese aircraft since the mid-1980s has ranged between outright failure to modest success. Co-production of foreign systems (most likely, through provision of Russian aviation technology, thereby replicating the patterns of the 1950s) represents the most likely near-to-mid-term solution, though this will necessarily constrain China's technological options for many years to come.

Why have the Chinese not been able to do better on their own? The failures are rooted in a highly "stovepiped," heavily subsidized research and development process that provides few incentives for genuine innovation. Production rates for aircraft are desultory at best, though this may partially reflect a recognition by the Chinese that they have little reason to continue to produce weapons systems that would leave them extraordinarily disadvantaged in combat and find only a limited market to customers in the third world. However, even assuming an enhanced ability to acquire, absorb, and integrate an array of more advanced aircraft technologies from abroad, it is likely to be another decade before the Chinese aircraft industry is able to begin producing 1980s generation aircraft in more than very limited numbers. This outcome would nevertheless be a significant accomplishment, since it would measurably advance China's aviation industry beyond where it stands today. The construction of an occasional prototype, however, tells us that large numbers of engineers assigned to a specific project can after many years of effort fashion an experimental, hand-crafted product. But it tells us next to nothing about the capacity to design and produce the reliable, more capable aircraft that the Chinese air force wishes to fly, let alone take into combat.

Why was more not achieved by China's designers and engineers? Presumably Chinese technical specialists are not intrinsically incapable of doing better. Two factors stand out. First, the Chinese research and development system does not permit effective horizontal communication and integration, without which meaningful innovation (especially in highly dynamic areas of technology) is impossible. This is as much a question of communication within China as it is between China and the outside world. It reflects the highly sequestered character of those portions of the industrial system that remain under exclusive control of the state. Second, sufficient incentives for risk-taking do not exist, at least in the military sector. The behavior of Chinese scientists and engineers therefore remains more self-protective than innovative.

Under what conditions might change prove possible? And are the observable patterns in the closed world of military research and development representative of the Chinese economy as a whole? These are among the pivotal questions with which Chinese leaders have grappled over the past decade. When Deng Xiaoping moved into a position of preeminent power after Mao's death, he sought to overcome the widespread inertia and insularity evident in China's industrial economy, though only after first launching major reforms in the agricultural sector. Deng did not assume that Chinese industrial enterprises could reform from within. He saw China's laggard industrial and technical development as a source of national embarrassment that put China's well-being and security at risk. That China lagged well behind the developed world was perhaps understandable; that it could not keep pace with China's smaller, highly dynamic neighbors undermined the stature of the Chinese state. Deng believed the key was to change the motivational environment within existing enterprises while simultaneously encouraging new forms of industrial organization that could employ the rapidly growing pool of younger workers. In addition, major efforts to solicit foreign investment (especially from overseas Chinese) were expected to generate vitally needed capital and to provide new sources of technology and know-how from abroad.

Absent the intervention of a determined, authoritative leader atop the system, would China's industrial economy have continued to limp along without discernible improvement? The answer is not certain, but it is very likely that the reform process would have been much more laggard and halting. In a profound sense the citizens of China still took their cues from the social and economic structures that had long defined their world, and these structures still took their guidance from senior political leadership. The prevailing frame of reference remained internal, even inertial: the conceptualization of "economic space" was severely constrained by accumulated habit and by the absence of the resources and information that would spur economic growth. In the absence of means to erode or transform this highly constrained view of the world, the prospects for meaningful economic change remained very bleak.

The transformation of China's economic landscape over the past decade or more testifies to a transition that is as much cultural as it is institutional. Unhinged from the moorings of the state-controlled industrial system that defined the universe of economic possibility for decades, tens of millions of new entrants into the Chinese labor force perceive different horizons and opportunities. Though far less secure and certain than under the entrenched industrial system, China's shifting economic dynamics have redefined the relationship between citizens and the state.

However, some dimensions of this change, while nominally reflecting the capacity for adaptation and entrepreneurship, have taken on a life of their own, often in ways that many Chinese find deeply troubling. The proliferating business activities of the Chinese armed forces represent an especially telling example (Bickford 1994; Joffe 1995). Though the emergence of an entrepreneurial army as a new entrant into domestic and overseas markets seemingly reflects the seizing of commercial opportunities, it also highlights how those at the upper reaches of the system can requisition resources for personal as well as institutional gain. The aggrandizement of the power and the financial assets of such upper-level elites has bred pervasive cynicism about privilege and corruption atop the system. In an equally ironic way it has reconfigured the Chinese military establishment, making it far less of a military institution and much more an agglomeration of financial and corporate interests.

However, even in the context of rapid economic growth the old system still persists. The smaller-scale industrial enterprises in China's dynamic coastal provinces have emerged alongside an existing system that (for reasons of social stability rather than economic efficiency) is still maintained on life support (Stepanek 1991). Some of these enterprises, to be sure, continue to serve related functions that facilitate Chinese social stability, if not always the efficient utilization of economic resources. For example, numerous large state-owned enterprises provide the "throughput" for major financial transactions, as a wide array of bureaucratic interests (while nominally on their own) are sustained through loans that are recycled and rarely repaid (Steinfeld 1995).

The contrast between the treatment accorded sunset industries in Korea and Japan and their status in China is telling. In the former cases, emerging industries reached a level of export activity such that social welfare functions in declining industries were no longer pivotal concerns. Indeed, much of the recent history of Asia's industrial food chain finds firms from Korea, Taiwan, and Hong Kong relocating their production lines to China. China's continental proportions, however, have dictated a different logic, though for reasons that are decidedly nonrational in economic terms. Heavily subsidized enterprises remain among China's largest and least efficient economic institutions. They persist as generally unproductive appendages of a system that (especially for younger, unaffiliated workers from China's inland provinces) can no longer provide either economic well-being or social security.

But the economic inefficiencies of the state-owned economy have helped sow the seeds of widespread social change. By no longer guaranteeing job security, the established industrial enterprises (as the embodiment of the state) have imparted a powerful signal to vast numbers of Chinese: higher-level political or economic authority will not ensure their well-being. Under these conditions Chinese citizens must pursue alternative means and methods to provide for their livelihood, and (at least potentially) to achieve increased prosperity.

This diffusion of labor and skills and the enhanced opportunities for individual initiative have transformed China's industrial landscape. As a consequence of export-led growth and (to a lesser extent) the increased purchase of consumer goods in China, the country's industrial output has exploded over the past half decade. Unlike the past, however, this increased output bears only indirectly on the economic capabilities of the Chinese state (or, more accurately, the industrial and technical capabilities that can be mobilized on behalf of the state). Whether and how central authorities will effect a satisfactory political bargain with the new economic power wielders at the local level represents a preeminent transition challenge that national leaders and China's emergent industrial elites have yet to address.

The Paradox of Chinese Power

These observations underscore the paradox of Chinese power. Even prior to the onset of the economic reforms the absolute scale of China's industrial establishment (including its pool of scientific manpower) was very large. But size can represent an enormous inhibiting factor if there are no means to ensure the rational allocation and application of productive resources. Failures to meet "market tests"—be it combat aircraft, telephones, or baseball gloves—loom as huge challenges, especially as China seeks to compete in the global economic arena.

China in aggregate terms looms increasingly large in the global economic equation.[3] But how does absolute economic performance translate into specific competitive advantage? To be sure, Chinese factories have demonstrated an ability to produce credible lower- and mid-range consumer items where skilled manufacture (as opposed to local assembly) is not a prerequisite and where Chinese labor costs confer comparative advantage upon Chinese enterprises. The pace of economic activity—especially in export-oriented industries—has exploded over the past five years. Over time this is likely to result in an appreciably more skilled and motivated labor force.

---

3. Though the scholarly community has followed China's economic emergence on a continuous basis, there has been a post-Tiananmen rediscovery of China's role and standing in the international economy by numerous foreign observers. But the assessments of the nonspecialists continue to wax and wane. Compare, for example, the two surveys in China published by *The Economist* in recent years: "When China Wakes" and "A Vacancy Awaits."

But the challenges are profound. A more productive China will generate increased material well being in certain regions, with the role of overseas Chinese being especially critical. But how will China be defined as an economic system? In whose hands will wealth and the capacity for innovation principally reside? Toward what purposes will it be directed? For example, will a taxation system ensure the provision of resources to the state in a manner commensurate with the leadership's convictions about China emerging as a leading scientific, technical, and military power? Can the Chinese leadership reduce the vast regional asymmetries in the country's economic conditions? Will sufficient numbers of Chinese workers be motivated either through personal or institutional interest to produce and compete according to international standards, especially as China's labor costs rise? Or, given China's absolute size, will an internally driven logic again predominate once China achieves a certain level of development? Despite the facile assumptions about the implications of rapid economic growth in China, we need to understand far more systematically how power in a wide variety of forms—financial, technological, institutional, and industrial—will be harnessed, channeled, and controlled.

Ownership and affiliation will both be critical factors in this process of economic and institutional change. Despite widespread claims of privatization in China, the meaning of this label is far from clear. Some of the principal beneficiaries of the privatization process, for example, have been local and provincial elites, many closely linked to the current power structure. To be sure, there is no reason why a Chinese version of the private sector has to follow the logic of a Western model. In view of the continued power of central government in China and the priority attached to national-level goals, the large state-supported industrial enterprises will very likely persist, though they must achieve a fundamental transformation if they are to be competitive and fully relevant to China's industrial future. But future economic possibilities will also be rooted in personalistic, family and clan-oriented patterns akin to those seen in Taiwan and Hong Kong. Unlike either Taiwan or Hong Kong, however, this development will be embedded within an economy of continental proportions. A crucial consideration, therefore, is whether intermediate institutions positioned between the family-run firms and major industrial conglomerates can develop and proliferate, for such enterprises may prove far more adept at technical advancement and industrial innovation.

For example, the virtual explosion in the growth of township and village enterprises, much of it taking place independent of meaningful government control or oversight, suggests adaptiveness and resourcefulness that would not have seemed possible a few years ago (Naughton 1994). Though many of these firms remain very small, some are of more substantial size, and are employing a growing portion of the work force, especially younger Chinese. Such experiences could fundamentally redefine the relationship of Chinese citizens to their political institutions at all levels.

Indeed, these changes speak to the malleability of culture and institutions, as well as the capacity of new economic actors to develop different norms and behavior patterns. Tu Wei-ming, for example, argues that the rise of industrial East Asia out of a Confucian tradition that supposedly inhibited innovation suggests a need to reconceptualize Chinese culture. As he notes:

> [The] Confucian ethic . . . does not take the quest for material wealth as intrinsically valuable . . . . If we assume that the rise of industrial East Asia represents a process significantly different from the West and yet historically and structurally linked to the "spirit of capitalism" . . . . [We need] to explore the spiritual resources, as well as the institutional innovations, that underlie the work ethic, authority patterns, social cohesiveness, motivational structure, value orientation, and world view . . . . I am not looking at institutions as static structures but as value-laden processes . . . [representing] networks of human interaction, arts of negotiation, patterns of symbolic control, and rules of social discourse (1991: 32–33).

Tu's observations reinforce practical economic necessity. Absent sufficient employment opportunities for younger Chinese, the capacity of the central authorities to retain effective control over the country as a whole could prove increasingly problematic. In the longer term the dispositions and expectations of China's younger workers will prove crucial to the country's future institutional development. Citizens may maintain loyalty or at least nominal acquiescence to the prerogatives of the Chinese state, but their relationship to governmental authority could undergo profound change, especially as their economic expectations and opportunities broaden. The test will be where their principal loyalties reside. For example, even in the context of continued familial and local bonds, it is difficult to imagine authority not ultimately attaching to particular institutions, perhaps an admixture that blurs the distinction between public and private, and in some instances between Chinese and non-Chinese.

None of these observations necessarily presumes a weak Chinese state. The complex webs of affiliation and authority in China seem very likely to ensure the persistence of powerful connections between the economy as a whole, or at least critical sectors within it, and provision of resources to the center. Even under circumstances where central decision makers are less able to lay effective or automatic claim to productive resources, the scale of these resources will grow appreciably over time, though this does not necessarily guarantee their effective use.

At the same time rapid technological change, increased labor mobility, and accelerating internationalization could induce larger changes in our concepts of China as a political and institutional entity. Boundaries have lost much of their relevance and meaning, at least in terms of economic transactions. In the 1950s the grafting of Soviet economic methods onto China was shaped principally by the central political and economic bureaucracies. The fact that the implanting of Soviet models took place immediately after the Chinese Communist victory enabled a more centrally guided process to take shape, all with a decidedly anti-Western flavor.

The circumstances today are very different. Central institutions, though still powerful, do not possess equivalent reach, control, and legitimacy. The flow of information and know-how from abroad (though still nominally subject to oversight and regulation from Beijing) may well be far too ample and diversified to permit meaningful control from the center. The reemergence of China's coastal cities as part of the internationalization of markets and commercial cultures represents an especially daunting challenge to the state-centered political order, since "the nature and political culture of trading cities (but not necessarily their wealthy elites) tend over time toward greater autonomy from political control and, thus, from the constraints of sovereignty" (Rohlen 1995: 19). The proliferation of economic actors in the Chinese development process will thus render effective management of resources by the center a far more difficult task. The question is how such change will reconfigure perceptions and expectations of individual Chinese toward those who govern them, and how government in turn will respond to such change.

However, the absolute scale of resources flowing into China and the new economic patterns they have induced may be somewhat misleading. To the degree that the preponderance of economic power shifts to local or provincial elites and institutions, the viability of national-level structures and institutions could be challenged. How power would then aggregate could have profound implications not only for the Chinese state but the international system as a whole.

We thus end where we began. In broad terms we can compare China to other major states, drawing judgments about the absolute and relative magnitude of Chinese economic capabilities. But this knowledge, data, and understanding instructs us very imperfectly about the requisites and consequences of economic growth and technological innovation in systemic, institutional, or sociocultural terms. In the future as in the past a more comprehensive sense of China must rest on "knowing the territory" and in imparting to specialists and the attentive public alike a more accurate sense of China in its larger economic and social context. It is only then that China's continuing economic and institutional evolution can be defined more fully and more realistically. It reminds us again why scholars are frequently drawn to China as an individual case, albeit one of major proportions and consequence. True understanding of China in its complexity and variation represents ample justification for the knowledge to which students of China must continue to aspire.

References

Allen, Kenneth W., Glenn Krumel, and Jonathan D. Pollack. 1995. *China's Air Force Enters the 21st Century*. Santa Monica: RAND, MR-580-AF.

Bickford, Thomas J. 1994. "The Chinese Military and Its Business Operations." *Asian Survey* 34, no. 5 (May): 460–74.

Economist. 1992. "When China Wakes." November 28.

————. 1995. "A Vacancy Awaits." March 18.

Fukuyama, Francis. 1995. *Trust—The Social Virtues and the Creation of Prosperity*. New York: The Free Press.

Joffe, Ellis. 1995. "The PLA and the Chinese Economy: The Effect of Involvement." *Survival* 37, no. 2 (Summer): 24–43.

Krieger, Silke and Rolf Trauzettel, eds. 1991. *Confucianism and the Modernization of China*. Mainz: Von Hase and Koehler Verlag.

Krugman, Paul. 1994. "The Myth of Asia's Miracle." *Foreign Affairs* 73, no. 6 (November/December): 62–78.

Lewis, John Wilson and Xue Litai. 1988. *China Builds the Bomb*. Stanford: Stanford University Press.

Lieberthal, Kenneth G., and David M. Lampton, eds. 1992. *Bureaucracy, Politics, and Decision Making in Post-Mao China*. Berkeley: University of California Press.

Naughton, Barry. 1988. "The Third Front: Defense Industrialization in the Chinese Interior." *The China Quarterly* 115 (September): 351–86.

————. 1994. "Chinese Institutional Innovation and Privatization From Below." *American Economics Association Papers and Proceedings* 84, no. 2 (May): 266–70.

Perkins, Dwight H., ed. 1975. *China's Modern Economy in Historical Perspective*. Stanford: Stanford University Press.

Perry, Elizabeth J., and Christine P. W. Wong, eds. 1985. *The Political Economy of Reform in Post-Mao China*. Cambridge: Harvard University Press.

Pollack, Jonathan D. 1988. "A Chinese Achievement." *Science*, September 23: 1691–92.

Rohlen, Thomas P. 1995. *A "Mediterranean" Model for Asian Regionalism: Cosmopolitan Cities and Nation-States in Asia*. Stanford: Asia/Pacific Research Center.

Schurmann, H. Franz. 1968. *Ideology and Organization in Communist China*. Revised edition. Berkeley: University of California Press.

Shirk, Susan L. 1993. *The Political Logic of Economic Reform in China*. Berkeley: University of California Press.

Steinfeld, Edward. 1995. "China's Cash Cow Dinosaurs." *The Asian Wall Street Journal*, February 7.

Stepanek, James B. 1991. "China's Enduring State Factories: Why Ten Years of Reform Have Left China's Big State Factories Unchanged." In Joint Economic Committee, Congress of the United States, *China's Economic Dilemmas in the 1990s: The Problems of Reforms, Modernization, and Interdependence*. Volume 2: 440–54. Washington, D.C.: U. S. Government Printing Office.

Tu Wei-ming. 1991. "A Confucian Perspective on the Rise of Industrial East Asia." In *Confucianism and the Modernization of China*, edited by Silke Krieger and Rolf Trauzettel. Mainz: Von Hase and Koehler Verlag.

Walder, Andrew G. 1986. *Communist Neo-Traditionalism: Work and Authority in Chinese Industry*. Berkeley: University of California Press.

World Bank. 1993. *The East Asian Miracle—Economic Growth and Public Policy*. New York: Oxford University Press.

Rice, Culture, and Growth in East Asia: Testing for a Linkage between Effort and Tenurial Relations in Agriculture

BRUCE L. REYNOLDS

Union College and *Cornell University*

1. East Asian Growth: Proximate versus Underlying Causes

In the past two decades East Asian economies have grown at annual rates which are roughly four percentage points faster than the rest of the world, in both gross and per capita terms (Table 1). Attempts to explain Asia's success at "catch-up industrialization" have by now generated a gargantuan literature, which I will not attempt to cite.

Table 1
GDP Growth, 1970–1991
(Annual Percentage Increase)

	GDP *(1970–1980)*	*GDP* *(1980–1991)*	*Per Capita GDP* *(1980–1991)*
Low Income	*4.5*	*6.0*	*3.9*
People's Republic of China	5.2	9.4	7.8
Indonesia	7.2	5.6	3.9
Middle Income	*n.a.*	*2.3*	*0.3*
Thailand	7.1	7.9	5.9
Malaysia	7.9	5.7	2.9
Korea	9.6	9.6	8.7
High Income	*3.2*	*2.9*	*2.3*
Hong Kong	9.2	6.9	5.6
Singapore	8.3	6.6	5.3
Japan	4.3	4.2	3.6
United States of America	2.8	2.6	1.7
World	3.5	3.0	1.2
East Asia	7.4	7.0	5.5

Source: World Bank (*1993*: 238, 241).

I follow Henry Wan (1993), Erik Thorbecke (1994), and others in understanding the catch-up process as one of technology acquisition and diffusion,

317

whose pace is determined in part by the effectiveness of the economic policies employed. A commonly accepted list of effective policies includes macroeconomic stability (high taxes/low public spending/restrained money creation), openness to world trade (incentives to compete at world prices), state infrastructural investment, and wage restraint.

Does correct policy choice explain East Asia's rapid growth? The usefulness of policies like these is well known, and yet relatively few developing countries embrace them, because implementation is painful. The adoption of appropriate policies is therefore only the proximate cause of growth. It leaves us with the deeper question: Why are these policies accepted and implemented in East Asia more readily than in other parts of the world?

In what follows I explore an answer to that question, within a broad social science framework in the tradition of Vernon Ruttan (1995) and Yujiro Hayami (1993). The argument goes as follows. The policies which have generated rapid growth in East Asia, and which would plausibly do so elsewhere, have distributional consequences which fall unevenly across social groups. This unevenness in turn creates political resistance to policy implementation. But East Asian societies seem to bring to this struggle a cultural/institutional repertoire which makes hard policies politically palatable. One underlying source of that cultural differentiation may be rice cultivation, through the population density, land ownership forms, and other social structures which it has engendered over the last twelve centuries.

Consider the eight Asian nations (Table 2) where rice is at least 25 percent of cultivated acreage. Their average Gini coefficient for inequality of land distribution is 0.54, compared with 0.80 for the thirteen non-Asian nations in the sample. Now consider a particular pro-growth policy—for example, stimulating growth of labor-intensive rural industry, which will eventually drive up the demand for rural labor and hence the rural wage. This policy hurts landowners and favors laborowners. Where land ownership is highly concentrated, a cohesive interest group may emerge to oppose this policy. But Asian land ownership is more evenly distributed among households. Hence the negative impact of the policy is widely diffused, and opposition will be more tractable.[1]

Some might consider the distribution of land ownership to be exogenous and end the story here. Others might attribute egalitarian distribution to post-World War II land reforms in East Asia, making an "effective policy choice" story. I argue that relatively equal land distribution in East Asia flows not from policy but from the nature of rice technology, which (more than other forms of agriculture) requires that the cultivator have an equity interest in the land.[2]

---

1. I am indebted to Valerie Bencivenga for this idea.

2. In addition to the argument presented here, latecomer growth in East Asia is advan-

Consider Table 3. It indicates that China's population nearly doubled between A.D. 600 and 1000, and nearly quadrupled in the following eight centuries, while population growth elsewhere was dramatically slower. This essay tells the story of the agricultural technology which made that growth possible and begins the story of the social and cultural institutions which that technology demanded.

After exploring the reasons for the dominant place of rice in East Asian agriculture, I then argue that it made Asia's enormous population densities possible and that in its wet-rice form rice cultivation requires a relatively high level of effort from the cultivator. When a cultivator's work is effortful, a land-tenure form which minimizes monitoring costs will be most efficient. Specifically, hired wage-labor will be least efficient, owner-cultivation most efficient, and rental or share tenancy relations somewhere in between. If efficient institutions tend to displace inefficient ones over time, rice-cultivation societies will shy away from wage-labor and tend toward owner-cultivation.

2. Why Rice Grows Mainly in East Asia: The Geophysics of the Monsoon[3]

Climate

Consider sunlight falling on a land mass and an adjacent ocean. The sun's heat dissipates more quickly into the subsurface mass of water than into the subsurface soil. After December 22 (the winter solstice) each new day brings more sunlight than the day before. Both water and land gradually grow warmer, compared to the sea's surface, the soil will stay hotter and will heat the air above it. The hot air over the land expands, rises, and draws in cool moist sea air, which precipitates its moisture onto the land through "Walker cell" circulation. In winter all this reverses; dry winds blow from land to sea.

Three constraints combine to make this monsoon effect particularly pronounced in Asia. First, below 15 degrees latitude,[4] seasonal variation is insuffi-

---

taged by the legacy of wet-rice agriculture in at least the following four key ways: (1) the historic role of government in water control at all levels creates a precedent for an activist government economic policy; (2) the wet-rice agricultural labor force is preconditioned to factory employment; (3) households have a high propensity to save and to invest in human and physical capital; and (4) population density lowers interurban transport costs and the task of absorbing underemployed rural labor.

3. This section draws on DeDatta (1987) and on conversations with K. Cook, R. Barker, and R. Coffman.

4. Manila, Da Nang, Rangoon, Madras.

cient, while above 35 degrees,[5] the planetary Coriolis effect disrupts monsoon weather systems. Second, a coastal mountain range will also disrupt the formation of Walker cells. Precipitation will be reduced and will be coastal.[6] Third, sheer land mass is important. The larger it is, the stronger the monsoon effect.[7] Thus strong seasonal high and low pressure systems, sharp seasonal wind shifts, and the concentration of precipitation into half the year or less are substantially unique to Asia, as Figure 1 demonstrates.[8]

Figure 1
Monthly Precipitation by World Region
(inches per month)

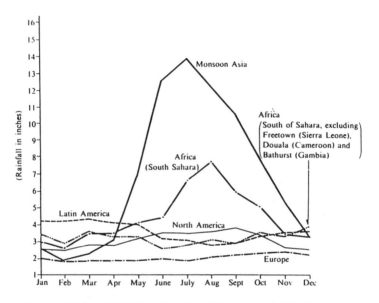

Source: Oshima (1987), based on Royal Meteorological Society data.

---

5. Kyoto, Busan, Xi'an, Islamabad.

6. Thus the Rocky Mountains, for example, curtail the monsoon effect while the Himalayan massif enlarges it.

7. The Mediterranean Sea lies north of Africa and east of Arabia, mimicking the relationship between the Himalyas and monsoon Asia—but undermining any possible monsoon effect instead of accentuating it.

8. Fig. 1 shows the highly seasonal nature of precipitation in Asia. Barry and Chorley (1990) show that this seasonality comes from Asia's seasonal extremes of barometric pressure (118) and the consequent shift in prevailing wind direction (240).

Native Rice (*Oryza*) and Domesticated Rice (*Oryza Sativa*)

The rice plant was already present on the Gondwanaland supercontinent, and was widely disseminated by that land mass's fracture (Chang 1976). It was closely adapted to monsoon conditions of rainfall, temperature, and seasonality. As a marsh plant, it grows well in the standing water resulting from heavy rains concentrated in one season. It requires high temperatures for germination: 10–20 degrees C., versus 1–10 degrees for all other grains. But the absence of a dry season would slow maturation; hence, relatively little rice is grown near the equator, where the monsoon effect is weak (Wickizer and Bennett 1941: 18).[9]

Figure 2
Diffusion of *Oryza Sativa*

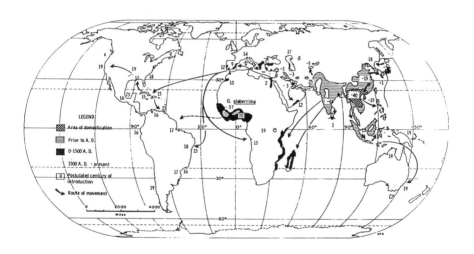

Source: Huke (1976: 32).

_____

9. Of course factors other than these also influence where rice grows well. In Indonesia, for example, rice cultivation is heavily concentrated on the one island of Java, whose weathered volcanic soils are more fertile than the granitic/slate base of Sumatra, Kalimantan, and Sulawesi (Thorbecke 1993:36).

Linguistic, genetic, and archaeological evidence clearly demonstrate that rice was first domesticated in Asia, most probably in the northern part of the Southeast Asian peninsula, at least seven thousand years ago.[10] This domesticated species, *oryza sativa*, was carried to Europe, Africa, and the Middle East as early as 2,000 years ago, and to North and South America in the sixteenth century (Figure 2). Yet as Table 4 shows, even in the postwar period, more than 90 percent of the world's rice is grown in Asia.

Table 2
Land Concentration and Rice Cultivation

Rice-Growing Societies	Land Concentration Gini coefficient for inequality	Percentage Land in Rice
Bangladesh	0.47	116
South Korea	0.39	65
Indonesia	0.62	64
Sri Lanka	0.66	78
Philippines	0.50	77
India	0.59	25
Thailand	0.46	57
China	0.64 (1930)	33
Average	0.54	64
Other Societies		
Kenya	0.82	
Dominican Republic	0.80	
Colombia	0.86	8
Costa Rica	0.78	
Panama	0.74	
Turkey	0.63	
Paraguay	0.93	
Venezuela	0.94	
Brazil	0.84	9
Uruguay	0.82	
Iraq	0.90 (1958)	
Egypt	0.72 (1951)	18
Pakistan	0.63	6
Average	0.80	

Sources: El-Ghonemy (1990: 30, 189, 220, 230); Huke (1990: 11). Bangladesh exceeds 100 percent due to double-cropping.

---

10. See Barker (1983), Bray (1986), Chang (1976), DeDatta (1987), Huke and Huke (1990), and Wickizer and Bennet (1941). Bray cites archaeological evidence from the Yangzi delta and in northeastern Thailand dating to 5000 B.C. as the earliest known rice cultivation (1986: 10).

Other Societies (continued)	Land Concentration *Gini* coefficient for inequality	Percentage Land in Rice
Sri Lanka	0.74	
Nepal	0.65	
Malawi	0.39	
Madagascar	0.41	
Rwanda	0.41	
Bangladesh	0.47	
Ethiopia	0.46	
Togo	0.47	
Sierra Leone	0.48	
Mauritania	0.59	
Yemen	0.66	
Kenya	0.51	
Philippines	0.53	
Jamaica	0.81	
Reunion	0.65	
Thailand	0.45	
Pakistan	0.56	
Niger	0.32	
Jordan	0.69	
Guatemala	0.85	
Panama	0.84	
Belize	0.71	
Uruguay	0.80	

(Calculated from assorted FAO census bulletins: Barrett 1994.)

Egypt	0.43	
South Korea	0.30	
Indonesia	0.72	
Saudi Arabia	0.83	
India	0.62	
Pakistan	0.54	
Dominican Republic	0.79	
Columbia	0.86	
Honduras	0.78	
Costa Rica	0.83	
Panama	0.84	
Turkey	0.58	
Paraguay	0.94	
Iraq	0.39	
Venezuela	0.92	
Brazil	0.86	

Sources: From El Ghonemy 1990: Table 1.5: 1978–84, except Indonesia 1973 and five South American countries 1971–73, largely taken from FAO World Agriculture Census.

Is rice cultivation concentrated in Asia simply because it was first domesticated there, or does the region's climate provide a unique ecological niche?

Some early specialists were ambivalent on this issue.[11] The modern consensus view is that if rice were well-adapted for cultivation outside its home region, then surely it would have spread more widely than it has done to date. Instead, rice remains remarkably immobile. Its consumers—one-third of the human race, who depend on it for food and spend over 30 percent of their income on it—are overwhelmingly Asian. Where 25 percent of wheat is traded internationally, only 3 percent of rice is, and half of this is from the small fraction grown outside Asia (Barker 1983: 1).

We have now established that rice, East Asia's core crop, is uniquely Asian. Rice technology also has a special characteristic: it has an intrinsic potential for very high output per hectare, and so can support very high population densities, but only if labor is effortfully applied.

3. Why is East Asia so Densely Populated? (Technology and Effort)

The single most important characteristic of wet-rice technology is its extraordinarily high yield. This high productivity of cultivated land in turn supports Asia's astonishingly high population densities (Table 5). Using FAO data, Oshima (1987: 20) has calculated that Monsoon Asia has nearly ten persons per cultivated hectare, thirty to forty times as high as Africa or Europe, and ninety times higher than North and South America.

Table 3
Population in China and the Rest of the World
A.D. 600, 1000, 1800, 1992
(in millions)

Year (A.D.)	(1) China	(2) Other	(3) World
600	55	182	237
1000	100	180	280
1800	373	517	890
1992	1150	4201	5351

Sources: (1) China: A.D. 600 and 1000, from Fairbank (1992: 89); 1800, from Perkins (1969: 216). (3) World: 600, 100, and 1800, from Grigg (1980: 1). (2) = (3) - (1). 1992 data from World Bank (1993). Implied annual population percentage growth rates: China 600 to 1000, 0.15 percent; China 1000 to 1800, 0.16 percent.; Other 1000 to 1800, 0.11 percent.

---

11. Wickizer and Bennett (1941: 25) write: "Even in Monsoon Asia the climatic zones apparently adapted to rice culture extend beyond the areas where it is much practiced, and this is even more apparent in other parts of the world. ... Whether and in what degree the obstacles to expansion of rice culture in such regions are natural (soil and topography), demographical, historical, or economic are questions not to be answered easily, if at all."

High levels of effort and skill on the part of rice cultivators are of central importance to the high yields. But let me first deal with a basic question of causality. Is it productive technology which has led to population growth, or the other way around? Much of my argument smacks of biological determinism, and indeed I argue below that the sources of rice's high yields could not be duplicated by any other plant. But in fact my position is that of Ester Boserup (1965, 1981), Dwight Perkins (1969), and others: that as Perkins puts it (23), "the major engine generating this rise in yields was population growth." Both Perkins (for China circa 1400–1800) and Boserup (for much broader time periods and areas) presume that over time, population pressure has driven human inventiveness so as to move preindustrial societies from right to left along the rectangular hyperbola shown in Figure 3.

Figure 3.
The Boserup Hyperbola
(Rising Population Density, Rising Yields,
and Constant Per Capita Output)

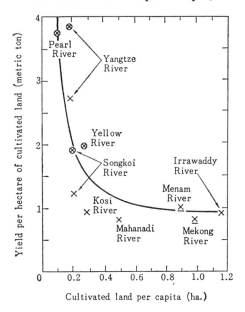

Cultivated land per capita (ha.)

Cultivated land per capita (hectares)

Source: Ishikawa (1967: 83). The fitted line represents the equation $Y = 0.3417X(-1) + 0.5062$. $R2 = 0.73$. While these data are cross-sectional, Boserup would argue that over time human society has moved from right to left along this curve.

Table 4
World Rice Production
(percentage)

	1950		1978	
Asia	93.0		91.1	
East Asia		44.1		42.6
Southeast Asia		20.0		19.3
South Asia		28.9		29.1
Africa	2.2		2.1	
North America	1.4		2.2	
South America	2.5		3.3	
Europe	0.9		1.4	
Total	100.0		100.0	

Source: Lu and Chang 1982.

Why does rice produce such high yields? There are four main reasons. First, each rice plant produces about 2,000 grains, compared with 400 or so for wheat or other grains. This 5:1 ratio by itself cuts seed grain requirements by 80 percent (one rice seed doing the work of five wheat or rye seeds). Coupled with the use of seedling beds (instead of wastefully broadcasting the seed), rice requires that only 1–2 percent of this year's crop be set aside to produce next year's, compared with 25–30 percent for wheat (Bray 1986: 15). This alone gives rice a yield 33 percent to 40 percent above its rivals.

Second, rice variegates more rapidly than other grains. This flows in part from the same 5:1 ratio. A farmer who observes a desirable variant can cull out and carry over that plant's genetic material into five times as many identical offspring. But in part the tendency to variegate appears to be intrinsic to the plant. The range of variation among rice subspecies is so great that no internationally recognized system of classification has yet been devised, despite several attempts since 1914. Rapid variegation, in turn, means that farmers over the centuries have been able to raise yields by optimally adapting *oryza sativa* to their particular growing conditions.[12]

Third, rice is the only grain that grows in standing water. Critical nutrients—in particular, nitrogen—are brought to and absorbed into the plant by water flow, in an entirely different and vastly more efficient manner than for dry-grown crops. The impact on yield is well-nigh miraculous. One experimental rice plot in the Philippines, for example, has produced four crops per year for over three decades, with no fertilizer applications.[13] Thus wet-rice cul-

12. Variegation also made possible the development of "miracle rice" strains in the modern era, but this essay concerns the characteristics which Asian societies brought with them into that era.

13. Personal communication from Ronnie Coffman. Of course, zero fertilizer application is not economically efficient, but it is certainly eye-catching.

tivation eliminates the need for a field to lie fallow. With greater cropping frequency, yield rises. For example, growing a crop twice as often on any given field, with yield per crop held constant, doubles yield per hectare.

Finally, the seedling-bed/transplanting technology, first developed in Vietnam and China 2,000 years ago, raises yields in many ways. It conserves time in the main field and so makes double-cropping more feasible. It strengthens the root system, which encourages the production of multiple heads of grain. The regular spacing of transplanted plants facilitates weed and pest control. Overall, yields rise by perhaps 40 percent (Bray 1983, citing Grist 1975: 149).

Now let us make three main observations about this high-yield rice technology. First, all four aspects are intrinsic to the particular plant in question; that is, the story is not just one of a continually intensified agricultural technology, but it is more narrowly about rice. Second, although all four aspects inhere as potential within the plant, they have been drawn out and perfected only over a long period of time—the historic time spans examined by Perkins (1969), Boserup (1981), and others. Third, and most important, each aspect of rice technology depends on great effort from the cultivator.[14] Single-stalked grain with heavy panicles is prone to lodging or shattering and must be carefully harvested.[15] Rice variegates only insofar as the careful farmer, in harvesting, spots and propagates useful variants. In an environment of many seed types, seed selection is more complex. Water control is notoriously a complex matter of close timing and cooperation.[16]

The link between effort and yield from rice cultivation can be further supported in two ways. First, rice specialists uniformly attest to the major role of effort. Randolph Barker (1983) reports the observation that rice yields decrease as distance from the cultivator's house increases.[17] Francesca Bray (1986) and Mark Elvin are rich in similar anecdotal evidence of the importance of effort.[18]

---

14. I use effort and skill interchangeably. More properly, one might wish to think of skill as a stock of human capital which the cultivator brings to the task, and effort as the energy with which even an unskilled cultivator might work. But since skill is built up out of past effort (particularly mental effort), the two will be highly correlated. Since both are hard to monitor, I treat them here as a single phenomenon.

15. The traditional rice-harvesting tool—a hand-held blade, not an arm's-length sickle—testifies to this fact.

16. Geertz (1980: 82), describing the religious customs adhered to by the Balinese *subak* (village irrigation coooperative), writes: "This developed ritual pattern, matching with fine precision the actual flow of irrigation activity, is one of the major regulating mechanisms in the whole, marvelously intricate econological system."

17. Personal communication.

18. Elvin (1982: 13) quotes an eighteenth-century missionary description of the "multitudinous adjustments" made by Chinese farmers as follows: "The little extra efforts and

Evelyn Rawksi (1972: 13), in a careful study of this issue for the Ming-Qing period, notes that "yields are very sensitive to skill and additional effort on the part of the cultivator."

Table 5
Population Densities
(persons per sq. km.)

	Population (millions)	Area 1000 sq. km.	Density (1)/(2)
East Asia	1323	10040	130
China	1150	9560	120
South Korea	43	100	430
Japan	124	378	328
Southeast Asia	370	3750	100
Indonesia	181	1905	95
Philippines	63	300	210
Thailand	57	513	110
Malaysia	18	330	55
South Asia	1130	4488	250
Bangladesh	110	144	764
India	867	3290	260
Pakistan	116	800	145
Africa	441	16623	27
North America	363	21307	21
South America	331	17330	19
World	5351	111306	48

Source: World Bank (1993: 238).

Second, one can make an *a priori* argument that effort level must be rising as output per hectare rises through a shift toward wet-rice techniques. Boserup (1981: 167) presents evidence that hours worked per day increase and/or per capita consumption falls as yield rises, and argues (1965: 41) that this must necessarily be so. Her argument is that if effort were lower and per capita output higher in intense, high-yield agriculture, then one would predict a switch to the new technology as soon as it becomes known. But we observe more- and

---

knacks, inventions and discoveries, resources and combinations, which have caused people to exclaim at miracles in [European] gardens, have been transported on a large scale out into the [Chinese] fields and have done marvels."

less-intensive technologies coexisting side by side. This suggests that the more intensive technology is either more effortful or yields lower per capita output, or both.[19]

To summarize: rice technology exhibits highly distinctive characteristics, all of which call forth a high level of effort on the part of the cultivator. Those characteristics have enabled rice-growing societies to move along the Boserup curve, achieving very high population densities.

At this point a significant and informative literature (the "equilibrium trap" story) argues, "Yes," and therein lies the key to Asia's *failure* to modernize.[20] That literature asks the question: Why did Asia not industrialize before or simultaneously with Europe? This is quite different from the question I pose: Why is Asia modernizing *more* rapidly than other *non*-European "latecomers to development"? I believe that rice cultivation provides part of the answer, through a story which links effort, tenurial relations, and the success of postwar policymaking.[21]

---

19. One could also look for evidence of higher effort in rice cultivation by asking whether rice farmers are paid more. Unfortunately, detailed micro data sets which include both rice and non-rice cultivation are scarce.

20. Oshima (1987) argues that seasonality made for "underutilization" of off-season labor which could not enter factory employment because of peak season labor demand. Bray (1986) stresses the nontransferability of Western agricultural technology and also notes that the larger-scale European farms fostered development of capitalist modes of organization. A broader literature [Perkins (1975: especially chapters by Elvin and Dernberger), Tang (1980), and Chao (1983)], focuses on the fact that by 1850 or at the latest 1900 China ran out of arable land, and found itself in a high-level equilibrium trap.

21. Barker (1983: 12) takes the core element of the equilibrium trap school (exhaustion of arable land) and implicitly links it to a latecomer argument of the sort I am making here. He notes that the "frontier" of arable but not yet cultivated land, which had disappeared in East Asia by 1900 at the latest, in tropical Asia persisted up to World War II or beyond. He then makes the following comment:

> By contrast, the community structures in South and Southeast Asia, moulded under the traditional land-surplus economy of the 19th century, could not accommodate the rapidly emerging need for leadership, organization and discipline required to mobilize the community to undertake cooperative action in the post World War II period. Such a lag in the institutional adjustment represents a major factor explaining the underinvestment in rural infrastructure at the community level in South and Southeast Asia.

4. Why is Land Distribution in Asia Egalitarian?
Effort and Tenurial Relations in Agriculture

What is the relationship between agricultural technology on the one hand and choice of contractual form on the other? After some general comments, I will make an intuitive argument that an "effortful" technology such as rice cultivation will be least likely to employ landless labor for a wage, somewhat more likely to employ share-cropping, and most likely of all to employ rental contracts for a fixed fee, or owner-cultivation.

Imagine an agricultural society with abundant land. The scale on which farming takes place—family farming, small plantation, or agribusiness—will be determined by technology. Assume that monitoring and other transactions costs make family farming the optimal choice. Then each household provides its own labor to agricultural production on its own land. Labor is the household's only asset, since land is free.

Now suppose land becomes scarce because population is increasing. Suppose that technology changes in a way which raises per hectare yields, but that the optimal scale of production is still the household. We would expect to observe family farming by households evenly endowed with two assets, labor and land. Still no factor market transactions occur.

Suppose now that some perturbation—a localized drought or flood, say—leaves some households so destitute that they must borrow from others, using land as collateral. Now wealth is unequal, and hence so is income, and (given a rising propensity to save as income rises), the initial perturbation will generate increasing concentration of land ownership.[22]

There must now arise some new institutional arrangement, some sort of market in land or in labor, which transcends the family farm and brings land and labor together in production. The following alternatives present themselves:

1. Each landless household borrows and purchases an optimal amount of land. If owner-cultivation is the most efficient institution, such purchase should be possible at some nonzero interest rate, assuming a perfect capital market on which landless peasants could borrow. But suppose that such a market does not exist.[23] This leaves us with

---

22. This process cannot continue without limit, because as landlessness grows, the landless are increasingly likely to combine, rebel, and redistribute wealth, as occurred at the end of each Chinese dynastic cycle.

23. This is not meant to be flippant. In principle such a market should exist; and it is useful to ask why in the real world it does not. Such an approach strongly suggests that the central question of tenurial relations in agriculture is the cause(s) of market failure of this sort—in the words of Sen (1981), the causes of "the system's inability to com-

2. *land rental*: landless households farm others' land and pay a fixed annual fee, in cash or in kind. The renters bear all risk and claim all residual output.

3. *sharecropping*: landless households farm others' land and pay a fraction of the crop to the landowner. Risk and reward are split between the two parties.

4. *wage labor:* landless households farm others' land in return for a fixed annual fee. The landowner bears all risk and claims all residual output.

There presumably exists a wide range of variations on these forms. But data are typically collected under these headings.[24] Which form will be chosen?

Will "society" "choose" the contractual form which is optimal or efficient?[25] The New Institutional Economics literature often makes just such an assumption. But others argue that for social institutions in general, the most that one can confidently predict is that the institutions chosen will not actively impoverish the society.[26]

But contracts, such as those governing land and labor relations, are a social institution with a special characteristic: individuals may be both motivated and fully empowered to change the contractual institution they use. If a landlord can do better by offering a rental contract in preference to a sharecropping one, he will presumably do so (Basu 1990: 26). In what follows I assume that the dominant contractual form in agriculture will be that which maximizes agricultural production.

The literature on this subject nominates a wide variety of factors as affecting contractual choice. Risk-sharing, the incentive to innovate, transactions costs, and interlinked markets may all play a part.[27] Consider only the impact of effort, which cannot be well monitored, on the choice among wage labor, sharecropping, or rental contracts.[28]

A wage-labor contract will depress agricultural output, since the worker receives a fixed amount regardless of effort. If effort carries disutility, and cannot be monitored, the laborer has no incentive to work effortfully, and so output

---

bine the abundant labour of the poor with resources owned largely by the rich."

24. Western-trained social scientists are culturally prone to impose these categories on Asian forms of property rights. But we do so at our own peril. Beneath the familiar labels, something else entirely may be going on. The current literature on China's township and village enterprises reflects this tension.

25. In the sense, presumably, of maximizing individual utilities within the society— although this leaves us with the problem of interpersonal utility comparisons.

26. Basu (1990: 23) calls this a "minimal functionalist position": if we observe a society which has existed for a long period, we can conclude that the institutions of that society "are functional above a certain cut-off point."

27. See Hayami (1993), Basu (1990), and Binswanger (1984).

28. The approach used here is in the spirit of Basu (1994) and (1984: 132).

will suffer. A sharecropping contract introduces some incentive to work hard, since the laborer now gets a share of the extra crop which results from extra effort. But a rental agreement provides the laborer with the most incentive of all three forms. Do both parties gravitate toward the contractual form which will maximize utility for both?

If an agricultural technology involves effort, sharecropping dominates wage labor and land rental dominates sharecropping. Indeed, the only contractual form we should observe would be land rental. But now imagine other factors in agricultural production which pull in the other direction. For example, if only the landlord can undertake output-increasing innovation, this taken alone argues for an exactly reversed ranking. Then the absolute rankings based on effort are transformed into tendencies: *to the extent* that a technology is effortful, as rice cultivation is, we are *more likely* to observe tenurial relations which accord to labor a relatively large share of residual reward.

Tables 6 and 7 present data for China in the 1930s which permit a rough test of this conjecture.[29] There is a clear tendency for wagelabor to be less prevalent, and for rental to be more prevalent, in the rice-growing southern provinces.[30] This suggests that careful empirical work, using both inter- and intra-country comparisons, may find good support for this hypothesis.

---

29. The literature on this subject suggests alternative tests and evidence. Rawski (1972: 10) notes for the Ming-Qing period in China that "since rice was Fukien's major crop, the ecology of its cultivation, particularly its labor intensive aspects, led to the development of tenure and rent conditions favorable to the tenant." Chao (1982) shows the gradual disappearance in China of wage labor and a movement from share tenancy toward rental. Perkins (1969: 87) states that Chinese tenurial institutions were settled by the Sung Dynasty (A.D. 1000); landowners "were well on their way to becoming similar to those existing in the 20th century. In the Sung, their principal claim was a share of the harvest and little else." Thorbecke (1994) tells a story of Indonesian industrialization, compared with the Philippines, which suggests the importance of a landowning class in explaining the different experiences of these two countries.

30. The adjusted R-squared for a regression linking percentage acreage sown to rice to incidence of wage labor is 0.25, and for rental contract 0.36. In both cases the coefficient is significant at the 99 percent level.

Table 6
Tenure Form by Province: China, ca. 1935
(percentage)

Province	L1 Wage-Labor	L2 Share-crop & Rental	L3 Owner-Cultivator	L21 Rental (kind)	L22 Share-crop	L23 Rental (cash)
Shaanxi	0.57	21.00	78.43	59	26	15
Shanxi	7.39	17.00	75.61	46	27	27
Hobei	4.41	13.00	82.59	22	26	52
Shandong	2.26	12.00	85.74	31	39	30
Honan	2.54	23.00	74.46	40	44	17
Jiangsu	0.60	32.00	67.40	53	19	28
Anhui	0.58	40.00	59.42	53	33	14
Zhejiang	2.03	44.00	53.97	66	7	27
Hubei	0.56	38.00	61.44	80	13	7
Hunan	0.84	56.00	43.16	74	18	7
Jiangxi	0.42	37.00	62.58	80	13	7
Fujian	0.21	39.00	60.79	56	25	19
Guangdong	0.61	47.50	51.89	58	18	24
Guangxi	2.00	37.50	60.50	65	29	6
Guizhou	1.42	38.00	60.58	40	51	10
Yunnan	1.64	30.00	68.36	61	25	14
Sichuan	1.58	53.50	44.92	58	16	26

Notes and Sources: L1: households providing wage labor to others. China Land Commission, p. 35, in Chao (1983: 308). Last three provinces interpolated based on partial data. L2: households renting all of their land. Perkins (1969: 91) presents three data sets. I average them after throwing out provinces with 6 or fewer observations. L3: households owning at least some of their land. L3=100-L1-L2. L21, L22, L23: Li et al. p. 245, in Perkins (1969: 105).

6. Summary and conclusions

I have presented five linked propositions about Asia. First, the monsoon climate, which is so strikingly conducive to wet-rice cultivation, is so prominent in Asia because of its geographic and topographic features which appear nowhere else on earth. The January Himalayan low, at 35 degrees latitude, is as low as Iceland (18 degrees latitude). The July high of 1035 millibars is the highest pressure on the globe (Barry and Chorley 1990: 118, 240).

Second, the biotechnology of rice underlies Asia's success in sustaining extraordinarily high population densities.[31] The Chinese population growth seems to coincide with the shift from the dry-farming North China to the rice-growing South beginning under the Sung. More work needs to be done to clarify this relationship, in China and elsewhere. More work is also needed on the third

---

31. The word "success" is meant here only in a biological sense, of course. Sichuan Province at the end of the sixteenth century was "successfully" feeding a population ten times that of Spain. But Spain's five million were "successfully" spreading Spanish culture and power around the world.

proposition: that wet-rice cultivation is highly intensive in unmonitorable effort by the cultivator.

Table 7
Acreage, Yields, and Population Density
China, circa 1935

Province	Acreage in Rice (percent)	Rice Yields	Corn Yields	Soybean Yields	Population Density (per mou)
		national average = 100			
Shaanxi	0.038	0.82	0.84	0.70	0.187
Shanxi	0.002	0.21	0.73	0.67	0.212
Hobei	0.008	0.57	0.86	0.82	0.247
Shandong	0.001	0.27	0.95	1.15	0.268
Honan	0.013	0.74	0.69	0.83	0.233
Jiangsu	0.256	1.08	1.12	1.11	0.271
Anhui	0.252	0.85	0.91	0.87	0.224
Zhejiang	0.489	0.98	0.88	0.83	0.414
Hubei	0.325	0.89	0.83	1.01	0.329
Hunan	0.683	1.13	1.04	1.12	0.485
Jiangxi	0.602	0.97	0.79	0.90	0.310
Fujian	0.686	1.09	1.35	1.06	0.409
Guangdong	0.815	1.00	N/A	1.10	0.408
Guangxi	0.602	0.90	N/A	1.32	0.322
Guizhou	0.379	0.85	1.22	N/A	0.597
Sichuan	0.321	0.93	0.75	1.45	0.340
	0.338	1.12	1.40	1.42	0.408

Notes and Sources: Acreage: calculated from Perkins (1969: Appendix 217). Yields: Perkins (1969: Appendix 266). Density: population (Perkins 1969: Appendix A) divided by cultivated acreage (Perkins 1969: Appendix B).

The fourth proposition is that because rice-growing requires the cultivator's effort, it will be carried on under those land tenure forms which most closely approximate owner-cultivation. Thus rental will be chosen over sharecropping, and both over wage labor. One would hope to see further work, either with country-level data or with regional data sets from countries other than China, to follow up on the suggestive Chinese data presented here.

The fifth proposition is that in societies like those in East Asia, where most land is owned by the cultivator, pro-growth policies will be implemented more effectively than in South America, for example, where land ownership is concentrated in a few hands. For this conjecture, I have offered no direct test. But effective implementation is unmistakably concentrated in Asia. Here, at least, is one way of understanding why that might be so.

References

Barker, Randolph, and Robert Herdt. 1983. *The Asian Rice Economy*. Ithaca: Cornell University.

Barrett, Christopher. 1994. "Peasants, Prices and Markets in Madagascar." Ph.D. diss., University of Wisconsin–Madison.

Barry, Roger C., and Richard Chorley. 1990. *Atmosphere, Weather and Climate*. New York: Routledge.

Basu, Kaushik. 1984. *The Less Developed Economy: A Critique of Contemporary Theory*. Oxford: Blackwell.

———. 1987. "The Growth and Decay of Custom: The Role of the New Institutional Economics in Economic History." *Explorations in Economic History* 24, no. 1 (January).

———. 1990. *Agrarian Structure and Economic Underdevelopment*. New York: Harwood.

———. 1994. "Rural Credit and Interlinkage: Implications for Rural Poverty, Agrarian Efficiency and Public Policy." London: Development Economics Research Programme, London School of Economics.

Binswanger, Hans, and M. Rozenzweig, eds. 1984. *Contractual Arrangements, Employment and Wages in Rural Labor Markets in Asia*. New Haven: Yale University Press.

Boserup, Ester. 1965. *The Conditions of Agricultural Growth: The Economics of Agrarian Change under Population Pressure*. Chicago: Aldine.

———. 1981. *Population and Technological Change: A Study of Long-Term Trends*. Chicago: University of Chicago Press.

Bray, Francesca. 1986. *The Rice Economies: Technology and Development in Asian Societies*. New York: Blackwell.

Chang, T. T. 1976. "The Origin, Evolution, Cultivation, Dissemination, and Diversification of Asian and African Rices." *Euphytica* 25: 425.

Chao, Kang. 1982. "Tenure Systems in Traditional China." *Economic Development and Cultural Change* 31, no. 2: 195–314

China Land Commission. 1937. *A Summary Report of the National Land Survey*. Nanjing: National Land Commission.

De Datta, Surajit K. 1987. *Principles and Practices of Rice Production*. Malabar: Krieger.

Dernberger, Robert F. 1975. "The Role of the Foreigner in China's Economic Development, 1840–1949.". In *China's Modern Economy in Historical Perspective*, edited by Dwight Perkins, 19–49. Stanford: Stanford University Press.

El-Ghonemy, M. Riad. 1990. *The Political Economy of Rural Poverty*. New York: Routledge.

Elvin, Mark. 1973. *The Pattern of the Chinese Past*. London: Eyre Methuen.

———. 1975. "Skills and Resources in Late Traditional China". In *China's Modern Economy in Historical Perspective,* edited by Dwight Perkins, 85–115. Stanford: Stanford University Press.

———. 1982. "The Technology of Farming in Late-Traditional China." In *The Chinese Agricultural Economy,* edited by Randolph Barker. Boulder: Westview Press.

Epstein, T. S. 1967. "Productive Efficiency and Customary Systems of Rewards in Rural South India." In *Themes in Economic Anthropology,* edited by R. Firth. New York: Tavistock Publications.

Fairbank, John King. 1992. *China: A New History.* Cambridge: Harvard University Press.

Geertz, Clifford. 1980. "Organization of the Balinese Subak." In *Irrigation and Agricultural Development in Asia,* edited by Walter Coward. Ithaca: Cornell University Press.

Griffin, Keith. 1974. *The Political Economy of Agrarian Change.* Cambridge: Harvard University Press.

Grigg, David. 1980. *Population Growth and Agrarian Change: An Historical Perspective.* New York: Cambridge University Press.

Grist, D. H. 1975. *Rice.* London: Longmans.

Hart, Oliver, and Bengt Holmstrom. 1988. "The Theory of Contracts." In *Advances in Economic Theory,* edited by Truman F. Bewley. New York: Cambridge University Press.

Hayami, Yujiro, and K. Otsuka. 1993. *The Economics of Contract Choice: An Agrarian Perspective.* Oxford: Clarendon Press.

Huke, Robert. 1976. "Geography and Climate of Rice." In International Rice Research Institute, *Climate and Rice,* 31. Los Banos, Philippines.

———, and Eleanor Huke. 1990. *Rice Then and Now.* Los Banos, Philippines: International Rice Research Institute.

Ishikawa, Shigeru. 1967. *Economic Development in Asian Perspective.* Tokyo: Hitotsubashi University Institute of Economic Research.

Kato, Shigeshi. 1953. "The Totals of Landowning and Tenant Households in the Sung Dynasty." *Shina keizai shi kosho* (Tokyo).

Li Wen-zhi et al. 1987. *Zhongguo jindai nongye shi ziliao* (Historical materials on agriculture in modern China) Volume III. Beijing: Zhongguo nongye chubanshe.

Lu, Jonathan J., and T. T. Chang. 1982. "Rice in Temporal and Spatial Perspective." In *Rice: Production and Utilization,* edited by Bor S. Luh. Westport: Avi Publishing.

Matthews, R. C. O. 1986. "The Economics of Institutions and the Sources of Growth." *Economic Journal* 96 (December): 903–18.

Oshima, Harry. 1987. *Economic Growth in Monsoon Asia: A Comparative Survey.* Tokyo: University of Tokyo Press.

Perkins, Dwight H. 1969. *Agricultural Development in China, 1368–1968.* Chicago: Aldine.

———. 1975. *China's Modern Economy in Historical Perspective.* Stanford: Stanford University Press.

Popkin, Samuel L. 1979. *The Rational Peasant: The Political Economy of Rural Society in Vietnam.* Berkeley: University of California Press.

Rawski, Evelyn S. 1972. *Agricultural Change and the Peasant Economy of South China.* Cambridge: Harvard University Press.

Roumasset, James A. 1976. *Rice and Risk.* New York: North-Holland.

Ruttan, Vernon W. 1995. "Cultural Endowments and Economic Development: Implications for the Chinese Economies." *China Economic Review* 6, no. 1.

Sen, Abhijit. 1981. "Market Failure and Control of Labour Power: Towards an Explanation of 'Structure' and Change in Indian Agriculture." *Cambridge Journal of Economics* 5: 201–28.

Tang, Anthony. 1979. "China's Agricultural Legacy." *Economic Development and Cultural Change* 28, no. 1: 1–23.

Thorbecke, Erik. 1994. "The Political Economy of Development: Indonesia and the Philippines." Inaugural Frank Golay lecture, Cornell University.

———, and T. van der Pluijim. 1993. *Rural Indonesia: Socio-economic Development in a Changing Environment.* New York: New York University Press.

Twitchett, Dennis C. 1963. *Financial Administration Under the T'ang Dynasty.* Cambridge: Cambridge University Press.

Wan, Henry, Jr. 1993. "On the Mechanism of Catching Up." *European Economic Review* 38: 952–63.

Wickizer, V. D., and M. K. Bennett. 1941. *The Rice Economy of Monsoon Asia.* Stanford: Food Research Institute.

Wittfogel, Karl. 1957. *Oriental Despotism: A Study in Total Power.* New Haven: Yale University Press.

World Bank. 1993. *World Development Report.* New York: Oxford University Press.

Selected Writings
of Donald J. Munro

"The Yang Hsien-chen Affair." *China Quarterly* (London) (April-June 1965).

"Dissent in Communist China." *Current Scene* (Hong Kong), 1 June 1966.

"Chinese Communist Treatment of the Thinkers of the Hundred Schools Period." *China Quarterly* (London) October-December 1965. (Reprinted in *History in Communist China*, edited by Albert Feuerwerker. Cambridge: M.I.T. Press, 1968.)

"Maxims and Realities in China's Educational Policy." *Asian Survey* 8 (April 1967).

"Comments on 'China and the West in the Thought of Mao Tse-tung' by Benjamin Schwartz." In *China in Crisis*, edited by Tang Tsou and Ho P'ing-ti. Chicago: University of Chicago Press, 1968.

The Concept of Man in Early China. Stanford: Stanford University Press, 1969.

"Humanism in Modern China." In *Works in Honor of Liu Yu Yun*, edited by Frederick Wakeman. Taipei: Chinese Materials and Research Aids Center, 1970.

"Egalitarian Ideal and Educational Fact in Communist China." In *The Management of a Revolutionary Society*, edited by John Lindbeck. Seattle: University of Washington Press, 1971.

"The Malleability of Man in Chinese Marxism." *China Quarterly* (London) (October-December 1971).

"Man, State and School." In *China's Developmental Experience*, edited by Michel Oksenberg. New York: Praeger, 1973.

"The Chinese View of Alienation." *China Quarterly* (London) (July-September 1974).

"The Chinese View of Modeling." *Human Development* (Basel) no. 18 (1975).

"Belief Control in China: The Psychological and Ethical Foundations." In *Social Control and Deviance in China*, edited by Richard W. Wilson and Sidney Greenblatt. New York: Praeger, 1976.

The Concept of Man in Contemporary China. Ann Arbor: University of Michigan Press, 1977.

"Chinese Values Through the Eyes of an American Philosopher." In *The China Difference*, edited by Ross Terrill. New York: Harper & Row, 1979.

"The Concept of 'Interest' in Chinese Thought." *Journal of the History of Ideas* (March 1980).

"Philosophy in China." In *Humanistic and Social Science Research in China.* New York: Social Science Research Council, 1980.

"Academic Research, Psychology, and the Social Sciences." In *Culture and Science in China,* edited by John Merson. Sydney: Australian Broadcasting Commission, 1981.

"Intellectual Freedom, The Individual, and the Laws." In *Culture and Science in China,* edited by John Merson. Sydney: Australian Broadcasting Commission, 1981.

Editor, *Individualism and Holism: Studies in Confucian and Taoist Values.* Ann Arbor: University of Michigan Center for Chinese Studies, 1985.

"Introduction" to *Individualism and Holism: Studies in Confucian and Taoist Values.* Ann Arbor: University of Michigan Center for Chinese Studies, 1985.

"The Family Network, the Stream of Water, and the Plant: Picturing Persons in Sung Confucianism." In *Individualism and Holism: Studies in Confucian and Taoist Values.* Ann Arbor: University of Michigan Center for Chinese Studies, 1985.

"'The Mirror and the Body': Values Within Chu His's Theory of Knowledge." *Tsing-Hua Journal of Chinese Studies* (1987).

Images of Human Nature: A Sung Portrait. Princeton: Princeton University Press, 1988.

"The Confucian Moral Sense in the Modern Period" (Rujia di daodegan: Ta zai xianzai Zhongguo di yichan). In *Ruxue guoji xueshu taolunhui lunwenji,* edited by Zhongguo Kongzi jijinhui and Sinjiapo Dongyang zhexue yanjiuso, vol. 2, 1273–77. Ji'nan: Qilu shushe, 1989.

"The Fact-Value Fusion." In *Zhexue yanjiu* (Philosophical investigations) (Beijing) (June 1990).

"Foreword" to Livia Kohn. *Taoist Mystical Philosophy.* Albany: State University of New York Press, 1991.

"Afterword" to Brian Bruya. *The Music of Nature.* Princeton: Princeton University Press, 1992.

"One-Minded Hierarchy versus Interest Group Pluralism: Two Chinese Approaches to Conflict." In *New Approaches to Conflict in World Politics,* edited by William Zimmerman. Ann Arbor: University of Michigan Press, 1994.

"Preface" to Liu Xiaogan. *The Classification of the Zhuangzi Chapters.* Ann Arbor: University of Michigan Center for Chinese Studies, 1995.

The Imperial Style of Inquiry in Twentieth-Century China: The Emergence of New Approaches. Ann Arbor: University of Michigan Center for Chinese Studies, 1996.

"Chinese Marxism." In *Encyclopedia of Philosophy.* London: Routledge, forthcoming.

Selected Writings
of Albert Feuerwerker

"A Draft Biography of Sheng Hsuan-huai, Official and Industrialist." *Papers on China* 8 (1954): 1–37.

"From 'Feudalism' to 'Capitalism' in Recent Historical Writing from Mainland China." *The Journal of Asian Studies* 18, no. 1 (1958): 107–16.

China's Early Industrialization: Sheng Hsuan-huai (1844–1916) and Mandarin Enterprise. Cambridge: Harvard University Press, 1958. [Chinese edition: *Zhongguo zaoqi gongyehua—Sheng Xuanhuai yu guandushangpan qiye,* translated by Yu Hesheng, with a new introduction; preface by Wang Qingcheng. Beijing: Chinese Academy of Social Sciences Press, 1990.]

"Sheng Hsuan-huai." In *Men and Politics in Modern China,* edited by H. L. Boorman, 109–14. New York: Columbia University Press, 1960.

"China's History in Marxian Dress." *The American Historical Review* 66 (January 1961): 323–53.

"Materials for the Study of the Economic History of Modern China." *The Journal of Economic History* (March 1961): 41–60.

"Rewriting Chinese History: Interpreting the Past in the People's Republic of China." *University of Toronto Quarterly* (April 1961): 273–85.

Chinese Communist Studies of Modern Chinese History, with S. Cheng. Cambridge: Harvard University Press, 1961.

"La storia della Cina in abito Marxista." *Mercurio* (Rome) 5, no. :3 (March 1962): 11–20.

Editor and contributor, *Modern China.* New York: Prentice-Hall, 1964.

"China's Nineteenth-Century Industrialization: The Case of the Hanyehping Coal and Iron Company, Limited." In *The Economic Development of China and Japan,* edited by C. S. Cowan, 79–110. London: Allen and Unwin, 1964.

"The Ideology of Scholarship: China's New Historiography," with H. L. Kahn. *The China Quarterly* 22 (April-June 1965): 1–13.

"China's Modern Economic History in Chinese Communist Historiography." *The China Quarterly* 22 (April-June 1965): 31–61.

Editor, *Approaches to Modern Chinese History,* with Rhoads Murphey and Mary C. Wright. Berkeley: University of California Press, 1967.

"Industrial Enterprise in Twentieth-Century China: The Chee Hsin Cement Co." In *Approaches to Modern Chinese History,* edited by Albert Feuerwerker,

Rhoads Murphey, and Mary C. Wright, 304–41. Berkeley: University of California Press, 1967.

Editor and contributor, *History in Communist China.* Cambridge: M.I.T. Press, 1968.

The Chinese Economy, 1912–1949. Michigan Papers in Chinese Studies, no. 1. Ann Arbor: University of Michigan Center for Chinese Studies, 1968.

"Comment (on Political Integration in Nineteenth-Century China)." In *China in Crisis.* Vol. 1. Edited by Ping-ti Ho and Tang Tsou, 179–93. Chicago: University of Chicago Press, 1968.

"Modern Chinese History." *Encyclopedia Americana.* Vol. 6. 1968.

The Chinese Economy, ca. 1870–1911. Michigan Papers in Chinese Studies, no. 5. Ann Arbor: University of Michigan Center for Chinese Studies, 1969.

"Handicraft and Manufactured Cotton Textiles in China, 1871–1910." *The Journal of Economic History* 30, no. 2 (June 1970): 338–78.

"Modern China?" *Michigan Quarterly Review* 11, no. 1 (Winter 1972): 1–5.

"Chinese History and the Foreign Relations of Contemporary China." *The Annals of American Academy of Political and Social Science* (July 1972): 1–14.

"Relating to the International Community." In *China's Development Experience,* edited by Michel Oksenberg, 42–54. New York: The Academy of Political Science, 1973.

Rebellion in Nineteenth-Century China. Michigan Papers in Chinese Studies, no. 20. Ann Arbor: University of Michigan Center for Chinese Studies, 1975.

State and Society in Eighteenth-Century China: The Ch'ing Empire in Its Glory. Michigan Papers in Chinese Studies, no. 27. Ann Arbor: University of Michigan Center for Chinese Studies, 1976.

The Foreign Establishment in China in the Early Twentieth Century. Michigan Papers in Chinese Studies, no. 29. Ann Arbor: University of Michigan Center for Chinese Studies, 1976.

"Economic Aspects of Reform." In *Reform in Nineteenth-Century China,* edited by Paul A. Cohen and John E. Schrecker, 35–40. Cambridge: Harvard University Press, 1976.

Economic Trends in the Republic of China, 1912–1949. Michigan Papers in Chinese Studies, no. 31. Ann Arbor: University of Michigan Center for Chinese Studies, 1977.

"Discussion." In *Conference on Modern Chinese Economic History,* 45–46, 497–99. Taipei: Institute of Economics, 1978.

"A White Horse May or May Not be a Horse, But Megahistory Is Not Economic History." *Modern China* 4, no. 3 (July 1978): 331–39.

Zhongguo jin bainian jingji shi (1870–1949) [China's economic history of the last hundred years]. Taipei: Hua-shih Publishers, 1978.

"China in the Last Decades of the Twentieth Century: Problems and Prospects of Modernization." *China Today,* Maxwell Summer Lecture Series, Syracuse University, 1979.
"History." In *Science in Contemporary China,* edited by Leo Orleans, 507–13. Stanford: Stanford University Press, 1980.
"Economic Trends in the Late Ch'ing Empire, 1870–1911." In *The Cambridge History of Modern China.* Vol. 11, edited by J. K. Fairbank and Denis Twitchett. Cambridge: Cambridge University Press, 1980. [Chinese translations: "Wan Qing di jingji qushi (1870–1911)." *Jianqiao Zhongguo shi, wan Qing pian.* Taipei: Southern Materials Center, 1986; and "1870–1911 nian wan Qing diguo di jingji quxiang." *Jianqiao Zhongguo wan Qing shi.* Beijing: Chinese Academy of Social Sciences, 1985.]
"China's Reaction to the Penetration of Western Commerce, 1839–1949." XVe Congrès international des sciences historiques, Bucarest, 1980, *Rapports* 2: 479–87.
"Characteristics of the Chinese Economic Model Specific to the Chinese Environment." In *China's Development Experience and the Other Developing Countries,* edited by Robert F. Dernberger, 261–305. Cambridge: Harvard University Press, 1980.
"Wan Qing shiqide jingji zhuangkuang" [Late Qing economic conditions], *Jingji xueshu ziliao* [Economic research materials], Shanghai Academy of Social Sciences (25 December 1980): 40–46.
"Ershi shiji chuqide haiguan, youju, yanzheng" [The customs, post office, and salt gabelle in the early 20th century]. *Jingji xueshu ziliao* [Economic research materials]. Shanghai Academy of Social Sciences (July 1981): 45–50.
"Ouzhou 'zhungongyehua' he Zhongguo zibenzhuyi mengya jinxing bijiao di lunshu" [European proto-industrialization and China's sprouts of capitalism]. *Jingji xueshu ziliao (Economic Research Materials).* Shanghai Academy of Social Sciences (November 1981): 36–42.
"Songdai yilai Zhongguo zhengfu yu Zhongguo jingji" (Chinese government and the Chinese economy since the Song dynasty). *Zhongguo shi yanjiu* [Studies in Chinese history], Institute of Historical Research, Beijing (December 1981): 60–73.
"Some Problems in Studying the Economic History of the Ch'ing Dynasty." In *Proceedings of International Ch'ing Archives Symposium,* edited by Ch'en Chieh-hsien, 81–109. Taipei: National Palace Museum, 1982.
Editor and contributor, *Chinese Social and Economic History from the Song to 1900.* Michigan Monographs in Chinese Studies, no. 45. Ann Arbor: University of Michigan Center for Chinese Studies, 1982.
"Lun ershi shiji chunian Zhongguo shehui weiji" [On the social crisis in early twentieth-century China]. In *Qingmo Mingchu Zhongguo shehui* [Chinese

society in the late Qing and early Republic]. Shanghai: Fudan University Press, 1983.

"Economic Trends, 1912–1949." In *The Cambridge History of China*. Vol. 12, edited by J. K. Fairbank. Cambridge: Cambridge University Press, 1983. [Chinese translation: "Jingji qushi (1912–1949)." *Jianqiao Zhonghua ming guo shi.* Shanghai: Renmin, 1991.]

"The Foreign Presence in China in the Early Twentieth Century." In *The Cambridge History of China.* Vol. 12. Edited by J. K. Fairbank. Cambridge: Cambridge University Press, 1983. [Chinese translation: "Waiguo shili zai Hua cunzai." *Jianqiao Zhonghua mingguo shi.* Shanghai: Renmin, 1991.]

"Academe in Contemporary China." *Michigan Quarterly Review* 22, no. 4 (Fall 1983): 579–93.

"'Proto-industrialization' and China's 'Capitalist Sprouts': A Comparative Discussion." In *Studies in Sinology,* 395–414. Seoul: Korea University, Asiatic Research Institute, 1983.

"The State and the Economy in Late Imperial China." *Theory and Society* 13, no. 3 (May 1984): 297–326.

"Chūka minkoku no keizaiteki chōryū" [Economic trends in the Republic of China]. Translated by Uchida Tomoyuki. *Ajia keizai jumpo* [Asian economic report] nos. 1306–1310 (September-October 1984): 1–19, 1–24, 1–29, 9–20.

"Aspects of the Transition from Qing to Republican China." *Republican China* 10, no. 2 (April 1985): 1–21.

"Introduction: perspectives on modern China's history," with Mary B. Rankin and John K. Fairbank. In *The Cambridge History of China.* Vol. 13. Cambridge: Cambridge University Press, 1986.

Editor, with John K. Fairbank, *The Cambridge History of China,* Vol. 13. Cambridge: Cambridge University Press, 1986.

"Qingdai jingjishi yu shijie jingjishi" [Qing economic history (1644–1911) in a world context]. In *Ming Qing dang'an yu lishi yanjiu* [Studies on the archives and history of the Ming and Qing dynasties], edited by First Historical Archives, 1: 390–408. Beijing: Zhonghua Press, 1988.

"Japanese Imperialism in China: A Commentary." In *The Japanese Informal Empire in China, 1895–1937,* edited by P. Duus, R. H. Myers, and M. R. Peattie, chap. 13. Princeton: Princeton University Press, 1989.

"China's Economic History in Comparative Perspective." In *The Heritage of China,* edited by Paul S. Ropp, 224–41. Berkeley: University of California Press, 1990.

"An Old Question Revisited: Was the Glass Half-full or Half-empty for China's Agriculture Before 1949?" *Peasant Studies* 17, no. 3 (Spring 1990): 207–16.

"State and Society in Twentieth-Century China." *The Centennial Review* 36, no. 2 (Spring 1992): 373–86.

"Questions About China's Early Modern Economic History That I Wish I Could Answer." *The Journal of Asian Studies* 51, no. 4 (November 1992): 757–69.

Studies in the Economic History of Late Imperial China: Handicraft, Modern Industry, and the State. Michigan Monographs in Chinese Studies, no. 70. Ann Arbor: University of Michigan Center for Chinese Studies, 1996.

The Chinese Economy, 1870–1949. Michigan Monographs in Chinese Studies, no. 71. Ann Arbor: University of Michigan Center for Chinese Studies, 1996.

Selected Writings
of Norma Diamond

"Some Aspects of Change and Continuity in Communist China." *Annals of the Michigan Academy of Arts and Sciences* (1965): 299–306.

K'un Shen: A Taiwan Village. New York: Holt, Rinehart and Winston, 1969.

"Fieldwork in a Complex Society." In *Being an Anthropologist,* edited by B. Spindler, 113–141. New York: Holt, Rinehart and Winston, 1970.

"The Middle Class Family Model in Taiwan." *Asian Survey* 13, no. 9 (September 1973): 853–72.

"Pye, Solomon and the Spirit of Chinese Politics," with Richard Kagan. *Bulletin of Concerned Asian Scholars* (July 1973): 62–68.

"Women in Taiwan: One Step Forward, Two Steps Back." In *Women in China,* edited by Marilyn Young, 211–42. Michigan Papers in Chinese Studies, no. 15. Ann Arbor: University of Michigan Center for Chinese Studies, 1973.

"Women in Traditional China" and "Women in Revolutionary China." Annotated bibliography. In *Women in China,* edited by Marilyn Young, 243–55. Ann Arbor: University of Michigan Center for Chinese Studies, 1973.

"Women Under Kuomintang Rule." *Modern China* 1, no. 1 (January 1975): 3–45.

"Collectivization, Kinship and the Status of Women in Rural China." In *Toward an Anthropology of Women,* edited by R. Reiter, 372–95. New York: Monthly Review Press, 1975.

"Collectivization, Kinship and the Status of Women in Rural China." *Bulletin of Concerned Asian Scholars* 7, no. 1 (1975): 25–32.

"Women in Industry in Taiwan," and editor's Introduction. *Modern China* 5, no. 3 (1979).

"China." Entry for *World Book Encyclopedia.* Chicago: World Book, 1979.

"Some Thoughts on American Literature." In *Xiandai Meiguo Wenxue Yanjiu* (Studies on Contemporary American Literature), no. 2. Jinan: Shandong, 1979.

"Model Villages and Village Realities." *Modern China* 9, no. 2 (July 1983): 163–81.

"Taitou Revisited: Prospects for Community Restudies." In *The Social Sciences and Fieldwork in China,* edited by A. Thurston, 123–42. Boulder: Westview Press, 1983.

"Household, Kinship and Women in Taitou Village." In *Agricultural and Rural Development in China Today*, 78–96. Ithaca: Cornell University Program in International Agriculture, 1983.

"Teaching American Literature in Shandong." *Asian Survey* (November 1983): 1194–99.

"Taitou Revisited." *International Journal of Sociology* 14, no. 4 (1984).

"Rural Collectivization and Decollectivization in China." *Journal of Asian Studies* 44, no. 4 (August 1985): 785–92.

"Taitou Revisited: State Policies and Social Change." In *Chinese Rural Development: The Great Transformation*, edited by W. L. Parish, 246–69. Armonk, NY: M. E. Sharpe, 1985.

"The Miao and Poison." *Ethnology* (January 1988): 1–25.

"Security and Alienation in Contemporary China." *Reviews in Anthropology* 17 (1991): 123–30.

"Cultural Revolution" and "China: People's Republic." In *Women's Studies Encyclopedia*, edited by H. Tierney. Vol. 3. New York: Greenwood Press, 1992.

"The Hua Miao of Southwest China." In *Ethnicity and the State*, edited by J. Toland, 55–78. Political and Legal Anthropology Series, no. 9. New Brunswick, NJ: Transaction Publishers, 1993.

Introduction on China, and short articles on Dauer, Drung, Jing, Maonan, Mulam, Nusu, and Miao. *Encyclopaedia of World Cultures*. Vol. 6, *Russia, China and Eurasia*. Edited by Norma Diamond and Paul Friedrich, xxxv–xlvii, 469–73. Boston: G. K. Hall, 1994.

"Defining the Miao: Ming, Qing and Contemporary Views." In *Cultural Encounters on China's Ethnic Frontiers*, edited by S. Harrell, 92–116. Seattle: University of Washington Press, 1995.

"Building Socialism with Chinese Characteristics." In *Women and International Development Review #4*, edited by R. Gallin et al., 147–72. Boulder: Westview Press, 1995.

"Christianity and the Hua Miao: Writing and Power." In *Christianity in China from the Eighteenth Century to the Present*, edited by Daniel H. Bays, 138–57. Stanford: Stanford University Press, 1996.

Selected Writings
of Robert F. Dernberger

"The Role of Nationalism in the Rise and Development of Communist China." In *Economic Nationalism in Old and New States*, edited by Harry Johnson, 48–70. Chicago: University of Chicago Press, 1967.

"Foreign Trade, Innovation and Economic Growth in Communist China." In *China in Crisis*, edited by Tsou Tang and Ping-to Ho. Vol. 1, book 2, 739–52. Chicago: University of Chicago Press, 1968.

"Prices, the Exchange Rate, and Economic Efficiency: Communist China." In *International Trade and Central Planning*, edited by Alan Brown and Egon Neuberger, 202–45. Berkeley: University of California Press, 1968.

"China's Foreign Trade: The See-Saw Pattern." *Columbia Journal of World Business* 3, no. 6 (November-December 1968): 17–26.

"Prospects for Trade Between China and the United States." In *China Trade Prospects and the United States Policy*, edited by Alexander Eckstein, 185–319. New York: Frederick A. Praeger, 1971.

"Radical Ideology and Economic Development in China: The Cultural Revolution and Its Impact on the Economy." *Asian Survey* 12, no. 12 (December 1972): 1048–65. Also reprinted in *Comparative Economic Systems: Models and Cases*, edited by Morris Bernstein, 349–66. Homewood, IL: Irwin, 1974.

"The People's Republic of China: The Market of the Future?" In *U.S. Trade in the Sixties and Seventies*, edited by Roger Skurski and Kenneth Jameson, 43–52. New York: D. C. Heath & Co., 1974.

"The Role of the Foreigner in China's Economic Development." In *The Chinese Economy in Historical Perspective*, edited by Dwight Perkins, 19–47. Stanford: Stanford University Press, 1975.

"Sino-American Trade Prospects." *Problems of Communism* (July-August 1975): 78–83.

"The Economic Consequences of Defense Expenditure Choices in China." In Joint Economic Committee, U.S. Congress, *China: A Reassessment of the Economy*, 467–98. Washington: U.S. Government Printing Office, 1975.

Co-author, with Dwight Perkins, Alex DeAngeles, et al. *Rural Small-Scale Industry in China*. Berkeley: University of California Press, 1977.

Co-author, with Alan Whiting. *China's Future*. New York: McGraw-Hill, 1977.

"Economic Development and Modernization in Contemporary China: The Attempt to Limit Dependence on the Transfer of Modern Technology from Abroad." In *Technology and Communist Culture*, edited by Fred Fleuron, 224–64. New York: Praeger, 1977.

"The Program for Agricultural Transformation in Mainland China." *Issues and Studies* (October 1978): 59–97.

"Prospects for the Chinese Economy." *Problems of Communism* (September–December 1979): 1–15.

"Agricultural Development: The Key Link in China's Four Modernizations Program." *American Journal of Agricultural Economics* 62, no. 2 (May 1980): 331–38.

"Quantitative Measures and the Analysis of China's Contemporary Economic Evolution: Problems and Prospects." In *Quantitative Measures of China's Economic Output*, edited by Alexander Eckstein, 1–43. Ann Arbor: University of Michigan Press, 1980.

Editor, *China's Development Experience in Comparative Perspective.* Cambridge: Harvard University Press, 1980.

Economic Consequences and Future Implications of Population Growth in China. Papers of the East West Population Institute, no. 76. Honolulu: East-West Center, 1981.

"Agriculture in Communist China's Development Strategy." In *The Chinese Agricultural Economy*, edited by Randolph Barker and Radha Singha, 65–79. Boulder: Westview Press, 1982.

"The Chinese Search for the Path of Self-Sustained Growth in the 1980's: An Assessment." In Joint Economic Committee, U.S. Congress, *China Under The Four Modernizations*, part I: 19–76. Washington: U.S. Government Printing Office, 1982.

"Micro-economic Analysis of the Farm in the P.R.C." In *Agricultural Development in China, Japan, and Korea*, edited by Chi-ming Hou and Tzongshuan Yu, 377–429. Taipei: Academic Sinica, 1982.

"China's New Economic Development Model: Problems and Prospects." In *China: The 80's Era*, edited by Norton Ginsburg and Bernard A. Lalor, 99–143. Boulder: Westview Press, 1984.

"The Domestic Economy and the Four Modernizations Program." In *China Policy for the Next Decade*, 139–79. Atlantic Council's Committee on China Policy. Boston: Oelgeschlager, Gunn & Hain, 1984.

"The State Planned, Centralized System: Comparative Analysis of China, North Korea, and Vietnam." In *Asian Economic Development: Present and Future*, edited by Robert Scalapino, Seizaburo Sato, and Jusuf Wanandi, 13–42. Berkeley: University of California Institute of East Asian Studies, 1985.

"Economic Policy and Performance." In Joint Economic Committee, U.S. Congress, *China's Economy Looks Toward the Year 2000*, 15–48. Washington: U.S. Government Printing Office, 1986.

Co-editor, with Kenneth DeWoskin, Steven Goldstein, Rhoads Murphey, and Martin Whyte. *The Chinese: Adapting the Past, Building the Future*. Ann Arbor: University of Michigan Center for Chinese Studies, 1986. Second edition published as *The Chinese: Adapting the Past, Facing the Future*. Ann Arbor: University of Michigan Center for Chinese Studies, 1991.

"Economic Developments in China and Sino-American Relations." In *America's New Competitors: The Challenge of Newly Industrialized Countries*, edited by Thornton F. Bradshaw, Daniel F. Burton, Richard N. Cooper, and Robert D. Hornats, 103–16. Cambridge: Ballinger, 1987.

Co-author, with Richard S. Eckhaus. *Financing Asian Development: China and India*. Washington: University Press of America, 1988.

"Economic Cooperation in the Asia-Pacific Region and the Role of the P. R. C." *Journal of Northeast Asian Studies* 7, no. 1 (Spring 1988): 3–21.

"The Vietnamese Economy." *Occasional Papers*, 15–30. Washington: The Wilson Center, 1988.

"The Economies of China, North Korea, and Vietnam: A Comparative Study. In *Asian Communism: Continuity and Transition*, edited by Robert Scalapino and Dachung Kim, 241–67. Berkeley: University of California Institute of East Asian Studies, 1988. Also published in Korean.

"Reforms in China: Implications for U.S. Policy." *American Economic Review* 79, no. 2 (May 1989): 21–25.

Co-author and co-editor, with Charles Morrison. China in the Reform Era. Special Issue on China of the Annual Report of the East-West Center, *Asia-Pacific Report*. Honolulu: East-West Center, 1989.

"The Chinese Economy in the New Era: Continuity and Change." In *Chinese Economic Policy: Economic Reform at Midstream*, edited by Ilpyong J. Kim and Bruce Reynolds. New York: Paragon House, 1989.

"Agriculture in U.S.-China Economic Relations." In *U.S.-China Relations: Present and Future*, edited by Richard Holton and Wang Xi, 261–85. Berkeley: University of California Institute of East Asian Studies, 1989. Also published in Chinese.

"China's Mixed Economic System: Properties and Consequences." In Joint Economic Committee, U.S. Congress, *China's Economic Dilemmas in the 1990's: The Problems of Reforms, Modernization, and Interdependency*, 89–101. Washington: U.S. Government Printing Office, 1991.

"The Drive for Economic Modernization and Growth: Performance and Trend." In *China in the Era of Deng Xiaoping: A Decade of Reform*, edited by Michael Ying-mao Kau and Susan H. Marsh, 155–215. Armonk, NY: M. E. Sharpe, 1995.

"Capitalism and The East Asian Miracle." In *Asia's New World Order*, edited by George Yu, 43–75. New York: Macmillan Press, 1996.

"China's Transition to a Market Economy: Back to the Future, Mired in the Present, or Through the Looking-Glass to the Market Economy." In *China's*

Economic Future: Challenges to U.S. Policy, 57–69. Washington: U.S. Government Printing Office, 1996.

.

Contributors to *Constructing China*

ANN ANAGNOST is Associate Professor of Anthropology at the University of Washington. Her book *National Pastimes: Narrative, Representation and Power in Modern China* will be published by Duke University Press in Fall 1997.

DANIEL H. BAYS is Professor of History and Chairman of the Department at the University of Kansas, Lawrence. He is editor of *Christianity in China, the 18th Century to the Present.*

SIN YEE CHAN is Assistant Professor of Philosophy at the University of Vermont. Her research interests include Chinese philosophy, feminist ethics, and emotions.

ROBERT ENO teaches Chinese philosophy and history at Indiana University. He is the author of *The Confucian Creation of Heaven.*

HILL GATES is a Lecturer in the Anthropology Department at Stanford University. She is formulating a unified theory of gender and political economy from field materials collected in Taiwan, Sichuan, southern Fujian, and the Jiangnan. She is the author of *China's Motor: A Thousand Years of Petty Capitalism.*

CHAD HANSEN is Professor of Chinese Philosophy and Chair of the Department at the University of Hong Kong. He is author of *Language and Logic in Ancient China* and *A Daoist Theory of Chinese Thought*, along with numerous articles on Classical Chinese philosophy.

LI XUN is currently a visiting researcher at the Institute of East Asian Studies of the University of California at Berkeley.

LILI LIU is an Economist at the World Bank. Her research work and resulting publications focus on links between policy reform, market structure, and productivity of firms in developing countries. She is currently working on policy reform in transition from planned to market economies.

ANDREA McELDERRY is Professor of History at the University of Louisville. She is the author of *Shanghai Old-Style Banks (Ch'ien-Chuang), 1800–1935* and several articles, most recently "Securing Trust and Stability: Shanghai Finance in the Late Qing" in *Chinese Business In Asia: A Long Term Perspective*, edited by Rajeswary Brown. She has been co-editor of *Chinese Business History* since it began publication in 1990 and is currently co-editing a book on the historiography of Chinese business history.

ELIZABETH PERRY is Professor of Government at Harvard University. Her books include *Rebels and Revolutionaries in North China, 1845–1945*; *Shanghai on Strike: The Politics of Chinese Labor*; and *Proletarian Power: Shanghai in the Cultural Revolution*.

JONATHAN D. POLLACK is Senior Advisor for International Policy at RAND, where he specializes in Chinese strategic and foreign policy and in East Asian international relations. He is currently engaged in research on Chinese military development, U.S. Export control strategies, and the prospects for major political change on the Korean peninsula.

BRUCE REYNOLDS is Professor of Economics at Union College and Visiting Professor of Economics at Cornell University. His main body of research concerns economic planning and reform, as published in the volumes *Chinese Economic Reform: How Far, How Fast?* and *Economic Reform at Midstream*. His current research explores the linkages between culture and growth in East Asia.

WILLIAM T. ROWE is currently John and Diane Cooke Professor of Chinese History at The Johns Hopkins University. He has written two books on the social history of nineteenth-century Hankou, as well as many articles, and is editor of the journal *Late Imperial China*. He is currently at work on a biography of the eighteenth-century scholar-official Chen Hongmou.

R. KEITH SCHOPPA is Chair of the Department of History and the East Asian Studies Program at Valparaiso University. His latest book is *Blood Road: The Mystery of Shen Dingyi in Revolutionary China*. He is currently at work on a study of the Sino-Japanese War (1937–1945) in Zhejiang province.